Reason Obscured

Reason Obscured

Nine Plays by Ricardo Monti

Edited and Translated, with an Introduction, by

Jean Graham-Jones

Lewisburg
Bucknell University Press

Associated University Presses
2010 Eastpark Boulevard
Cranbury, NJ 08512

The paper used in this publication meets the requirements of the American National Standard for Permanence of Paper for Printed Library Materials Z39.48-1984.

Cataloging-in-Publication Data
is on file at the Library of Congress

PRINTED IN THE UNITED STATES OF AMERICA

Contents

"A Broader Realism":
The Theater of Ricardo Monti

ALTHOUGH RICARDO MONTI HAS PRODUCED FEWER PLAYS THAN MANY OF HIS COM-patriot dramatists, he is widely regarded as Argentina's most distinctive, innovative, and influential contemporary playwright. His plays have been staged in Brazil, Uruguay, Venezuela, Puerto Rico, Spain, France, Italy, Portugal, Germany, and the United States. They have represented Argentina at international theater festivals in Latin America and Europe, and many have been translated into French, German, and English. Monti's theater has been described as a social spectacle. Indeed, his plays mix allegory, tragedy, farce, and mystery play; they intermingle religious and mythological motifs, characters, and plots; and they cross and recross multiple historical zones. The result is a body of work possessing a dynamic and truly theatrical tension.

Norberto Ricardo Monti was born in Buenos Aires on 2 June 1944 to Ricardo Victorio Monti and María Pujalka, the children of Italian and Polish émigrés. He and his two older sisters (Lilia Mercedes, born 1934, and Matilde Noemí, born 1939) were raised in Villa Celina, a lower-middle-class neighborhood on the outskirts of Buenos Aires. At that time it was an area surrounded by fields, giving Monti what he would later describe, in personal correspondence with this author in 2001, as "a sensation of open space and great freedom."[1] These fields were gradually covered by today's low-income apartment buildings.

Monti acknowledges having always thought of himself as a writer, and he produced his first poem at the age of eight. His initial contact with the theater also came at an early age, despite his family's apparent lack of interest in the stage. As a preadolescent, he was taken to the Variedades Theater to see the old-style comic Charmiello perform. More than twenty years later, in a 1979 interview with Charles Driskell, Monti recalled the experience: "I remember the performance perfectly, the set design, the characters. The stage's strange luminosity had a great effect on me. . . . And I still can see the main character in his red wig."[2] This single exposure was inspirational, because shortly thereafter, at the age of fourteen, Monti began

7

to study acting at two of Buenos Aires's best-known independent theaters, the Nuevo Teatro and the Fray Mocho. He also began attending plays, including the Instituto de Arte Moderno's landmark production of *Waiting for Godot*, which Monti saw two or three times. During this period, too, he made his first attempt at writing for the theater, as he told Driskell: "At 14 or 15 I entered a one-act play in a contest, and of course it didn't win anything" (44).

In pursuit of a writing career, Monti left the theater behind as he focused on poetry and narrative. He published one poem in a literary journal and produced many short stories, none of which was published. He began several novels, which were never completed. In the mid-1960s he wrote for cultural programs broadcast on municipal and national radio. He studied various languages, becoming fluent in German. Monti then entered the National University of Buenos Aires. At the university, he first studied philosophy, but after six or seven courses, he switched to psychology. His university career would be interrupted by the premiere of his first play, and when he returned later to study literature, he was able to endure only one class. As he stated in the 1979 interview, "I ran away horrified because it wasn't what I wanted or needed. I've never gone back . . ." (44).

Notwithstanding Monti's negative academic experience, a "literary" motivation can be seen in all of his plays. For Monti, theater mixes both theatrical and literary genres, an opinion he made pointedly clear in a 1989 interview with Jorge Conti:

> Theater belongs to two aesthetic spheres: on the one hand, [there is] the written text, which falls within the territory of literature. And on the other, there is the sphere of representation. At some determined point, these two spheres intersect. . . . Grotowski reduces theater to the relation between actor and audience. I believe [instead] that it is a relation between the actor, the word he incarnates ([i.e.,] the written text), and the audience.[3]

A one-time avid reader of the "moderns" (from Henrik Ibsen to Samuel Beckett) as well as fellow twentieth-century Argentinean playwrights (Armando Discépolo, Defilippis Novoa, Roberto Arlt, and Griselda Gambaro), today Monti prefers historical texts.

Monti's first produced play, *Una noche con el señor Magnus e hijos* [An evening with Mr. Magnus & Sons], has its origins in a fragment of one of his incomplete novels. Monti began writing the play in 1966 and finished it three years later at the age of twenty-five. The 1970 premiere of *Una noche con el señor Magnus e hijos* not only marked the debut of a great Argentinean playwright; by melding sociopolitical realism with avant-garde experimentation, the production also signaled a change in Buenos Aires theatrical aesthetics at a moment of enormous sociopolitical upheaval. *Una noche con el señor Magnus e hijos* self-consciously ritualizes behavior, emphasizing not only the familial ceremonies but also the power relations between the dominator and the dominated. The theatrical event itself becomes foregrounded as the play's internal performances cycle through such forms of theater and ritual as absurdism, naturalism, tragedy, expressionism, farce, mystery play, and even children's games. Among the play's themes that would be developed more fully in the dramatist's later works are: authoritarian paternal figures as impostors; youthful responses to repression; the redemptive power of the feminine; performances within performances and the easily erased boundary between representation and reality; and the hero and villain, equally relativized.

Una noche con el señor Magnus e hijos sets up the middle-class family home as a theater for the staging of the struggles between the patriarch and his children, rivals, and lovers. The patriarch Magnus is a Western capitalist, engaged in the business of selling images and identities. He obtains his power by offering up himself as the center of meaning, a defining mirror whose reflection not only seduces his subjects but also beats them into submission: "My success lay in anticipating everything. As soon as I saw something being born, I swallowed it up. And only later I offered it up as mine. I was a mirror all my life. A polished, empty surface. I made a fortune selling everyone back their own images. Of course, to all of you, too."[4] When Magnus confesses that he has tricked everyone with his illusion-making and that he intends to abdicate his power, his three sons decide to kill him. The play ends in parricide, the sons aided by Magnus's girlfriend and his old rival.

Yet even as *Una noche con el señor Magnus e hijos* stages authoritarianism and the response to such repression, it critiques that very response. Magnus is the villain, but he is also at times sympathetic, convincing in his assertions, and quite possibly a victim of the very system he defends. The three sons heroically overturn the old order, but they themselves are perverse and frustrated beings, rendered impotent by the privileged order of Magnus's house. Gato, the family intellectual, is Magnus's chief opponent, and the character's name emphasizes his function as the "cat" chasing after the Rat-Magnus. Wolfy, the second son, is an artist, like his beloved namesake Mozart. The youngest son, Santiago, is a narcissistic sensualist. Both Wolfy and Santiago have floating loyalties: Wolfy runs back and forth from his brothers' collective resistance to the protective shadow of Magnus; and Santiago, often aloof from the family situation, alternates between self-absorbed sexual pleasure and revolutionary solidarity with Gato. Gato himself is torn between his desire to annihilate Magnus and craving to obtain his recognition. The fifth member of the household is Magnus's former rival, Lou. The old man has been reduced to the status of family dog after having lost to Magnus in business as well as love. Lou belongs to Magnus's world and accepts its rules; he begs his way back into the house, preferring its repressive order to the outside's uncertain freedom.

One night Magnus, the feared master of the family universe, brings home Julia, a figure as ambiguous as the others. It is never clear whether she is an innocent virgin or an opportunistic prostitute, but her doubly disruptive condition, as outsider and woman, weakens the patriarchal system's toughness and ultimately questions it. It is Julia, of the same age as the sons, who introduces the possibility of actively overturning Magnus, and with her as catalyst the oppressed sons inaugurate their dreamed-of liberation movement. Julia also functions as a substitute for the dead mother Bibí (whose name homophonically recalls *viví*, literally "I lived" or the familiar command "live!"), and the sons identify her as such, but her questionable purity and innocence resist such easy spiritual idealization and annihilation at Magnus's hands. Magnus seduces Julia, as he does everyone else, by offering her a defining image of herself. In the process, he nearly destroys her, and the resulting disorientation leads her to join the sons in their struggle.

The text is structured in four parts: a prologue and two acts, with the first act divided into two scenes. Structural convention notwithstanding, the play contains numerous multiple internal performances that supply the family prehistory while confounding narrative continuity and beginning to erase the boundary separating reality and representation. The confluence of the two worlds of real life and theater will gain momentum until it culminates in Magnus's death, the event that Monti declared, in his introduction to the 1993 revised edition, the play's "only moment of absolute truth."[5] The play ends with the five victors separated and in various states of confusion: vomiting, moving around the stage in disgust, and howling. Only Santiago remains with Magnus's putrid corpse, staring with "obstinate attention."

Although not initially well received by Buenos Aires critics and traditional theater audiences (despite a very positive out-of-town premiere in southern Argentina and a modest box-office success during the 1970 season), *Una noche con el señor Magnus e hijos* forced the critics to reevaluate its revolutionary theatricality when the original cast production opened the first Patagonian National Theater Festival in the southern coastal city of Comodoro Rivadavia. After the performance, thousands of spectators applauded for fifteen minutes as they called Monti to the stage. *Una noche con el señor Magnus e hijos* went on to receive two major awards that year, and Monti was declared Buenos Aires's great new playwright.[6]

The new aesthetics exemplified in *Una noche con el señor Magnus e hijos* defied easy compartmentalization. Yet the play's destruction of repressive powers echoed the complex politics of its time, a moment when social protest against General Juan Carlos Onganía's ongoing military dictatorship was becoming increasingly open. Monti has said that he wrote *Una noche con el señor Magnus e hijos* to protest the Onganía dictatorship and growing authoritarianism within Argentine society. In 1970 Argentina, Magnus and his old rival Lou stood in for the older generation and the established bourgeoisie's desire to maintain control at any cost. The three sons, together with the young guest Julia, epitomized various responses available to the younger generation. With its theme of parricide, *Una noche con el señor Magnus e hijos* is not unlike many of its contemporary Latin American plays, such as fellow Argentinean Guillermo Gentile's successful and very direct *Hablemos a calzón quitado* [Let's speak frankly] (1970) or the Cuban playwright José Triana's *La noche de los asesinos* [The criminals] (1965), in which three siblings plot the murder of their parents by acting out the ritual in an apparently never-ending cycle of rehearsals.

The great achievement of *Una noche con el señor Magnus e hijos* is its unmasking of politics as theater, of reality as performance, at a time when realism was considered to be political theater's only vehicle and avant-garde experimentation was condemned as "apolitical." From our postmodern vantage point, the play's metatheatrics may seem perfectly natural, but its cautionary note still jars. There are never any easy answers in Monti's theater, and his first play harshly questioned its own solution.

In his 1992 *Página/12* article on political theater, entitled "Una nueva utopía" [A new utopia], Monti wrote:

> [T]he first object of reflection has to be the intellectual himself . . . because we cannot continue on mechanically as if nothing had ever happened here. I think that we have to look for a theater with a more problematized vision, . . . go deep into it to see what happened to that generation that was so committed and, although it may be hard, now must ask itself if it truly was right or if it made a mistake.[7]

One year after the premiere of *Una noche con el señor Magnus e hijos*, Monti wrote his most "political" play to date: *Historia tendenciosa de la clase media argentina, de los extraños sucesos en que se vieron envueltos algunos hombres públicos, su completa dilucidación y otras escandalosas revelaciones* [A biased history of the Argentinean middle class: About the strange events in which certain public figures found themselves involved, the complete elucidation of these events, and other scandalous revelations] (1971). *Historia tendenciosa* is the only text the playwright has not wished to have translated into any other language, saying that it is "too Argentine" for the foreign reader-spectator.[8] *Historia tendenciosa* is further exceptional within Monti's oeuvre for its collectively developed text. Building upon his own initial idea as well as a basic plot and characters, Monti worked with the actors and director in various phases to create the performed text. Finally and possibly most importantly, *Historia tendenciosa* marked the first of Monti's collaborations with the noted Argentinean director Jaime Kogan.

The overt politics of *Historia tendenciosa* constitute a departure from the earlier *Una noche con el señor Magnus e hijos* and Monti's later play, *Visita* [Visit] (1977), which he began writing that same year. Premiering at the height of militant resistance in twentieth-century Argentina, its lengthy title recalls the contemporary German theater tradition of Brechtian epic theater and its successor, the documentary theater associated with the dramatist Peter Weiss (and especially Weiss's best-known play, *Die Verfolgung und Ermordung Jean Paul Marats, dargestellt durch die Schauspielgruppe des Hospizes zu Charenton unter Anleitung des Herrn de Sade* [The persecution and death of Jean-Paul Marat, as presented by the inmates of the Charenton Hospital under the direction of the Marquis de Sade], or *Marat/ Sade*). In general, Monti's theater shares postwar German theater's mixing of historical detail with mythic structures, and *Historia tendenciosa* is his play that most closely resembles European documentary theater.

Nevertheless, the play transcends mere imitation of the documentary model, becoming an allegorical overview of Argentine history from the nineteenth century through the early 1970s. The text is structured on three levels: allegorical, historical, and personal. The main plot allegorizes Argentinean history through multiple characters, representing various socioeconomic sectors of the country. Even the Argentine nation itself is allegorized in the figure of the prostitute Pola. Marcelo Boñi García, the landowner and representative of the oligarchy, is the Europeanized *criollo* who enters into a series of agreements, first with the English (depicted by the character Mr. Hawker), then with the Americans (in the character of Mr. Peagg, pronounced "Pig"), and finally with the military forces of the General. Boñi García appears willing to go to any length in order to consolidate his control over the petite bourgeoisie (personified by the lawyer Matías Bonafede), who have in turn aligned themselves with the liberal Radical party and their leader, "el Peludo" (the nickname given to the country's former president, Hipólito Irigoyen). A middle-class family, the Filipeaus, makes an appearance later in the play, and they exemplify the impact on the average Argentinean family of this unholy alliance of oligarchs, foreigners, and military: the father as failed and ultimately eliminated intellectual; the mother that, like Brecht's Courage, seeks to rise above her class; and the son that unwittingly enters into a blood pact with Boñi García and ends up co-opted by the oligarchy. The working classes make intermittent appearances, in the character of the Obrero [Worker], but he is always silenced because, as another character says to him, "This play is about the middle class. You have nothing to do here."

The first act of *Historia tendenciosa* traces the last decades of the nineteenth century, the first military coup of the twentieth century and the "infamous" 1930s, and the rise and fall of Juan Perón, ending with the 9 June 1956 execution of twenty-seven Peronist military members. The second act recounts the consolidation of United States power assisted by Argentina-Pola, the League of Pro-Development Ladies (the three "mannequins" Pulcinelle, Dorotée, and Gaby), and the Council of Native Industrialists (the two clowns Anselmo and Nicanor). The victorious do not have the final word, however; rather, the actors, discarding their characters, repeat the command "Escuchen" [listen], as they talk to each other and the audience about the winners' value-system, and propose alternatives that are immediately questioned:

> —Each one of us carries the fight within us.
> —But that's also outside.
> —We're split in two.
> — . . . we have to take it easy . . .
> —We have to look around.
> —We must place comfort above all else.
> —But how much will that comfort cost us?

Throughout this allegorized story, Monti and company interweave two other historical threads: "real" history and "personal" histories. The characters listen to a radio transmitting speeches by Perón and Evita; and historical and fictitious characters intermix. The "personal" makes itself present in two ways: at play's end, as mentioned above, the actors directly address the audience and each other; and there are other moments, which the playtext calls "implosiones" [implosions], based on the actors' memories of lived experiences and either written down by Monti or improvised in performance. Thus, in *Historia tendenciosa,* each actor plays at least three roles: real, historical, and symbolic. The metadramatic effect is accentuated by the omnipresence of the character Teatro [Theater], who—much like the Emcee of Monti's later play *Marathón* [Marrathon] (1980)—plays the role of director, controlling and intervening whenever he deems it necessary.

Monti, like Weiss, sees history as an immediate and subjective confrontation and not some obscure object of study disconnected from the present. By choosing to dramatize his analysis of modern Argentine history through metadramatics, intertextuality, and multiple theatrical levels, Monti moved "political theater" away from the realist-naturalist aesthetics so often associated with the theater of dissent and toward his own obsessions with issues of history, myth, truth, fiction, reality, and representation.

Throughout the 1970s, Monti continued to work with Jaime Kogan and the Payró Theater. He directed two plays: *El contratiempo* [The contretemps] (1973), by Argentinean playwright Diana Raznovich, and Brecht's *The Days of the Commune* in 1974. He also began leading playwriting workshops, which he would continue well into the 1990s. Monti was by now married (in 1970) and the father of Lila (born 1972), and the workshops provided a needed source of income. They also became the training ground for some of Argentina's better-known playwrights. In these workshops, Monti developed his own image-based system. He refused to impose any precepts on his students, attempting instead to help each one discover his or her own world of imagery, without preconceived models. In the 1985 article "El teatro, un espacio literario" [Theater, a literary space], Monti explained his position:

> I consider the image (i.e., that which exists, in the writer's case, prior to its translation into words) the central nucleus of the writing process. . . . The playwright, for his part, has to rework his initial, spontaneous images, relocating them in an artificial space—the scenic space—that will then transform [these images], magnifying some and expelling others. Characters, environments, and actions will thus lose in freedom what they gain in intensity. Condensation: this is the term that best reflects the alchemy proper to the scenic space.[9]

Monti's dramatic system of images would have the most influence on his own generation of Argentinean writers (whom he has termed the "'70s" generation), including Mauricio Kartun, Eduardo Rovner, and the deceased Hebe Serebrisky.

In its original staging, *Historia tendenciosa* ends with a handsome young man, "Criatura" [Creature], entering the stage with a machine gun. For Monti, the image meant nothing more than a warning to the old order, but when it was interpreted by many spectators and critics as a prophetic call to armed revolution, Monti excised the final image from the printed edition. Monti's next play, *Visita*, also has two endings: that of the early performances of director Jaime Kogan's original staging, included in the play-text's first edition but labeled as "rejected," as well as the ending adopted during the original production and included in all subsequent printings.[10]

The 1977 production of *Visita* ran for three years, achieved national and international recognition (by being acclaimed Buenos Aires's best "drama" of the season and receiving Spain's Carlos Arniches prize in the same year) and represented Argentina at the 1978 International Festival of Theater of the Nations in Caracas, Venezuela. Such success notwithstanding, it still remains perhaps the least studied of Monti's major plays and, when discussed, is often regarded as a hermetic reflection on the limits of human existence. Nevertheless, its two endings point, much like the endings of *Una noche con el señor Magnus e hijos* and *Historia tendenciosa,* to a meditation on the possibility of sociopolitical transformation. Indeed, much of the hermeticism cloaking *Visita* stems from the circumstances of its premiere during the first and darkest years of Argentina's most repressive military dictatorship to date.

Monti's writing of *Visita* was inspired by a newspaper article about a young man who specialized in breaking into the houses of elderly couples and, over the course of the evening, forcing the couples to treat him as if he were their son. The intruder would leave the next morning with whatever he had stolen. In 1979 Monti recalled to Driskell, "I closed the newspaper and saw the play."[11] Like *Una noche con el señor Magnus e hijos, Visita* takes place in a strangely lit, enclosed space—the run-down apartment of an old, possibly dead couple named Perla and Lali. Three days have passed since an intruder, Equis (whose name is the Spanish pronunciation of "X"), has arrived, and the old couple appears to have been engaged in a cat-and-mouse game with their uninvited guest. It is unclear if Equis is a murderer, a thief, a prodigal son, or a replacement for the fourth character, Gaspar, who is equally unidentified as the elderly couple's adoptive son, servant, slave, or lover.

The two-act play's action is built upon a series of power struggles among the four characters, and almost every battle ends in the death and resurrection of one of the characters. Conflicts are multiplied during the sections entitled "acciones simultáneas" [simultaneous actions], in which paired characters engage in parallel struggles. Alliances are made, broken, and remade. Each character plays, or attempts to play, roles within roles: Perla at times is sweetly maternal and at others a despot; Lali is a helpless old man, a magician, and a seducer; Gaspar serves invisible yet rancid cookies; and even the outsider Equis, copying Perla's death performance that ends the first act, pretends to die, but he is tortured back to life by Lali and Gaspar under Perla's direction. Nevertheless, the stage directions leave it unclear as to whether or not the characters are pretending. Identities remain confused even as the play ends: Are Perla and Lali immortal? Is Equis the prodigal son, the messiah, or a murderous burglar? Is he the next Gaspar, a younger Lali, or an alternative to the old couple's obsolete but still powerful order?

Visita ends with the visitor draped across his hostess's lap. He is apparently sleeping, but his eyes are still open. This Pietà-inspired image contrasts with the play's original ending, in which Equis murders Perla and Lali, only to assume their reign upon finding that the outside door is locked. When Gaspar, now Equis's manservant, goes to investigate a sound heard outside, he sees that someone is watching from the other side of the door. The houselights then come up to reveal the theatrical spectacle. This earlier, rejected ending is very similar to the parricide staged and critiqued in *Una noche con el señor Magnus e hijos* and quite likely stems from Monti's having begun writing *Visita* in 1970. Both plays reflect the 1960s generation's self-critical preoccupation with revolution as a means for effecting sociopolitical change. In both plays the son (albeit symbolic in Equis's case) kills the father but is incapable of constructing his own alternative world. By the time of *Visita*'s premiere, Monti had witnessed the state's violent, negative reaction to his generation's "parricidal tendencies." In all, some thirty thousand people "disappeared" during the 1976–83 military dictatorship, and most of them were abducted during the regime's first three years.

The life/death dichotomy present in all of Monti's plays is perhaps most concentrated in *Visita*. Although *Visita* stages the debate as a metaphysical problem in Perla and Lali's closed world, this world is part of the same national struggle that was taking place outside the theater. The original ending is both too neat and too fatalistic. Much like Magnus's sons, Equis acts, but there is no fundamental change to the power structure. In the original ending, Equis assumes Perla and Lali's power (and even makes himself up in their image), and Gaspar continues as a servant. Equis's revolution has failed. In the second ending, the parricidal ceremony remains unfulfilled; the intruder is in an apparent trance, but he remains vigilant with his revolutionary potential intact even under repression.

Visita premiered at the height of the military dictatorship. Although several plays had already been officially banned and some theaters closed, theater practitioners were subjected to primarily anonymous acts of aggression. Such was Monti's experience. In the late 1970s, he began writing for motion pictures. With the filmmaker Ricardo Wulicher, he adapted Roberto Arlt's 1936 play *Saverio el cruel* [Saverio the Cruel] for the screen; he also cowrote (with Wulicher and the novelist Vlady Kociancich) the dramatic scenes for a documentary on the Argentinean writer Jorge Luis Borges, entitled *Borges para millones* [Borges for millions]. Although Monti was never officially censured and during the dictatorship did not see his name on any unofficial blacklist circulating (learning only in the late 1990s that his name had been listed), he was the victim of unofficial, state-sponsored censorship on at least two occasions during the late 1970s. The filmmaker Mario Sábato had hired Monti to cowrite the screenplay for *El poder de las tinieblas* [The power of shadows] (1979), based on a portion of the novel *Sobre héroes y tumbas* [On heroes and tombs] by the filmmaker's father, Ernesto Sábato. Monti cowrote the script, but his name would not appear in the credits, because Sábato had been told that the censors would not approve a movie project with Monti's name attached. The second instance occurred when Monti, following *Visita*'s international success, was invited to the 1979 New York Theater Festival. Well in advance of the travel dates, Monti applied to have his passport renewed; nevertheless, the renewed passport did not arrive until after the festival had ended, thus denying Monti the opportunity to attend. During this dark period, his second child, Matías, was born (in 1978).

Monti's next play premiered under continuing military repression. After four years, the Argentine people were exhibiting signs of a collective anguish, and *Marathón* [Marrathon] tapped into both this ongoing suffering under repression and a growing critical awareness regarding what have been called the guiding fictions that had led the country to such an end.[12] Indeed, the premiere of *Marathón* was greatly anticipated (and later awarded that year's Argentine Writers Association prize for best dramatic play). It was Monti's first play in three years as well as the Payró Theater's inaugural production (once again under Jaime Kogan's direction) at the new Teatros de San Telmo, in a theater designed especially for the premiere by the noted architect and set designer Tito Egurza.

The design recreated a 1932 suburban Buenos Aires ballroom, in which six couples are participating in a dance contest. Monti took the idea from discussions with director Kogan about working with music to adapt Horace McCoy's novel (later made into a Hollywood movie) *They Shoot Horses, Don't They?* The six couples represent different socioeconomic, cultural, and even age groups. The dancers are: an aging poet (Homero Estrella) and his aging muse (Elena García); a young couple with the assumed names of Tom Mix and Ana D.; an unemployed office worker and his wife (Héctor and Ema Expósito); a bankrupt industrialist (who uses the initials "NN" to maintain his anonymity) and a prostitute (Pipa) he has hired as his contest partner; and a tubercular bricklayer and his wife (Pedro and Asunción Vespucci). These five couples are later joined by a sixth couple, two wealthy siblings looking to experience "real-life" drama. Another ominous pair, the Guardaespaldas [Bouncer] and the Animador [Emcee], oversee the contest. One physically abuses the contestants while the other inflicts psychological punishment yet both are revealed by play's end to be nothing more than middlemen in the repressive order of the dance-hall regime.

When the play begins, the couples have already been dancing for an undetermined yet very long time. They are "lifeless dolls covered in dust and cobwebs." Throughout the play they dance, take short breaks, visit the Emcee's platform to endure various abuses, are beaten by the Bouncer, argue among themselves and then reconcile, witness the death of one of their own and the departures of several others, and end the play continuing to dance as the never-ending marathon drags on. The audience plays multiple roles—the Emcee at times speaks to the spectators as if they were the audience in his 1930s ballroom; at other times, he addresses an invisible, imaginary audience. The real spectator is both included and excluded, participant as well as witness.

This doubling mechanism undergirds the structure of *Marathón*, and the device allows the play to avoid censorship even as it forces the audience to take a distanced, more critical stance. As Monti explained in an interview published in 1992, "In order to talk about the present, I went back to the past, to an equivalent period, the unhappy decade of the 1930s."[13] The play's structure, nevertheless, is far more complex than this simple flashback strategy would suggest. *Marathón* is divided into twenty-three episodes in which multiple levels of reality are interwoven: the 1932 dance marathon itself, including the contest events and the dancers' private individual dreams, spoken aloud, and five *mitos* (myths), which function as critical transformations of an Argentinean collective historical memory— Conquest, Independence, Pastoral America, Industrial America, and Fascism. The play's flashback strategy thus both avoided censorship and created a double text for 1980's Buenos Aires spectators, forcing them to read their present circumstances through the context of 1930s repression and corruption. With the *mitos*, Monti takes his play even farther by drawing attention to the relation between history and mythmaking. The dance contest participants play the characters in the five mythic episodes, transforming themselves into historical and symbolic, even composite, figures. In the first myth, that of the Conquest, the tubercular bricklayer Pedro Vespucci is transformed into the Spanish conquistador Pedro de Mendoza and quite possibly Amerigo Vespucci. In the Independence myth, the contestant calling himself Tom Mix (the hero of the Hollywood Western movies) plays a composite character, who is both Argentinean Independence hero Mariano Moreno and an anonymous twentieth-century freedom fighter. When the wealthy siblings arrive, the dancers transform themselves into a herd of cattle. The image not only points to class distinctions but also alludes to Esteban Echeverría's nineteenth-century allegorical novella *El matadero* [The slaughterhouse], in which the slaughtered cattle are identified with the Argentinean people oppressed by the mid-nineteenth-century dictator Juan Manuel de Rosas. The fourth myth dramatizes the transformation of the bankrupt "NN" into an investor willing to exploit everyone else for his own gain. Finally, in the fifth myth, the Bouncer is transformed into an authoritarian, antidemocratic nationalist who is easily identified with the Emcee's glorification of fascism. All five myths portray degrading transformations and suggest certain universal negative traits present in both individuals and the national culture. There is no single positive, transformative myth.

In a later interview (1992), Monti said that the true hero of the play is the one dance contestant who chooses to stay—Héctor Expósito. As his surname suggests (the Spanish noun *expósito* means "foundling" and, as an adjective, "abandoned"), Héctor, like Equis and Gaspar in *Visita*, is alone, abandoned, and isolated but not necessarily powerless. His "mythic" transformation occurs during the dance contest and does not require its own episode, because his countermyth is a parable for daily life: he is the one who stays, who chooses to live with the uncertainties, and who rejects the easy answers offered by mythologization. Unlike Tom Mix (and the revolutionary "parricidal" characters of Monti's earlier plays and rejected endings), Héctor is the only contestant to question the Emcee's and the Bouncer's actions, and he is the only dancer who consciously chooses to stay to fight their repression. His heroic stance constitutes a call to human solidarity and the final awakening from isolated private dreams and collective mythical nightmares. Such heroism notwithstanding, Héctor is alone at the end of *Marathón*; the younger dancers are gone, and the rest are lost in their dreams. The Emcee has the last word: "Ladies and gents, if this weren't so ridiculous, it would be a tragedy. On with the dance, ladies and gentlemen, on with the dance!"

A final comment must be made about the title's deformed spelling of the Spanish word for marathon, *maratón*. At the time of the play's 1980 premiere, Monti stated in an interview published in the Buenos Aires daily newspaper *Clarín*: "It's about a real marathon and at the same time a metaphor. The 'h' [included in the play's title] is a form of distancing, it's a kind of signal that the thing is not as real as it appears."[14] Monti's inclusion of the *h* reinforces his play's use of Brechtian epic theater conventions by encouraging his spectators to question what is often taken for (historical) fact.

The last play Monti wrote under dictatorship is noteworthy for both its revision of an earlier play and its presence within one of Argentina's most important mass cultural responses to dictatorship—the 1981 Teatro Abierto festival. Monti was a founding member of Teatro Abierto and edited the group's short-lived journal. His play *La cortina de abalorios* [The beaded curtain] was one of three one-act plays that opened the festival on 28 July 1981 in the Picadero Theater. In total, twenty plays were staged in this festival of "open theater for a closed country," with three plays presented each afternoon during the seven-day cycle. When on 6 August an "accidental" fire destroyed the Picadero, the festival was moved to the Tabarís, a much larger commercial theater, where it continued its run until the end of September. Approximately twenty-five thousand spectators attended the festival.

Although the importance of Teatro Abierto as an act of cultural resistance lies beyond debate, the majority of the plays, notwithstanding their common defiant oppositional stance, replicated a fairly conventional theatrical aesthetic. *La cortina de abalorios* both built upon and transcended dominant naturalist aesthetics. A play that can easily be read as "political," it overtly focuses on Argentina's discourses of power even as it presents the clearly ambiguous and problematical character of a brothel madam. In the 1981 original staging, this character carried an even greater importance within the work's power balance, as she was played by the well-known actress Cipe Lincovsky, recently returned from political exile.

La cortina de abalorios found its inspiration in a scene straight out of Monti's earlier *Historia tendenciosa*: the conspiratorial meeting of the local landowner, the Englishman, and the prostitute. The action of *La cortina de abalorios* takes place in a "ghostly and dusty brothel from the late nineteenth century," the setting for a sinister coming to terms between the Argentinean oligarchy and foreign interests. Here the landowner is named Pezuela and the Englishman, Popham. Both bear traces of historical characters from Argentina's colonial past: in 1806, the British Admiral, Sir Home Popham, acting on his own initiative, invaded and occupied Buenos Aires. Joaquín de la Pezuela was a late-eighteenth-century Spanish general who later became viceroy of Peru. Once more, Monti makes symbolic use of historical names to dramatize a national mythology. The cattleman Pezuela, recently returned to the brothel after "butchering Indians," receives a visit from Popham, from whom he has borrowed money. The Englishman is dragging a trunk, in which he claims there are jewels, feathers, and various stock certificates for "a bit of everything. Mines, trains, banks . . ." They gamble for the debt, and Pezuela loses everything he owns to the Englishman's cheating. The loss triggers a physical fight between the two men, but they finally end in agreement when Pezuela offers up the madam along with millions of others like her–"[r]egiments of cows, an entire layer of them covering my lands, fucking like bunnies . . ." Popham begins to conduct behavior-modification experiments on a fourth character, the Mozo [Servant], and when the Servant resists Popham's needle, the madam stabs him with a scalpel. The play ends with the three conspirators exhausted from a brief celebratory orgy under the table.

The brothel's madam remains unnamed in the text (Pezuela calls her "mamá," and she in turn refers to him as "bebé" [baby]), but she plays a role similar to Pola's in *Historia tendenciosa* in that she is culturally pretentious and willing to prostitute herself to anyone who will help her rise in power. The Servant's allegorical role as the masses victimized by the controlling powers resembles that of the Worker in *Historia tendenciosa*. In *La cortina de abalorios*, the Servant is first knifed by Pezuela; he comes back to life only to be shot by Popham; and once more he brings himself back to life only to be stabbed by the madam. At the end of the play, the

Servant will once again gather himself up and leave the stage as the madam calls for someone to wait on her.

La cortina de abalorios is clearly a critique of turn-of-the-century colonialism. Its indictment of alliances made to keep the populace subjugated as the country is sold off to the highest bidder is also a none-too-veiled reference to the military dictatorship and its neoliberal economic policies. Even so, the play's allegorical symbolism is less explicit than that of the earlier *Historia tendenciosa*, and perhaps such ambiguity can explain the mixed critical response to the character of the madam. She has been interpreted as representing the history of Argentina, French corruption of local culture, and the country itself as commercial goods. It is clear that she is not simply a prostitute: she runs the brothel in which the play's action takes place, claims to have traveled around the world, speaks French, and quotes, at times badly, Mallarmé. Nevertheless, the two men in power take full advantage of the madam, referring to her as a cow and even treating her as such, having her get down on all fours to be milked. This rather unsubtle image is a clear reference to Argentina's cattle industry and, by extension, the entire country's natural resources. The question arises, does this madam carry the same allegorical weight of the nation that Pola did in the earlier play? In *La cortina de abalorios*, the brothel itself is clearly the national "scene," replete with nefarious meetings, human corpses, and the remains of discarded beasts. Could the madam not then represent *Historia tendenciosa*'s Argentinean middle class, otherwise absent from *La cortina de abalorios*, with its ideologies borrowed from the upper class and "high" foreign culture and its historical willingness to affiliate itself with any social group but the working class?

At the end of *La cortina de abalorios*, the three accomplices seem to be incapable of leaving the brothel. The madam is slowly expiring; Popham lies on top of his own trunk, claiming that he is dying; and Pezuela has his head stuck in the cow's skull, with which he had earlier crowned himself, and confuses a mirror with his beloved "mamá." They have been abandoned by the Servant, apparently the only character now capable of going through the beaded curtain that separates the madam's room from the rest of the world. Inside the room is an invented Argentina, and it is a world of cheap fantasy, not unlike the curtain's beads, that ends up destroying its own inventors. Once more Monti focuses on Argentina's guiding fictions, invented and maintained by the various discourses of power.

Monti's plays written during the 1976–83 military dictatorship shared several concerns: the possibility or impossibility of a truly "revolutionary" act; individual complicity in collective historiography; and the presence of power structures in all political movements, oppressive and resistant. In later plays, he began to open up the border, moving away from the specifically

Argentinean historical referents present in the earlier plays and toward a more "American" context. His later plays engage in direct dialogue with the canonized models of Western culture: tragedies, passion plays, and even divine comedies.

Monti's next play, *Una pasión sudamericana* [A South American passion play], marked his first attempt to look at America as a frontier. Even though the play takes place in "the hall of what remains of a ranch located in the plains outside Buenos Aires," its title has crossed the national border. Monti's expansion of his demythologizing project is also reflected in his theatrical language. In *Una pasión sudamericana*, Monti's theater is even more hybrid, his story lines are more fragmented, and his characters are more mediated. It comes as no surprise, then, that transvestism would appear here for the first time in his work. In Monti's later plays, all identity would be constructed and all constructions subject to dismantling. Monti's critique of Argentina was soon to become a revision of the modern Western tradition.

Monti began writing *Una pasión sudamericana* while his country was still under dictatorship, but he did not finish it until the late 1980s. The play premiered in November 1989 in the largest theater-hall of Argentina's largest theater complex, Buenos Aires's General San Martín Municipal Theater (where Monti also served as artistic advisor for a short time). After a falling out with Kogan, Monti took over the staging of his play. While most spectators (and even Monti himself) were dissatisfied with the production, *Una pasión sudamericana* is regarded by many critics as Monti's greatest play to date.

Una pasión sudamericana appears to tell the story of Camila O'Gorman and her lover, the Jesuit priest Ladislao Gutiérrez. By 1989, their tragic romance had already been the subject of many Argentinean plays, novels, poems, and even films, and their story has often been revisited as a metaphor for youthful romantic individualism and martyrdom at the hands of a repressive status quo. The nineteenth-century historical account is as follows: Camila O'Gorman was the pampered daughter of a prominent Buenos Aires Federalist and the personal friend of the daughter of General Juan Manuel de Rosas, the Federalist dictator of Argentina at the time the events took place. Camila fell in love with her confessor, and the two ran away together to live on the Argentine coast. They were discovered, imprisoned, and executed in 1848. Camila was twenty years old and, by popular account, pregnant. Despite the attraction of such an emotionally charged story and unlike most other fictionalized treatments, *Una pasión sudamericana* subverts the romantic tradition entirely by telling the lovers' story from the executioner's point of view. On the eve of a decisive battle with his enemy (referred to in the play as simply the Loco [Madman]), the Brigadier must decide if he will execute Camila. During the course of the evening, his five fools (or "crazies") reenact Camila and Ladislao's "passion" as an inverted *Divine Comedy*.

Monti took great pains to distance *Una pasión sudamericana* from its own historical subject.[15] Some of the characters reinforce the play's nine-teenth-century Argentine setting, especially in the play's initial version: the Brigadier, assisted by an aged Edecán [Aide-de-camp], is and is not Rosas; the Madman's letters that are read aloud include fragments of texts from famous Argentinean politicians (and opponents of Rosas). Other char-acters refer back to different historical moments: the British minister Can-ning (best known for his associations with the government preceding Rosas's) calls upon the Brigadier, and the biblical criminal Barrabás [Barabbas], now an enormous gaucho, is chained in the Brigadier's quar-ters. The lead "crazy" goes by the name of Farfarello but says his real name is Pedro de Angelis (the Italian intellectual known best as a Rosas apolo-gist), and two other buffoons bear historical names as well: San Benito (Saint Benedict), whose monastic order has been credited with pulling Western Europe out of the Dark Ages, and the warring Murat, Napoleon Bonaparte's marshal. The final two buffoons are the murderous Biguá and Estanislao the foundling. Once again, Monti creates a collective mythocultural past that fragments, multiplies, and even contradicts simple historical diachrony. Such "contradiction" reaches its height with what has been perhaps the play's most contested modification—the birth of Camila's son. *Una pasión sudamericana* ends with the newborn swaddled in the Brigadier's poncho.

A brief prologue sets the play's foreboding, mystically heightened mood with the four wet and muddy "crazies" circling trancelike around Farfarello as he sings the Neapolitan song *Madonna della Grazia*. The five then whirl offstage before the play's sole act begins. Throughout the course of the play, the Aide-de-camp comes and goes, delivering reports and pleading mercy for Camila. The Brigadier dictates letters to his general Flores; these letters are recorded by the two Escribientes [Scribes] and serve as medita-tions on the war and the Brigadier's own role in the struggle. As a diversion from the next day's battle, the Brigadier tells the buffoons to create a farci-cal "theater of dreams," which the crazies transform into the four-part story of Camila and Ladislao. They begin their story in Inferno, where they tell the legend of the young maid (Camila) that aroused a priest's lust. The Brigadier at first does not want to participate in the buffoons' "madness of love" and halts the performance. Yet he is already swept up in the story and wants to know what happened: "Why do you suppose that a young woman from a good family . . .? It's a mystery, don't you think?" His questions lead the buffoons into their passion play's second station, the World, site of the mystery of the flesh. Estanislao plays Camila, wearing a crown of transparent roses whose thorns cause blood to trickle down his face. The buffoons recite a reworked Song of Solomon to stage the awakening of erotic passion in the two lovers. Once again the Brigadier stops the performance, but once more he cannot resist and allows the buffoons to go on. The mystery of the flesh reaches its climax in the third station, Purgatory. The Mystic Rose and the sexual act fuse together in the buffoons' language; the Brigadier, now horrified, tries to stay the performance but is instead so completely caught up that he becomes an actor. Wearing a crown of red roses, he enters the crazies' dreamworld. Blood trickles down his temples and cheeks. The Brigadier, brought back to his own immediate reality, asks the Aide-de-camp for details about "those children," which the Aide-de-camp, ever hopeful for Camila's pardon, provides. The buffoons then arrive at the final station, the lovers' escape to Paradise and a return to the moment before the fall from grace. Nevertheless, the lovers' future has already been predicted by the fools: "We're the remains, Genesis undone, green." When their performance has finally ended, the Brigadier is calm: "What peace! What enormous and simple peace! Now everything has its order." The Aide-de-camp continues to pressure the Brigadier for an answer and, after recommending that they send the priest to jail and Camila home to her parents, listens in horror to the Brigadier's decision: "Shoot them . . . How could you possibly think that I wouldn't give a response worthy of their bravery?" The play ends in temporary stasis: Camila's newly born son holds promise for a utopian future, but the Brigadier has also unchained the criminal Barrabás, who flees into the violent early dawn as the distant firing of rifles and cannons is heard.

For the first time in any fictionalization of this famous story, the executioner assumes his own tragic role. The Brigadier's identification with Camila's tragedy (and death and martyrdom) is witnessed in their shared crowns of thorns, but whereas her roses are innocently transparent, his are violently red. So strongly has the Brigadier identified with the lovers and their heroic flight that he finally arrives at the decision to execute them. In the Brigadier's world of individualism, law, and honor, the only way to respect and punish Camila's behavior would be to execute her like a soldier. Just as the lovers consciously decide their tragic destiny within society by choosing to run away together, the Brigadier consciously chooses his future as barbaric monster. Each is the appropriate tragic ending in a world of polar opposites where there are only two options: civilization or barbarity.

Una pasión sudamericana, with its mediated and atomized text, precludes any identification, empathy, or catharsis on the part of the audience as it analyzes, from a carnivalized distance, the lovers' plight and the executioner's thought processes. In this play, a product of both dictatorship and postdictatorship, Monti attempts to separate his theater from all models of dialectical opposition, theatrical or historical. The text thus manages to cross national borders and examine the theme of "America" without resorting to the models of polarization that have perpetuated violence and withheld any understanding. By forcing the spectator to witness the symbolic and concrete events that lead the Brigadier to his final decision, Monti introduces his audience into what his fellow Argentinean playwright Eduardo Pavlovsky has called the collective subconscious of victims and victimizers. *Una pasión sudamericana* dramatizes and comments on the tragic outcome of the authoritarian episteme confronting the mystery of passion. Furthermore, by exploding Camila's story and the way in which it is told, the playwright rejects both the diachrony of tragedy's "historical" causality as well as the synchrony of the passion play's "mythical" eternal return. In this way, *Una pasión sudamericana* initiates Monti's search for an alternate means of representing and interpreting recent, and not so recent, Argentine-American history. Monti so identified with his project that he named his third child, born earlier that year, Camila.

Despite a flawed original production, *Una pasión sudamericana* was critically well received and awarded the 1989 ARGENTORES (Argentine Association of Writers) and Pepino el 88 prizes for best drama; and Monti received that year's María Guerrero award for outstanding playwright. Four years later, in 1993, Monti would be awarded the First National Award for authoring the best drama, tragedy, or historical play during the 1988–91 period.

Even as Monti continued to write new plays, he often revisited and reworked his own texts. In 1990, he adapted his 1980 play *Marathón* for the opera. With music written by Pompeyo Camps, the opera was staged that year in the Colón Theater by Jaime Kogan. In 1990 also, Monti produced a new version of the 1971 *Historia tendenciosa*, which he called *Una historia tendenciosa* [A biased (hi)story] and subtitled "Moralidad en un acto" [A one-act morality play]. Modifications made to this new version, as yet unstaged, can be summarized as follows: The basic story has been streamlined but not significantly altered (except for the elimination of extraneous characters such as the three mannequins), and the one-act play focuses more on historical events and less on characters and performers commenting on those events. In a similar vein, several of the earlier version's more Brechtian elements have been eliminated, most notably the improvised "implosions" and the actors' direct address to the audience that ended the original. The first version's second act has been modified considerably more than the first, to reflect historical events that took place after the earlier play's premiere. In *Una historia tendenciosa*, the General (who makes

only a brief appearance in the first act of *Historia tendenciosa*) takes over
the clown Nicanor's temporary role as national hero. The change is clearly
justified as a comment on Argentina's 1976–83 military dictatorship, whose
takeover occurred some five years after *Historia tendenciosa* was written.
The prostitute (before named Pola and known in the later version merely as
the Madame) more clearly assumes her role as *madre patria*, the Argentine
nation itself. There are also significant changes in the narrator/director character of Teatro: the character plays fewer roles outside his own and comments far less on the significance of the staged events. Instead, Teatro con-
sistently brings the other characters back to the idea of their production as
theater and not as life. He limits himself to only veiled allusions to any
correlation between on- and offstage worlds (a correlation overtly present
in the earlier text) until the play's end, when he addresses the audience in
newly added lines:

> Curtain, I said! Are you asleep? You're ruining my grand finale! [*He's si-
> lent as if he were listening to someone from offstage.*] What? What do you
> mean? It's not over? We have to keep going? [*Pause.*] Begin all over again?
> [*Pause. Perplexed, he addresses the audience.*] But how many times are
> we going to have to repeat the same [hi]story?

As these final lines make clear, *Una historia tendenciosa* is indeed a didac-
tic morality play.

Monti's next new play, *Asunción*, continued his "American" project.
The one-act play's subtitle summarizes the action of what is principally a
monologue: "The mystical delirium, passion, and death of Doña Blanca,
once the concubine of Don Pedro de Mendoza and now ill with syphilis,
agonizes in the still Paraguayan night, while at her side, Asunción, an Indian girl, gives birth to the land's first *mestizo*, in the Year of Our Lord
1537." Doña Blanca is a woman who, similar to Pola of *Historia tendenciosa*
and the madam in *La cortina de abalorios*, has been co-opted by the masculine world. She first allied herself with the conquering Pedro de Mendoza,
only to take up with a lesser conquistador, Domingo de Irala. Mendoza, the
great initial "founder" of Buenos Aires, has died of syphilis, a disease he
most probably passed on to the now-dying Doña Blanca. Irala, who would
go on to spend some thirty years in Paraguay, is the supposed father of
Asunción's child. Like so many characters in Monti's plays, Doña Blanca
is not easily categorized. Clearly a victim of a masculinist society, she has
participated in her own victimization. As she sits on her large thronelike
chair next to an enormous baroque cross, she tells her life story, stabbing
the palms of her hands with a dagger so that her blood will continue to flow
and she will continue to live. The image of flowing liquid dominates this

very lyrical text, and Doña Blanca's self-created stigmata suggest her martyrdom at her own society's hands. Straddling life and death, the Old World and the New, Doña Blanca's life and destiny are inscribed in her body. *Marathón* staged the demythologization of the syphilitic conquistador Mendoza's delirium of power; in *Asunción*, Mendoza's concubine seeks her own assumption into heaven and transcendence of her borderline condition.

The premiere of *Asunción*, on 2 November 1992, as part of a festival of new Latin American one-act plays ("Voces con la misma sangre" [Voices with the same blood]), tragically coincided with the sudden, unexpected death of Monti's second wife, Teresita, to whom *Una pasión sudamericana* had been dedicated. Monti would be left alone to raise his young daughter Camila.

Running through most of Monti's plays is a strong masculine/feminine dichotomy, but the dialectic comes center-stage in his plays of the late 1980s and early 1990s. At times, the split has been dramatized in a single character, as seen in Estanislao's performance of Camila in *Una pasión sudamericana*. Other times, a female character is "masculinized"; such are the cases of Doña Blanca in *Asunción* (and indeed that of all the "prostitute" characters appearing in Monti's plays) and Perla in *Visita*, both of whom participate in the perpetuation of the patriarchal status quo. The feminine in Monti's theater, incarnated by Julia (and the absent mother Bibí) in *Una noche con el señor Magnus e hijos*, carries a redemptive and revolutionary power. Much like Camila's nonappearance in the man's world staged in *Una pasión sudamericana*, the feminine is often silenced or mediated but still present. For Monti, the feminine constitutes what the French philosopher Jacques Derrida has called the *supplément*, the ever-present, potentially subversive trace. Monti's dramatic world is overwhelmingly masculine, because such is the Western world. The feminine, always present but not always represented by female characters, offers the promise of redemption, of change.

The redemptive power of the feminine is perhaps most present in Monti's next play. Under the direction of Jaime Kogan, *La oscuridad de la razón* [The obscurity/darkness of reason] premiered 8 September 1993 in the Payró Theater. Both the play and production would receive almost every Buenos Aires award accorded a dramatic play (including a municipal award for outstanding contribution to the theater and the Association of Theater Critics awards for best director, music, and dramatic play).

La oscuridad de la razón is an inverted *Oresteia*, in which the Virgin Mary (costumed in the original staging as Eva Perón and referred to in the play-text simply as Mujer [Woman]) makes appearances together with various "types" from nineteenth-century Argentine history. *La oscuridad de la razón* celebrates the death of modern individualism and Western modernity's preferred dramatic genre, tragedy. Monti stated, in a 1992 personal conversation with this author, that Aeschylus's classical tragedy represents "the passage from a matriarchy to a patriarchy and the establishment of reason . . . , which culminated in Positivism's arrogant domination of Nature."[16] Indeed, according to Monti (in an interview with Susana Freire published in the Buenos Aires newspaper *La Nación* at the time of play's 1993 premiere), the play's historical moment is roughly 1830, a year he regards as "the birth of modernity, where the cultural turn was made that produced our world."[17]

The three-act play begins, as do many of Monti's works, with a brief, strange prologue. The young Mariano (an Orestes who also bears not only a striking resemblance to the nineteenth-century Argentinean independence hero Mariano Moreno but also echoes of *Marathón*'s Tom Mix) returns from France to his homeland, now lying in ruins. There he meets the Woman, who promises to lead and "enlighten" him about himself. The first act opens with Mariano's sister, Alma (a woman's name common in Spanish whose translation is "soul"), surrounded by a chorus of Weeping Women. Like her classical counterpart, Aeschylus's Electra, Alma mourns her father's death and vows to avenge his murder. Mariano approaches her, but she does not recognize her French-speaking brother. When he finally speaks to her in Spanish, she unexpectedly stabs him with her knife and then fails again to recognize her own responsibility in inflicting this wound, which Mariano will keep bandaged in a bloodstained cloth throughout the rest of the play's action. It is only when the Women's Chorus demands that "blood recognize blood" that Alma finally recognizes her brother. They are soon joined by their mother, María, who, like Clytemnestra, has taken up with her husband's younger brother and murderer, the local *caudillo* Dalmacio. Dalmacio, accompanied by the Men's Chorus, attempts to ascertain Mariano's motives in returning. The first act ends with the return of the women characters, who crown Mariano as everyone cries,

> Glory be to our lost brother,
> glory be to our found son,
> to our pilgrim,
> our stranger,
> our hero,
> glory.

The second act moves indoors and brings the struggle between light and darkness to its climax. A dreamlike cloud still envelops the play, blurring the line between the rational and irrational as it dramatizes Mariano's slow awakening from his dream of reason. In the first scene, Alma urges

Mariano to kill both Dalmacio and their mother. The second scene stages a confrontation between María, lying next to a sleeping Dalmacio, and the ghost of her dead husband. María unrepentantly confesses to having participated in his murder. Dalmacio awakes to profess his innocence, justified in his desire to bring "freedom" to his land. The act ends with everyone awake, meeting in the debris, as María, Dalmacio, and the Ghost reenact his murder for Mariano and Alma. The Ghost hands Alma's knife to Mariano, who fulfills his destiny by killing Dalmacio.

The third and final act takes place in an old abandoned church, ruined by the ongoing civil war. Mariano, alone and overwhelmed by the horror of what he has done, wonders aloud, "Father, father! Why have you forsaken me?" He is joined by Alma, who brings him out of his delirious state (in which he has confused her with Mary Magdalene), as the Men's Chorus, now pale, ferocious, armed specters resembling Aeschylus's Furies, clamor for revenge. Mariano now refuses Alma's knife, saying:

> I wasn't born to kill.
>
> . . . .
>
> No, sister,
> I was born to engender,
> to give life.
> Now I understand.
> And if I should die tonight,
> I no longer wish
> new shadows
> to drag along with me.
> I will die my death,
> that's enough,
> and no others.

Alma insists, and Mariano is about to take the knife when the Woman reappears. She goes to him and removes the bloodied bandage from his hand; the two, free of the cycle of violence, begin to ascend. Nature appears to reign once more over America as the Woman/Virgin Mary returns Mariano/Jesus to the Holy Trinity. The Men's Chorus attempts to stop them by arguing, "But that way there's no tragedy." They continue, "So let him pay for it, pay for that destiny," to which the Woman responds, "Now destiny belongs to everyone." The play's final image, echoing the last scene of *Visita*, is a Pietà that leaves no doubt as to Mariano's imminent resurrection, made explicit in the final stage directions: "Mariano, resting motionless on the Woman's lap, appears to wake up; he slowly gets up, smiling, and submerges himself, dancing in the ever-growing light." This image of triumphant immortality does not necessarily foretell a utopian return; Alma is still alive and, electing to sleep in "defeated obscurity," completes this American family portrait. She waits, clutching her knife.

Monti's plays of the late 1980s and early 1990s constitute a deconstructive take on "America." They consciously avoid falling back on the traditional polarized models that have perpetuated a split, binarized view of the world as, in Argentina's case, either civilized or barbaric. Nevertheless, at the same time, these plays recognize the impossibility of returning to a utopian state of grace. Plays such as *Una pasión sudamericana* and *La oscuridad de la razón* mix various classic Western dramatic models to comment on the tragedy of Western rationality when confronted with passion's mystery. Monti expressed as much in a personal conversation with this author in 1992:

> I don't know if we can call *Una pasión sudamericana* a tragedy, yet there is at least a tragic movement, a tragic point, but it's crossed and cut up by the mystery play, which in turn produces a very strong structural and aesthetic tension, because tragedy by definition is dynamic while a mystery play by definition is static. There's a tremendous tension. In the case of *La oscuridad de la razón*, it's a tragedy framed by a mystery.[18]

Earlier in the same conversation, Monti made clear his own awareness of the "American" project: "I believe that there is a common destiny for America. . . . We are living in a period of incredible transformations, of the dissolution of nation-states. Let's not talk about an absurd, romantic, nineteenth-century nationalism at a moment when it's obvious that larger structures are breaking through." In these later plays, Monti has begun to question the relevance of Western modernity itself.

In 1994, Monti and Kogan again joined forces (with their usual set designer Tito Egurza) to work on a stage adaptation of Julio Cortázar's landmark 1963 novel *Rayuela* [Hopscotch]. The Payró Theater project was underwritten by the Argentine Mercantile Bank Foundation, whose president had contacted Kogan with the idea of celebrating the tenth anniversary of Cortázar's death (and the eightieth anniversary of his birth). Although the initial proposal suggested adapting selected short stories by the famous writer, Monti proposed that they stage Cortázar's challenging novel. The book's length (at over six hundred pages) was not Monti's only obstacle; the text is structured in such a way that it requires the reader's participation in its own reconstruction. (One can elect to read the first two-thirds of the novel alone, or interweave the "dispensable" chapters that make up the other third of the text, following the author's suggested order, or even invent a new reading sequence.) Despite such challenges, Monti said that, upon rereading *Rayuela*, he clearly saw dramatic "nuclei." The dramatic version is almost entirely faithful to the language of the original novel, with the addition of only a couple of phrases.

Monti focused his adaptation on the relationship between Buenos Aires and Paris, the respective earth and heaven present in the hopscotch pattern. Building upon what the playwright called this "speculative" relationship, he dramatized the two romantic triangles in which the novel's protagonist, Horacio Oliveira, finds himself entangled. In Buenos Aires, Oliveira loses the love of Talita, but he wins the love of la Maga in Paris, and, because of his relationships with the two women, his friendships with Ossip Gregorovius and Traveler are severely tested. Monti furthered the parallels between the two affairs by having the same actor and actress play both the Buenos Aires and Paris characters. True to the spirit of Cortázar's experimental text, Monti's version condensed space and time to capture the novel's lyricism and magic. The Buenos Aires production was sadly the last time Monti and Kogan collaborated before Kogan's untimely death in 1996. Together they had premiered five of Monti's plays.

During the mid-1990s, Monti worked on several adaptations. In 1995, the Colón Theater staged an operatic version of *La oscuridad de la razón*, with music once again composed by Pompeyo Camps. Rubén Szuchmacher (who had played the role of Gaspar in the original production of *Visita*) was the regisseur for Monti's adaptation of his own play-text. The following year, Monti provided a translated version, from the French, of Eric-Emmanuel Schmitt's 1993 play *Le Visiteur* [The visitor]. Monti's version, entitled *El visitante del doctor Freud* [Dr. Freud's visitor], was directed by Víctor García Peralta and presented in the Auditorium Theater of the Bauen Hotel.

In recent years, Monti has begun work on a series of one-act, two-character plays, provisionally entitled "Encuentros ejemplares" [Exemplary encounters]. The first of the series has been published under the original title of *No te soltaré hasta que me bendigas* [I will not release you until you bless me] with its alternate title, *Hotel Columbus*, in parentheses.[19] In this "thriller," a security agent for the president of an unnamed South American country has a strange encounter with a transvestite, who may or may not have come to assassinate the head of state. Over the course of an evening in the Columbus Hotel's presidential suite, "Roca" and "Sarah" play a cat-and-mouse game during which each threatens to kill the other and him- or herself with Roca's pistol.

The play opens with Roca receiving a humiliating phone call from his superior. Filled with impotent violence, he begins to drink whiskey as Sarah mysteriously enters from another room in the suite. At first, she perceives Roca to be the president; it is a confusion Roca will exploit until nearly the play's end. When Sarah suddenly takes Roca's gun, he fears she is an assassin. Sarah responds that, on the contrary, she has come to propose a union, "To us. Art and power. Politics and theater." Sarah appears to be lost in a dream, or the mad delusion, of a previous love affair, during which she, as the famous actress Sarah Bernhardt, performed for Roca and his troops. Roca accompanies Sarah in her invented memories, playing the role of his namesake, General Julio Argentino Roca, the nineteenth-century hero of the "Conquest of the Desert," in which the Argentinean government displaced or killed thousands of gauchos and indigenous peoples and cleared the way for white settlers and investors.

Their fiction-making takes more and more serious turns. Roca's actions oscillate between sudden, violent outbursts of anger and absolute exhaustion even as he maintains his fictitious presidential role and makes several attempts to tell Sarah the story of his violent "bodyguard." Sarah prefers to revisit their old love affair. Bemoaning the absence of romantic artistic glory in the modern world, Sarah begs Roca to kill her. Roca in turn suggests that the only way his quest for political power can be stopped is if she kills him, warning her that she will probably die in the attempt. Sarah responds, "I always knew you'd do it, that you were my fate. I always saw in you, in your black eyes, my own murderous double."

These games of death and memory continue, interrupted several times by the telephone. When the final call informs Roca that the real president is on his way to the suite, the bodyguard finally drops the presidential fiction. As if he were telling a police officer, he recounts the afternoon he discovered his son in his dead mother's clothing and makeup:

> The thing that hurt me the most was that he was identical to his mother. So I lifted my arm, like this, way up, and I hit him as hard as I could with my fist, hit that beautiful, fragile face I loved so much . . . And a second before I turned away, I saw the blood start pouring out of his nose, his mouth. . . .
> I don't know how much time went by.
> Then it was like thunder hit the house. . . . I ran to my room.
> My son, sir, my son was there, dead, sprawled out, his beautiful head destroyed. Blood, brains, bones scattered everywhere, spattering everything.

Sarah takes the gun from Roca just as he is about to demonstrate his son's suicide. She asks him to hold her, and, in the middle of the embrace, the gun discharges. Sarah's body slowly falls to the floor. Monti repeats his favored final image of the Pietà as Roca pulls Sarah onto his lap, saying "mi hijo" [my son/child]. He kisses her on the lips as the lights fade to black and the phone begins to ring once again.

Monti's play *Finlandia* [Finland] is as yet unpublished but premiered in 2002. The manuscript version made available to this author reveals a streamlined version of his earlier *Una pasión sudamericana*. Although the basic story line remains unchanged, there are no longer any specific references to Argentine history. Rather, the action now takes place in "the frozen plains of Finland, covered by a thick blanket of snow, at the end of the Middle Ages or the beginning of the Renaissance." The cast has been reduced to four characters: the military leader Beltrami, with his Aide, is entertained by the Mezzogiornos, brother and sister twins conjoined genitally and in a state of perpetual orgasm. Transcending the freak-show oddness of their physiological condition, the Mezzogiornos afford Monti the opportunity to explore gender construction; the twins often do not know which one is performing their *Divine Comedy* turned upside down. Both *No te soltaré hasta que me bendigas* and *Finlandia* fall squarely within Monti's larger investigation into Western modernity and modernism as they also extend his critique of modern binaristic authoritarianism to incorporate gender construction and categorization.

In recent years, Monti has continued to write for television and motion pictures as well as for the theater, with two plays in development: *Crucigrama* [Crossword puzzle], another work in the "Exemplary Encounters" series (and involving two elderly sisters living alone in an apartment); and *Genoma Elektra* [Elektra genome], which the author describes as a mix of "classicism, the 'absurd,' and science fiction."[20] His plays have won every major municipal and national award available to an Argentinean dramatist. Monti himself has received various awards for his overall achievement in the theater, including the prestigious Diploma of Merit from the Konex Foundation in 1994.

In his search to create what he has called "a broader realism," Ricardo Monti has traced the enduring presence of nineteenth-century myths in contemporary Argentina in order to dramatize the perceived failure of Western modernity and its aesthetic counterpart, modernism. Even Monti's earliest plays demonstrate a rejection of totalizing systems of power and an attempt at experimenting with alternative structures. There are other constants in Monti's plays: the mixing of religious and mythological motifs, the fusion of multiple dramatic genres, and the confluence of historical moments and references. Time and again, Monti has revisited classical formulas and images (and even his own earlier texts) in his critical dialogue with Western tradition. This unrelenting impulse to transform (texts, genres, motifs, and histories) has resulted in a body of work rich in dynamic, theatrical tension and worthy of inclusion in the Western dramatic canon.[21]

NOTES

An earlier version of this essay appears in the *Dictionary of Literary Biography: Latin American Dramatists,* edited by Adam Versényi (Columbia, S.C.: Bruccoli Clark Layman, forthcoming), s.v. "Ricardo Monti," by Jean Graham-Jones.

1. Ricardo Monti, personal e-mail correspondence with Jean Graham-Jones, 17 July 2001. All English translations from the Spanish are my own.

2. Ricardo Monti, "Conversación con Ricardo Monti," interview by Charles B. Driskell, *Latin American Theatre Review* 12, no. 2 (spring 1979): 44.

3. Ricardo Monti, "La difícil enseñanza de la libertad," interview by Jorge Conti, *Crisis* 75 (December 1989): 40.

4. The translation of *Una noche con el señor Magnus e hijos* included in this collection is based on the revised version published in *Del parricidio a la utopía: El teatro argentino actual en 4 claves mayores,* edited by Osvaldo Pellettieri (Ottawa: Girol Books, 1993), 3–54.

5. Ricardo Monti, "Presentación," in *Del parricidio a la utopía,* 2.

6. There are several newspaper accounts of *Magnus*'s reception at the Comodoro Rivadavia festival. See, for example, the local chronicles published in *El Patagónico* (e.g., "Con extraordinario éxito inicióse la Primera Muestra Patagónica de Teatro," 7 September 1970) and especially fellow playwright Germán Rozenmacher's reevaluation of *Magnus,* published in *Siete Días Ilustrados* (c. 1970). For an evaluation of Monti as rising theatrical star, see the unsigned article "El primer triunfo de un dramaturgo joven," published in the cultural magazine *Visión: Revista Internacional* (c. 1970).

7. Ricardo Monti, "Una nueva utopía," *Página/12,* 28 June 1992, 26.

8. For this reason, a translation of *Historia tendenciosa* is not included in this collection.

9. Ricardo Monti, "El teatro, un espacio literario," *Tiempo Argentino. Cultura,* 17 February 1985, 5.

10. A translation of *Visita*'s original ending immediately follows the translated playtext. See "Rejected Ending," pp. 130–32.

11. Monti, "Conversación con Ricardo Monti," 48.

12. The phrase "guiding fictions" comes from Nicolás Shumway, *The Invention of Argentina* (London and Los Angeles: University of California Press, 1991).

13. Ricardo Monti, "Entrevista," interview with Juan A. Arancibia, in *Teatro argentino durante el Proceso (1976–1983),* edited by Juan A. Arancibia and Zulema Mirkin (Buenos Aires: Vinciguerra, 1992), 249.

14. Ricardo Monti, "Con 'Marathón vuelven Monti y Kogan,'" interview with R. G., *Clarín* , 18 June 1980.

15. Later versions of *Una pasión sudamericana* (including the version upon which the translation included here is based) are more streamlined. In these versions Monti eliminated the fool Biguá as well as the characters of the British minister Canning, the chained criminal Barrabás, and one of the scribes.

16. Ricardo Monti, personal conversation with Jean Graham-Jones, September 1992.

17. Ricardo Monti, "Ricardo Monti y el sueño de un Orestes moderno," interview with Susana Freire, *La Nación,* 8 September 1993.

18. Ricardo Monti, personal conversation with Jean Graham-Jones, September 1992.

19. The title comes from Genesis 32: Jacob's refusal to release God without having been blessed.

20. Ricardo Monti, personal conversation with Jean Graham-Jones, August 2001.

21. The translator wishes to acknowledge the following persons and organizations

without whose contributions this project might not have been completed: Tabitha Combs, Paul Miller, and Rosita E. Villagómez for assistance in editing the plays; Robert Romanchuk for help in tracking down Mayakovsky; Graciela Castellanos, Mónica Viñao, David William Foster, and the late Jaime Kogan for their recollections of earlier stagings of Monti's plays; Alec and Trish Hargreaves, Jorge Huerta, Kirsten Nigro, Mario Rojas, Margarita Vargas, Adam Versényi, and members of the Mickee Faust Club for their careful readings of the translated plays; Bruccoli Clark Layman, Inc., for permission to revise and republish an earlier study; Florida State University for producing 1995's English-language premiere of *Visit* as well as granting research leave to work on the translations; and Brian Graham-Jones, for much more than can ever be expressed here. Final recognition must be paid to Ricardo Monti, with appreciation for his "obstinate clarity" and unfailingly enthusiastic support of bringing this project to completion. Any incompleteness is the translator's exclusive responsibility.

Selected Works by and about
Ricardo Monti

PLAYS BY RICARDO MONTI

Una noche con el señor Magnus e hijos. Buenos Aires: Talía, 1971. Premiered, Buenos Aires, Teatro del Centro, 1970 (premiered earlier in Neuquén, 1970); restaged as *Magnus & Hijos, S.A.* by the Venezuelan troupe Rajatabla, in Madrid, Barcelona, and Rome, 1975. Author-revised version published in *Del parricidio a la utopía: El teatro argentino actual en 4 claves mayores*, edited by Osvaldo Pellettieri, 3–54. Ottawa: Girol Books, 1993. Republished in *Teatro II*, edited by Osvaldo Pellettieri, 81–145. Buenos Aires: Corregidor, 2000.

Historia tendenciosa de la clase media argentina, de los extraños sucesos en que se vieron envueltos algunos hombres públicos, su completa dilucidación y otras escandalosas revelaciones. Buenos Aires: Talía, 1972. Premiered, Buenos Aires, Payró Theater, 1971. Author-revised version published as *Una historia tendenciosa*. Ottawa: Girol, 1993. Republished in *Teatro II*, edited by Osvaldo Pellettieri, 147–200. Buenos Aires: Corregidor, 2000.

Visita. Buenos Aires: Talía, 1977. Premiered, Buenos Aires, Payró Theater, 1977; produced in English in Tallahassee, Florida State University Conradi: Studio Theater, 1995.

Marathón. In *Teatro argentino. 16. Cierre de un ciclo*, edited by Luis Ordaz, 57–122. Buenos Aires: Centro Editor de América Latina, 1981. Premiered, Buenos Aires, Teatros de San Telmo (Payró Theater), 1980; produced in German in Stuttgart, the Theaterhaus, 1988; operatic version (with music by Pompeyo Camps) premiered, Buenos Aires, Colón Theater, 1990.

La cortina de abalorios. In *Teatro Abierto 81: Veintiún estrenos argentinos*. Buenos Aires: Teatro Abierto, 1981. Republished in *Siete dramaturgos argentinos*, edited by Miguel Angel Giella, Peter Roster, and Leandro Urbina, 139–73. Ottawa: Girol Books, 1983. Republished in *Teatro Abierto 1981: Veintiún estrenos argentinos*, edited by Miguel Angel Giella, 207–33. Collection Dramaturgos Argentinos Contemporáneos. Buenos Aires: Corregidor, 1992. Premiered, Buenos Aires, Teatro del Picadero, later Tabarís Theater (Teatro Abierto Festival), 1981.

Una pasión sudamericana. Teatro/Celcit 2, no. 3 (fall 1992): 67–95. Premiered, Buenos Aires, General San Martín Municipal Theater, 1989. Revised and republished in *Una pasión sudamericana, Una historia tendenciosa*, edited by Osvaldo Pellettieri, 31–89. Ottawa: Girol Books, 1993. Republished in *Antología del teatro argentino*, edited by Gerardo Fernández. Madrid: Centro de Documentación Teatral, Ministerio de Cultura, 1993.

Asunción. Hispamérica 22, no. 64/65 (April–August 1993): 149–65. Republished in *Teatro I*, 251–70. Buenos Aires: Corregidor, 1995. Premiered, Buenos Aires, Presidente Alvear Municipal Theater ("Voces con la misma sangre" Festival), 1992.

La oscuridad de la razón. In *Teatro I*, edited by Osvaldo Pellettieri, 131–270. Buenos Aires: Corregidor, 1995. Premiered, Buenos Aires, Payró Theater, 1993; operatic version (with music by Pompeyo Camps) premiered, Buenos Aires, Colón Theater, 1995.

Rayuela (stage adaptation of novel by Julio Cortázar). Unpublished manuscript. Premiered, Buenos Aires, Payró Theater, 1994.

El visitante del doctor Freud (translated version of *Le visiteur* by Eric-Emmanuel Schmitt). Unpublished manuscript. Premiered, Buenos Aires, Bauen Auditorium Theater, 1996.

Finlandia. Unpublished manuscript. Staged reading in Teatrísimo series, Buenos Aires, Presidente Alvear Municipal Theater, 2000. Premiere, Buenos Aires, La Trastienda, 2002.

No te soltaré hasta que me bendigas (Hotel Columbus). In *Teatro II*, edited by Osvaldo Pellettieri, 201–35. Buenos Aires: Corregidor, 2000. Premiere, Buenos Aires, Cervantes National Theater, 2003.

EDITIONS AND COLLECTIONS OF PLAYS BY RICARDO MONTI

Una pasión sudamericana, Una historia tendenciosa. Ottawa: Girol Books, 1993. Introduction by Osvaldo Pellettieri.

Teatro I. Edited by Osvaldo Pellettieri. Collection Dramaturgos Argentinos Contemporáneos. Buenos Aires: Corregidor, 1995. Comprises *Una pasión sudamericana, Asunción, La oscuridad de la razón*. Introduction by Osvaldo Pellettieri and critical bibliography by Liliana López.

Teatro II. Edited by Osvaldo Pellettieri. Collection Dramaturgos Argentinos Contemporáneos. Buenos Aires: Corregidor, 2000. Comprises revised *Una noche con Magnus e hijos*, revised *Una historia tendenciosa, No te soltaré hasta que me bendigas*. Introduction by Osvaldo Pellettieri.

PRODUCED SCRIPTS BY RICARDO MONTI

With Ricardo Wulicher. *Saverio el cruel*. Motion picture. 100 mins. Based on the play by Roberto Arlt. Directed by Ricardo Wulicher. Buenos Aires: Cañas-Flores Productions/Patagonia Films, 1977.

With Ricardo Wulicher and Vlady Kociancich. *Borges para millones*. Motion picture. 60 mins. Directed by Juan Carlos Victorica and Milton Fontaina. Buenos Aires: Distrifilms, 1978.

With Mario Sábato. *El poder de las tinieblas*. Motion picture. 90 mins. Based on a fragment ("Informe para ciegos") from the novel *Sobre héroes y tumbas* by Ernesto Sábato. Directed by Mario Sábato. Buenos Aires: Productores Americanos/Producciones del Plata, 1979.

Roberto Arlt en escena. For the television series *DNI* (National Identity Card), 1994.

OTHER TEXTS BY RICARDO MONTI

With Jaime Kogan. "Nacimiento y vida." In *Historia tendenciosa . . .* , 5–6. Buenos Aires: Talía, 1972.

"Teatro" (theater reviews). *Crisis* 38 (May–June 1976): 62–63.

"Teatro" (theater review). *Crisis* 39 (July 1976): 55.

"Teatro" (theater review). *Crisis* 40 (August 1976): 68.

"Prefacio." In *Extraño juguete* (a play by Susana Torres Molina), 7–9. Buenos Aires: Editorial Apex, 1978.

"Las imágenes en la creación literaria." In *Memoración de Sigmund Freud*, 43–47. Buenos Aires: Trieb, 1979.

"Prólogo." In *Teatro* (plays by Gabriel Díaz, Mauricio Kartun, Eduardo Pogoriles, and Víctor Winer), 7–11. Buenos Aires: Los Autores, 1983.

"El teatro, un espacio literario." *Tiempo Argentino. Cultura,* 17 February 1985, 5. Reprinted in *Espacio* 3, no. 5 (April 1989): 33–35.

"Teatro y libertad." *Asuntos Culturales* 4 (March 1989): 22–26.

"Una nueva utopía." *Página/12,* 28 June 1992, 26.

"Presentación." In *Del parricidio a la utopía: El teatro argentino actual en cuatro claves mayores*, edited by Osvaldo Pellettieri, 1–2. Ottawa: Girol, 1993.

SELECTED INTERVIEWS WITH RICARDO MONTI

"Reportaje a Ricardo Monti." Interview by Jorge Adip. *Fronteras* 1–2 (February 1979): 19–22.

"Conversación con Ricardo Monti." Interview by Charles B. Driskell. *Latin American Theatre Review* 12, no. 2 (spring 1979): 43–53.

"Con 'Marathón' vuelven Monti y Kogan." Interview by R.G. *Clarín,* 18 June 1980.

"Un teatro de reflexión." Interview by Osvaldo Pellettieri. *La Escena Latinoamericana* 2 (August 1989): 75–78.

"La difícil enseñanza de la libertad." Interview by Jorge Conti. *Crisis* 75 (December 1989): 38–42.

"La pasión como enigma: Entrevista a Ricardo Monti." Interview by Peter Roster. *La Escena Latinoamericana* 5 (December 1990): 34–40.

"Entrevista." Interview by Juana A. Arancibia and Zulema Mirkin. In *Teatro argentino durante el Proceso (1976–1983)*, edited by Juana A. Arancibia and Zulema Mirkin, 247–52. Buenos Aires: Vinciguerra, 1992.

"Ricardo Monti y el sueño de un Orestes moderno." Interview by Susana Freire. *La Nación*, 8 September 1993.

"Una noche con Ricardo Monti e hijos." Interview by Miguel Angel Giella. In *De dramaturgos: Teatro latinoamericano actual*, 118–26. Collection Dramaturgos Argentinos Contemporáneos. Buenos Aires: Corregidor, 1994.

"El valor de la representación." Interview by Carlos Pacheco. *La Nación*, 11 February 2002.

CRITICAL STUDIES OF RICARDO MONTI'S PLAYS

Adler, Heidrum. "Marathón de Ricardo Monti." *La Escena Latinoamericana* 1 (April 1989): 26–31.

Arlt, Mirta. "Los '80–Gambaro–Monti–y más allá. . . ." *Latin American Theatre Review* 24, no. 2 (spring 1991): 49–58.

Cosentino, Olga. "Misterio, poesía y tragedia de América Latina." In *Teatro contemporáneo argentino (Antología)*, 1015–21. Madrid: Fondo de Cultura Económica, 1992.

Foster, David William. "Semantic Relativity in Ricardo Monti's *La visita*." *The American Hispanist* 4, no. 34–35 (March–April 1979): 17–20.

GETEA (Grupo de Estudios del Teatro Argentino). *De Bertolt Brecht a Ricardo Monti: Teatro en lengua alemana y teatro argentino, 1900–1994*, edited by Osvaldo Pellettieri. Buenos Aires: Galerna, 1995.

Giella, Miguel Angel. "*La cortina de abalorios*, de Ricardo Monti." In his *Teatro Abierto 1981: Teatro argentino bajo vigilancia*, 177–90. Buenos Aires: Corregidor, 1991.

Giustachini, Ana Ruth. "El teatro de la resistencia: *Una pasión sudamericana* y *Postales argentinas*." In *Teatro argentino actual*, Cuadernos Getea 1.1, 55–72. Ottawa: Girol/ Revista Espacio, 1990.

González, Horacio. "Ricardo Monti, su pasión y el combate por la historia." *Nuevo Sur,* 1989.

———. "El teatro de Ricardo Monti: El misterio y la carne." Unpublished manuscript.

Graham-Jones, Jean. "*Camila* y *Una pasión sudamericana:* Bemberg, Monti y un paraíso perdido argentino." In *Segundas jornadas internacionales de literatura argentina-comparatística, Actas*, 102–10. Buenos Aires: Universidad de Buenos Aires, 1998.

———. "De la euforia al desencanto y al vacío: La crisis nacional en el teatro argentino de los 80 y los 90." In *Memoria colectiva y políticas de olvido. Argentina y Uruguay, 1970–1990*, edited by Adriana J. Bergero and Fernando Reati, 253–77. Buenos Aires: Beatriz Viterbo, 1997.

———. "*Magnus*, a los (casi) 30 años." In *Indagaciones sobre el fin de siglo*, edited by Osvaldo Pellettieri, 143–49. Buenos Aires: Galerna, 2000.

———. "1976–1979: Theater 'Metaphorizes' Reality" and "1980–1982: Myths Unmasked, Unrealities Exposed." In her *Exorcising History: Argentine Theater under Dictatorship*, 25–54, 55–88. Lewisburg, Pa.: Bucknell University Press; London: Associated University Presses, 2000.

———. "Ricardo Monti." Bio-bibliographical entry in *Dictionary of Literary Biography: Latin American Dramatists*, edited by Adam Versényi. Columbia, S.C.: Bruccoli Clark Layman, 2004.

López, Liliana. "Bibliografía crítica sobre Ricardo Monti." In *Teatro I*, by Ricardo Monti, edited by Osvaldo Pellettieri, 271–83. Buenos Aires: Corregidor, 1995.

———. "Las máscaras del poder en la dramaturgia de Ricardo Monti." *Arte y poder*, 467–74. Buenos Aires: Centro Argentino de Investigadores de Artes, 1993.

———. "Los paradigmas de la alteridad en *Asunción*, de Ricardo Monti." In *Actas de ACITA*, 78–82. Buenos Aires: Asociación de Críticos e Investigadores de Teatro Argentino, 1993.

———. "Poéticas refuncionalizadas. Mito e historia en *La oscuridad de la razón*, de Ricardo Monti." In *El teatro y los días*, edited by Osvaldo Pellettieri, 3:101–9. Collection Estudios sobre Teatro Iberoamericano y Argentino. Buenos Aires: Galerna, 1995.

Monteleone, Jorge. "El teatro de Ricardo Monti." *Espacio de Crítica e Investigación Teatral* 2, no. 2 (April 1987): 63–74.

Moretta, Eugene Lawrence. "Reflexiones sobre la tiranía: Tres obras del teatro argentino contemporáneo." *Revista Canadiense de Estudios Hispánicos* 7, no. 1 (fall 1982): 141–47.

Ordaz, Luis. "Ricardo Monti y el juego de los símbolos." In *El teatro argentino*, edited by Luis Ordaz, vii–x. Buenos Aires: Centro Editor de América Latina, 1981.

Pellettieri, Osvaldo. "Cuatro textos de nuestro tiempo o la continuidad de una voluntad modernizadora." Introduction to *Del parricidio a la utopía: El teatro argentino actual en cuatro claves mayores*, edited by Osvaldo Pellettieri, i–xvii. Ottawa: Girol, l993.

———. "Historia y teatro." *Todo es Historia* 212 (December 1984): 32–44.

———. "Un microcosmos del país." *La Escena Latinoamericana* 2 (August 1989): 12–13.

———. "El teatro de Ricardo Monti: De la rectificación de la historia a la historia propia." Introduction to *Una pasión sudamericana, Una historia tendenciosa*, by Ricardo Monti, edited by Osvaldo Pellettieri, 1–29. Ottawa: Girol, 1993.

———. "El teatro de Ricardo Monti (1989–1994): La resistencia a la modernidad marginal." Introduction to *Teatro I*, by Ricardo Monti, edited by Osvaldo Pellettieri, 6–60. Buenos Aires: Corregidor, 1995.

———. "El teatro de Ricardo Monti (1970–2000): La resistencia a la modernidad marginal." Introduction to *Teatro II*, by Ricardo Monti, edited by Osvaldo Pellettieri, 9–79. Buenos Aires: Corregidor, 2000.

———. "Una tragedia sudamericana." *La Escena Latinoamericana* 5 (December 1990): 28–34.

Podol, Peter L. "Surrealism and the Grotesque in the Theatre of Ricardo Monti." *Latin American Theatre Review* 14, no. 1 (fall 1980): 65–72.

Previdi Froelich, Roberto. "Víctimas y victimarios: Cómplices del discurso del poder en *Una noche con el sr. Magnus e hijos* de Ricardo Monti." *Latin American Theatre Review* 23, no. 1 (fall 1989): 37–48.

Ramos Foster, Virginia. "Theatre of Dissent: Three Young Argentine Playwrights." *Latin American Theatre Review* 4, no. 2 (spring 1972): 45–50.

Sagaseta, Julia Elena. "La dramaturgia de Ricardo Monti: La seducción de la escritura." In *Teatro argentino de los '60—Polémica, continuidad y ruptura*, edited by Osvaldo Pellettieri, 227–41. Buenos Aires: Corregidor, 1989.

———. "Los límites del poder: En torno a *Una pasión sudamericana* de Ricardo Monti." *Boletín del Instituto de Artes Combinadas* 8 (1990): 19–21.

———. "El placer del texto." *Teatro 2* 3, no. 4 (July 1993): 20–22.

Scheinin, Adriana. "Sobre *Una pasión sudamericana*, de Ricardo Monti." *Boletín del Instituto de Artes Combinadas* 8 (1990): 22–26.

Taylor, Diana. "Staging Battles of Gender and Nation-ness: Teatro Abierto 1981." In her *Disappearing Acts: Spectacles of Gender and Nationalism in Argentina's "Dirty War,"* 223–54. Durham, N.C.: Duke University Press, 1997.

Tirri, Néstor. "Los parricidas: Monti y Gentile." In his *Realismo y teatro argentino*, 185–92. Buenos Aires: La Bastilla, 1973.

Trastoy, Beatriz. "El teatro argentino de los últimos años: Del parricidio al filicidio." *Espacio* 2, no. 2 (April 1987): 74–82.

———. "Teatro político: Producción y recepción (notas sobre *La cortina de abalorios* de Ricardo Monti)." In *Teatro argentino de los '60—Polémica, continuidad y ruptura*, edited by Osvaldo Pellettieri, 217–23. Buenos Aires: Corregidor, 1989.

Tschudi, Lilian. *Teatro argentino actual*, 81–93, 107–14. Buenos Aires: García Cambeiro, 1974.

Zayas de Lima, Perla. "Historia, antihistoria, intrahistoria en *Una pasión sudamericana* de Ricardo Monti." *Boletín del Instituto de Artes Combinadas* 8 (1990): 16–18.

———. "El neorrealismo en dos tiempos: de Gorostiza a Monti." In her *Relevamiento del teatro argentino (1943–1975)*, 109–18. Buenos Aires: Rodolfo Alonso, 1983.

Reason Obscured

An Evening with Mr. Magnus & Sons

(revised 1993 version)

Una noche con el señor Magnus e hijos was first staged by the Grupo Laboratorio de Teatro (of Buenos Aires) in Neuquén, Argentina, on 2 May 1970 and on 25 June that same year in the Teatro del Centro, Buenos Aires.

Original Cast

JULIA	Graciela Castellanos
MAGNUS	Carlos Catalano
AMANCIO (EL GATO) [KIT]	Alfredo Sosa
GUALTERIO (WOLFI) [WOLFY]	Adelfo Bianciotto
SANTIAGO [JIMMY]	Alberto Sosa
EL VIEJO LOU [OLD LOU]	Raúl Manso
Set Design	Leonor Puga Sabaté
Direction	Hubert H. Copello

Translator's note: At the author's request, the present translation is based on the revised 1993 version of *Magnus*, from which several sections of the text were excised. For reasons of historical documentation, the playwright's original staging instructions have been appended to the play-text.

PROLOGUE

The stage is completely dark. There is only a tenuous light coming in through the upstage window. The only sound is a record playing Mozart. Then a voice speaks.

KIT *(hissing and whispering)*: Wolfy. *(No one responds.)* Wolfy, little brother, where are you? The game's over. *(No response. KIT searches around in the darkness.)* If I catch you, Wolfy . . . *(There's a sound of someone tripping and falling. KIT's strangled moan. With barely contained fury:)* Wolfy, you son of a bitch, where are you? I can hear you salivating, you shit . . . Your hands must be covered in horny sweat. *(KIT lets out a whoop. Silence. Moans. Suddenly, there's the sound of a leap, confused noises, objects falling.)* Ow, Wolfy! *(Silence.)* For Chrissakes, bro. I dislocated my finger, I'm going to die. *(Silence. Quickly, without interrupting.)* Wolfy, don't leave me alone in the dark, Wolfy, don't leave me alone in the dark, Wolfy, don't leave me alone . . . in . . . the . . . dark! *(Silence. KIT howls.)* Wolfy, this music is making my head explode! *(Someone turns off the record. There's a bit more light that will gradually grow in intensity, but it already allows us to make out the figures on stage. KIT is on his knees at center stage. Tall, very thin, unshaved, his clothing dirty and worn-out. There is something feline about his movements. Thick, dark eyebrows, walleyed. WOLFY is standing, over to one side. He is biting his nails as he observes KIT. WOLFY is the exact opposite of his brother. Pudgy, with a rosy complexion and short, almost shaved blond hair. He dresses with modesty, precision, and cleanliness. He has a grating, shrill voice. WOLFY's eyes are round, wet, and frightened. Quickly, KIT speaks, with no change of tone.)* This must never happen again, Wolfy; I'm not saying that to hurt you because I know that your soul is wretched, petty, and small, but if there's anything that can stop you, it should be the horrible things that the laws of this city reserve for those who violate their sacred norms, and don't you know there's no worse atrocity and stupidity than provoking the atrocity and stupidity of others, I beg you, you disgusting pig, I beg you, never again to blanket my eyes in darkness. *(Now slower, tired, bothered.)* Because you'll be paid back with death one hundred times over. *(Silence.)* Wolfy, I had those nightmares again tonight. *(Silence.)*

WOLFY *(screeching):* I don't want to hear about them!

KIT *(paying no attention to his brother):* It happened right here. In this very room. But the light was different . . . At first it was kind of . . . but then it became red. Redder and redder and then heavier . . . just like blood.

WOLFY: Winston, I'm not going to listen to you! I'm not listening to you!

KIT: It was suffocating . . . The window was jammed . . . There were three people here . . . It was us but we couldn't make each other out. I called to Jimmy, Jimmy called to Wolfy, Wolfy called to me . . . and even so, we couldn't recognize each other . . .

WOLFY: I mean it, Kit, I'm not listening anymore.

KIT: It was becoming heavier, and heavier . . . it suffocated us, it flattened us . . . We were going to choke to death, Wolfy, I swear, when suddenly the rat came out of nowhere . . .

WOLFY: Shut up!

KIT: It was really huge and fast, this rat . . . but it jumped out of a crack at just the right moment and we understood then . . .

WOLFY *(calling toward offstage):* Help, Jimmy, help!

KIT: That's when we understoood that the rat was the one poisoning the air and not letting us breathe . . . that fat, piggy rat . . . *(WOLFY moves around the stage, blind and dizzy.)* The rat realized that we were going to kill it and so it hid, over in that corner . . . *(He points to the exact spot where WOLFY is standing. WOLFY lets loose a scream and runs to the opposite corner.)* Its hard little eyes were spying on us . . . Jimmy threw a chair at it and the rat ran away . . . with Wolfy in hot pursuit.

WOLFY: No, not me! Not me! Not me!

KIT: And Kit gave it a good clawing in the backside . . . The rat began to bleed . . . Wolfy bit into it with his sharp little teeth . . .

WOLFY: I'm going to throw up, Kit!

KIT: And Jimmy gave it a slam, pow, right there, in the middle of its head. Slammed it over and over. Pow, pow, pow!! Blood splattered everywhere . . . Boom! The walls were covered in rat blood. Boom! Our bodies all bloody from the blood of the rat. Pow!

WOLFY: Stop it! Please, stop it, I can't take any more! Stop.

(Silence. WOLFY, worn-out, falls backward onto the sofa. JIMMY appears. He stands motionless next to the wings. The youngest of the three brothers, he possesses an artificial and satanic beauty. His eyes are shiny, blue. Blond hair, curly and long. He dresses narcissistically. KIT observes WOLFY in silence. Then he goes over to him and softly caresses his closely shaved head.)

KIT: Feelin' bad, little bro?

(WOLFY gets up, angry. He notices JIMMY's presence, and suddenly throws himself on top of him and starts beating the hell out of him.)

KIT *(speaking at the same time):* When I lie down I say, 'When shall I arise?' But the night is long, and I am full of tossing till the dawn. My flesh is clothed with worms and dirt. Therefore I will not restrain my mouth; I will speak in the anguish of my spirit. How long wilt thou not look away from me, nor let me alone till I swallow my spittle? For now I shall lie in the earth; thou wilt seek me, but I shall not be.[1]

(WOLFY finally leaves his brother alone. JIMMY's on the ground, out of breath; WOLFY goes over to one side of the stage and violently paws through some records. He chooses one and then turns to JIMMY.)

WOLFY *(shrieking hysterically):* That'll teach you to masturbate!

KIT *(neutral, without looking at his brother):* Wolfy, don't put on that record.

WOLFY: I'll play anything I feel like! *(He turns around to put on the record. KIT, calmly, goes over to him. A brief fight. The record falls to the ground, breaking. Silence. WOLFY kneels, slowly.)* Mozart! The concerto in B-flat major, for bassoon and orchestra!

(KIT moves away. JIMMY, seated on the ground, straightens his clothing and checks his bruises.)

KIT: Wolfy, the nightmare went on.

JIMMY *(with a hoarse voice):* It's still going on.

(After a brief silence, WOLFY and KIT break out into simultaneous shouts.)

WOLFY: But it was clear! Completely clear! That's why I wanted to throw up! Parriciiiiide!

KIT: Who threw us into this jail? Who buried us in this cave? Doesn't anyone know his name?

JIMMY *(intervening, passionate):* I know who it is, Kit!

WOLFY: Parricide!

KIT: Shut up, bitch!

WOLFY: Parricide!

(KIT pounces on WOLFY, who escapes.)

KIT: Because I say what you two only think!

WOLFY: Lies! Sacrilege!

JIMMY: I think about it, Kit! *(Silence. He speaks while the others are silent.)* I think about it. When I'm alone. When I look out the window at the women going by in the street. When he caresses my hair. Kit, in the kitchen . . .

KIT: The big knife.

JIMMY: Every time I see him.

KIT: I think.

JIMMY: That it could.

KIT: Serve us.

WOLFY: Help! Parricide!

KIT: What a party that would be, Jimmikins!

(KIT and JIMMY look at each other, and each takes the other's hands.)

JIMMY: A great party!

(WOLFY appears to have suddenly gone into a trance.)

KIT: Finally our own bosses!

JIMMY: Alone and free!

KIT: What a beautiful nightmare, Jimmy!

WOLFY: I smell . . . *(Suddenly silent. JIMMY and KIT also remain motionless.)* I smell a rat. *(He quickly corrects himself.)* I mean, Magnus.

(JIMMY runs over to the window.)

JIMMY: Magnus is home! He's crossing the street . . . with a woman!

(After a brief pause, complete disorder overtakes the three SONS.)

ALL THREE: Here comes Magnus!
                  With a woman!
                  The lights!
                  He saw us!
                  Turn off the lights!

We've got to clean this up!

He's going to find out!

Help me, you morons!

Madly, they dash off and onto the stage. They carry different objects and disappear. Everything suddenly goes dark again, with the exception of the window, through which we can see the face of OLD LOU. His face disappears as the lights for act 1 *begin to come up.*

ACT ONE
SCENE ONE

Lights up. There are a few seconds of emptiness and silence. Then JULIA slowly enters. She has a gray or brown suede jacket over her shoulders and a half-smoked cigarette in her hand. Long, chestnut hair. Large dark eyes in a hard and pointy face. She's eighteen years old. Her voice has many nuances: from deep, hoarse tones to irritating shrieks. She stands motionless at center stage. MAGNUS enters, putting his keys back in his pocket. His appearance is brutal. Fat, at times imposing. Eagle-eyed, rapid and incisive looks. Thick red lips. Balding, but with very black hairs on the back of his hands, which are small, nervous, and sensitive. His complexion is ruddy, and his five o'clock shadow gives a bluish cast to his cheeks. Thick, black eyebrows.

MAGNUS: So, what do you think of the house? A little large, isn't it? Sometimes even we get lost in it. This is the living room. Or the stage, as the boys call it.

JULIA: What boys?

MAGNUS: My sons. You'll get to meet them soon. They're delightful creatures. A teeny bit extravagant, but I know how to keep them in check. Are you nervous? Make yourself at home. I've got this feeling that if I touch you, you'll fall to pieces. And end up a little pile of dust on the floor. Give me your hand. Courage! Confidence! Come on, give me that little hand .. . *(He takes JULIA's hand.)* That's it . . . Now give me a smile. A beautiful smile for this bossy but inoffensive fatty.

JULIA *(biting off every word):* Please don't act the clown, do you mind?

(Pause. MAGNUS lets go of her hand.)

MAGNUS *(smooth):* No, no. It's not time yet for the tragedy to begin. That would be a mistake. You're feeling prematurely overcome by sin and guilt. The first rule is to free oneself from all preconceived notions. Deliver oneself up, white and naked, to the moment. Right?

(Pause.)

JULIA: Get me something to drink.

MAGNUS: Of course. A little shot of the hard stuff? To get the blood flowing, hmmm? *(He calls toward offstage.)* Ratlets! *(Humming to himself, he takes out a bottle. WOLFY appears.)* Ah, here's Walter. He calls himself Wolfgang, for Mozart. Among us, Wolfy. He's the most loving. Daddy's favorite, right, Wolfy? A sensitive soul. With an enviable musical ear. Come on, Wolfy, greet the young lady. From now on, she's going to be our friend. Her name is . . .

JULIA: Julia.

MAGNUS: Julia, that's right. Wolfy, I want Julia to be like a mother for you, understood?

WOLFY: Yes, Papa.

JULIA: Hello, Wolfy.

WOLFY: How are you, Miss Julia?

MAGNUS *(looking at the two of them, with a fatherly smile):* You're both so lovely. Here you go, Julia. It's sweet and strong. *(Toward the wings.)* Come out here, you beast, didn't I teach you any manners? *(KIT appears.)* This is Winston, though I know the boys call him Kit.

WOLFY: Papa, please . . .

MAGNUS: Come on, come on. We're among family. Did you think Papa wasn't aware of that? He knows lots of other things, too . . .

WOLFY: Please, Paaa . . . What's Miss Julia going to think?

KIT: Good evening, Miss Julia.

JULIA: Hello, Winston.

MAGNUS: Don't trust this one; he's a son of a bitch, a traitor, and a bum.

JULIA: I think he's delightful.

MAGNUS: I'm telling you this because I'm his father. But one thing's for sure, he's intelligent. The family intellectual. Between us, I prefer Wolfy. A little retarded, but that's the reason I prefer him . . . Ah, here's Jimmy.

JULIA *(dazzled):* Ah.

(Silence.)

MAGNUS *(objective):* Handsome, isn't he? Come in, Jimmy. Give the young miss your hand, let her feel the sweet touch of your skin.

JULIA: He's still a child.

MAGNUS: Well, we're all here. Tonight our family is going to celebrate.

(JULIA lets loose a shriek. Silence.)

MAGNUS: What's the matter, dear?

JULIA: Nothing . . .

MAGNUS *(smooth):* Jimmy, you grabbed the young lady's ass.

JULIA: Please, I don't want to . . .

MAGNUS *(slowly advancing toward JIMMY):* You grabbed the young lady's ass and that is bad, Jimmy.

WOLFY: Let him have it, Dad!

JULIA: Please, it would be terrible for me if . . .
(MAGNUS begins to beat JIMMY up. The rest watch with sadistic expectation.)
KIT: This time he'll draw blood.
(MAGNUS brings JIMMY to his knees, with one arm twisted behind his back.)
MAGNUS: Tell the young lady you're sorry. *(Tense silence. MAGNUS twists the arm a bit more.)* Tell the young lady you're sorry.
JIMMY: I'm sorry, miss.
(Pause.)
MAGNUS: Now give him a kick, Julia.
JULIA: I ummmm . . .
MAGNUS: Come on, don't be shy.
JULIA: I ummmmm . . .
KIT/WOLFY: Let him have it, Miss Julia!
(JULIA vacillates. Then with obvious satisfaction and ferocity, she kicks him in the ribs. MAGNUS lets go of JIMMY, who writhes on the ground. Silence. Suddenly, JULIA kneels down and clasps JIMMY's head to her chest.)
JULIA: He's so handsome.
JIMMY *(with a weak thread of a voice):* Water . . .
JULIA: A glass of water, please.
MAGNUS *(to KIT):* A glass of water, louse. The young lady is moved.
(KIT exits running. The following scene is evangelical and takes place in silence. KIT brings back a glass of water. JULIA gives JIMMY a drink.)
JULIA: My sweet baby.
(MAGNUS claps his hands.)
MAGNUS: Well, that's enough. *(JIMMY gets up.)* A family incident.
(OLD LOU's face appears in the window. He taps the pane with a coin.)
MAGNUS *(to OLD LOU):* Get out!
(OLD LOU disappears. The SONS and JULIA have formed a group, from which there emerges a guffaw. MAGNUS turns toward them. All movements are almost automatic, without any apparent motivation, and simultaneous. A kind of dreamlike change in the action.)
MAGNUS: Julia!
(The GROUP goes silent.)
JULIA *(rude):* Huh?
(Pause. JULIA goes to MAGNUS, with almost a hypnotic resignation. The SONS form a tight, envious group of spectators. When JULIA is at MAGNUS's side, he grabs her by the nape of the neck.)
MAGNUS *(smoothly):* Julia. *(Pause.)* I suddenly felt so anguished. *(JULIA smiles out of obligation. Silence.)* It's cold outside.
JULIA: Really? I get warm very easily. Besides, your sons are adorable.
MAGNUS: Careful. *(The SONS begin to protest. JULIA gestures, as if to defend the SONS. MAGNUS silences them.)* Your hands were blue. *(His hands move*

down JULIA's neck, her shoulder, her arms. He grabs her hands and chastely kisses them. JULIA directs a quick wink at the SONS. OLD LOU's face reappears, and he watches the scene pathetically.)

MAGNUS: You were so tiny, so helpless and fragile, standing there on the corner. The wind was moving the lamp, and the light came and went. And my Julia entered and exited the light. Motionless on the corner. And I was at the bar, holding a hot cup of coffee and a lit cigarette. And Julia out there trembling in the cold, all alone. So I get up. I cross the street. The wind beats my face. *(Slight laughter erupts from the SONS' group.)* Silence!

(The SONS begin to disperse, silently. Upstage, at the window, OLD LOU's face.)

MAGNUS *(justifying himself in front of the sons, or the audience):* I'm a softy. Each of us has his own weakness, and the best thing we can do is hide it. That's difficult for me. An abandoned child, a freezing puppy . . . everything moves me. *(Yelling to the SONS.)* And I already know that you don't believe me, you retards! *(To JULIA.)* I've trained them not to believe me. Their job is to doubt.

A VOICE *(in falsetto):* Pig!

MAGNUS *(smooth, warning):* No insults, my dear. *(He turns back to JULIA).* I got up. I crossed the street. A black wind beat me in the face. *(He moves away and then circles back to JULIA, who follows his movements with weariness.)* Are you lost, little one?

JULIA: No, I'm thinking.

MAGNUS: No, you didn't say anything, idiot! You were thinking in silence!

JULIA *(hysterical):* No, I was not thinking about anything! I was only standing on the corner, without thinking, without thinking about anything! My brain was completely empty! *(Because of the SONS.)* And those three, what are they doing?

MAGNUS: They're preparing the bar, what's it to you?

SONS *(protesting from upstage):* That's right, let us do our job in peace! Otherwise, we can't work!

JULIA: They're hurting my concentration!

MAGNUS: Be still for a minute! *(Jeering from the SONS and then silence.)* You were smoking.

JULIA: I was not smoking.

MAGNUS: You were smoking: I'm sure I saw you at that moment with a cigarette in your hand.

JULIA: I had a cigarette in my hand, but I was not smoking it. My fingers were stiff from the cold.

(The SONS stomp their feet and whistle.)

MAGNUS: Be quiet, you envious slime! *(He takes out a cigarette, places it in JULIA's mouth and lights it; JULIA accepts this action with a gesture of repugnance.)* Little one, are you lost? *(Giggles from the SONS. Furious look from MAGNUS, and then silence.)* It's cold, and the night is great and sinister like a mask. Dear, could you tell me where we are?

JULIA: Here or there. One side or the other. Only a step separates the two, one never knows.

MAGNUS *(his asides are stagy, grotesque)*: Another lost lamb. *(To JULIA.)* It's a long time 'til dawn. Are you a virgin? *(JULIA laughs. Aside.)* She's young like a drop of rain. I need her life. For her to bear witness for me. I'll go through her body like a gust of wind blowing over the earth. *(To JULIA.)* Sister, would you come with me?

JULIA: Where?

MAGNUS: What does it matter? Is it better to be here than somewhere else?

JULIA: No.

(The show is over. Ovations from the SONS. MAGNUS makes a triumphant circle around the stage, aroused by the enthusiasm.)

MAGNUS: Well done, Julia. It was almost real. I would say that it was even better than life itself.

JULIA *(with a touch of vanity)*: Please, Magnus. I was incredibly nervous. I almost dropped my cigarette.

SONS: Encore! Bravo! Encore!

MAGNUS: Are you up for going on, Julia?

JULIA: I'm . . . I really don't know . . . it's such a commitment. *(The SONS urge her on with eloquent gestures. JULIA shyly looks at them.)*

MAGNUS *(shoots her a pleading look)*: But I don't know . . . If my public wants me to . . .

SONS: Yes, yes, Julia! Come on, Julia! Ju-li-a! Ju-li-a! We love you, Julia!

JULIA: Welllllllll . . .

(The SONS go wild with applause.)

MAGNUS: That's how I like it, Julia. *(To the SONS.)* Now, careful. Pay attention. In a minute, you're going to come on. *(Nervous movements from the SONS.)* Same place as before. The light comes and goes over Julia's tiny, frozen figure. *(He clears his throat.)* Here's a warm place for us to bundle up. You're trembling like a leaf. Are you afraid?

JULIA *(somewhat affected)*: No, it's the cold. Anyway, I'm tired. Tired of walking the streets alone.

MAGNUS *(laughing)*: Let's go in. I'm going to ask for a tall glass of steamed milk. Quickly, Wolfy, Winston!

(The SONS immediately take on the roles of waiters.)

KIT: Here comes a couple.

WOLFY: They look like father and daughter.

KIT: She's no whore.

MAGNUS: Stop. Sit. A glass of milk for her. And for me, a cognac. You're pale, sister.

JULIA: I haven't slept for two nights. My shoes are so worn-out that water gets in.

MAGNUS: I'm going to buy you a new pair of shoes and a dress. I'm going to give you my bed.

JULIA: I miss my family. My parents don't know what's been going on. They're going to die of a broken heart.

MAGNUS: Nobody dies from that, little sister. And now it's too late to go back. Why did you leave them? Did they beat you? Did somebody knock you up?

JULIA: No, I was fed up. I just went drifting. I wanted to experience life.

MAGNUS: That's OK, sister. It's never too early.

JULIA: I'll drink my milk and go.

MAGNUS: Do I scare you?

JULIA: Yes.

MAGNUS: I have three sons at home. They're as innocent as little lambs. Their mother is dead. You'd be able to play with them.

JULIA: I don't trust you.

MAGNUS: My dear, I'm an angel.

JULIA: Well, then, why are you dressed in black?

MAGNUS: Because I'm going to die.

JULIA: You have sinister eyes. Purple lips.

MAGNUS: I'm a peaceful man.

JULIA: Are you going to slice my throat in some ditch?

MAGNUS: My sons need a companion.

JULIA: I don't like children.

MAGNUS: Can you cook?

JULIA: No.

MAGNUS *(dramatic):* Oh no, my little ones will die of hunger. (*JULIA shrugs her shoulders.*) Well, let's try it from another angle.

JULIA *(on the defensive):* You're not going to convince me.

MAGNUS: Silence, slut.

JULIA: I'm a virgin.

MAGNUS *(surprised):* Oh. (*Aside.*) Am I going to pass through this life without having deflowered the last virgin? (*To JULIA.*) Little one, I'm ill.

JULIA: Illness makes me sick.

MAGNUS: I'm strong as a bull.

JULIA: I'm not impressed.

MAGNUS: I have all my teeth. Muscles of steel. And baldness is a sign of virility.

JULIA: Don't touch my knees.

(Silence.)

MAGNUS: You've finished your milk. (*JULIA blinks her eyes, disconcerted.*)

So, why don't you leave? *(JULIA leans back. She looks at him.)* Well, I'm going to give you one more chance.

(MAGNUS gets up and exits the spotlight, strutting around like a peacock. He waits upstage.)

KIT: What a disgusting individual.

(MAGNUS moves back and forth, upstage.)

MAGNUS *(restless, in a stage whisper)*: Careful, Kit.

JIMMY: Shhhh.

KIT: He's fat. Looks like a seal in heat.

WOLFY: But she doesn't want to save herself.

KIT: He gave her her chance. But she's staying put, doesn't even budge. She's hesitating, she wants to flee. But something holds her back.

WOLFY: Come on, dummy! What's holding you back?

KIT: He can't do anything now. He's too far away. Julia, please, just get up and run away.

WOLFY: Run, Julia!

MAGNUS *(from upstage)*: No taking sides!

WOLFY *(turning around, furious)*: We demand to have freedom of speech.

MAGNUS: As long as you're objective.

WOLFY: The only possibility of our being objective is if we can say whatever we want!   .

MAGNUS *(stomping the floor once)*: I'm the only objectivity around here!

WOLFY: I protest!

MAGNUS: Get out!

WOLFY: But, Paaa . . .

MAGNUS: Get out! Jimmy, take his place!

(JIMMY gets up.)

JIMMY *(after a pause)*: Run away, Julia!

MAGNUS *(coming downstage, all-powerful)*: Enough! Give the actors a little rope, and they try to hang you with it. The show is over! Julia, that was your last chance.

JULIA: I still haven't decided.

MAGNUS: Oh, yes, you have. When I returned, you were still at the table. That cigarette between your fingers was burning down almost to the butt. I said to you, "Let's go, sister." And without a word, you got up and followed me.

JULIA: I said that I still haven't decided!

(Pause.)

MAGNUS: Let's go, sister.

(JULIA, without saying a word, gets up, stubs out the cigarette with her foot and follows MAGNUS offstage.)

JIMMY: I told you guys she's a whore!

(WOLFY, waving his fist in the air, runs over to the wings into which MAGNUS and JULIA have disappeared.)

WOLFY: When are you going to quit corrupting youth? *(He searches for the appropriate insult.)* Socrates!

(Suddenly the stage goes dark. Another part of the set is partially lit, giving it a murky luminosity. JULIA and MAGNUS enter, walking.)

JULIA: I can't take another step.

MAGNUS: We can rest here.

JULIA: I'm freezing to death.

MAGNUS: Well, let's go to my house.

JULIA: No. You don't mean that much to me. You're a fling, nothing more.

MAGNUS *(with a serious tone):* Of course, my little fool.

JULIA: Tomorrow, you'll be nothing more than a dream.

MAGNUS: A bad dream.

(MAGNUS stomps the floor and rubs his hands.)

JULIA: My hands are blue.

MAGNUS: Bad circulation. *(JULIA puts her hands under her armpits. MAGNUS makes a sweeping gesture.)* Ah, dark night of merciless specters and dead dogs.

JULIA: It's necessary that everything be absolutely on the up and up.

MAGNUS: Fine. *(Silence. MAGNUS continues moving around, trying to keep warm. JULIA is motionless.)* And now what, sister?

JULIA: I'm afraid I'll regret this later. *(MAGNUS laughs.)* Don't laugh.

MAGNUS: You look so tiny and far away. So tiny that it's as if you were in the palm of my hand. But it's cold. Let's go.

JULIA: Just a minute. What do you think I am?

MAGNUS: Nothing.

JULIA: You must have some opinion of me.

MAGNUS: Not right now.

JULIA: It has to be right now.

MAGNUS *(with a giggle):* So you can slip out of my hands? Give me some time. Until tomorrow morning.

JULIA: I cannot go on unless I know what I mean to you.

MAGNUS *(smiling):* A whore. Is that what you want? An angel. A lost little lamb. A woman of the world. Anything. What a relief! But no, I don't have any idea. *(Pause.)* You can stay.

(He moves away from her. The stage lights come up full. JULIA blinks, disconcerted. She looks around her. The SONS, having followed the action from the shadows, display an indifferent and hostile aspect.)

KIT *(To JULIA, without looking at her):* Yes, you're already here.

JULIA: It all happened so fast.

WOLFY: We warned you.

JULIA: It was too fast. I didn't have time.

JIMMY: But here you are. And now it's hard to leave.

(JULIA takes a few steps, looking around the place, perplexed. MAGNUS goes over to her, putting his keys back in his pocket, just as he did at the beginning of the scene.)

MAGNUS: So, what do you think of the house? A little large, isn't it? Sometimes even we get . . . *(He interrupts himself, doubting.)* I already said that, didn't I?

(OLD LOU appears at the window and taps on the pane with a coin.)

OLD LOU *(plaintive, as if from far away):* Magnus, it's cold tonight. I'm freezing and I'm hungry. Please, Magnus.

(The reaction of the SONS is uniform.)

SONS: Don't let him in, Magnus!
　　　Make him deal with it!
　　　He's dirty!
　　　He stinks!
　　　He's old!
　　　He could die in here and then we'd be responsible, Magnus!

(Pause.)

MAGNUS: Come in, Lou.

(OLD LOU enters, through the window.)

OLD LOU: Thank you, Magnus.

(Slowly, in the middle of this general silence, OLD LOU collapses, with a humble smile on his lips, until he is on all fours, like a dog. He crawls on all fours over to MAGNUS.)

SONS *(in a stage whisper to one another):*
　　　He's a disgrace!
　　　He has no dignity!
　　　He's lost his self-respect.
　　　Arf-arf-grrr!

MAGNUS: Don't pay any attention to them, Lou. *(He pats OLD LOU on the head.)* They don't understand that, at your age, there's no such thing as indignity. *(To the SONS.)* Hey! Show a little more respect for Old Lou! *(Looking at the old man.)* He's as old as time. *(With sadistic sarcasm, hypocritically.)* And he's suffered greatly, isn't that right, Lou?

OLD LOU *(by way of answering, beginning to howl plaintively, like a dog):* Owwwww . . .

LIGHTS OUT.

SCENE TWO

The lights come up. JULIA is seated near one side of the stage. At the extreme opposite, OLD LOU is on the floor, delousing himself. He then stretches out his body and gives a great canine yawn. JULIA lights a cigarette. OLD LOU pricks up his ears and sniffs in the direction of JULIA. He gesticulates, trying to get her attention.

JULIA: What do you want?

(OLD LOU motions to her for a cigarette. As JULIA looks for a cigarette in her purse, OLD LOU goes over to her on all fours. JULIA throws him a cigarette. OLD LOU catches it in midair and sits down. He puts the cigarette in his mouth and begins to puff away on the still unlit cigarette. He takes it out, observes it, and begins to puff once more, unsuccessfully. JULIA doubles over in laughter.)

JULIA: What a stupid old fool!

(OLD LOU, panting contentedly, trots over to her side and embraces her legs. JULIA screams and gives him a kick. OLD LOU howls and runs over to his old spot. From there, he shoots fiery looks at JULIA, showing her his teeth and growling.)

JULIA *(calling out, terrified):* Magnus!

(OLD LOU rushes at JULIA, barking at her like a little puppy. JULIA shrieks, takes off one of her shoes, and brandishes the heel at OLD LOU, threatening him. From different wings, WOLFY, JIMMY, and KIT stick out their heads, fleetingly, and then disappear. JULIA and OLD LOU stalk each other fiercely, bitterly. Suddenly, OLD LOU's attitude changes; he sits down on the floor and contemplates JULIA with a desolate expression.)

OLD LOU *(struggling to articulate):* B-b-bi-b-bi.

JULIA *(without abandoning her defense, indignant):* So, now you can talk, huh?

OLD LOU *(sadly):* Bibi!

JULIA: Who are you calling for, you disgusting old thing? *(OLD LOU repeats the same word, silently. JULIA, in an excess of ire.)* My name is Julia! Do you understand? Ju-li-a!

(WOLFY enters on tiptoe. He puts on a record and disappears immediately.)

JULIA: Wolfy, what's the meaning of this?

(We hear, at a deafening volume, the first drumbeats of a requiem. JULIA is petrified, her shoe still in her hand. When the music explodes in funereal apotheosis, MAGNUS storms onto the stage, buttoning up his pants. With an irate yell, he takes the record off.)

MAGNUS: Aha, you rotten bums! What were you trying to do, sons of bitches? Poor Julia, just look at her . . .

JULIA *(shaking it off):* Magnus!

(MAGNUS grabs his SONS from offstage, shoving and pushing them. The SONS cluster together, fearful. They're wearing baggy, black cloaks, and they are sweating. MAGNUS beats them, indiscriminately.)

MAGNUS: Taking advantage of the slightest carelessness! Huh! Sons of bitches! So that somebody can't even take a simple dump around here! Huh! Can't let one's guard down even for a moment! Huh! *(JULIA is sobbing and seeks MAGNUS's protection. He puts his arms around her, while he continues to kick the air in the direction of his SONS.)* Just look at how you've left her! Reduced to shit! Her nerves ruined!

JULIA *(pointing to OLD LOU, hiccuping):* He . . . He . . . He . . .

(MAGNUS appears to have received an electric shock. He looks at OLD LOU, stupefied, and then goes over to the old man.)

MAGNUS: Him? What did he do to you? What did you do to the young lady? *(OLD LOU, when he sees MAGNUS approaching him, begins to pant and wag his tail, making a fuss over him, on all fours.)*

MAGNUS: Don't play the dog with me!

(MAGNUS hits OLD LOU, who starts to run away; suddenly, OLD LOU straightens up, like a snake, and confronts MAGNUS.)

OLD LOU: Enough, Magnus!

MAGNUS *(amused):* He's rising up against me! *(MAGNUS, his SONS, and JULIA burst out guffawing.)* Here, doggie, doggie, doggie . . . *(Vanquished, OLD LOU slowly collapses until he is once again on all fours. MAGNUS pats his flank.)* Good dog. *(He slowly turns around to face his SONS, who take a step back.)* As for you . . . *(He looks at them threateningly, but then adopts a paternal tone.)* Couldn't you have waited for me? You wanted to keep all the fun to yourselves?

SONS *(relieved):*

We were going to tell you about it, Magnus.

Yes, we were going to tell you all about it.

It's more fun to have it told to you.

MAGNUS: Well, it's alright. *(Feigning a sudden severity.)* Take off those clothes right now. *(The SONS begin to leave quickly. MAGNUS detains them with a single gesture.)* But leave them nearby.

SONS *(overcome by enthusiasm):* Long live Magnus!

(They exit, running. Pause.)

MAGNUS *(to JULIA):* I told you not to trust them.

JULIA *(somewhat upset):* What were they trying to do, Magnus?

MAGNUS *(evasive):* Nothing . . . *(OLD LOU is seated in a corner, with a look of resentment. MAGNUS goes over to him, threatening.)* And as for you . . . *(OLD LOU does not flinch. Pause.)*

OLD LOU *(sullen):* Why do you take it out on me, Magnus? If you're trying to find out how far you can go . . . But you know there's no limit. I can take anything. So? Sure, now it's easy to beat up old Lou . . . A piece of old flesh . . .

MAGNUS *(impatient, interrupting him):* Alright, it's . . . possible that I went too far.

JULIA: Too far, Magnus! He's a monster!

MAGNUS: Silence, you shit! *(JULIA gives a start. Then, confused, she curls up in a chair. Pause.)* You know that I don't like to ask for forgiveness.

OLD LOU *(smoothly):* I'm not asking you to apologize, Magnus.

MAGNUS: So . . . all over?

OLD LOU: All over.

(MAGNUS is visibly relieved. Now he goes over to OLD LOU in an open, light manner.)

MAGNUS: Lou, dear . . . I don't want to hurt you. Whatever I do to you, you can be sure, it's going to be involuntary.

OLD LOU: That's enough for me, Magnus.

MAGNUS: Dear Lou, my faithful Lou. Your wrinkles choke me up. How long have we known each other?

OLD LOU: Centuries.

MAGNUS *(sighing):* Centuries! It's all so fleeting. You've wasted away, Lou! Time's really given you the shaft!

OLD LOU: Well, I can't deny that it's been rough.

MAGNUS: I'm a kid next to you. And, nevertheless, when we met Bibi, we were the same age.

OLD LOU *(painfully):* For some of us, the years go by faster.

MAGNUS *(with a slight giggle):* Come on. The coup de grâce was Bibi. You can't deny that.

OLD LOU: Why bring up the past, Magnus?

MAGNUS: What, are you still in love with her? *(Pause.)* I took her right out of your mouth, huh, Lou? At the exact moment when you were about to swallow her up, huh, Lou? You closed your mouth and nothing . . . *(He laughs, happily.)* I, on the other hand, enjoyed her fully. For five, ten years I had her lovely flesh at my full disposal. At my full disposal, Lou. *(Pause.)* But what does that matter. She no longer exists. She's just a little pile of rotting dust lying around somewhere. And I'm in love with matter, with what's real. With something that will put up a fight, something that I can conquer.

OLD LOU: I already know that, Magnus.

MAGNUS: Remembering these things really gets my blood flowing, Lou. My old butcher's spirit begins to stir again. I need a little action.

OLD LOU: Our battle ended a long time ago, Magnus.

MAGNUS: There's always hope. Let's make something up.

OLD LOU: Without an audience?

MAGNUS: She's here.

OLD LOU: She doesn't want to watch.

(JULIA turns her back to them.)

MAGNUS: So what? She's here, she's a body, that's enough. And anyway, we can't always count on the intelligence of others. Let's go. The plaza downtown. A bench. *(They line up two chairs at center stage.)* And a touch of beauty: trees . . . Ready, Lou?

OLD LOU: Ready.

(OLD LOU sits down on one of the chairs.)

MAGNUS: During the morning, I was young. I jumped without a care in and out of the puddles. Now it's getting cold. A white moon hides in the still-white sky. Silence, here comes someone. May I?

OLD LOU: You may speak with me, but on the condition that you treat me with respect.

MAGNUS: Absolutely.

OLD LOU: What are you selling?

MAGNUS: How did you know? *(OLD LOU smiles knowingly.)* I sell anything they'll buy from me.

OLD LOU: Shall I tell you the story of my life?

MAGNUS: Today was a killer.

OLD LOU: I was born at the beginning of the last century, during the winter, after a long and complicated embryonic gestation. My ontogeny summed up my phylogeny.

MAGNUS: I couldn't sell a thing.

OLD LOU: My childhood was both lucky and tragic. But I managed to grow up like any other kid.

MAGNUS: Something's broken. Some imperceptible thread.

OLD LOU: Do you have a cigarette? *(MAGNUS gives him one. OLD LOU puts it away.)* Smoking is a nasty habit.

(The SONS enter, without the oversized cloaks. They observe the scene.)

MAGNUS: How old are you?

OLD LOU: Show some respect, kid!

MAGNUS: You must have lived a lot.

OLD LOU: I was born at the beginning of . . . *(He vacillates.)* I sometimes lose my memory. *(He smiles.)* But it's agreeable. Not remembering any-thing, not knowing anything, not seeing anything. *(Giggles.)* Revenge is sweet. Here I am, I don't know any of you, I don't see any of you. How do all of you know you even exist?

MAGNUS: How did you know I was a salesman?

OLD LOU *(mysterious):* Two days ago someone came by at the same time. He sat down there. He was a salesman. *(He looks meaningfully at MAGNUS.)* Understand?

MAGNUS: Not yet.

OLD LOU: Yesterday another person came by. At the same time. He was a salesman. Do you understand now?

MAGNUS: No.

OLD LOU: It always happens! Gimme a cigarette!

MAGNUS: It's my last one.

(OLD LOU takes the cigarette and stores it away.)

OLD LOU: Don't you have anything to say?

MAGNUS: This morning something strange happened. *(OLD LOU begins to hum, quietly.)* I got up early as always. I shaved, brushed my teeth, I performed my usual morning ritual. I left the house fresh, happy, and young. I jumped over the puddles without a care. Around noon, the sun was high up. My right hand was sweaty. I was uneasy, nervous.

OLD LOU *(interrupting him):* Yesterday you certainly made me laugh.

(One of the SONS imitates a rooster's cry.)

MAGNUS *(slowly):* I wasn't here yesterday.

OLD LOU: Come on, you want to take advantage of an old man?

(Another rooster cry.)

MAGNUS: I wasn't here yesterday.

OLD LOU: And the day before that.

(A third rooster cry.)[2]

MAGNUS: You're mistaken.

OLD LOU: Show some respect, young man! You spoke to me of your wife. *(Confidential.)* Her little dove breasts. Her velvet lips. Come on, don't you remember?

MAGNUS: I just killed my wife.

OLD LOU *(hitting the palm of his hand with his fist):* I knew you were a murderer! *(He thinks it over.)* Listen, you're not on the run from the cops, are you?

MAGNUS: No way. It was a clean job.

OLD LOU *(thoughtful):* I always wanted to kill my wife. Poor thing . . . *(With sudden vehemence.)* Tell me.

MAGNUS: What?

OLD LOU: How did you do it? Tell me.

MAGNUS: Oh . . . it was easy. Give me your hand. I took her hand. Look at me. I looked her in the eyes. I took her pulse softly . . . until it stopped beating.

(Silence.)

OLD LOU *(experiencing a chill. He jumps up from the chair, howling):* Son of a biiiiiiiitch!

MAGNUS: But no . . .

OLD LOU *(rubbing his wrist):* Murdererrrrrrr!

MAGNUS: If you don't shut up, I'm going to strangle you with your own guts. *(OLD LOU shuts up. MAGNUS smiles professionally.)* Now, please sit down. *(OLD LOU sits down, obedient.)* How could you think that with a smile like this, I would be capable of killing someone? Not even a fly . . .

OLD LOU: I'm so ashamed.

MAGNUS: Friend, friend.

OLD LOU: It's just that you don't understand. Nervous tension . . . the stress of modern living . . . I'm very unhappy . . . My life is hell. My children hate me . . . My grandchildren torture me . . . I'm underfoot at home . . . I'm a bother . . . They don't love me . . . Why do they keep feeding me chicken soup?[3]

MAGNUS: I'm restless. It's too quiet.

OLD LOU: Sell me something.

MAGNUS: You do not have any expendable income, you're on Social Security.[4]

OLD LOU *(angry):* Bullshit. Come on, give it a try.

MAGNUS: What do you want to buy?

OLD LOU: No, first you offer me something. I'm the client.

MAGNUS *(mechanically):* If you don't know what you need, I cannot tell you what it is. After an absolutely objective analysis of your life, desires, aspirations, your social, natural and spiritual milieu. And after endless scientific research; after centuries of sweat and tears, of hunger, revolutions, wars, modern technology has made a supreme concentration of forces in order to offer you the essence of your own dreams and projects, the culmination of forty centuries of culture.

OLD LOU *(belligerent and hysterical):* I don't want anything, I don't want anything! Don't badger me! Go away!

(OLD LOU pushes MAGNUS away. They wrestle briefly.)

OLD LOU: Help!

(MAGNUS moves away. He is livid, and he mops up the sweat on his brow. Silence.)

MAGNUS: There it is. It's over.

OLD LOU: Keep trying, I still might buy something from you.

MAGNUS: Impossible. I can't waste any more time.

OLD LOU: Loser!

MAGNUS: Au revoir, mister.

OLD LOU: Wait! *(MAGNUS disappears. OLD LOU sighs.)* If only he'd tried just a little bit harder . . .

(OLD LOU gets up, concluding the performance. The SONS applaud.)

SONS *(mockingly):*

    Oh, very good.

    Now that's avant-garde theatre!

    A brilliant game.

    Subtle.

    Definitely a little gem.

JULIA *(venomous):* I didn't understand a thing.

SONS: It has nothing to do with understanding.

She meaning is not important, you understand?

Don't understand it, live it.

She's playing the dummy.

(MAGNUS reappears.)

WOLFY: Here comes our genius!

SONS: Bravo!

(But MAGNUS has returned in an obvious bad mood. He knocks over one of the chairs with a single kick.)

MAGNUS: Do I look like a moron? *(Pause.)* I asked you if I looked like a moron? *(He flashes a terrifying look at his SONS. Pause.)* Were you trying to be clever, huh, Lou?

OLD LOU *(with just a thread of a voice):* I don't understand, Magnus.

MAGNUS *(mocking him):* "I don't understand, Magnus." *(To the SONS, with his fists on his waist.)* What do you think? He doesn't understand.

SONS *(not understanding what MAGNUS is up to):*

He's playing the fool!

Ha . . . ha . . . ha . . . !

He doesn't understand!

But in any case, it's obvious.

Poor man!

MAGNUS *(to OLD LOU):* Even they get it!

SONS: Of course!

It was a . . . horrible experience!

I'm still trembling!

(Brief pause.)

MAGNUS: You accused me in public, Lou.

SONS *(covering their eyes in horror):* Oh!

OLD LOU: *I* accused . . . *you*?

MAGNUS: In front of my own sons, without any sense of propriety. You took advantage of the opportunity to sow discord. You slandered my good name.

SONS: Shameful!

It's an outrage!

We told you he was a bad seed, Magnus!

MAGNUS: You vilely insinuated that I was a wife-killer. That I had murdered Bibi!

(This time the SONS keep quiet, stunned. MAGNUS notices their nonreaction and fixes them with a stare. Under such pressure, the SONS begin to react, but without much enthusiasm.)

SONS: It's slander.

Who would've thought, Magnus!

You can't trust anybody these days.

MAGNUS: Do you have anything to say, Lou?
OLD LOU *(terrified):* It was just a . . . misunderstanding, Magnus.
(MAGNUS throws himself on top of the old man and grabs him by the throat.)
MAGNUS: Cunning snake!
SONS *(bloodthirsty):*
> Harder, Magnus!
> Give it your all!
> Crush him!
> Like a worm, Magnus!
> Don't hold back!
> Let him have it!

MAGNUS *(squeezing OLD LOU's neck):* I let you keep going in order to see just how far your cynicism went, you rat! *(Suddenly, MAGNUS lets go of OLD LOU, who collapses like a rag. MAGNUS moves away.)* I could have strangled you!
SONS *(like a distorted echo):* He could have strangled you, Lou!
MAGNUS: But you make me sick! *(The SONS make varied gestures indicating disgust.)*
SONS: It's best if you don't take him on, Lou.
> You're dead meat.
> He's not kidding.

MAGNUS: I know exactly where your hatred comes from, Lou. *(MAGNUS's movements become feline. He moves around like a cornered panther.)* We competed for Bibi, and I won! We competed in business, and I won! Year after year fighting tooth and nail, stalking each other like jungle tigers! We were young and strong. We were a match for each other! And I won! Not only against you, Lou; no, against the whole world! I fought against everyone! And I won! Because I was tough! Because I was merciless! Because I was a machine, Lou! *(Pause.)* Bibi, on the other hand, was so fragile . . . She wasn't built to stand up to such . . . She used to look at me, pale, silent . . . I think she was afraid of me. I could never find out. I held her in my arms for a time and then, finally, she crumbled apart in my fingers, like a dried flower, like a moth . . . *(Pause.)* Yes, I killed her. *(Pause.)* What was my alternative? Become weak myself along with her? They would have overtaken me like wild beasts . . . Everyone . . . You would have devoured me, Lou . . .
(OLD LOU nods gravely in agreement. The SONS begin to stir, restless. They clear their throats, they softly call to MAGNUS, etc.)
SONS: Psst, Magnus.
> It's our turn.

MAGNUS *(without looking at them, tired):* Yes, I know. So, get started.
SONS: Thanks, Magnus!

(WOLFY quickly puts on a record and is pushed offstage by his brothers, who also disappear.)
MAGNUS: Don't be afraid, Julia. *(With a gesture of rationalization.)* What do you want me to do? I can never say no to them . . .
(We hear the first notes of the requiem. KIT appears, solemn, in his oversized black cloak.)
KIT *(announcing):* "The funeral for our dearly departed mother!"
(He slowly moves forward. Behind KIT, forming the procession, follow WOLFY, carrying a small urn in his hands, and JIMMY, with a lit candle. They are wearing oversized black cloaks, too.)
KIT: They placed her in a little plastic urn.
JIMMY: Tiny as a sugar cube.
WOLFY: They placed her ashes.
KIT: Tiny as the eye of a needle.
WOLFY: They placed her ashes.
KIT: Still warm . . .
WOLFY: Like bread fresh out of the oven.
KIT: On the ground.
(WOLFY places the small urn on the ground.)
JIMMY: Our hallowèd mother.
WOLFY: Hallowèd be our mother.
KIT: On Earth as she is in Heaven.
JIMMY: Her ashes gave off a thread of smoke.
WOLFY: Which they called Psyche.
KIT: Which they called Soul.
JIMMY: And up to the pale sky her smoky thread ascended.
WOLFY: It rose up.
KIT: Up to the Milky Way.
JIMMY: Her ashes grew cold.
WOLFY: They faded and grew cold.
KIT: And Psyche died once more on Earth.
(KIT bends over and picks up the urn.)
JIMMY: As her sons continued to call her.
WOLFY: Soul!
JIMMY: Where are you, Soul! *(The SONS begin to leave, led by KIT, as WOLFY and JIMMY continue calling, "Soul!")*
WOLFY: Soul!
JIMMY: Soul!
(MAGNUS, full of sorrow, follows the procession. OLD LOU, on all fours, brings up the rear, rounding off each call with a plaintive howl. They all exit. Silence.)
JULIA: This is a nuthouse! *(Nervous, JULIA puts the jacket over her shoul-*

ders, grabs her purse, and looks for the exit.) How do you get out of here? *(She calls out, in a controlled tone.)* Wolfy! Jimmy! I want to leave! Could you please show me the way out? Wolfy!

(The Sons appear, looking like actors who have just finished a show. They go to different areas of the stage. They are still wearing their oversized costumes, which they lift up in order to walk, giving them a ridiculous air.)

JIMMY *(indifferent):* Don't wear yourself out, Julia.

KIT: We told you it would be difficult to leave.

JULIA *(calmly):* It makes no difference to me, hon. If I feel like going, I'm going to leave. I'm a free spirit.

WOLFY: But of course, Julia.

KIT: Do you have a smoke, Jimmy?

JIMMY: She has some.

(JULIA has gone over to the Sons. She sits down on the ground near them, gives a cigarette to KIT and offers the other two a cigarette. They decline.)

JULIA: I don't think you dears understood me. I'm a little tired and tomorrow I have to work. The gathering was truly lovely, but now it's time for me to leave.

KIT *(to his brothers, paying no attention to JULIA):* These things wipe me out.

JIMMY: You get too involved.

KIT *(to JULIA):* Give me a light. *(JULIA gives him a light.)* Wolfy, as usual, was sloppy.

(MAGNUS's face appears from the wings. He grimaces and then disappears.)

WOLFY *(on the defensive):* Why don't you ask her?

JIMMY: And what would she know?

KIT: What did you think, Bibi?

JULIA: Reeeeeaaaaally lovely, but now I have to . . . *(She stops herself. Pause.)* What did you call me? *(Silence. Somewhat hysterical.)* I asked you what you called me!

KIT: What does it matter?

JULIA: My name is Julia! Ju-li-a!

KIT: It's alright, Ju-li-a. It was just a joke.

(JULIA calms down.)

JULIA: Nobody likes to lose their identity.

WOLFY: Of course not.

(Silence. OLD LOU's face appears from the wings. He grimaces and then disappears.)

KIT: I have something to show you, Julia.

(His brothers become tense.)

WOLFY: Don't do it, Kit.

(Pause.)

KIT *(smoothly):* Why not, Wolfy?
WOLFY *(with the same tone):* Because we'll catch hell, Kit.
KIT: We'll catch hell no matter what, Wolfy. She'll understand.
(KIT backs up a little.)
WOLFY: Please, Kit, don't.
(WOLFY covers his eyes.)
KIT: Don't be afraid, Wolfy. And don't cover your eyes. We're blind any-
way. *(He brusquely turns away. He stomps out the cigarette on the floor,
lifts up his oversized cloak, mysteriously takes something out and returns
with the object clutched to his chest. He hands the ancient photograph to
JULIA.)* This is Bibi, our mother . . .
*(JULIA observes the photo for some time. MAGNUS crosses upstage on tip-
toes.)*
JULIA *(smoothly):* She's beautiful.
KIT: Isn't she?
JULIA: She looks like me, doesn't she?
KIT: Doesn't she?
JULIA: It's the hair, isn't it?
(KIT caresses JULIA's hair.)
KIT: So dark and so warm. *(He slowly moves his nose to JULIA's hair and
inhales, deeply.)* And you smell the same . . . like a warm night . . . like rain
. . . like the womb . . .
*(His brothers grow restless, and they begin to move blindly around the
stage.)*
WOLFY *(in a broken voice):* Bi-bi.
JIMMY: She disappears . . . into the night . . . She leaves us behind, sniffing
after her tracks as she goes farther and farther away . . . Like little pups
lifting their muzzles up into the air . . .
(KIT slips and falls onto the ground next to JULIA's body.)
KIT: Your open . . . knees . . . Heat . . .
JIMMY: All alone, in this wasteland.
*(JULIA has her knees wide open. Her aspect is one of an idol, a primitive
totem from some fertility cult. KIT has his head embedded between her legs.
JULIA softly caresses his hair. The others, meanwhile, wander around the
stage, articulating inaudible words. A kind of general murmur, and then a
sudden shriek. It's WOLFY, running downstage, fleeing from something.)*
WOLFY: Kit! *(His terror prevents him from speaking.)* Knife!
*(Indeed, JIMMY, upstage, brandishes an enormous knife. JULIA screams and
holds on to WOLFY. KIT, delighted, goes over to JIMMY.)*
KIT: Aha, but what do my eyes see here?
JIMMY *(with pride):* It's beautiful, isn't it, Kit?

KIT *(admiring the knife with JIMMY):* Fabulous. *(He runs his finger along the knife's edge.)* Nice edge.

JIMMY: Razor-sharp.

(He hands the knife over to KIT.)

KIT *(feinting):* The handle's strong.

JIMMY: Made special, for carving up pigs.

(KIT and JIMMY laugh.)

WOLFY: Stop it!

KIT: Very special, Jimmy.

JIMMY: Somebody could trip and . . .

(JIMMY mimes tripping and stabbing himself in the belly. KIT joins his brother in laughter.)

WOLFY: We're going to die of starvation! Have you thought about this? Have you even thought about that if he disappears, we'll have condemned ourselves to starving to death?

(Silence.)

JIMMY: We'll go out and work, or beg, or steal!

WOLFY: Where? Out there?

JIMMY: Wherever.

(Silence.)

KIT *(indicating WOLFY):* He's right, Jimmy.

JIMMY *(hysterical):* He's wrong! We'd be free, we'd be powerful!

WOLFY: Have you ever gone into the outside world? Have you ever even opened that door?

JIMMY: I'd do it! I swear! I'd do it!

WOLFY: No, you wouldn't!

KIT: We've never done it! *(To JIMMY.)* And do you want to know why?

JIMMY: Chickenshit rats!

KIT: Exactly! That's why! Because we're afraid! Fear has paralyzed us!

JIMMY *(spitting):* You make me sick!

WOLFY: Have you ever even thought about the outside world? About walking through streets that are always open and deserted, around trashcans, at dawn, until you froze? Have you ever thought about being hungry?

JIMMY: We'd be free!

KIT: Free? Free? Like who? *(An instant earlier, OLD LOU has begun to cross upstage on all fours. KIT refers to OLD LOU.)* Like that animal? *(OLD LOU stops, surprised, howls plaintively, and continues his cross.)* Sleeping in some ditch? Being at the beck and call of another Magnus . . . ? The world belongs to them . . . you stupid dreamer . . .

(Silence.)

JIMMY: Well then . . . we could become . . . one of them . . . like them . . .

WOLFY: Traitor!
KIT *(with a smile):* You'd dare do it?
WOLFY: All bow to the new Magnus!
KIT: You'd really do it?
(Silence.)
WOLFY: There's the door, Magnus. Go on. The world awaits you.
KIT: Come on, Jimmy. Who's stopping you from leaving?
(Silence.)
WOLFY: Come on!
JIMMY, with an impetuous burst of energy, runs over to the door and then stops. There's a pregnant silence. The action that follows is nearly simultaneous: JIMMY turns and faces his brothers, letting out a cry of rage and impotence. OLD LOU howls plaintively from offstage. MAGNUS, with an evil expression on his face, crosses upstage on tiptoes. LIGHTS OUT.

ACT TWO

Music from a Renaissance banquet, slightly distorted. A table on top of which is a lustrous white cloth covered with food. Seated behind the table, from left to right are: KIT, WOLFY, MAGNUS, JULIA, and JIMMY. MAGNUS, who is slightly higher than the rest, gobbles his food down, without pausing, vulgar and voracious. WOLFY watches MAGNUS and tries to imitate him, in a gross fashion. OLD LOU, on all fours, waits at the foot of the table, anxious for anyone to throw him some scraps. JULIA eats delicately. JIMMY eats in a sensual and refined manner, detached from what is going on around him. KIT looks attentively at the glass of red wine he is holding in his hands. He moistens his fingers in the wine.
KIT: Res est arduissima, vincere naturam,
       In aspectu virginis mentem esse puram:
       Juvenes no possumus legen sequi duram
       Leviumque corporum non habere curam.
MAGNUS *(elbowing WOLFY):* What's he saying, Wolfy?
WOLFY: Crap, Magnus. It's an old poem by some vagabond priests.[5]
KIT: Quicquid Venus imperat, labor est suavis . . .
(Another elbow-jab from MAGNUS.)
WOLFY *(with a giggle):* "What Venus commands us to do is sweet work . . ."
(MAGNUS and WOLFY laugh with their mouths full.)
KIT: Meum est propositum in taberna mori . . .
WOLFY *(translates quickly into MAGNUS's ear):* His plan is to die in some tavern.
KIT: Ut sint vina proxima morientis ori . . .

WOLFY: Where wine is near the dying man's mouth.

KIT: Tunc cantabunt letius angelorum chori . . .

WOLFY: Later, the angels will descend, singing.

KIT: Sit deus propitius huic potatori . . .

WOLFY: May God look favorably upon this . . . drunkard.

(KIT drains his glass.)

MAGNUS: Not bad, my dear. But you intellectuals are mighty stingy. *(He chews and drinks.)* When you're hungry, the only thing that occurs to you is to think about the transience of life. When you're full, you rationalize it away with a quote. It's alright, Lou, don't yell. *(He throws something to OLD LOU. To WOLFY.)* When did those people live?

WOLFY: What people, Poppy?

MAGNUS: The ones who wrote that poem.

WOLFY: At the end of the Middle Ages.

MAGNUS: That's what it sounded like. *(Throwing something to OLD LOU.)* When the world is coming to an end, carnal appetites rise in value. *(He pontificates, with a chicken leg in his hand.)* The blood is clever, sons. It wants to live even the last traces of its experience. *(He raises his glass of wine.)* To all that is concrete in our human existence: Cheers!

ALL *(like a distorted echo)*: Cheers, Magnus!

JIMMY: Now it's my turn. *(He raises his glass, and brings it to his ear.)* Inside this glass is the ocean . . . *(He takes a sip.)* Now I have the ocean inside my body. At one with the universe, each fiber of my flesh vibrates inside me . . . My organs, viscera, and muscles. Our body reveals a subtle harmony: we are beautiful. *(He looks at his reflection in the surface of the wine.)* I look at myself in the wine's surface. My face is reflected shining. I kiss my own lips in the wine. I'd like to dive in and penetrate myself. Be my wine and drink it, too.

(JIMMY slowly drains his glass. When he finishes, he falls flat on his face on top of the table. MAGNUS continues eating. The rest cannot eat another bite. WOLFY tries to keep up with MAGNUS until the end, with obvious repugnance. KIT sits down on top of the table. He holds out to one side a piece of grilled meat, dangling it in front of OLD LOU's nose. KIT entertains himself by foiling OLD LOU's attempts to grab the meat with his teeth.)

KIT: No. No. Hey! Over here, over here. No!

(JULIA tries to get up, heavily.)

JULIA: I'm . . . full. Up! *(She laughs, like an idiot.)* I think I need to empty my . . . *(She laughs. Finally she manages to get up. She wobbles, and grabs on to the back of her chair.)* I'm . . . sloshed!

(JULIA takes a few steps, vacillating, until she finds a place on the floor where she can stretch out.)

KIT: Over here, over here! No!

(JULIA sits up slightly. MAGNUS continues to eat, indifferent.)
JULIA: Magnus, you make me sick!
(MAGNUS looks at her briefly and, with a shrug of his shoulders, continues eating. WOLFY has used up his resistance. He is nauseated. He gets up and staggers upstage, where he apparently vomits. MAGNUS bursts out guffawing.)
MAGNUS *(with his mouth full):* Hey, little pup, you've got a long ways to go to match up to your old man's stomach!
JIMMY *(in a high-pitched voice):* The old man's cow stomach!
KIT: Now over here, over here. No!
JULIA *(directing her question to the SONS):* How can he gorge himself that way?
KIT: It's all a matter of filling oneself up and then emptying oneself out, Julia. *(KIT finally gives OLD LOU the scrap, and OLD LOU takes his prey over to the corner. KIT jumps off the table.)* The more you fill yourself up, the more you empty yourself out. *(MAGNUS lets loose a sarcastic guffaw.)* That's how it is with everything. Even love.
JIMMY: I could use some loving.
(JULIA has sat up on the floor; she fans herself with her skirt.)
JULIA: Oh, I am so hot!
(WOLFY returns, in a bad mood. OLD LOU crosses his path and receives a foot jab as his reward. Plaintive howls. WOLFY goes back and sits in his old chair and looks at MAGNUS, with rancor. MAGNUS has finally finished. He takes a last swallow, lets out a belch, and wipes his hands and face on the napkin. He stretches out in his chair.)
MAGNUS: That's some good eating, huh? Now a little ideology would do us some good. *(KIT clears his throat and tries to leave unnoticed.)* Where're you going, my dear?
KIT: Personal business, Pops.
MAGNUS: What, you can't control your sphincter, kid? Just when your old dad has asked you to join him in a little father-son chat?
KIT: I'm going to pee my pants, Magnus.
MAGNUS: Ah, youth. You offer them a place in society and they respond with biological needs. Deep down, they just don't want, they just don't want to be heard.
KIT: It's hard to think with a full bladder.
MAGNUS: If you're truly free, you can think under any circumstances.
KIT: So this is about having a freewheeling chat?
MAGNUS: Of course.
KIT: I'd rather go to the bathroom.
(He makes signs of leaving.)
MAGNUS *(smooth):* Kit.
KIT *(stopping):* Yes, Dad?

MAGNUS: Come on, don't be a coward. Your father only wants a little bit of fantasy. A nice, after-dinner chat.

KIT: My fantasy, Magnus, is not very nice.

MAGNUS: Would you call it terrible?

KIT: Yes.

MAGNUS: Don't be afraid, son. Up until now nothing has ever been destroyed by fantasizing. *(Pause.)* But what could you possibly want to destroy? *(Pause. KIT makes an ambiguous, tired gesture indicating their house.)* This? The house? *(KIT halfheartedly shakes his head no.)* You obviously indicated the house. *(To WOLFY.)* Or did he not?

WOLFY *(objectively):* Yes, he pointed to the house.

MAGNUS: Incidentally, *our* house. But why? Aren't you happy here?

KIT: It's not the house . . .

MAGNUS: Well, then, what is it? *(KIT points to his head.)* Suicide? *(KIT shakes his head no. MAGNUS grows impatient.)* Well, enough, Kit. A chat, no matter how intergenerational, may not be conducted with gestures. I command you to speak to me in full voice and tell me what you would like to destroy in your fantasy.

KIT *(fed up):* Your world, Magnus.

MAGNUS *(with histrionic alarm): The* world? But why?[6]

KIT: Too many victims.

MAGNUS: What victims?

KIT: *Your* victims.

MAGNUS: *My* victims? Who are my victims?

KIT: You're not going to like it.

MAGNUS: Don't be ridiculous.

KIT: Promise?

MAGNUS: Yes, of course.

KIT *(quickly):* People dying from hunger.

(Brief pause.)

MAGNUS: Could you be more specific, Kit?

KIT: I'm talking about the people that built your house . . .

MAGNUS: But, what's this obsession, Kit! What does it mean that they built my house? Didn't I pay them? Wasn't there a contract? On the other hand, who's going hungry in this blessèd land? It may be that here and there . . . In ancient countries, India maybe,[7] or . . . But that's the tradition! You can't go against tradition!

(A shriek from JULIA. MAGNUS turns violently to JIMMY, but then contains himself and takes on a tone of compromise.)

MAGNUS: Jimmy, you're a son of a bitch. Yes, you're a son of a bitch, Jimmy. You take advantage of the fact that your old man is busy talking to someone else and that is bad manners. Julia, come here, dear.

(JULIA goes to sit next to MAGNUS. She has the attitude of a "daddy's girl."
MAGNUS makes a gesture of endearment toward her.)
MAGNUS: Are you alright, my beauty?
JULIA: Now I am, Magnus. *(Giving JIMMY an accusatory look.)* Jimmy is
obscene.
(Nevertheless, during the course of the following scene, JULIA will continue
to communicate with JIMMY through signs, winks of complicity, silent giggles,
etc. Finally, almost accidentally, JULIA will get up and go over to JIMMY.)
MAGNUS: Well, where was I?
WOLFY *(whispering the answer):* People dying from hunger, Magnus . . .
MAGNUS: Oh yes . . . Winston, briefly: opportunity for all, today it's yours,
tomorrow it's mine, money can't buy happiness, one day you're on top and
the next you're on the bottom, don't cry over spilt milk, the higher they
climb, the harder they fall, don't put all your eggs in one basket, a bird in
the hand is worth two in the bush.[8] Popular wisdom, my dear! You've got
to know how to suckle at the udders of the masses.
KIT *(venomous):* And you're the expert, Magnus.
MAGNUS: In other words, there are no victims here, Winston. Period. Nothing to fear!
(Obstinate silence from KIT.)
MAGNUS: Well, let's just suppose that there were victims . . .
KIT: Let's just suppose it, Magnus . . .
MAGNUS: Victims don't think, pup. They're too busy being victims. They
pose absolutely no threat. *(Pause.)* The victim and his victimizer form a
system, a structure that melds together perfectly. There's nothing wrong
with that. *(Pause. Moved.)* Kit, your naïveté moves me. Your panic moves
me. I would like to give you some of my security, this sense of security that
I've had my entire life. *(Pause.)* And even if there were a real threat, don't
we have our defenses ready, aren't we prepared for any eventuality? Let's
leave to one side brute force—there will always be someone out of line—,
well, but . . . *(An ambiguous gesture.)* Don't we always have one more card
up our sleeve? And do you know what that card is, Kit? *(Pause.)* Man,
sonny, man himself. In all his weakness and misery. The possibility of forming images, illusions in his brain. And that possibility is fantastic! Objects,
pup! He who has the most toys wins! And as for us, all we have to do is
show them our playroom, just show it to them. Our way of life doesn't
offend them, pup! They'd love to live like us. They're just as corrupt as we
are, worse than we are! It's all the same game! And the same trap!
(Silence.)
KIT *(in a low, smooth voice):* And then where is your great victory, Magnus?
If, in order to keep your toys, you have to corrupt others, awaken useless
and petty anxieties in others, where then is your victory?

(Pause.)

MAGNUS: Well, it's not a question of objects and nothing more. Man does not live by bread alone. We also need you, the martyrs, the idealists, the intellectuals. You're our critical side, you're the ones who keep us from falling into inertia and death. *(Jovial.)* How many times have you upset our digestion! *(He jokingly threatens KIT with his finger.)* And not only you intellectuals. The artists, too. *(MAGNUS and WOLFY bow reverentially to each other.)* The artists! How could we possibly forget the artists, they who enrich our lives, who give it variety and sensitivity! What would you like, Winston? Sublime art in the paws of the sinister hordes?

(Silence.)

KIT *(enlightened and smooth):* Someday, some clear morning, we will wake up from this long dream. We will look at ourselves, unable to believe it. All the open wounds will be erased. And eternity, hidden to us before, will burst open in the sky, glowing.

(Brief pause.)

MAGNUS: Well, but that will be after a very long time. Now it's called extremism.

WOLFY *(pounding the table with his fist):* Agitator!

KIT: I told you, Magnus, you wouldn't like it.

MAGNUS *(under his breath to WOLFY, shrugging his shoulders):* I don't have any problems.

KIT *(exalted):* And that's not the worst of it, because the truth is, the truth is that your world is insane, Magnus, and your house is a lie!

MAGNUS *(to WOLFY, under his breath):* Same old story.

KIT *(calm):* You promised us the world, Pops.

MAGNUS *(to WOLFY):* I didn't promise you anything.

KIT: We followed you, we trusted you. You told us: "It's here." But we never made it to any promised land. In reality, we never made it to anywhere.

JULIA: Amen.

KIT: And we began to rot alive. We looked fearfully out at the world through this window. And on the other side, a parade of contorted faces. That's our handiwork. Their hunger, their frustration, their greed.

JULIA *(rejecting JIMMY):* No! I want to listen! Go on, Kit. I'm on your side.

KIT: For how long? Every day I look out that window and I think: Today's the day.

JULIA: Exactly! You can all go to hell!

KIT: Magnus?

(Silence.)

MAGNUS: Yes . . . You asked me a question? I don't know, Kitten. You're the ones with the questions. So it's up to you to find the answers. *(Very deliber-*

ately.) Get by . . . any way you can. *(Pause.)* And that's enough debate for today. I'm tired. *(Brief pause.)* Lou?

OLD LOU: Yes, Magnus?

MAGNUS: Nothing, dear. I just wanted to hear a human voice. *(Pause.)* The child always bites the nipple that feeds it.[9] This beast has upset my stomach. *(Brief pause.)* Lou?

OLD LOU: Yes, Magnus?

MAGNUS: What are they protesting? I don't understand them, Lou! When I took Bibi away from you, did you protest?

OLD LOU: No, Magnus.

MAGNUS: And when I ruined your future, taking over the business, reducing you to misery, and pushing you to the edge of suicide, did you protest?

OLD LOU: No, Magnus. Those were the rules of the game. Free enterprise. It happened to me. It could have happened to you. And now I would be in your place. With a house and children. And you would be in the streets, shivering with cold, eating scraps.

MAGNUS: Absolutely, Lou! That is equal opportunity for all. It's the way things are. Oh, Lou, what a disappointment!

OLD LOU: Our generation was better, Magnus.

MAGNUS: That's what I also suspect, my dear old Lou. We had the firmness of our convictions. Solid moral values!

OLD LOU: We were geniuses, Magnus!

MAGNUS: Strong and vigorous. Full of life. *(Sighing.)* Oh! What a fucked-up mess, Lou! *(Pause. OLD LOU lets MAGNUS know, through signs, that KIT has stayed in his place, with a confused expression on his face. MAGNUS adopts a cold attitude. The OTHERS imitate him. Icily.)* Did you have something else you wanted to say, Winston?

KIT *(with a gesture of firmness):* Yes! *(He takes a step forward.)* I . . . *(His expression is at once perplexed and dazzled.)* I . . . *(He vacillates.)* I protest! And . . . ·

(The group's tension eases. They whisper among themselves.)

MAGNUS: Now he's doing better.

WOLFY: More human, don't you think?

KIT: I said that . . . I protest! I seek . . . that which . . . *(Always with firm gestures that contrast with his incoherence.)* Pity and violence! I seek . . . a violence that's destructive . . . and full of pity. I . . . Protest! Emphatically!

(Pleasant applause from the others.)

JIMMY: You tell 'em, Kit!

MAGNUS: At least say something!

(Pause. KIT is motionless, his head down, humiliated. THE OTHERS whisper to each other, as if they were watching a performance.)

JULIA: What's wrong with him? Hasn't he finished?

JIMMY: Yes, he's finished.

JULIA: Well, then, why is he still standing there? Is there something wrong?

WOLFY: He's overcome with emotion.

JIMMY: The same thing always happens. The effect of what he says stays with him.

(KIT lifts up his face. He looks wild.)

KIT: Everything around me is empty. An immense city, dead, devastated. Shadows pass by quickly, the silhouettes of men outlined by a pale moon. And I'm all alone. I extend my arms out into the layers of air, layers that disintegrate and dissolve when I pierce them. I walk on the rubble, fragile debris that sinks under the weight of my shoes. Reality shatters without a sound behind me, and I breathe in the fragile light of illusion.

(Pleasant applause from the rest.)

JULIA: Is he ill?

MAGNUS: No, he's acting.

JULIA: He's worrying me.

KIT (to the audience): I beg you to believe me. I hear their voices coming to me from far away, but I can't seem to escape from this no-man's land.

(Everyone, except JULIA, applauds pleasantly.)

JULIA (worried, anxious): He's ill. We have to help him.

MAGNUS: Don't be so naïve. And don't interrupt him.

WOLFY: It's just a play.

KIT (to the audience): And that's exactly what I'm begging you to save me from. Because I've lost control of my performance. Help me, please.

(Applause from the OTHERS.)

JULIA (getting up): We have to help him! He's suffering! Can't you see that he's suffering?

THE OTHERS: Shhhh. Dumb bitch. How can she be so stupid? Ignoramus. Can't tell the difference between a simple performance and reality. Moron.

JULIA (terrified, sits down): And what if he's telling the truth?

(THE OTHERS burst out in stifled, repressed laughter.)

MAGNUS (drying his eyes): The truth . . .

(JULIA looks at the others, disconcerted and confused. THE OTHERS are falling apart with laughter, but when they see that KIT is continuing to speak, they motion each other to be quiet, and try to compose themselves and fake seriousness. KIT no longer addresses the audience. He slowly crumbles and ends up nestling on the floor in the fetal position.)

KIT: Worms and rats, now I'm with you. In your mundane world of the material, in the tangled and spongy womb of Mother Earth.

(OLD LOU finishes off KIT's last words with a canine howl. Applause, with JULIA joining in timidly. KIT immediately joins the others.)

MAGNUS *(getting up):* Well, this after-dinner divertissement has gone on long enough.

JULIA *(seizing the opportunity):* It certainly has. *(She gets up, too, with an air of "mission accomplished," and smoothes her clothing.)* What time is it? It must be getting close to dawn. Also . . . You eat dinner so late. Did anyone see my little jacket?

(The expression on everyone else's face is evidently one of sarcasm.)

JIMMY: Did anyone see Julia's little jacket?

KIT: Julia's little jacket, Wolfy.

WOLFY: Now, where did I last see Julia's little jacket?

MAGNUS: Let's get looking, boys!

(Everyone begins to move around in an apparent search.)

WOLFY: But are you sure that you brought a little jacket, Julia?

JIMMY: I don't remember seeing one.

JULIA: But how could you not? It's . . . brown . . . suede . . .

KIT *(snapping his fingers):* With green fringe?

JULIA: No, no . . . More like . . . plain! It's plain brown.

KIT: Well then, no, I haven't seen it.

JULIA: How awful! I remember perfectly well . . .

WOLFY: Lou, you haven't seen a little brown jacket . . . made out of suede?

OLD LOU: Bibi had one just like it.

JULIA: This is ridiculous, I had it over my shoulders the entire . . .

JIMMY: It's always this way. When you look for something, you can't find it.

WOLFY: It happens even in the best of families!

MAGNUS *(who has been sarcastically observing the scene up to now):* I believe you had it over your shoulders in the park.

JULIA *(with a nervous giggle):* In the park?

MAGNUS: Yes, just before you came in the house. *(A giggle from JULIA and then silence.)* In front of the house, there's a park, Julia. *(Pause.)* Don't you remember?

JULIA: I . . . I d-don't remember any park.

WOLFY: It's always been there.

KIT: As far as we know.

JIMMY: It could have disappeared during the night, but . . .

WOLFY: It would be very strange for a park to disappear like . . . that.

KIT: You can see it from the window.

JIMMY: You can go take a look for yourself, Julia.

JULIA: No, no, I believe you. If there's a park over there, then it still must be there. But I don't remember . . . having been in any park . . . tonight.

MAGNUS: Come on, Julia. Use your memory.

JULIA: I'm trying to remember, Magnus.

MAGNUS: We walked along in silence.

JULIA: Yes, yes.

MAGNUS: There was a red wall.

JULIA: Which I remember perfectly.

MAGNUS: When we got to the house, you began to hesitate again.

JULIA: Yes . . .

MAGNUS: I suggested that we go sit in the park . . . You agreed . . . There was a fountain . . . A bench. *(Someone sets a pair of chairs together.)* You sat down at the very end of the bench. *(JULIA sits down, rigid.)* You were wearing your jacket over your shoulders. *(Someone places the jacket over JULIA's shoulders.)* Your silence is getting on my nerves, sister.

JULIA: I have nothing to say.

MAGNUS: Do you see that little window all lit up? That's where my sons are. They're waiting for us. All you have to do is cross the street. *(Silence. JULIA doesn't move.)* You're so pale, sister!

(Pause.)

JULIA: I'm tired. I can't organize my thoughts.

(Pause.)

MAGNUS *(without looking at JULIA, as if he were talking in his sleep):* I look into your eyes. Your lips are white. Your hand barely pulsates between my fingers. A dry, snapping beat. The only thread that keeps you alive.

JULIA *(without looking at MAGNUS, as if she were talking in her sleep):* I'm going to get up now, and I'm going to go away forever.

(There is absolutely no contact between the two; it's a sleepwalking scene.)

MAGNUS: You were far away, dead, but now you're taking on form. I recall you, detail by detail. I'm rescuing you from obscurity.

JULIA: I'm going to go away forever.

MAGNUS: Now you wouldn't be able to, sister. I've found you. *(Brief pause.)* In the street.

JULIA: In reality I never saw you. I saw some lips steaming, an enormous head, cold, piercing eyes. At first you looked grotesque, deformed. But later on . . .

MAGNUS: My life is ending. There's no room for coincidence. I am a memory that swallows everything up. And it's too strong for you. *(He suddenly turns toward the woman, and with a brusque, voracious gesture of possession, he takes her hand. The dream ends.)* Little slut.

(She shudders and looks at him. Her face takes on a sharp and ironic expression. MAGNUS, for his part, softens, and becomes gentle, astute.)

JULIA: Come on, what's the matter? Why don't you take off your mask? So many twists and turns just to sleep with me? Why the need to justify your morality as a family man? It's alright, I assure you that afterwards you'll be just as respected as you are now. *(MAGNUS looks at her with astuteness.*

JULIA *lets out a quick, nervous guffaw.)* Well, I'd be less afraid if I knew who you were. A whore at least arranges the price with the client. I want to know what I'll have left after it's over. And I don't accept money.

MAGNUS: Resentment.

JULIA *(laughing):* That's not much.

MAGNUS: Don't you believe it. When you have it, you begin to hold on to things. And you have to be a miser even with your own life.

JULIA: Who wants to hold on to things?

MAGNUS: Hah, it's inevitable. As inevitable as no longer being young. *(Pause.)*

JULIA: I do not accept. What else can you offer me?

MAGNUS: Words. Horrible words, whispered in your ear. And as time passes, they'll be joined by other words. They'll slowly form a net. And that will be your life: an unbearable net, woven by everyone else.

(Long pause.)

JULIA *(sarcastic):* So, you want to define me?

MAGNUS: I'll give you form.

JULIA: You're using me.

MAGNUS *(objective):* Yes, that, too.

(Pause.)

JULIA: I've already started to hate you.

MAGNUS: That means that you've made your decision. *(Pause.)* That's all. You've made the deal. Now you have to honor it.

(Pause.)

JULIA *(hysterical):* I have not accepted any deal.

MAGNUS *(authoritarian and definitive):* Wolfy! Jimmy!

(WOLFY and JIMMY carry a sofa onto the stage. JULIA looks at them in desperation.)

JULIA *(brusquely):* Everything's so dirty, Magnus. It makes me sick. Such a mess . . .

MAGNUS: Jimmy! Kit!

(JIMMY and KIT carry on a screen, which they place in front of the sofa.)

JULIA: Magnus! *(Pause.)* Don't you think that I should do the dishes? Seriously, I'm a fanatic about cleanliness. At home, every day . . .

MAGNUS: Jimmy! Wolfy! Kit!

(The SONS place chairs in front of the screen and sit down on them.)

JULIA: And what are they doing?

MAGNUS: Turn your back, Lou!

(OLD LOU goes to a corner and turns his back to the screen.)

JULIA: But no, the old man is so nice. Lou, you can stay! I, on the other hand, I've got to . . .

MAGNUS: Let's go, Julia!

(Silence.)

JULIA *(shrieking):* Just a moment! *(Pause.)* Can I go over and look out the window just . . . to make sure . . . that . . . ? *(MAGNUS has disappeared behind the screen. JULIA docilely follows. She disappears. Suddenly half of JULIA's body appears.)* Wolfy! Could you bring me a glass of wa . . . ? *(She abruptly disappears, as if someone had pulled her back. Long silence.)*

WOLFY *(sighing):* Well, here we are.

KIT: At the edge of dawn.

JIMMY: The dirty dawn of winter. *(Silence.)* When is this going to end, Kit?

KIT: What, Jimmy?

JIMMY: This waiting, or this searching.

KIT: I don't know.

(WOLFY gets up and stretches. His brothers watch him.)

KIT *(severe):* Where're you going, Wolfy?

WOLFY *(excusing himself with a shy smile):* No . . . where, Kit. I only wanted . . . *(A severe look from the other two. WOLFY, ashamed, sits back down. Silence. JIMMY begins to laugh softly.)* What's going on, Jimmy?

JIMMY: Nothing . . . I just remembered something . . . But it's nothing important.

KIT: What's it about, Jimmy?

JIMMY: Sometimes, when I'm just about to fall asleep, in that brief instant . . . Sometimes . . . I feel afraid . . .

KIT: Afraid of what, Jimmy?

JIMMY: It's ridiculous . . . I'm afraid . . . that one of these days I'll wake up . . .

(Silence.)

KIT: That would be absurd. *(Silence. Suddenly, KIT gets up.)* I think they called us. *(Icy look from the other two.)* You didn't hear anything?

(KIT, ashamed, sits back down. Silence.)

JIMMY *(singing the "Marseillaise"):* Allons, enfants de la patrie, Le jour de gloire est arrivé . . .

(Silence.)

WOLFY: Well, anyway, she's beautiful . . .

KIT: Who is, Wolfy?

WOLFY *(lyrical):* Our land, Winston. *(Dreamy, with broad and clumsy gestures.)* Forests . . . and hills . . . green fields . . . where . . . with the plow . . . the seed . . . wheat grows and grows . . . her valleys and . . . folds . . . Her anatomy . . . so exuberant . . . *(Silence. JIMMY gets up.)* Where are you going, Jimmy?

JIMMY: I wanted to see if . . . it was dawn yet . . .

(Severe looks at JIMMY, who, ashamed, sits back down.)

KIT: My dear little brothers . . . *(Pause.)* I believe the sun has just come up.

(A sharp whistle from behind the screen. The Sons jump to their feet. They move around, agitated and nervous, running into each other. JIMMY and KIT remove the screen. WOLFY puts on a record: a slow and erotic jazz number. The lighting is crude: every element makes one think of a naturalistic melo-drama. JULIA is seated on one of the ends of the sofa, in her slip, looking like a prostitute. MAGNUS, with his undershirt out. The Sons move away on tiptoe. JULIA, with languid and sensual gestures, lights a cigarette and with one foot brings her purse from one of the chairs to her side; she does the same thing with her clothing, also on one of the chairs. She opens her purse and takes out her compact, lipstick, etc. She puts red lipstick on, exaggeratedly, and does the same with mascara and powder. The scene transpires in a slow rhythm, before the great expectations of the Sons. When JULIA finishes with the makeup, she unsuccessfully tries to look at herself in her compact mirror. She gives up and looks around her, with half-closed eyes.)

JULIA: Boys, I'd like a larger mirror. *(The Sons go off, nervous. They return with a big mirror, which they hold up at a certain distance from the sofa. JULIA gets up and goes over to the mirror, with a wiggle in her hips. The Sons whistle in admiration. One says, "Wow.")* Goodness me, well, here we are! *(Giggles from JULIA and the Sons.)* So that's what I looked like? *(Nervous giggles.)* Well, well. *(Giggles.)* I am! *(She moves away from the mirror. Swaying her hips.)* Goodness me! I never would have thought that I'd feel so . . . light! I feel light . . . as a feather! *(She goes over to JIMMY.)* I'm going to eat you up, arrroooommmmm! *(The other two elbow each other, smiling beatifically. JULIA embraces JIMMY. They dance a few steps, clutching each other, following the jazz song's beat. JULIA lifts her hair up, because of the heat, just like an on-screen Rita Hayworth.)* It's hot as hell, boys! Get me a drink! *(WOLFY leaves quickly. He returns pouring some whiskey into a glass and gives it to JULIA, who's still in JIMMY's embrace. JULIA takes a drink, at the same time as JIMMY whispers something in her ear. JULIA, her mouth full of whiskey, breaks into an obscene guffaw and pushes him away.)* You're a pig, boy! *(Still laughing, with the glass in her hand, she moves downstage, hesitates, and begins to collapse, sensually, laughing and hiccuping, with a little bit of hysteria. She rolls around on the floor. Then she sits up slightly.)* Gotta have some fun, boys! *(The Sons respond with nasal giggles of understanding.)* Didn't you hear me? I said you gotta have some fun! *(Rough, abrupt.)* I want to fuck around! *(Silence.)*

SONS *(compassionate, pitying):* We heard you, Julia. It's alright, Julia.

JULIA: Sons of bitches! Give me more whiskey!

SONS: It's alright, Julia.

We understand you, Julia.

We feel your pain.

Don't drink any more, poor Julia.

Don't drown your sorrows in booze.

JULIA *(hysterical):* Whiskey! Whiskey! Whiskey!

WOLFY *(who has hidden the bottle, acts like he's looking at it against the light):* Uh-oh, there isn't any more!

JULIA *(abrupt):* FUCKING FUN!

(She collapses, worn-out.)

SONS: Poor Julia.

She's fucked up.

She needs our compassion.

(They go over to her, kneeling at her side, as they hold her head.)

JULIA *(hiccuping):* My God, what have I done? What have I done, dear God?

SONS *(sympathetic, consoling her):*

There, there.

Ga ga, goo goo.

It's OK.

Nothing's wrong.

B-b-b-b-baby.

(They help her get up.)

JULIA: I'm just a sad whore.

(During this scene, MAGNUS has remained reclining on the sofa, indifferent to everything going on. The SONS and JULIA form one group. For some time, we've been listening to the phonograph needle stuck on the final part of the record, the music over. JULIA suddenly turns on MAGNUS, her mascara running, melodramatic.)

JULIA: Magnus! Magnus! Give me back my virginity! I'm begging you on my knees, Magnus! I want nothingness! I want to go back to being free! I want to go back to being a virgin! Give me my virginity, Magnus! My virginity!

SONS *(in a high-pitched voice):* Her virginity, Magnus!

(ALL FOUR, a chorus of supplicants from a Greek tragedy, raise their open arms to MAGNUS. A grotesque tableau. MAGNUS takes a long pause to prepare.)

MAGNUS *(cynical, brutal, rough):* Your virginity? *(Pause.)* Your virginity? *(Pause.)* That fine and fragile little ring? Your virginity envelops me, shelters me.

(The SONS, making a circle around JULIA, begin to sing in falsetto, like a boys' choir.)

SONS: Her virginity, her virginity . . .

MAGNUS: Your virginity gives me power!

(The scene is now transformed into a true pandemonium. All the charac-
ters, except for MAGNUS, erect like a phallic idol in the middle of the stage,
run around speechless, shrieking. KIT begins to scream out a Goliard song
in Latin. JIMMY chases after JULIA, who is laughing scandalously. WOLFY
has become possessed by demonic, epileptic convulsions. OLD LOU, finally,
jumps on all fours and gesticulates.)

OLD LOU: Bibi! Bibi! Bibi!

KIT: O fortuna
     velut luna
     statu variabilis,
     semper crescis
     aut decrescis;
     vita detestabilis
     nunc obdurat
     et tunc curat
     ludo mentis aciem,
     egestatem,
     potestatem
     dissolvit ut glaciem.[10]

MAGNUS *(shouting in the midst of the uproar):* Who is the being of beings, the great, the invincible!

ALL: Magnus!

MAGNUS: Who is the sun, the universe, the point of all reference!

ALL: Magnus!

WOLFY *(with a distorted voice):* Magnus, der Groooossse!

KIT: Heil, Magnus!

ALL: Heil!

MAGNUS: Who has you tied up in the subtle threads of your own complicity!

ALL: Magnus!

MAGNUS: Who gives you life, who illuminates you and rescues you from oblivion!

ALL: Magnus!

(MAGNUS lets fly a guffaw. There follows a profound silence.)

MAGNUS: And now, Magnus . . . The great, invincible, and sovereign Magnus will bequeath to any and all who would desire and dare to hear . . . his last confession of weakness.

(WOLFY gives out a shriek and throws himself at MAGNUS's feet.)

WOLFY: No, Magnus! For God's sake, don't do it! They'll destroy you! Hunger and revenge nestle inside them! I beg you, Magnus! Don't allow the monstrous to rise up in us!

MAGNUS *(smooth):* Easy, Wolfy. Have I ever done anything that I didn't want to do and that wasn't for my own benefit?

WOLFY *(whiny):* All I ask is that you do something now for our benefit.

MAGNUS: That's asking a lot, Wolfy. Go join your brothers. I need to be alone right now.

WOLFY: I can't, Magnus. I see myself reflected in them and I feel afraid.

MAGNUS *(smooth):* Come on, Wolfy, don't be hardheaded. Don't make me lose my patience.

WOLFY: I want to be at your side, Magnus, at this time of great . . .

MAGNUS *(with a stomp on the floor):* Get out! *(WOLFY flees like a rat. He stays curled up in a corner, wringing his hands and groaning in anguish. He looks back and forth from MAGNUS to the group. The rest observe with absolute coldness. MAGNUS signals for silence and concentrates.)* Night has come; now all fountains speak more loudly.[11] *(He clears his throat.)*

KIT *(commenting to the OTHERS):* Nietzsche, of course.

(MAGNUS, with an expression of exhaustion, turns toward his SONS.)

MAGNUS: My little sons, I feel worn-out. To be precise: I am rotten. Everything has gone just as I wished. I traced a plan: it turned out perfectly. And now? Years and years of effort. Hardening oneself has its price. And I achieved it. I transformed myself into stone. It's useless to try to find a single feeling in me: they don't exist. I'm bored. *(Pause. Suddenly melodramatic.)* My little ones, I fooled everyone!

KIT *(fed up):* Big news flash, Magnus!

(The others laugh, pleasantly.)

MAGNUS *(reciting Nietzsche):* Light am I . . . But this is my loneliness that I am girt with light. Ah, that I were dark and nocturnal! How I would suck at the breasts of light!

SONS *(uncomfortable):*
> And what do you want us to do, Magnus?
> If it were up to us . . .
> We already know that you're alone.
> That's the fate you chose.
> The fate of all great ones.

MAGNUS *(laughing):* Bravo, great Nietzsche. *(Serious.)* Well, it's over. There are no more secrets. *(Shouting.)* Confession! *(He laughs. Pause.)* My success lay in anticipating everything. As soon as I saw something being born, I swallowed it up. And only later I offered it up as mine. I was a mirror all my life. A polished, empty surface. I made a fortune selling everyone back their own images. Of course, to all of you, too.

(Silence.)

JULIA *(somewhat hysterical):* Wha-what is he talking about? *(She shakes KIT.)* Kit!

KIT: Don't go hysterical on us. Explain yourself better, Magnus.

MAGNUS: There's nothing to explain. I give everything back. *(He laughs.)* I deliver unto God my soul, pure, intact. Absolutely empty. I only reflected others. The mirror has closed. To each his own soul.

JULIA: Help!

(Panic begins to take over the SONS.)

KIT: One moment, one moment . . . I want to understand this better . . .

JIMMY: He wants to dump it on us.

JULIA: Don't you see, Kit? He wants to make us responsible for everything!

KIT: Calm down . . . I don't want to stop thinking . . .

WOLFY: I told you! I told you that we shouldn't let him talk!

JIMMY: He's a Machiavelli.

KIT: This is a . . . conspiracy.

JULIA: Help! They tricked me!

MAGNUS *(rubbing his hands together, content):* What's up? What's up, Lou, how are things going?

OLD LOU: Getting by, Magnus.

MAGNUS: Getting by, huh?

KIT: Our world was beautiful, Magnus! Why do we have to lose it?

MAGNUS *(without looking at him):* Your world was a comfortable one. And now you're on your own.

WOLFY: Kit, there's still something that can save us!

KIT: What, Wolfy?

(The SONS and JULIA huddle together in a worried council upstage. We see them make large gestures, etc.)

MAGNUS: And now I'll return to my world. All the past belongs to me. It pertains to me. No one can take that away from me, eh, Lou?

OLD LOU: Nobody. Now nobody can touch it. That's the only thing that belongs to you, Magnus.

MAGNUS: Come, come to my side, Lou. My knees are weak. *(OLD LOU goes over to him on all fours.)* Not like that, Lou. Upright. Now we're equals.

OLD LOU: I can't, Magnus. I've become too fond of the ground. Closer every time. I want to be like that: sniffing the dust and dirtying my hands.

MAGNUS: As you wish, Lou. *(Pause.)* What was Bibi's voice like?

OLD LOU: A little hoarse, slightly shy. Her breath barely escaped her lips.

MAGNUS: Yes, it was like that. It was like listening to her breathe or to her heart beat.

(Silence. The SONS come back with the attitude of having arrived at some serious decision.)

KIT: We have decided to kill you, Magnus.

MAGNUS: I already knew that. *(Pause.)* And may we know why?

(The SONS and JULIA look at each other.)

WOLFY: It doesn't matter to you!

KIT *(with a smile):* It's easy, Magnus . . .

WOLFY: Don't tell him, Kit!

(KIT *motions for* WOLFY *to be quiet.*)

KIT: A crime is something, Magnus. A life can be constructed around a crime. The other way around is unbearable. "Nothing" is unbearable. The last image, Pops. At least you'll leave us that. (*Pause.*) Are you resigned?

MAGNUS (*with a shrug of his shoulders*): I only ask that you let me smell my own blood . . .

JULIA: Your egomania is monstrous, Magnus!

MAGNUS (*with a giggle*): Yes, I've loved myself like an animal.

JIMMY: Poor Magnus, your useless life has finally come to an end.

MAGNUS: No, little Jimmy, my life has come to an end because it has become something useless.

WOLFY: And what about us, Magnus?

MAGNUS (*deliberately*): Get by . . . as best as you can.

KIT: Straighten up, Magnus! You have only a few more seconds.

(*Profound silence. For the first time, the enormous knife is displayed, it shines.* MAGNUS's *eyes grow very large.*)

MAGNUS (*suddenly*): Hey, you're not serious?

(*Stupor in the group.*)

WOLFY: Magnus! Magnus! You were fooling!

MAGNUS: Of course, you pack of fools. What did you think?

KIT: Don't believe him! Don't believe him, it's another trap!

JULIA (*hysterical*): Magnus, don't play with us!

MAGNUS: Jesus fucking Christ! You're all nuts!

JIMMY: It's too late, Magnus!

MAGNUS: Help, Lou!

(OLD LOU *washes his hands in the air.*)

JIMMY: Let's go, Kit! No regrets!

(KIT, *as if hypnotized, goes over to* MAGNUS, *the knife in his hand.* MAGNUS *lets loose a shriek.* KIT *raises the weapon above his head, holding on to it with both hands, as if it were some ritual sacrifice. He trembles all over. Suddenly he turns around and drops the knife.*)

KIT: I can't! You just can't kill a man like that!

(JIMMY *pounces on the knife and picks it up. After looking at it in his hands for an instant, he ferociously points it at his own body.*)

JIMMY: I would stab myself!

(JULIA *grabs the knife away from him, with a cry. During this scene,* MAGNUS *has been silently laughing, sitting on the floor.*)

WOLFY: He's laughing at us!

ALL: Let him have it, Julia!

(JULIA *steps back, the knife in her hands.* MAGNUS *springs to his feet.*)

MAGNUS (*triumphant*): Magnus is eternal! He will never die! (*Completely*

drunk on himself, he gesticulates and rehearses demagogical gestures in front of an imaginary mirror. He speaks incoherently, somewhat hoarse.)
Magnus is . . . eternal . . . Moi . . . le General . . . Salt . . . of the earth . . . Signed . . . the King . . . I . . . His Holiness . . .
(On the rest of the stage the following actions have begun developing. JULIA cradles the knife in her arms, as if it were a baby, cooing and caressing.)
JULIA: Little one . . . sweet little one . . . my little one . . .
(WOLFY wanders around the stage, listing names in a deliberate manner, as if dealing with a soccer team.)
WOLFY: Mozart, Beethoven, and Stravinsky, Bach, Handel, Copland,[12] and Mussorgsky . . .
(JIMMY has sunk into a state of autistic trance. He hugs and cradles himself with a sound coming from his closed mouth. OLD LOU is chasing his own tail, like a dog. We begin to hear music, with an obsessive rhythm, whose volume will gradually increase.)
KIT *(strong, dominating the rest):* I have had . . . beautiful visions . . . The entire earth . . . began . . . to bud again . . . and was resplendent. The light . . . was an ocean . . . out of which . . . sprang . . . unceasingly . . . forms . . . trees . . . of a green beauty . . . beaches . . . and stars . . . that descended . . . and that got caught up . . . in the tresses . . . of the multitudes . . . who laughed . . . and embraced each other . . . in the great . . . universal . . . harmony . . . I have had . . . visions . . . of rivers . . . of milk . . . that fed . . . small . . . children . . . in a sky . . . filled . . . with bliss . . . I have returned . . . to see . . . the great mother . . . rocking us . . . eternally . . . in the great . . . reconciliation . . . of all . . . men . . . I have seen . . .
(These words of KIT act like a magnet over the two BROTHERS and JULIA, who have imperceptibly gone nearer to KIT. Finally, KIT's voice is drowned out by the music. The SONS and JULIA form now a compact line, a type of military formation, out of which rises a ritual sound, through closed mouths, and that, advancing and retreating rhythmically, closes in on MAGNUS. From the other side, OLD LOU takes on the appearance of a bloodthirsty mastiff and also goes toward MAGNUS in a rhythmic, ritual manner. MAGNUS begins to be suspicious and retreats, but he finds himself closed off by OLD LOU, who growls at him. The FATHER attempts different forms of claiming control over the SONS, who, nevertheless, inexorably close in on him.)
MAGNUS: Just a minute . . . Come on, boys . . . What's going on here? Wolfy! A little bit of common sense, hey . . . Well, the game's over . . . I told you that was enough . . . Jimmy! Julia, please, tell them that . . . Get the hell out of here . . . Wol . . . Jim . . . Lou!
(When the rhythm has become unbearable, the military formation takes two quick steps and covers MAGNUS. There is a sudden, heavy silence. Then,

we hear a subhuman howl. The line of the Sons circles again and we see the spectacle of Magnus's agony. The bloody knife lies on the floor. Magnus takes a few hesitating steps and falls. At this moment, the compact group of the Sons falls apart. Wolfy runs upstage and vomits.)
Kit *(moving away, holding his nose):* Ugh! He was rotten!
Julia also moves away. Only Jimmy remains, staring at the body with obstinate attention. Old Lou sits down on the floor and howls plaintively. Silence. All remain motionless during a few long seconds in the middle of blindingly white light. Then, a quick and complete BLACKOUT.

The following staging suggestions appeared in the original version of *Una noche con el señor Magnus e hijos* (Buenos Aires: Talía, 1971) but have been omitted by the author from subsequent editions.

Some Suggestions

Set design: This is left entirely up to the designer's imagination. One might assume that the setting is the interior of an old house. Sumptuous objects. The only requisites: a window upstage; an open scenic space that allows for simultaneous games in different acting areas; a "clearing" at center stage, such that the rest of the playing space might have different levels; and a screen—red on one side and an erotic "pop" painting on the other.
Makeup: All the actors (except for the person playing JULIA—at least until the screen-scene in act 2) should have a sort of "mask," drawn with makeup on their faces. The masks will have exaggerated and clownlike traits. After all, *Magnus*, deep down, is really a circus show.
Acting style: It is important to achieve an acting style that corresponds to the play's proposed aesthetic. For example, furtive gestures, or falsely pathetic ones; the imagination's arbitrary sway over any object; the multiplication of internal allusions or inside jokes in an infinite game of mirrors; savage breaks in the action's rhythm; unexpected jumps to different zones of reality, without any transitions. In sum, every gesture must be invented.
Music: Use a sound track with clear and distinct factory sounds, that become more perceptible at different moments and, at the end of the play, explode onto the lit stage, after a few moments of absolute silence and stillness on the part of the actors. The following musical selections should be incorporated, as indicated in the text:
   a)   a limpid, playful piece by Mozart;
   b)   a requiem;
   c)   circus music;

d)   Renaissance banquet music (perhaps a little distorted);
e)   an old jazz piece, morose and extremely erotic; and
f)   "Beat" instrumental music, with an obsessive rhythm, almost ritualistic.

—R. M.

TRANSLATOR'S NOTES

1.   Kit quotes from Job 7:4–5, 11, 19, 21 (Jerusalem Bible).
2.   The reader will note that this is the sons' third rooster cry and a possible biblical allusion to Peter's denial of knowing Jesus Christ (the "cock's crow" of Luke 22:6–11).
3.   In the original text, the reference is to angel-hair pasta soup, fed to sick children and the elderly.
4.   In the original Spanish version, the reference is made to "passive sectors of society," i.e., retirees.
5.   Kit quotes from the ribald, satirical songs ascribed to the Goliards, the name given to "scholar-poets" that wandered throughout England, France, and Germany in the twelfth and thirteenth centuries. The Goliards were notorious for their conviviality and riotous behavior, and Goliardic verse characterized itself as: "(1) satiric, directed against the church and the Pope and (2) profane, devoted to the pleasures of the bed and the tavern in a spirit of reckless hedonism" (*Princeton Encyclopedia of Poetry and Poetics*, edited by Alex Preminger [Princeton: Princeton University Press, 1974], 324). Their name supposedly derives from the Old French word for glutton (*goliard*). The best-known collection of Goliardic Latin verse is the *Carmina Burana*. Kit first quotes from the "Vagabond's Confession" by the Goliard known only as the Archpoet (c. 1130–67). John Addington Symonds's translation is as follows: "'Tis most arduous to make nature's self surrender; / Seeing girls, to blush and be purity's defender! / We young men our longings ne'er shall to stern law render, / Or preserve our fancies from bodies smooth and tender" (*Wine, Women, and Song* [New York: Cooper Square Publishers, 1966], reprinted http://www.auburn.edu/~downejm/sp/rabfw/media/confession.htm).
6.   A line is omitted from the revised version: "WOLFY: I caught him reading Marx, Poppy." Kit-Marx debates Magnus-Nietzsche.
7.   In both versions of the original text, there is an additional phrase ("or in Tucumán"), a reference to one of the more important cities of Argentina's interior.
8.   The literal translation of the proverbs cited in the original text is as follows: "Opportunity for all, today for you, tomorrow for me; money cannot buy happiness; today you're on top and tomorrow on the bottom; it hurts harder to fall than to climb; he who reaches for too much grabs too little; and a bird in the hand is worth more than one hundred flying."
9.   The original Spanish plays on the traditional proverb "Cría cuervos y te sacarán los ojos" (Raise crows and they'll rip your eyes out): "Cría hijos y te comerán las entrañas" (Raise children and they'll eat your guts out).
10.   The words are from the medieval poem "Fortuna, imperatrix mundi" [Fortune, empress of the world], known to contemporary audiences as the chorus that opens and closes Carl Orff's 1936 oratorio *Carmina Burana*: "O Fortune, you are changeable, ever

waxing and waning; hateful life first oppresses and then soothes, as fancy takes it; poverty and power, it melts them like ice."

11.   Magnus quotes from "The Night Song" of Friedrich Nietzsche's *Thus Spoke Zarathustra* (second part), English translation by R. J. Hollingdale (Harmondsworth, England: Penguin Books, 1961).

12.   The U.S. composer Aaron Copland stands in for the original text's (Alberto) Ginastera, Argentina's best-known experimental "classical" composer at the time of the play's 1970 premiere.

Visit

Visita premiered in the Payró Theater (Buenos Aires) on 10 March 1977, and later represented Argentina at the Fourth International Festival of Theater of the Nations (Caracas, Venezuela) in July 1978.

Original Cast

EQUIS [EX]	Antonio Mónaco
	(replaced by Patricio Contreras)
PERLA [PEARL]	Felisa Yeny
LALI [LOLLY]	Aldo Braga
GASPAR [CASPER]	Rubén Szuchmacher
Costumes	Graciela Galán
Assistant Director	Francisco Díaz
Direction and Lighting/	
Set Design	Jaime Kogan

ACT ONE

The living room of an old apartment. High walls and no windows. A ceiling with moldings. Unpleasant and cold ambience. Only a few pieces of furniture: an armchair, an ottoman, a chest of drawers, a couple of chairs. A couple of ornate antiques remain; the walls are stained with the marks of objects that are no longer there. Several doors. Upstage, an arch or wide entryway leading to a foyer.

    A figure can barely be made out in the middle of the murky light. It is Ex, scouring the room. He caresses in passing the few objects that remain. He goes to the chest and attempts to open the drawers but is unsuccessful. A cough offstage is heard and Ex disappears rapidly into the upstage space. A door opens, a light is switched on, and PEARL enters, with quick steps. She is an old woman, tall and thin, with an upright and rigid posture. Her

93

movements are extremely agile and energetic. Her face is a white mask, and exaggerated makeup accentuates her already cadaverous looks. Lips painted an intense, gaudy red; a harsh face; icy eyes. She stops briefly center stage, as if she sensed something, but then she goes to the chest and looks for something inside it. Ex appears momentarily from inside the room upstage. PEARL *interrupts her search and rapidly goes to where he was. Seconds later, Ex opens a door, crosses the room on tiptoes, and disappears through another door.* PEARL *returns, heading toward the center of the room. She stops suddenly and, after a brief pause, begins to sniff the air, her eyes half-shut, as if she were following the trail of scent left by Ex. When she gets to the door through which Ex has exited, he appears once more from inside the room upstage.*

PEARL *(furious, stomping the floor):* Well, enough! What are you looking for? What do you want to do? Give me a heart attack? *(Pause.)* Come out! I know you're here! I can feel you! I can smell you! I've been smelling you for three days! I have the sense of smell of a blue-blooded aristocrat, my dear. I know all the smells of my house, and yours is not among them! It's acidic, like . . . piss and sweat . . . And you think that if you throw on some of our cologne you've covered it up? Impossible! It is out of your control! You've been given away! For three days I've been going mad because of this repulsive smell . . . of a man! No, dear, you don't fool me; you don't smell like here. *(Pause.)* And now what shall you do? I know you're here! But don't think that I will come for you, my child. You shall come to me. *(Pause.)* Listen to me. If you don't come out, if you don't appear before me like a civilized and normal person, within five seconds, exactly five seconds, I am going to go into hysterics.

(Short pause. Ex appears upstage in the doorway of the room. He is a rather enigmatic individual. Delicate features, almost feminine. White, transparent skin; thin, red lips that are now drawn into a tenuous, shy smile. Dark eyes, heavily shadowed. Long, white hands. He wears a bluish suit that is too small for him, thus giving him a slightly ridiculous look. All the buttons are done up. The tie's tight knot suffocates him. PEARL, *up to now twitching nervously, relaxes, relieved, when she sees him. She examines him carefully. Pause.)*

PEARL *(clearing her throat):* I didn't expect you to be like this, exactly. I mean, I imagined you differently. More . . . On the other hand, you appear to be clean. In principle, you appear to be clean. That's important. And shy. You appear to be shy. *(Short pause.)* A girl. But come closer. Come, come, don't be afraid. We've already met. In a way, everything has returned to normal. *(Ex takes a few steps toward the center of the room.)* Your situation was slightly . . . irregular. But now everything is much simpler. Infinitely much simpler. *(Pause.* PEARL *turns a certain distance from him, examining*

him coldly from head to foot, as if he were an object.) Hmmmm, you bite
your nails. *(Ex tries to hide his nails.)* And your cuffs are very worn . . .
And your clothing's too small. Do you have dandruff? What's the matter?
Why don't you speak? I can't stand people who don't speak. *(Brief pause.
She moves with quick steps toward the chest, but before she gets there, she
turns around.)* Deep down you have deceived me. You weren't what I was
expecting. For example, you showed yourself too quickly. That's alright,
you didn't have any choice. But I would have liked to have had a little
more of a struggle. After all, it was pleasant to have a secret for three days.
And if it hadn't been for my feminine curiosity . . . You would have stayed
there, hidden, all your life. And finally you would have died. Everyone dies
. . . And we would have found you because of the rotting stench . . . In a
closet, for example . . . And we would have thrown you in the incinerator
. . . *(Pause.)* But, anyway, here you are. *(Sighs.)* Make yourself comfortable. *(Pause.)* Did you hear me? You don't have to remain standing, like a
post. Move. *(Pause. Ex does not move. PEARL once again goes toward the
chest. As soon as she turns her back, Ex walks toward her; but when PEARL
suddenly turns around, Ex once again freezes in midair.)* Did my old man
see you? *(Ex does not respond.)* No, Lolly surely knows nothing of this. I
would have noticed it. The only thing I can say is that you must be careful
around him. Over the years, he has acquired a repulsive vice. *(She weighs
him with her eyes.)* And you will be a bocato di cardenale for him. Last
month they found him with the mongoloid downstairs . . . A disagreeable
subject . . . On the stair-landing . . . Anyway, they're respectable people,
incapable of creating a scandal over nothing. But after all, he is my husband. I have forbidden him. Except . . . under certain circumstances . . . It's
just that I, years ago . . . On the other hand, poor Lolly . . . It would appear
to be the exact opposite. But that's not really normal, is it? At his age . . .
Actually, it makes me rather sick. Because I don't believe it is a physical
need but rather something . . . purely mental. *(Long silence.)* What are you
thinking about? No, don't tell me. I prefer to read your mind. *(Pause.)* But
you're so stiff. Are you always like that? Loosen up, come on, loosen up.
Say something. Speaking is a way of releasing tension. A way of forgetting. In general, my memories last exactly one minute. Why? Because I
speak. It would be unbearable to keep so many memories locked up inside.
One must empty oneself out, evacuate . . . For example, how did it happen
that we are here talking? I don't know, I don't remember. I don't remember, either, what you said your name was. I swim, as they say, in oblivion,
between reflections and fleeting sensations . . . I'm also a poet, a dreamer,
as you must have guessed from my earlier sentence . . . *(Brief pause. Suddenly, without any transition, she turns toward the chest, opens a drawer,
and begins to rummage around frantically inside.)* Where the fuck are they?

. . . *(Ex goes toward her and looks over her shoulder.)*
Ex: What are you looking for?
PEARL: My cigarettes.
Ex: Over there, under the album . . .
PEARL: Oh . . . *(She takes out a cigarette and slams the drawer shut. Ex barely has time to pull his hand out. PEARL looks around nervously, searching for something. Ex comprehends what she is looking for and lights her cigarette. PEARL accepts the light, looks first at the lighter, and then gives Ex a penetrating stare.)* Where did you get that lighter?
Ex: I found it.
PEARL: Where?
Ex: I don't remember.
PEARL *(sarcastically)*: You don't remember. From now on, my little one, you shall light *my* cigarettes with that gold lighter that has *my* initials engraved on it. Do you understand? *(Pause.)* Now put it away. *(Shifting position.)* And you, my dear, don't you smoke?
Ex: Yes.
PEARL: But I didn't offer you one, did I?
Ex: No.
PEARL: It would have been a mechanical gesture. Should it ever happen, do not accept. These cigarettes are British, and therefore expensive. And I only smoke British cigarettes. *(She inhales and has a coughing fit. She throws the cigarette on the floor and destroys it with her foot. She goes over to the armchair and sits. Ex picks up the bits of the cigarette; during the following dialogue, he will finish crumbling it up, mechanically, in his fingers.)* Dear, you remind me of someone, but I don't know who. What did you say your name was? *(Pause.)* Dear, you are a mystery. But if only I knew your last name, the mystery would be over. Let's suppose that it is Gómez or . . . Jones. What mystery could there be in being a Jones? This city is full of such trivial mysteries. *(Pause. Offstage, a fight of some sort begins and ends abruptly: confused screams, whines, the sudden racket of breaking glass and objects falling down. Silence.)* There is a detail that's engraved in my memory. When you . . . appeared, it was a radiant day. However, you were wet. I found trails of water and the marks from your footsteps. So I looked out the window, and it was a radiant day. *(Pause. The same ruckus as before is heard offstage. Silence.)* Have you already been to the other apartments? *(Ex does not respond.)* Surely not. Surely you began from the top of the building. If you had begun on the ground floor, you wouldn't have gotten all the way to us. You would have been satisfied. Our neighbors are all people of noble birth. Hah, we don't have anything to do with them now. But I remember the old receptions, cause-

ries, magnificent dinners. Even though that was long ago. It's possible that it's all changed, I don't know. It's possible that all of them, or at least the majority, have disappeared. Oh, what melancholia! In the salons of the fourth-floor apartment, opposite their mirrors, there were some beautiful tapestries. How many times I surprised myself seeing my image with a tapestry behind! My porcelain skin, my ample dresses . . . And I, surprised, flushed, I didn't know if the mirror had trapped me, or if one of the ladies in the tapestry had come to life. Oh, and in the apartment on the third floor, we'll be able to satisfy our thirst for exquisite goblets of worked silver, of old-fashioned colonial stock, upper Peruvian . . . Melancholia! *(Pause.)* And here? What can we offer you? As you see, there's very little. It's that we have slowly been stripping ourselves of our earthly goods . . . Well, over there you'll find an authentic Frederick Remington.[1] If it interests you, I'll make you a gift of it. It's awful. Now, in cash, deutschmark, I'm sorry but no . . . Anyway, they'll give you something for the Remington. I can recommend a good marchand . . .

Ex: Please . . .

PEARL: What? Don't be ashamed, please. I'm not blaming you. After all, what would a family like ours be like without robberies, kidnappings, swindles?

Ex: But you're wrong. I didn't come here to rob you.

PEARL: Oh. *(Pause.)* Then why did you come here? *(Ex smiles shyly, lowers his eyes, and then passes his thumb across his neck, with a slicing motion.)*

PEARL *(slightly disappointed):* Oh. *(Pause. Smiling.)* Well. *(Pause.)* Sit down. You must be exhausted. A decision like that . . . *(Pause. Ex doesn't move. The racket outside is heard again. PEARL smiles.)* They're trying to get our attention.

Ex: What?

PEARL: They feel excluded. I'm going to have to go establish a little order. If you'll excuse me . . .

Ex: Of course . . .

PEARL: I'll be back in a minute. Excusez-moi.

(PEARL exits through one of the side doors. As soon as Ex is alone, he goes quickly to the chest and tries to open a drawer. He is unsuccessful. He tries to force it open. While Ex is doing this, an old man enters through the same door through which PEARL exited. Both men look at each other for a few seconds, in silence. LOLLY is carrying an old magazine: the Saturday Evening Post. *His face resembles PEARL's. The makeup on top of the whitewashed skin emphasizes an infinite corruption. He is bald or has a closely shaved head. He wears a worn-out dressing gown and slippers. He stands motionless in the doorway.)*

LOLLY: Excuse me.

(LOLLY leaves, closing the door behind him. Ex goes over to the door and listens. He then returns to the chest and begins forcing the drawer once more. When he is convinced of his own impotence, he looks around for something to help him. He notices an old ornamental ax hanging on the wall. He takes it down and goes back to the chest. Just as he is about to bash in the lock, LOLLY appears again. They look at each other silently for a few seconds.)

LOLLY: Excuse me, but it's my reading hour. *(He indicates the magazine he has in his hands.)* I'm going to relax here, as long as you . . . But I don't wish my presence to be a . . . Go on, go on, don't interrupt your work. I have great powers of concentration. *(He sits down in the armchair and submerges himself in reading the magazine, which hides his face from the audience. In the old man's presence, Ex has slowly lowered the ax. Now, with careful steps, he returns the ax to its original location, hanging it up.)*

LOLLY *(without lowering the magazine):* The other way. *(Ex jumps and looks at the old man. The latter lowers his magazine, smiling.)* The head of the ax, you put it up backwards. It goes the other way. *(Ex quickly corrects the ax's position.)* Yes, now it's alright, even though . . . *(Pause. Ex looks at him expectantly.)* It's tilted too much. *(Ex modifies the angle.)* No, now you've made it too horizontal. Try to put it at a thirty-degree angle. *(Ex tries to do that.)* Thirty, my child, thirty! Don't you know what a thirty-degree angle is? No! Careful! It's going to fall! That's alright, leave it alone! Leave it as is! *(Ex leaves the ax alone. He is confused and humiliated. The old man gives him a hard stare.)* Now it's never going to be the same again. Do you understand? Why did you take it down? It's so easy to destroy order! Just by simply changing a detail! And the entire edifice comes tumbling down! A beautiful edifice minutely planned over centuries! *(Pause.)* But there it is. What are you going to do? It's irreparable. *(Pause.)*

Ex: Sir, I'm sorry . . .

LOLLY: You're contrite. *(Ex looks questioningly at him.)* That's good. Your contrition is enough for me. *(Sadly.)* This will never again be what it was, but . . . let's forget it! The forgiveness of oblivion . . . The mantle of . . . Mon fils, voudriez-vous m'approcher le pouf, s'il vous plaît? *(Ex looks at him; he doesn't understand. LOLLY enunciates in an exaggerated fashion and points to the object.)* L-e p-o-u-f. *(Ex brings it to him.)* Thank you, son. Is it too much to ask you to help me put my feet up? *(Ex rushes to help him and kneels at his feet.)* Oh, thank you. When you are old, my dear, if that day ever comes, you'll understand . . . Age brings so many humiliating things. The body doesn't respond, and one has to begin relying on others. And not all strangers are so understanding. Alas . . . Now, please, will you permit me to read? *(LOLLY hides himself behind his magazine. Ex remains at his side, watching him. Then, with a quick, stealthy move, he takes off one of LOLLY's slippers and hides it away. The old man's stocking is very dirty and full of holes.)*

LOLLY *(quickly, without lowering the magazine):* Tell me, my child, whose side are you on? The Boers' or the British? *(Ex does not respond. LOLLY lowers the magazine.)* If this puts you in a compromising situation, don't respond.

Ex: I don't know.

LOLLY: You don't know what? *(Pause.)* It's very easy, you have to choose, simply, between two things. The Boers or the British. *(Pause.)* The Boers or the British. *(Pause.)* Surely you know what it's about.

Ex: No.

LOLLY: But how can that be, my dear, the Anglo-Boer War![2] Don't you read the papers, the magazines?

Ex: It's been a long time since . . .

LOLLY *(disappointed):* Oh. That's a pity, because this will limit our conversation. What can two strangers talk about? *(Pause. They look at each other.)* And if you were to choose at random?

Ex: I don't like chance.

LOLLY: Why not?

Ex: I need some facts . . .

LOLLY: Such as?

Ex: Who's right. *(LOLLY sits back in the armchair. He looks at Ex rather disconcertedly.)*

LOLLY: I've never thought about that. Who's "right." I guess that would be the British: they're so pragmatic. Is this detail very important to you?

Ex: Yes.

LOLLY: Of course. No, I'm very sorry that in this case I cannot . . . *(He suddenly lets out a guffaw.)* Who's right! How droll! Oh, how pathetic! *(He calms down. Brief pause. They look at each other.)* A bunch of blokes with their guts ripped out, and it was all over. Tout fini.

Ex: How do you know?

LOLLY: Oh, because I read it. *(He hits the magazine.)* Here, it's all in here, you see? What happened, and what's about to happen. Look, what's the date on it? *(He shows Ex the magazine cover.)*

Ex *(reading):* 1899.

LOLLY: I read only magazines that are at least half a century old; it's the only way to avoid surprises. I hate surprises. That's why I know everything: what's happened. *(Brief pause.)* And what will happen. Don't you realize that way one can be on top of everything? The motivations for what happens cease to be of interest. Things simply happen. *(Pause.)* Do you understand? *(Pause. Ex's look is impenetrable.)* No, you don't understand anything. Now give me back my slipper.

Ex *(with a jump):* What?

Lolly *(with unexpected violence):* Give me back my slipper!

Ex: What slipper?

Lolly: My left slipper!

Ex: I never saw your slipper!

Lolly: So you want to be a wise guy? *(Ex jumps up and throws the slipper at him violently. A long pause ensues, and the two look at each other. Lolly, his torso erect and his eyes burning with hatred, is like a serpent.)* That was a useless gesture, my son. Now you are going to pick up my slipper and put it back on my foot. *(Pause. Ex picks up the slipper, kneels at Lolly's feet, and puts it back on his foot.)* Thank you, son. *(He smiles at Ex. Then the smile evaporates from his face. A transformation comes over Lolly. He looks at Ex with interest. He swallows his saliva. He looks anxiously at the doors. His eyes shine with arousal. He takes out a cigarette, with nervous, effeminate gestures.)* Listen to me. *(He checks his pockets.)* Give me a light. *(Ex lights his cigarette with the lighter. Lolly grabs hold of his hand.)* What did she tell you about me?

Ex: Who?

Lolly: The bitch.

Ex *(freeing his hand with a single, strong tug):* To watch myself around you.

Lolly *(standing up, annoyed):* That bitch in heat! *(He looks over at the chest.)* What were you looking for over there?

Ex *(leaping to his feet):* Nothing!

Lolly: I saw you.

Ex *(slightly hysterical):* I wasn't looking for anything!

Lolly *(going over to the chest):* Couldn't you open it? *(He opens a drawer, rummages around inside. With a look of disgust, he pulls out a woman's stocking and throws it to one side. He then stands, motionless, observing Ex. Ex slowly approaches, but when he is beside the chest, Lolly slams the drawer shut. Ex throws him two punches, both of which Lolly evades.)* No, no! Hey! Control yourself!

(Ex remains motionless while the old man moves around the stage, prisoner of some violent agitation. Ex slowly lets himself fall down next to the chest. Lolly approaches. He kneels at Ex's side. He puts the cigarette in Ex's mouth. Pause.)

Lolly: Is it very cold outside?

Ex: Yes.

Lolly: Did you eat? Are you hungry?

Ex: No, I ate a slice of pizza. It made me sick to my stomach.

Lolly: You're just tired. You must have walked a lot.

Ex: Yes, I had to get here.

LOLLY: Here? *(Ex nods.)* But why, if this place is now nothing but a cave. Everything is dirty, cold, abandoned. If only you'd come here before . . . Before, the porcelain and the bronze gleamed, and the . . . Well, anyway, everything gleamed . . . Now everything is hidden. Nothing in sight. Nobody can steal it.

EX: I didn't come here to steal anything.

LOLLY: No, of course not. Besides, many thieves and murderers have already come through this place. *(Brief pause.)* And they're all dead. *(Pause. He goes to Ex.)* You're young, aren't you? I don't think you're more than thirty years old. Even though you do have those two little wrinkles around your mouth. *(He takes Ex by the chin and turns his head toward him.)* I like your face. It's a very . . . fleshy face. Yes, it's fleshy. It's full of evil. Full of death. *(He lowers his hand to Ex's neck, and then his chest. Ex, without flinching, pushes his hand away. The old man, somewhat indignant, moves away slightly.)* You're very proud, my dear.

EX: Your hands are cold.

LOLLY *(runs his hands over his lips):* You're right, my hands are cold. How about that? I'd never noticed it before. *(He goes right up to Ex.)*

EX: Get back.

LOLLY: Why? *(Ex does not respond.)* A matter of principles, is that it? *(Ex does not respond.)* That's alright. *(Pause.)* Principles. They all come here with principles. But why do they come here at all then, I ask? Do we call them? Do we need them? And with what pretensions! Tous grands hommes! Until one offers them a little of what they want and good-bye principles. Oh, I know what you all are like!

EX: I am incorruptible.

LOLLY *(making fun):* Oh, yes? Look, I still have some power left in me. Not as much as I had in my youth, but . . . Anyway, enough left. Besides, it's not only worldly things that I can offer you. *(Silence.)* You see? Now you're doubting. *(Ex remains imperturbable.)* Let's see, what is it that chains you to the Earth?

EX: The force of gravity.

LOLLY: What else?

EX: Nothing else.

LOLLY: And death?

(Pause.)

EX: Everything has to die.

LOLLY: Come on, don't be naïve. Why are you here then? Don't lie. I myself, for example . . . Well, at least under certain conditions. I have known immortality. *(Pause.)* So? What do you say?

EX: I don't believe you.

LOLLY: Naturally. It's difficult for you people to conceive of this.

Ex: Are you making fun of me?

LOLLY: Absolutely not, son. I'm already on the other side.

Ex: Well, then, give me some proof.

(Pause.)

LOLLY: Well, alright. But, careful, it'll be brief, only an instant.

Ex: Doesn't matter.

LOLLY: And besides, we'd have to go up.

Ex: Up where?

(Brief pause. An anonymous hand opens one of the doors, and from the room next-door come the chords of an out-of-tune clavichord, accompanying LOLLY's recitative. In this scene, the clavichord will give a flourish to certain passages, or, rather, it will create its own musical forms in the pauses.)

LOLLY *(reciting):*

 Friend of mine, there is a place
 In that abyss known as space,
 Where centuries are mere bubbles,
 That by the thousands explode,
 Disappear as they go.
 A most remarkable show!

Ex: You lie.

LOLLY: No, it's absolutely true.

 There twinkle the immortal stars
 and matter is a river transparent
 flowing forever, without bars.
 There all forms
 are but a single form
 that engenders itself
 eternally, immanent.
 One single form, inseparable,
 without limit, without a crack.
 There death has lost her knack.
 She cannot divide nor wear out nor disfigure.
 There are no others,
 just everything, one and the same.
 Let's go, are you game?
 Your decision requires only a word of it.

Ex: What is there to lose?

LOLLY: Nothing, it's all pure profit.

(Pause.)

Ex *(barely audible):* What do I have to do?

LOLLY: That depends on the time. What time is it?

EX: I don't know.

LOLLY: Grosso modo. Is it morning or afternoon?

EX: I think it's afternoon.

LOLLY: Oh, what a shame. I usually fly in the morning. It's healthier. But it doesn't matter. Today I'll make an exception. *(He gets down on all fours.)* Let's go.

EX: What?

LOLLY: You have to climb on top of me.

EX: No, I don't want to.

LOLLY: Come on, fool, it may be shocking down here, but once you're up above, what does it matter where you are? All of space just for us! Let's go! *(Pause. The old man is panting from arousal. Ex, slowly, climbs on top of him.)* That's good, hold on tighter with your thighs. Close your eyes. We're beginning to take off. *(He takes a few painful steps.)* So? What do you feel? Do you feel how the wind blows over your face? But don't open your eyes yet. You could become dizzy. Over there is a little white cloud. We're going to go through it. Doesn't it tickle? It's so cute . . . Now yes. We're floating in the middle of rays of sunshine. Open your eyes, I'm going to show you my domain. Do you see that strip of green earth? Over there's abundance. And that strip of golden earth? Over there's drought. And that strip of black earth? Over there's the beginning of night.

EX: I think I'm going to throw up.

LOLLY: Close your eyes. Up here the air is so pure, so transparent. Fill up your lungs. This is the air of immortality. Up here is where we begin to gain time. If you could see the Earth now! A little wound of light. Trembling in the darkness. It goes on, it goes off, it goes on . . . *(He laughs, panting.)* Do you know what I'm thinking? What if it never came back on . . . All that scab, all that misery, so many screams, so much desire . . . All lost, useless, swallowed up by the darkness . . . What a celestial joke!

EX *(spurring him on with his heels)*: Let's go! Let's go!

LOLLY: Alright, alright. It scares you, doesn't it? And anyway, that's what will happen. *(Pause.)* Are you trembling?

EX: It's cold up here.

LOLLY: We have to hurry up.

(They trot in silence. Ex carefully opens his eyes. He has his arms extended, as if he were floating.)

EX: And now where are we?

LOLLY: I don't know exactly. It's all the same. Emptiness, flashes of light, lost suns, luminous points floating in the darkness. Dissolution, gestation, birth, death. And in the middle of all of it, us. Oh, mon enfant, your thighs are so warm! Deep down the universe is cold and boring. Your thighs, however, are throbbing. Immortality is so boring! If I could only for an instant merge myself with your life, mon enfant!

Ex: But I'm not immortal.

LOLLY: And that's just why I desire you, mon enfant. If I could only for an instant merge myself with your death! *(He tries to turn over.)*

Ex: Careful!

LOLLY: Why? Nobody can see us up here.

Ex: We could fall!

LOLLY: Fall where? We're in the middle of everything.

Ex: Keep going! Keep going! I want to see more!

LOLLY *(annoyed):* But it's all the same. There's no variety. I'm tired.

Ex: I want to see more!

LOLLY: I told you that the trip wouldn't last long. We can't spend all eternity up here.

Ex: Why not? I've just barely had enough time to see anything. Keep going!

LOLLY: No, I'm staying here. Je suis fatigué.

Ex *(spurring LOLLY on with his heels):* Let's go!

LOLLY: Ow! No, I'm not going to if you act like that. After all, I'm not a horse. Get down.

Ex: Keep going!

LOLLY: No. Ow! Let go of my hair! Oh, no, dear. *(LOLLY tries to get up. Ex holds on to his hair and immobilizes him. LOLLY howls. Silence.)*

Ex *(very slowly, almost pinned to LOLLY's ear):* Now I'm in charge. And we're going to keep going until both of us are tired, for as long as I want.

LOLLY: That's what you think, my son. But we're already back. The trip is over. Because in reality, my dear, we never left.

(Pause. The anonymous hand slams the door shut. Ex lets go of the old man, who falls down; from the floor, between Ex's open legs, LOLLY laughs silently. Ex watches him. Then, with a growing ferocity, Ex begins to kick LOLLY. The old man tries to avoid him, laughing, until he is able to quickly grab Ex by the crotch.)

LOLLY: Aha! Now the bird's in its cage! *(Ex tries to push him, but LOLLY grabs his arm. Pause. They look at each other.)* In the back of my mouth I have two moldy teeth. Does that disgust you?

Ex *(manages to shove him away):* Rotten flesh! That's all there is around here!

(LOLLY, on all fours, moves quickly to Ex and wraps himself around Ex's waist. Ex knees him, but LOLLY then wraps himself around Ex's leg. Ex tries to get away and walks, dragging the old man along. He stops and manages

to disengage one of LOLLY's hands clinging to his ankle, but LOLLY holds on by the other, trying to force EX to the ground. It's a sordid battle; they're both panting. EX grabs LOLLY by the hair and slams his head against the floor. LOLLY tries then to grab EX by the arms, and EX closes his fingers around LOLLY's neck. He shakes him. PEARL enters quickly, with a box in her hands. Behind her enters CASPER.)

PEARL *(crossing the stage without stopping):* Ah, but what's going on in this room? Lolly, Lolly, the pitcher can only go so often to the well before . . . Why fuck around with strangers? *(She sits in a chair.)* Hey, Casper! *(CASPER the dwarf is on her knees in a single leap. PEARL hands him the box containing her cosmetics, and CASPER begins to do her nails.)* You can't say that I didn't warn you, Lolly. Don't ever get involved with strangers, one never knows how they'll react. *(The dwarf starts paying attention to the strangulation. PEARL slaps him.)* Pay attention, Casper. Scissors. *(Referring to LOLLY.)* Now he's slobbering. How disgusting! It makes me want to vomit. This time you've met your match, huh, Lolly? *(To CASPER.)* Trim the cuticle again, child. *(Thinking it over.)* But I'll be left a widow! During the best years of my life! Poor Lolly, who would've thought that it would turn out like this? What does destiny hold in store for us? No one knows. Life is uncertain, at the mercy of any kind of strange accident. Ow! *(She slaps the dwarf.)* You almost cut my fingertip, you son of a bitch! The file. And to think that I married him for his virility. His black mustache, his ferocious stare . . . And now he's just a filthy piece of rubbish. Nail polish.

LOLLY *(in a whisper):* Je suis mort.

(EX lets go of LOLLY, who collapses like a rag. Pause.)

PEARL: What did he say? *(CASPER gets down and goes over to the body.)* Is he breathing?

CASPER *(after probing LOLLY's body with his foot.):* No.

PEARL: Well then, it's all over. He will have all the rites as befit a man so dignified and of such an elevated rank. *(She turns to EX, who is looking at the body.)* And you, sir, are a murderer. Are you aware of that, young man? Did you ever think about what it cost to give that man life? It's obvious that you've never been a mother. And you seemed so shy, so innocent. But I should have suspected it! It's not rare for murderers to look so sweet, so childlike. *(EX begins to rub his hands together vehemently.)* What's the matter with you? Do you feel bad? Now it makes you sick, doesn't it? But you should've thought of that before, my dear. Please, you're making me nervous. Calm down, you don't have anything on your hands. You strangled him, that's all. There wasn't any blood. Would you like to wash up? *(CASPER suddenly is paying attention.)* My son, please, I asked you if you wanted to wash your hands.

CASPER: And where would he do that?

PEARL: Go on, dear. Through there, at the end of the hall. The door with the vitraux.

(When CASPER *hears this, he takes two jumps and places himself between* Ex *and the door. He extends his arms out exaggeratedly, à la Sarah Bernhardt.)*

CASPER: *Nevah! (Ex pushes him aside with a single shove and exits.* CASPER *is desperate.)* Pearl, it's an abuse of our trust! He's going to use our bathroom? Our sanctuary. He wants to displace us, don't you see? First the bathroom, then everything else.

(Brief pause.)

PEARL *(leaving her reverie):* What are you talking about, stupid?

CASPER: He's going to profane our sanctuary!

PEARL *(insulting):* The little trysting room, you mean. Or don't you think that I don't know who hides in there to commit who knows what disgusting acts?

CASPER: Come on, Pearl, we meet there to pray.

PEARL: To pray? Vile little verses that he teaches you! Obscene little chants!

CASPER: They're our hymns, Pearl.

PEARL: Obscene little chants! The one about the weenie and other vulgarities.

CASPER *(innocent):* What weenie?

PEARL: You know very well what weenie I'm referring to. *(LOLLY sighs.)* Help your adopted father.

LOLLY: Ah, mon Dieu, quelle bête! *(CASPER shakes the dust off his clothing.)* Careful, Casper! I'm broken!

PEARL: Lolly, our adopted son is nervous. We should give him a tranquilizer.

CASPER *(kicking the floor):* No tranquilizers!

PEARL: No scenes, please, Casper.

CASPER: No tranquilizers!

PEARL: They're good for you.

CASPER: They're not good for me. I lose all sense of time.

PEARL: So what? You're going to die anyway, dear.

CASPER *(with a sly smile, like someone who knows more than he is saying):* That remains to be seen.

PEARL: What remains to be seen? *(To LOLLY.)* This imbecile thinks he's the only servant we've ever had. *(To CASPER.)* Don't fool yourself, dear. We're not going to lift one finger to keep you from dying. To each his own cycle. Anyway, even if we wanted to, we couldn't do anything.

CASPER *(with the same sly smile):* You two can.

PEARL: No, no, we can't. And when all's said and done, dear, even if we could, why would we want to?

CASPER *(resentful):* Of course, I don't deserve any compensation, do I?

PEARL: Not *that* kind of compensation.

CASPER: I'm not interested in any other kind of compensation.

PEARL: How unbearable! A miserable life and no matter what, he clings to it.

CASPER: You two have made my life miserable. I was happy before. I didn't know anything. I was free. But here, I don't have any privacy. I don't get one moment of solitude.

PEARL: Solitude. For what?

CASPER: For thinking.

PEARL: About what?

CASPER: About many things. *(PEARL smiles sarcastically.)* Yes, sir, about many things. Because I am a sentient being. I have free will. But, nevertheless, here I am, wasting my life away in order to serve the two of you. And all the while, I'm getting older.

PEARL: You're still young, Casper. A boy.

CASPER: Yes, of course, but I'm still getting older.

PEARL: You look just the same to me.

CASPER: No, I'm aware of it. Time goes by. Sometimes I look at myself in the mirror, and I scare myself. But then I think: No, they're not going to let this happen to me. They will finally compensate me. Pearl, it would be so beautiful. The three of us together. Forever. And I would serve you both just as always, only better. We wouldn't even have to talk. We'd use signs to communicate. And I would always serve you. Just like a dog. Like a faithful little dog.

PEARL: Lolly, the tranquilizers.

CASPER: No tranquilizers! I know what you want to do to me! You want to drug me! You want to drug me so you can get rid of me easier and have the other one around!

PEARL: Well, after all, it would be an interesting change.

CASPER: Never! Before that, I'll kill him first!

LOLLY: Well, Casper, stop it. Enough, my dear, enough. *(He picks CASPER up in his arms and calms him.)* Nobody's going to replace you, stop it.

CASPER *(crying):* Lolly, she doesn't love me.

LOLLY: She does too love you, silly.

CASPER: No, she doesn't love me. She hates me.

PEARL: I'm fed up, fed up. Give me a cigarette. *(CASPER gets down and goes to look for her cigarette, wiping the snot from his nose.)* He's taking forever! Do you think he's committed suicide?

LOLLY: I hope he doesn't do that to us!

PEARL: He's a strange one.

CASPER: An underhanded enemy.

PEARL: Silence. Here he comes.

(Pause. They all get ready to receive Ex. Ex opens the door but doesn't enter, leaning instead against the frame.)

PEARL: Ah, here's our friend. Come in. What's the matter? Are you woozy? Your face is still wet.

Ex: There aren't any towels.

PEARL: That's possible. Since we never bathe . . .

Ex: There isn't anything, not even toilet paper.

PEARL: So? What's the matter? Are you woozy? I want to speak with you alone. Come in here. Don't stay rooted over there. What's the matter? This man's ill.

Ex: I'm going to die.

PEARL: Yes, it's horrible. But for the moment you look pretty healthy. Come, come over here. *(Ex takes a few steps.)* Someone dry his face! It's horrible! He looks as if he's been crying.

(LOLLY goes over to Ex. He unfolds a white handkerchief and applies it to Ex's face. Then LOLLY goes downstage and displays the handkerchief to the spectators, crossing from one side to the other, like a magician just before he performs a trick. There is nothing on the handkerchief. PEARL and CASPER have anxiously followed the action.)

PEARL: Is it he?

(LOLLY hands her the handkerchief. PEARL examines it, smells it.)

LOLLY: Nothing. Not even a trace. Absolutely white.

(PEARL gives him back the handkerchief.)

PEARL: Come to me, dear. Allow me to check your pulse. *(Ex goes to her. PEARL takes his pulse.)* Hmmm, it seems normal. Do you have heart murmurs?

Ex: Sometimes.

PEARL: Well, but that's normal. Let's see, turn around. *(Ex turns in place.)* No, you're alright. Nice tight little buns, eh? Wide pecs. You're healthy, dear! *(Pause.)* Humanity. *(Pause.)* Let's see, do this. *(She shows him her teeth. Ex repeats the gesture. PEARL leans in close to his face.)* A horse, dear, a horse. Open your mouth. *(Ex does so. PEARL looks inside.)* Ah, a cavity.

Ex: Where?

PEARL: Back there, dear. *(She has one finger inside Ex's mouth.)* Careful, don't bite me. Does it hurt? *(Ex shakes his head no.)* Well, that's enough. No such thing as perfect health! Something's always rotten in Denmark! Sit down. *(Ex does not move. To CASPER and LOLLY.)* He's obstinate, isn't he? *(Pause.)* Did someone send you?

Ex: No.

(Pause.)

PEARL: Then, how did you find our house?

(Pause.)

EX: Were you expecting me?

PEARL: No. That is to say, we weren't expecting anyone, but we weren't not expecting either. We just were. Sometimes someone comes here, for some reason. Generally, they come around asking for something. But people, you know, ask for the impossible. We don't have that much. Sometimes they come to rob us. Sometimes, too, they come and leave us provisions at our door . . . where they rot. They've never asked us to pay . . . They must think that we're very rich and that we'll settle up the entire account at the end . . . But it could also be that they're offerings . . . For something that they think, anyway, for some obscure reason that escapes us . . . In general it's very difficult to discover why people do things, don't you think? *(Pause.)* But you, dear, why? *(Pause. PEARL, questioningly, draws her thumb across her neck. EX nods yes. Pause.)* Well, but supposing that you're successful, why? *(Pause.)* Besides, why didn't you try to do it when you had the chance? *(Pause.)* Well, that's alright. You may leave. Casper, a mouchoir drenched in cologne.

EX *(taking a few steps toward PEARL):* Perhaps you accept dying . . .

PEARL: You don't need to come any closer. What did you say?

EX *(going closer):* Perhaps you accept dying . . .

PEARL: I said that was enough. I don't like hot-blooded animals to get too close. They affect my metabolism. We accept what?

EX: Dying.

PEARL: Not on your life. And don't come any nearer. I don't want to hear any more. I'm tired and nervous. You tire me. You're slippery, viscous. One can't use logic with you. And illogical things tire me out. The interview's over for today. Go back and hide yourself. *(She gets up. EX goes to her and grabs her by the arm.)* What are you doing? What is this insolent man doing? Let go of me! Disgusting! Get this thing off of me!

(CASPER returns with the handkerchief.)

LOLLY: Please. Behave yourself; show some decorum. She's a lady.

PEARL *(seeing CASPER):* The boy! The boy! Get the boy out of here! I don't want him to see this!

EX *(disconcertedly lets go of PEARL. After a pause):* What boy?

CASPER *(uncomfortable):* What boy? What boy? This boy. The only boy here.

PEARL: The foundling.

(Pause.)

CASPER: Yes, the foundling. Found-ling. Come on, Pearl, don't listen to him. *(He pulls on her dress.)*

PEARL: Calm down, dear. *(To EX.)* What's the matter? What don't you understand?

Ex *(pointing to* CASPER*): He*'s the . . . boy?

CASPER *(increasingly frantic):* Yes, yes, I'm the boy. So what? Let's go, Pearl. He's got the tongue of a serpent.

PEARL *(raising her tense hands over her head):* You're hiding something from me! I want to know what!

CASPER: There's nothing to hide! There's nothing to know! There's nothing new under the sun!

PEARL: What's going on with this boy? With this foundling? This foundling . . . that we pulled out . . . of the stream . . . in a cradle?

Ex: Well, this boy's a man.

*(*CASPER *screams and runs away.* PEARL *feigns laughter.)*

PEARL: How absurd! *(She stops laughing. Pause.)* Casper.

*(*CASPER *nears her cautiously, with a finger under his nose.)*

CASPER: What, Pearl?

PEARL: Come here. Closer. What are you hiding?

CASPER: Where?

PEARL: Under your nose.

CASPER: Nothing.

PEARL: Take your finger away.

CASPER: Pearl, please.

PEARL: Take your finger away! *(*CASPER *lowers his finger.* PEARL *goes to him and bends over. She looks at him, only centimeters away. With a howl.)* Hairs! *(She raises her arm, as if about to slap* CASPER's *face. But her hand hangs in the air. She has some kind of apoplectic fit and collapses. Silence.* CASPER *kneels and takes her pulse.)*

CASPER: The old bag kicked it.

LOLLY: What a tragedy! We'll have to give her a funeral.

ACT TWO

The same apartment. No one is on the stage. Nevertheless, one perceives a certain agitation and disorder. The few pieces of furniture have been cleared aside to make an opening in the middle of the room. Offstage can be heard LOLLY's *voice giving orders.* CASPER *enters, carrying two candelabra, old and unmatched. His movements are feverish, but by and large absolutely ineffective. He moves the candelabra from one place to another, moves furniture that doesn't need moving, etc.*

CASPER *(yelling excitedly toward one of the doors):* Come on, hurry up in there!

LOLLY *(offstage):* Alright, alright, we're almost finished.

CASPER: We can't waste so much time.

LOLLY *(offstage):* Don't worry, my dear. Ready? You take her by the shoulders!

(LOLLY appears in the doorway with EX, both carrying PEARL's body, which is decked out in a bridal gown, all in tulle, that serves as her shroud. CASPER moves frantically all around her, smoothing out the fabric.)

CASPER: Careful! Careful!

(Judging from the looks on LOLLY and EX's faces, PEARL's body must weigh a ton.)

LOLLY: Strength, my dear. Don't dump it all on me! You're the youngster!

CASPER: The chaise longue! The chaise longue's missing! Give me a hand in getting the chaise longue! *(He runs offstage. LOLLY and EX take a few painful steps.)*

LOLLY: Come on, don't give up. Just a few steps more. Casper, the chaise longue! What disorganization! If she were here, it would have been all different. Come this way, let's put her down on the floor for a moment. *(They get all tangled up.)* So? Why don't you pull? A little respect, dear, you're stepping on her tulle . . . Forza! *(They take two more steps.)* This's good. Gently, don't drop her all at once. Like this . . .

(They put her on the floor.)

EX *(exhausted and bewildered):* I didn't mean to do it.

LOLLY: Do what?

EX: Step on her dress. Really, I didn't mean to do it.

LOLLY: Yes, but it still was tactless of you. It's obvious that she's dead. It's like stepping on a bridal gown. *(He smiles and gives EX a couple of light slaps on the cheek.)* Well, don't get all worked up. You did a good job. Now we'll rest a bit and smoke a cigarette, eh? *(He flops down on the floor. EX remains standing. LOLLY offers him a cigarette.)* Don't you want one? It looks like this really affected you. One can tell that you aren't used to spending time with the dead. *(He exhales a mouthful of smoke.)* Ah, what a day! But I'm content. Not because she's dead, of course. That makes no difference. One day you're alive, the next you're not. Or vice versa. That's the way it must be. What excites me is that . . . these things generate forms, don't you realize? Rituals, theater, forms. It's like when you're walking absent-mindedly along and you trip. You suddenly realize that you were walking. Believe me, I feel alive. *(Pause.)* But you don't seem very excited.

EX: I wonder if she really is dead.

LOLLY: Like a rock.

EX: But something would have to have changed.

LOLLY: For instance?

EX: Suppose that I killed her.

LOLLY: That's vanity, pardon my frankness. She died from disgust. She was given to that kind of reaction. Now, if it's worth anything to you . . .

Ex: Nevertheless, she's stiff.

LOLLY *(looking tenderly at the cadaver):* Yes, she's beautiful. *(He arranges her skirts as he begins to sing a fragment from* La Bohème.*)* "Che gelida manina . . ." Surely you haven't guessed that this dress . . . I myself, on our wedding night, took it slowly off her, until her body burst forth, hot, full of secrets . . . She trembled . . . *(Transition.)* And now look at her. And look what this crummy fabric's good for . . . It's a mystery, don't you think?

(Ex, with an exhausted look, slowly collapses, until he's on his knees.)

Ex: Yes, a mystery . . .

LOLLY: What's the matter, dear?

Ex: My knees . . . are weak . . .

LOLLY: Well, come here, relax. Put your head on my lap. *(Ex does so, slowly. LOLLY caresses his hair.)* Poor little stranger. *(Brief pause.)* I'm going to save this dress. It might be of some use again.

(Pause. CASPER violently opens the door. Ex jumps up to his feet.)

CASPER: So you thought you could spend all afternoon lounging around, scratching your balls! Let's go! I need some help with the chaise longue. *(He leaves, slamming the door behind him.)*

LOLLY: Moron! I can't stand people who become obnoxious when they think they're important. You go on, dear, I'll take care of the candles.

(Ex exits. LOLLY takes some used candles out of one of the chest's drawers. He puts them in the candelabra. Then he changes his mind and removes some of the candles, putting them back in the drawer. Ex and CASPER enter with the chaise longue.)

LOLLY: Over here, in the middle. There should be some marks on the floor.

CASPER *(brusque and obnoxious):* Get out of my way! I know perfectly well what I have to do!

LOLLY: I'd like to give you a knock on the head!

CASPER *(after examining the floor, authoritatively):* Here. A little more forward. *(They move the chaise longue.)* The corpse! *(To Ex.)* You, grab here. *(To LOLLY.)* You, get out, bum! *(LOLLY looks at him with hatred. CASPER moves around feverishly but in reality doesn't do anything. It is Ex, sweating and looking like he's dragging a cross, who heaves the upper half of the cadaver onto the chaise longue, followed by her legs, at CASPER's orders.)* Now, here. *(LOLLY takes charge of arranging her skirts. To LOLLY.)* Are the candles ready? *(LOLLY does not respond. CASPER looks over at the candles.)* Why so few?

LOLLY *(evasive):* I couldn't find any more than these. I don't know what happened to them.

CASPER *(with pent-up anger):* Tightwad!

LOLLY *(with a hysterical scream):* Please, Casper, I'm not in the mood to put up with any more insults or needless offenses! There aren't any more candles other than what you see here!

CASPER: I counted at least ten at the last funeral! Where are they?

LOLLY: What, do you think I ate them?

EX: Excuse me, but what funeral?

CASPER: What you did with the candles is your business. I'm only saying that I counted at least ten of them.

LOLLY (*sarcastically, to Ex*): Look at that, now the lice want to take over the head.

CASPER: We either take this seriously or not at all. If this is a funeral, let it be a funeral.

LOLLY (*still sarcastic*): Did you see that? It looks like the bereaved is this gentleman and not I.

EX (*to CASPER*): When was the other funeral?

LOLLY: The widower is the gentleman. I am the one who cracks jokes at the vigil, and the one who cries is the gentleman. I'm not the one who is about to faint . . .

CASPER (*pushing Ex*): Grab him!

(*Ex runs to hold LOLLY up, and LOLLY collapses in his arms. CASPER spins to one side and heads toward one of the doors.*)

CASPER: Time to begin!

LOLLY (*suddenly rising halfway*): Just one moment, sir! I assume that you'll not want to begin with me still unconscious.

CASPER: No, sir, now that you aren't.

LOLLY (*confused*): Ah.

CASPER (*to Ex*): You, go stand over there, at the corpse's feet!

(*Ex does so. CASPER to LOLLY.*) And you, light the candles! Gentlemen, I now declare in session the funeral in memory of the deceased!

LOLLY: What do you mean, "in memory," animal, if the body is still here?

CASPER: But if we keep going on like this, not even the memory of this body will be left.

LOLLY: What are you saying?

CASPER: That it's going to start to rot!

LOLLY: How dare you, you worm?

CASPER: Please, Lolly, let's be rational.

LOLLY: *Reasonable*, you imbecile! (*To Ex.*) It just infuriates me that he doesn't have the slightest idea of what solemnity is! By the way, son, and not meaning to offend you, do you understand the gravity of this moment? That is . . . if you are aware of what a privilege this is for you.

EX: I think that I don't understand this exactly . . .

LOLLY: Excuse me, but don't you think she looks slightly emaciated?

Ex: That's natural, she's dead.

Lolly: And what's so natural about death? *(To Casper.)* Some rouge and lipstick! *(Casper reluctantly goes to the chest and takes out the cosmetic bag. He then straddles Pearl's corpse and smears makeup on her face, as he pays attention to the following conversation.)* I was referring, my child, to the fact that this is a very intimate ceremony . . . and it isn't often that a stranger . . .

Ex: Do you want me to leave?

Lolly: No, no, that's not necessary. Now that you're here, and anyway you were involved to a certain extent . . . Not that that constitutes any accusation toward anyone. We only expect from you a formal attitude. To be more explicit, there occurred here an everyday kind of accident, nothing out of this world, but then it gave way to a ceremony, and then everything changed. Because the ceremony transcends us, it brings us nearer eternity. And we, my child, we live only for eternity. Do you understand now?

Ex: No.

Casper *(looking at Ex in a strangely resentful way):* This is a godsend.

Lolly: Do you know how to pray?

Ex: I'm an atheist.

Lolly: I suspected as much. But I'm not referring to that. I mean, are you capable of any abstract attitude: of something that will keep your mind off your ego?

Ex: I could practice my multiplication charts.

Lolly: Well, I don't know if . . . In any case, the most important thing is to keep up appearances. Please, put your hands together like this. *(He demonstrates; Ex imitates him.)* Now, look up, in an attitude of ecstasy. *(Ex does so.)* Do you see anything special?

Ex: A water stain.

Lolly: Do me the favor of kneeling. *(Ex does so.)* Good. Now, don't move until I tell you to. That's it. Casper! Lights! *(Casper leaps over to the light switch and turns off the lights, while Lolly lights the candles.)* The book! *(Casper takes out of the chest an old, dusty book, which he hands over to Lolly. The old man opens it to the place marked by a ribbon, puts on his old glasses, glances over at Ex, who remains absolutely still, clears his throat, and begins to read in a solemn voice.)* Domine . . . *(Brief pause.)* We'll do without the Latin.

Casper: Why?

(Lolly stomps impatiently, once. Casper adopts a mortified expression.)

Lolly: Sir, before your august throne your creature comes today . . . *(He continues murmuring something under his breath.)* Well, we'll also do without the names, titles, positions, et cetera. I suppose that our Lord already knows all that. *(He turns the page.)*

CASPER *(suffocating from indignation, in a low voice):* Let the record show that this ceremony is following an irregular course. Nota bene.

LOLLY *(contemptuous):* Quid pro quo. *(He continues his reading, solemnly.)* Lord, gone the earthly scandal, gone the days and the splendors in whose delusion the flesh was wrapped up, gone the cycles, the seasons, and the resting places that imprisoned it, a weak and trembling soul seeks you, et cetera. Drive away, Lord, the din, the taste for battle, the taste for blood, and the tears from her eyes, so that this soul may not lose her way, et cetera. *(He skips a couple of pages.)* Interpolations without any importance.

CASPER: I would read everything.

LOLLY: Not necessary. *(He reads.)* With a tired and sad step . . . *(He murmurs something under his breath.)* Her immaculate offering . . . *(He murmurs again.)* Because, what is the body but painted cardboard and a base façade? What is the flesh but a momentary repugnant effervescence? A fragile skin that lasts only as long as it takes to corrupt and, in its vain arrogance, tries to separate us from the immutable and severe order of the spirit? And what is time but an illusion of the senses? And what is the history of the world, with all of its inexhaustible and feverish generations, what is history past and to come but the slow blinking of one of Your infinite eyes? *(Pause. He looks at Ex over the top of his glasses.)* Did he fall asleep?

(CASPER leaves the book on the floor and stealthily approaches Ex.)

Ex: I'm awake.

CASPER *(hurriedly turning around):* He's awake. *(LOLLY indicates to CASPER to pick up the book. He does so.)*

LOLLY: Let's shorten the formalities. *(He passes over several pages rapidly.)* Where were we?

CASPER: History.

LOLLY *(reading):* The Resurrection. But He who is master of all the roads is also master of the Other Road. And as it has been ordered that matter dissolves into spirit, has it not traced those lateral paths by which spirit returns to matter? Has it not created dreams? Has it not confronted the gross materiality of objects with the transparency of mirages? *(He skips a few more pages.)* Hmm, Lazarus, et cetera . . . Ergo, Domine, fiat voluntas tuam. The rest is just formality. Names, titles, properties. *(He slams the book shut.)* Amen.

CASPER: Amen.

LOLLY: On your knees. *(LOLLY and CASPER kneel.)* Sic transit gloria mundi. *(Brief pause. CASPER and LOLLY stare at Ex. PEARL suddenly sits up.)*

PEARL: Casper, prego, the chamber pot!

(CASPER and LOLLY keep staring at Ex, who falls heavily backwards and stays that way.)

CASPER: A miracle! A miracle! Our mother has come back to life!

CASPER/LOLLY *(matter of fact):* A miracle! A miracle!
PEARL: Hurry up!
(CASPER runs to the chest.)
LOLLY *(slowly taking off his glasses):* We can blow out the candles now.
CASPER *(returns waving in the air a porcelain chamber pot):* A miracle! A miracle! Our mother has come back from the dead!
LOLLY: *(automatically, absentminded):* A miracle, a miracle.
(CASPER places the chamber pot behind the chaise longue and moves away. PEARL nimbly jumps up from the chaise longue; only her torso is visible from behind the chaise. Pause. We hear the trickle into the chamber pot.)
PEARL: I almost peed my pants.
CASPER: Praised be our Lord!
PEARL: How disgusting!
CASPER/LOLLY: A miracle! A miracle!
PEARL: To be revived like that . . . How humiliating!
CASPER/LOLLY: A miracle! A miracle!
PEARL: Shut up, you fools! *(Short pause.)* Don't depress me any more than I am already. I feel as stupid as an incontinent old woman. Imagine, at my age, still a prisoner of my bodily functions! *(To CASPER.)* My little dove, a handkerchief or some such thing, from my makeup case. *(CASPER runs over to the chest.)* Who put me in this getup?
LOLLY: We thought you'd like it.
PEARL: I feel ridiculous. *(CASPER brings her the handkerchief.)* Merci, mon enfant. *(She blows her nose, etc. CASPER remains at her side, watching her expectantly. LOLLY gets up, tired, and begins to blow out the candles.)*
CASPER: So, Pearl?
PEARL: So what?
CASPER: So what did you see?
PEARL *(looking at herself in the mirror, primping and feigning indifference):* Nothing.
CASPER: What do you mean "nothing"?
PEARL *(mocking):* He's slobbering over me as if I were a bonbon. What do you want to know? Mystical experiences cannot be communicated to others.
CASPER: But if you made an effort . . .
PEARL: That depends . . . on if the effort is worth the effort . . .
CASPER: And why wouldn't it be worth the effort?
PEARL *(for LOLLY's benefit):* It would appear that not everyone is listening to me.
CASPER *(to LOLLY):* Stop it!
LOLLY *(violently):* The ceremony's over! I want candles for my funeral, too!
CASPER: She needs them for inspiration!

PEARL: The longer you argue the more time you're wasting . . . because the images are disappearing, just like dreams.

CASPER *(to LOLLY):* I'm going to kill you!

LOLLY: I already know your dreams by heart!

PEARL: Not this time, dear. You'll be surprised.

LOLLY *(moving away, disgusted):* You two do whatever you want.

CASPER: Come on, Pearl.

PEARL: A cigarette.

CASPER *(to LOLLY):* Didn't you hear her?

(LOLLY, fed up, throws him a cigarette. PEARL meanwhile looks at herself in her hand-mirror.)

PEARL: I think I still look a little the worse for wear. *(CASPER hands her the cigarette and a candelabrum to light it with.)* Thank you, dear. *(She exhales a mouthful of smoke.)* Oh, what can I tell you?

CASPER: Tell us everything, Pearl. What you saw. What it's like . . .

PEARL: What is it like . . . Strange, very strange . . .

CASPER: But start at the beginning.

PEARL: Yes, at the beginning. Well, after the events that are now in the public domain *(throwing a severe glance at CASPER)*, over which it is preferable to throw the compassionate mantle of forgetfulness . . . *(CASPER timidly lowers his eyes.)* After that miserable trick, I found myself being whirled away by some kind of wind . . . *(CASPER avidly devours her words.)* More than a wind it was something like a horrible hurricane. A tornado carried me away, and it irresistibly sucked me into its vortex . . . I tried to scream, but I couldn't . . . I tried to move, but my limbs were paralyzed . . . Oh! *(She closes her eyes. Pause.)*

CASPER: And then?

PEARL: I fell and I fell and I fell in this bottomless abyss . . . I fell for centuries, until finally, first very far away and then increasingly closer, I heard a voice, clear and powerful, and it called to me from the depths of the abyss . . . *(She pauses and then, in a solemn, deep voice.)* "Pearl, Pearl, is that you, dear?"

CASPER: British?

PEARL: Yes.

CASPER *(with a thick British accent):* Good God, why?

PEARL: I'm just telling you what I heard. An impeccable Oxford accent. "Pearl, Pearl, is that you, dear?"

CASPER: And then?

PEARL: I froze.

CASPER: And then?

PEARL: Everything turned supernaturally calm. Dopo, a deadly silence. I cautiously opened my eyes. *(Pause.)*

CASPER: And then?

PEARL: There she was.

LOLLY: Who?

PEARL: I'm not lying. The first thing I saw was a house, very turn-of-the-century, a cottage, small but cozy, recently served tea, some scones, and a servant in livery and a wig who announced: "Queen Victoria has been awaiting you."

CASPER: Queen Victoria?

LOLLY *(very British):* Jolly good!

CASPER: And then?

PEARL: She appeared. Very nice. We had tea. We chatted about this and about that. She gave me her recipe for scones. And, afterward, well, why hide it, we had a political discussion. I must say that the lady still has all her wits about her.

CASPER: But what did you talk about?

PEARL *(evasive):* Well, we exchanged general opinions in an open and cordial dialogue. I can't tell you more than that. It was a discussion of the highest order. Top secret! *(Pause. Pointing to Ex.)* Excuse me, but what is that?

(Pause. All three look at Ex with curiosity, as if they were seeing him for the first time. LOLLY turns on the light. They observe Ex in silence a few seconds more, until CASPER goes alongside Ex and flips him over with his foot.)

CASPER: It looks like a corpse.

PEARL: And what is this corpse doing here?

CASPER: I don't know him.

LOLLY: No one saw him enter?

(They all go over and examine him. LOLLY puts on his glasses.)

LOLLY: No sign of physical violence . . .

CASPER: His heart must have given out.

(Pause. They continue observing Ex.)

PEARL: There's something sad about this corpse. Maybe it's the worn-out clothes, the dandruff . . . or maybe his face all drawn up in pain . . .

LOLLY: There's a small grease stain on his lapel.

(PEARL squats down in order to see the stain better.)

PEARL: Yes, it must be left over from some meal.

CASPER: It's been a long time since his shoes were polished.

PEARL: What a curious face. All drawn up in pain, don't you find him vaguely familiar?

LOLLY: Yes, very vaguely . . .

PEARL: I wonder who he could have been.

CASPER: I think that it might be a waste of time, but we could ask him.

LOLLY: At least in order to shed our doubts . . .

(The two look at PEARL questioningly. PEARL, after reflecting for a few instants, nods her head and moves away. LOLLY and CASPER turn the "corpse" over onto his back, and CASPER pulls his head up by the hair.)

PEARL: Mais non, Casper, doucement, doucement. The soul is delicate. *(CASPER lets him go. PEARL yells as if EX were far away.)* Listen, dear, or whatever it is that's inside that greasy brain, do you hear me?

(Brief pause. CASPER pulls EX's hair again.)

CASPER: Did he hear you?

PEARL: If you heard us, give us a sign! *(Brief pause. LOLLY steps on EX's hand.)* We don't want to hurt you! It's merely curiosity! If you would only tell us who you were! *(Brief pause. At a sign from PEARL, CASPER and LOLLY let go of EX. PEARL goes over to him.)* Dear, we don't wish to interrupt your eternal rest. But you cannot go away like that, leaving us the thorn. Put yourself in our place. You came to die here, motu proprio. No one invited you. We have the right to know who you were. *(Brief pause.)* Are you listening to me? W-h-o w-e-r-e y-o-u? *(Brief pause. PEARL moves away. CASPER and LOLLY tower over the "corpse." CASPER pulls his hair. LOLLY twists his leg.)*

CASPER: Answer when you're asked a question!

PEARL: He moved his lips! *(CASPER and LOLLY put their ears to EX's lips.)* What did he say?

CASPER: Yes.

PEARL: Yes what?

CASPER *(yanking EX's hair):* Yes what?

PEARL: That's enough, Casper. *(To EX.)* My son, I know that you're listening. That means that there is something in your soul that's burdening you and keeping you from leaving your body behind. Share this burden with us, and you'll feel much better. Tell us, son. Did you commit some crime? *(Pause. There is no response. PEARL's face hardens, and she makes a sign to CASPER and LOLLY, who twist EX's limbs. EX moans for the first time. PEARL halts CASPER and LOLLY.)* Yes, dear? We didn't hear you. Did you commit a crime? Well, did you commit a crime? Something bad? Was it really bad? *(Impatient.)* But speak, dear, what did you do? Do you think we're innocent? We all have something on our conscience. What are you saying? *(EX moves his lips. The others anxiously lean toward him. Even PEARL kneels.)* What? *(They listen. PEARL stands up.)* Let him go. *(LOLLY and CASPER do so. EX collapses. PEARL sits again. She looks at herself in the hand-mirror, then looks severely at EX.)* So, you wrote obscenities on bathroom walls.

LOLLY: How disgusting!

CASPER: So, he was the one doing that!

PEARL: How disappointing, dear! Such a petty gesture! *(Pause. The three look at Ex with a mixture of repugnance and boredom.)* And for him, it's a tragedy! How unbearably tedious! *(Long pause during which the three remain motionless, terribly empty masks. Only Ex is a body, breathing heavily.)* Casper! This house is topsy-turvy! I want routine reestablished immediately! I want my tea! I want tea and cookies!

CASPER: At your service, madam! *(As if impelled by a whip, he runs off through one of the doors.)*

PEARL *(pointing to Ex):* And make this one disappear!

LOLLY *(taking Ex by the feet to drag him outside):* Any place special?

PEARL: To the garbage can!

LOLLY: He's heavy! *(He lets go of Ex, rubs his hands, looks at him.)* Poor thing, I liked him. He had something that touched me, a touching lack of humor. Well, fuck him! *(He takes Ex's feet once again. CASPER enters with a little table on wheels upon which there is an ostentatious tea service. Nevertheless, the tea and cookies are nonexistent. CASPER leaves this in front of PEARL.)*

CASPER: Served!

PEARL: Thank you, dear.

LOLLY: Casper, a hand here.

CASPER: We're taking him now?

LOLLY: Yes.

(CASPER goes to help LOLLY. PEARL serves herself the nonexistent tea.)

CASPER: Let's go! The sooner he disappears the better!

(The two pull Ex, one foot each. PEARL sniffs the little plate.)

PEARL: Casper?

CASPER: What?

PEARL: These cookies are stale.

(Ex opens his eyes.)

CASPER *(dumbfounded):* What are what?

PEARL: S-T-A-L-E. Stale.

Ex: Let me go.

CASPER: What do you mean they're stale?

LOLLY *(reacting to Ex):* Did you hear him?

PEARL *(turning in order to face CASPER):* Son, they're old.

CASPER: That can't be. They're the same ones as always.

LOLLY *(to Ex):* Are you looking at me or at someone else?

PEARL: They may be, but smell them . . .

Ex: Let me go.

(CASPER lets Ex's leg drop, goes over to the little table, and smells the cookies.)

LOLLY *(to Ex):* Dear, good thing that you reacted. We had already given you up for dead.

Ex: I'm fine. It's time for me to go.
LOLLY: Go? And where do you want to go?

[Simultaneous actions: A & B]

A	B
Ex: Outside. Good-bye. *(He begins staggering toward a door.)*	CASPER: I don't notice anything.
LOLLY *(holding him back):* Just a moment, dear. How can you leave like that, without saying good-bye to the others?	PEARL: But I do. I'm sick of consuming rotten food.
	CASPER *(livid):* Is that an accusation?
	PEARL: Take it any way you wish.
	CASPER: Do you pretend to insinuate that I serve rotten food?
Ex: I can't, I'm in a hurry. It's late.	PEARL: I'm not pretending, I'm saying it.
LOLLY: But this I cannot allow. Please, stop arguing and help me! He's trying to escape!	CASPER: Do you pretend to insinuate that I do not serve you adequately?
Ex: No. Let me go.	PEARL: Well, enough of this exasperating little tone!
(They struggle.)	CASPER: Excuse me, madam, what little tone?
	PEARL: This little tone of pretended offense.
	CASPER: Do you pretend to insinuate that I pretend to be the offended party, madam?
	PEARL: I'm going to rip out one of your eyes!
	CASPER *(jumping back a step):* Excuse me, madam?

Ex *(yelling):* Let me go, for God's sake! Do you think that I still haven't suffered enough humiliation!
PEARL: What's going on here?
(LOLLY lets go of Ex. Long pause.)
CASPER *(with rancor, to PEARL):* Do you think that I still haven't suffered enough humiliation?
(Without warning, PEARL slaps his face. CASPER screams and flees to a corner.)
LOLLY *(to Ex):* Alright. Do whatever you want, it's your business.
(Pause. Ex does not move.)
Ex: I have no choice but to leave. If I stay, I'll end up tearing you all into shreds . . .

PEARL: And who is this disgusting creature going to tear into shreds?

LOLLY: How would you like to moderate your tongue a little, eh?

Ex: Excuse me, I'll not bother you anymore. *(He makes signs of leaving. LOLLY takes him by the hand.)*

LOLLY: But why are you going?

Ex: Because I'm a body.

(Pause.)

PEARL: And what does that have to do with it?

LOLLY: You believe that you are a body, but it's only a moment, an illusion created by your mind.

PEARL: Naturally.

CASPER *(sobbing, in his corner):* Pearl . . .

PEARL: Get out of here. *(PEARL begins a sadistic game with CASPER. She pours out the "tea" with a vengeance and tosses the "cookies" off the plate. CASPER suffers.)*

Ex: I'm a body.

LOLLY: Well, let's suppose you are a body. So?

Ex: I sweat. I can die at any moment. And outside, things . . . I'm hungry.

LOLLY: Over there you have tea and cookies.

PEARL *(to CASPER):* Pick up the cookies.

(CASPER slowly obeys. Ex observes this as if it were a dream. Pause.)

Ex *(with anguish and worry):* I have to go. *(He heads toward one of the doors.)*

LOLLY: That way leads to the bathroom.

Ex *(stops, vacillating):* I still don't know my way around here.

LOLLY: That's natural. You only just arrived. And nevertheless, you already wish to leave.

Ex: It's late, and I left some unfinished business outside.

LOLLY: I understand, it was only a visit.

Ex: Yes.

LOLLY: And moreover, brief.

Ex: Yes.

LOLLY: Will we see you again around here?

Ex: I don't think so.

CASPER *(unwillingly throwing the plate with the "cookies" he's picked up onto the table):* There you go!

(PEARL takes off a slipper and throws it at him. CASPER hides. PEARL adopts an offended and concentrated expression. Ex observes it all.)

LOLLY: Well, are you leaving?

Ex: Yes.

LOLLY: What do you have to do outside?

Ex *(thinking about it for a few seconds, then smiling timidly):* Everything . . .

LOLLY: Are you an important man?

EX: No.

LOLLY: Then they are trivial matters?

EX: That depends on how you look at them.

LOLLY: Of course, it depends on how one looks at them. What is important? Scratching one's nose? *(Ex looks at him uncomprehendingly, and then mechanically he scratches his nose.)* Extending the species? *(Pause. Ex mechanically grabs his crotch.)* Regenerating the species? *(Pause. CASPER goes over to PEARL; he has the slipper in his teeth, like a little dog. PEARL pretends to ignore him.)* Creating empires? *(Brief pause.)* Abolishing injustice? *(Brief pause.)* Conquering the universe? *(Brief pause.)* Making war or revolution?

PEARL *(laughing, to CASPER):* Flatterer!

(In a flash, CASPER is sitting on PEARL's lap. The two begin to laugh and whisper, in complicity, commenting on the dialogue between Ex and LOLLY.)

LOLLY: Believe me, my son, those are trivial matters. Please accept the advice of a man who has lived much longer than you and who . . . well, there's no need to go into detail. Flee from worldly matters and aspire only to the eternal. Eternity is, how can I tell you? It is like dreaming with your eyes open. *(He goes to Ex and takes his hands. In a low voice.)* It is like masturbating. *(Ex moves away. LOLLY abruptly changes his tone.)* Now, if you wish to leave, go. You are an imperfect being. You were created that way. I forgive you. But what I will not forgive is when you, by a stroke of fate, by some strange privilege, manage to catch a glimpse of another life, and do not have the moral and spiritual integrity to . . . Anyway, ashes to ashes . . .

PEARL: Who said asses? *(Giggles between CASPER and PEARL.)*

EX: I see your point of view.

LOLLY: Then, choose.

EX: And you, what can you all offer me?

LOLLY: Well, you know, we are infinitely rich, in a certain sense. You would have your future assured. We would protect you from misery and pain . . .

EX: In exchange for what?

LOLLY: No, nothing. Well, you might possibly have to perform some small services for us . . . *(With an excusing smile.)* We're already old and . . . But not to worry, it's not important. Anyway, if this bothered you, you could limit yourself to a purely mental role. Mental services, you understand? *(Giggles from CASPER and PEARL.)* We hold your intellectual gifts in great esteem. You see, we aren't even afraid of your small criticisms. *(With a humble smile.)* One knows one isn't perfect. Perfection is a divine gift, and even if one has his affectations . . .

(Pause.)

Ex *(sharply):* No, it's impossible. *(He extends his hand to the old man in a gesture of farewell. The old man holds on to it. From now on, Ex will be constantly thinking about leaving even though he doesn't ever complete the action; every so often, he shoots a glance at the door.)*

LOLLY: Wait, wait! Why is it impossible?

Ex: I would like to explain it to you but I'm afraid that you won't . . . Please understand me! Ideas run away, and we wear ourselves out trying to catch them, and when we do, sometimes they're not . . . what we thought they were. But before that happens, I want to be outside. So I need to leave now. Give my regards to your wife.

PEARL: What, he's leaving now?

(Giggles of complicity from CASPER and PEARL. LOLLY holds on to Ex.)

LOLLY: Son, wait! If you were to explain yourself, it would help to free us. *(He winks at PEARL and CASPER.)*

Ex: It's through there, isn't it?

LOLLY: Yes, but . . .

Ex: Let me free, please! I don't want my deciding to be turned into a purely mental act!

LOLLY: You fool, that is what freedom's precisely about!

Ex: No, I am a body, that is what freedom's precisely about!

LOLLY: That's corruption and death!

Ex: But it's also my freedom!

(CASPER and PEARL split their sides with laughter. Ex vacillates and brings his free hand to his head, as if it were about to explode.)

Ex: Ah . . .

LOLLY: Go on, go on. Speak, and it will go away.

Ex: I need to go before it gets late. Out there, an act, even if it's minimal, even if it's useless, moving a finger, for example, that can contain me. It's enough. That's where life is.

(Brief pause.)

LOLLY: Go on.

Ex *(almost automatically):* I mean to say. Out there I'm in risk of dying at any moment. Just by my mere presence. And even the most innocent gesture can contain my death . . . I mean to say, each gesture contains as much my life as it does my death. But that is my condition. I can only exist if I put my existence at risk.

(Brief pause. Laughter from PEARL and CASPER.)

LOLLY: Go on. *(Suddenly, to PEARL and CASPER.)* Hey, can we quiet it down a bit! Can't one have a nice, quiet philosophical conversation around here?

PEARL *(brusquely):* Fuck philosophy!

CASPER: Yeah, fuck it!

(PEARL shoves CASPER violently, and he flies several yards.)

PEARL: Pig!

(CASPER, limping in pain, returns to his corner and, from there, watches PEARL with murderous and impotent hatred.)

LOLLY: Don't pay any attention to them, dear. Continue!

Ex: I don't have time. I need time! *(He begins to tug blindly.)* Time! Time!

LOLLY: Son, it hurts me to see you like this. How I wish I could take away your pain!

(Ex stops for an instant and looks at LOLLY sadly.)

Ex: Too late.

(The two begin a savage tug-of-war.)

[Simultaneous scenes: A & B]

A

(CASPER initiates a litany that will gradually grow in force.)

CASPER: They beat me, they abuse me, they torture me. That's the pay I receive. They have me go here and there, they martyr me, they trick me, they drug me, they rob me. That's the pay I receive. I sacrificed my youth, a home, children, the tranquility of old age, and this is the pay I receive! Thirty years serving them, subdued, mocked, and humiliated! And this is the pay I receive! The vilest jobs! Dead from hunger and cold! Without even raggedy clothes or a hitching post where I could scratch myself! And this is the pay I receive! Servant, lackey, buffoon! And this is the pay I receive! Why do I exist? What do I even exist for?

B

Ex *(during the struggle with LOLLY):* Let me go! This is the last time I'm going to warn you! I'll destroy you!

LOLLY: Shut up!

Ex: I'm going to leave! I'm going to look!

LOLLY: Help me gag his mouth!

Ex: I'm going to look! I'm going to see! Air! Air!

LOLLY: He's going to escape! Son!

(LOLLY falls. Ex drags him. He suddenly turns around and looks with fury at the old man. He kicks him and gets away. Pause. Ex looks at his hand and at the old man, as if he were surprised to find himself free.)

(Silence. LOLLY rolls on the floor, whimpering.)

LOLLY: Moron, why did you hit me?

CASPER *(softly):* Why do I exist? What do I even exist for?

LOLLY *(to Ex, violently):* Get out! Get out! I don't want to see you ever again! Ungrateful beast! I can't stand any of you! No more blood! No more bodies! No more rotten food! You make me sick! I want phantasmagoria!

(He jumps up and runs over to PEARL. He grabs her cosmetics case out of

her hand and begins to paint himself frenetically.) I want the spirit! The spirit! *(Finally, worn-out and with a pathetic appearance, he lets the case fall and leans against a wall, sobbing, completely disconsolate. CASPER, in turn, begins to roam around the stage, also desolate, repeating over and over the same litany: "Why do I exist? What do I even exist for?" PEARL has remained absolutely aloof to all this. Ex is next to a door, his eyes shining with tears.)*

Ex *(his voice slowly becoming audible over CASPER's litany):* Good-bye, visions! Good-bye, infancy! Shadows on the walls, lost nights, lost days! Good-bye, innocence! Good-bye and compassion! Good-bye for once and for ever and compassion! Good-bye and compassion! *(Pause. In the middle of the silence, in a hushed tone.)* Good-bye.

(Silence. No one moves. Suddenly, CASPER runs toward Ex and bites him on the leg, growling. Ex lets out a scream of pain and runs after CASPER, who now seeks PEARL's protection.)

PEARL *(confronting Ex while she protects CASPER):* Be still! Enough! How dare you?

(Pause. Ex, confused, looks at PEARL, holding on to his bitten thigh.)

Ex: He bit me.

PEARL: He must have had a good reason. You are to blame for everything that has gone on in this house. You have made everyone nervous, beginning with the boy, who never before disobeyed me as he has done today. Everything was in perfect order until you showed up. Furtively! Yes, sir! Furtively! Like a thief! Or a murderer! Impostor! What do you have hidden up your sleeve? Where is the murderer's weapon? What are you doing here? What are your intentions? Who knows your past? Are you a normal person? Are you unbalanced?

LOLLY: Pearl, please, let's not make a scene. The neighbors will show up.

PEARL: He exasperates me. This dog, this mystery exasperates me. Dog! Murderer! *(She spits on him.)* Murderer! *(LOLLY and CASPER hold her back. PEARL calms down immediately.)* It's alright, I was just letting off a little steam.

CASPER *(envious):* He doesn't deserve that much.

(Pause. No one moves. PEARL observes Ex. Finally, she takes out a handkerchief from her sleeve and hands it to him.)

PEARL: Wipe your face. *(Ex wipes the saliva off his face and gives the handkerchief back.)* I was too harsh.

Ex *(smooth):* No, it wasn't anything.

PEARL: I overreacted. It was out of line. It's a shame when an old woman like myself, who could even be your mother . . . What's the matter? You're pale. Do you need to go to the bathroom again?

Ex: No, I'm sorry. I think I'm going to throw up.

PEARL *(startled):* Go, go, dear. The only thing missing is for someone to throw up in here. Hurry, you know the way. Too much tension. Please, in the toilet! And flush it! *(Ex by now has gone.)* Nervous stomach. *(Pause. The three relax, loosen up, waiting. CASPER picks up all the objects thrown around by LOLLY and puts them back in the case. To LOLLY.)* Why did you yell so much?

LOLLY: I don't know; he got me going.

(PEARL looks at herself in the hand-mirror and fixes her makeup and hair.)

PEARL: And what did he say?

LOLLY: I don't know. I didn't understand it very well.

PEARL: Cracked.

LOLLY: Who?

PEARL: The mirror.

LOLLY: Oh, I'm sorry.

CASPER: Here he comes.

(They automatically change their attitude. Ex appears at the door. He leans against the frame as if he were dizzy.)

PEARL: Well, well, here's our friend. Did you get it all out? What's the matter? Are you woozy? Your face is still wet.

EX: There aren't any towels.

PEARL: That's possible. But come in . . . don't stay rooted over there. What's the matter? This man is ill.

EX: I'm going to die.

PEARL: Yes, it's horrible. Let's see, come here. *(Ex takes a few steps.)* Someone dry his face! Horrible . . . he looks as if he's been crying.

(LOLLY goes to Ex, unfolds a white handkerchief and applies it to Ex's face. Then LOLLY goes downstage and displays the handkerchief to the audience, crossing from one side to the other, like a magician just before he performs a trick. There is nothing on the handkerchief. PEARL and CASPER have anxiously followed the action.)

PEARL: Is it he?

(LOLLY gives her the handkerchief. PEARL examines it, sniffs it.)

LOLLY: Nothing, only . . .

(PEARL returns the handkerchief.)

PEARL: Come nearer, dear. Allow me to check your pulse.

(Ex draws near. PEARL takes his pulse.)

LOLLY: Pearl.

PEARL: Yes?

LOLLY: Nothing, it may be insignificant, but he has a mole . . .

(PEARL lets go of Ex.)

PEARL: A mole?

LOLLY *(meaningfully):* On his neck.

(CASPER becomes alarmed.)
PEARL: So?
LOLLY: Our son . . .
(Pause.)
PEARL *(to Ex, coldly):* Dear, without any obligation, show me your neck.
(Ex goes over to her and shows her his neck. PEARL lets out a choked cry. CASPER does also, but in his case, it's out of panic.)
PEARL: It is he!
LOLLY: Just a moment, Pearl, there still isn't enough proof.
PEARL: It is he, I'm sure! My heart tells me it is, and a mother's heart is never wrong!
LOLLY: Just a moment! Our son also had a mole on his left buttock. A mole as big as a coin. Drop your pants!
PEARL: Lolly, enough, one mole is sufficient.
LOLLY *(violent):* It is not sufficient! Anyone can have a mole on his neck! There's room for error!
PEARL: I forbid you to look at our son's buttocks!
LOLLY *(dogmatically):* Then I am not convinced!
(He leaves, slamming the door behind him. CASPER leaves by the other door.)
CASPER: Eppur si muove!³
(The door slams. Long pause. PEARL and Ex look at each other.)
PEARL: It would appear that they have left us alone. *(Pause.)* Life's strange, isn't it? *(Pause.)* I always dreamed about having a prodigal son, and now that I have one . . . I don't know what to do. Est-ce que vous savez? I can't imagine myself giving birth to you. I suppose that it must have disgusted me. Just like any excretion, from any other orifice. The strange thing is that that little event, that moment of disgust, if you will, has connected us forever. It's curious. You will always search for me and will keep returning until I accept you, devour you, reintegrate you once more into your longed-for unity. When all is said and done, you're luckier than I. *(With a trace of envy.)* You have someplace to return to. *(Pause.)* Why do you look at me like that?
Ex: I'm trying to remember you.
PEARL: What, son? You don't remember your mother?
Ex: Not exactly. The last image always erased the others so that I don't remember you. I simply see you and believe that it is you. But it's hard to know.
PEARL: But there must be something that seems familiar. Could there be something that would help you to recognize me?
Ex: Yes. *(Timidly.)* Your smell.
PEARL: In order to do that you need to come nearer. Come, smell me.
Ex *(soft):* No, no.
PEARL *(smiling):* You're always so shy. *(Pause.)* And I, do you know how I

could recognize you? Besides the mole, of course, that's a bureaucratic detail, typical of these cases. No, the thing that would confirm that you're my son is your weight on my lap. *(Pause.)* Are you sleepy?

Ex: Yes.

(PEARL, looking at him meaningfully, smoothes the pleats of her dress. Ex goes to her, yawning.)

Ex: Excuse me, may I?

PEARL: Yes, yes, of course.

Ex *(sitting on PEARL's lap):* Am I heavy?

PEARL: Yes, a little. But it doesn't matter. I hope you're not uncomfortable.

Ex: Oh, no, not at all.

(Pause.)

PEARL: You can rest your head on my shoulder, too, if you like.

(Ex does so. Pause.)

PEARL: Do I smell the same?

Ex: No.

(Pause.)

PEARL: Your weight isn't the same either.

(Pause.)

Ex: Before I fall asleep, I want to tell you . . .

PEARL: Yes, son?

Ex: If I really lived once . . . If it was really . . . They're nothing but fragments, without much sense . . . There's an afternoon, a face, a color, and they run together . . . the smell of bleach, of disinfectant . . . In an old, dirty bar . . . A dark afternoon, cold . . . A horrible silence . . . The buzzing of a fly . . . Someone yawns . . . And my suffering flattened me against the front window. And outside the afternoon was dying . . . And a yellowish old man with malignant eyes appeared. And he smiled at me . . . A dirty and tattered old man . . . He smiled at me hatefully and then disappeared . . . Now I don't even remember why I suffered so much that afternoon. *(Pause.)* A cluster of trees, crossing the countryside . . . mysterious trees . . . Someone calls me . . . I lie down on the straw . . . The big, motionless light . . . The warm earth . . . The sky faded by the light . . . A cloud stopped over me . . . Soft, fragile, infinitely white . . . Suspended . . . And then everything was pure, clear, logical, until it disappeared . . . And one day I thought that everything I had ever done since then, everything I had suffered, or committed was in order to recover that cl . . . *(Pause.)* And I wanted to forget all the sordidness, the dirt . . . That cloud that will never stop over me again . . .

(Pause. Ex appears to be sleeping but with his eyes open. His body has become slightly rigid. PEARL looks at him. Together, the two figures reproduce somewhat the Pietà. PEARL bends over Ex and slowly deposits a long kiss on his lips. Pause. LOLLY and CASPER appear at the same door.)

PEARL: Shh, he's sleeping.

CASPER and LOLLY come closer cautiously, on tiptoe. The three observe Ex for a long time. All three smiling, curious and distant. Ex looks straight ahead, motionless. Then, in the silence, the light diminishes, focusing on Ex, until everything is finally enveloped in darkness.

REJECTED ENDING

(Long pause. Ex appears to be sleeping but with his eyes open. His body has become slightly rigid. PEARL looks at him. Together, the two figures reproduce somewhat the Pietà. *PEARL bends over Ex and slowly deposits a long kiss on his lips. Pause. LOLLY and CASPER appear at the same door.)*

PEARL: Shh, he's sleeping.

LOLLY *(whispering):* Casper, our son's clothing.

(Cautiously, on tiptoes, CASPER goes over to the chest as LOLLY goes over to PEARL. From now on, the actions of all three characters will be rapid, furtive, and precise, as if they had been rehearsed over and over again. LOLLY and PEARL place Ex in a chair and begin to undress him. LOLLY dries the sweat on Ex's brow with a handkerchief. CASPER returns carrying a little sailor's suit, which is faded and covered with dust. The three begin to dress Ex. Ex resists, weakly, as if in a dream. The suit is ripping and tearing apart at the seams. Ex's resistance increases, causing PEARL to slap him.)

PEARL: Be still once and for all!

(Ex goes motionless. He is now dressed and slumped in the chair. His two hands cover his crotch; his head has fallen forward. LOLLY smoothes Ex's clothing, PEARL touches up Ex's makeup, and CASPER picks up Ex's original clothing.)

PEARL: How nervous he was!

CASPER: But he didn't go wee-wee.

PEARL: It must have been a nightmare.

LOLLY: Maybe he's hungry?

PEARL: Maybe.

CASPER: He's raised his head.

(PEARL closes the makeup case.)

PEARL: Son, you're finally born!

(No one moves. Ex looks around him with enormous sadness. Then he appears to have remembered something. He rummages through the pockets of his little suit and takes out a small, rusted penknife.)

LOLLY: What's that?

(Ex opens up the penknife. CASPER lets out a scream and runs toward one of the doors. PEARL and LOLLY, in a leap, are also at the doors.)

PEARL: Who left that in there?

LOLLY: I don't know; it's been a long time since anyone wore the suit.

PEARL: Well, it's dangerous. Someone could get cut.

LOLLY: Never mind, let's rejoice! Our son has been born!

(Ex stands up quickly, brandishing the small penknife like a sword, and rushes after them. The old couple and CASPER immediately disappear, slamming all the doors simultaneously. The stage is left empty for a few seconds until we hear PEARL shriek. Then one of the doors opens and LOLLY appears, covered in blood; he staggers forward a few steps.)

LOLLY: He killed her! He killed her! Murther! Murther!

(Ex appears at another door and quickly goes over to the old man, stabbing him with the small penknife. LOLLY takes a few more steps before he collapses. Ex does not move. He lets the penknife fall. PEARL appears at another door; she is covered in blood.)

PEARL: As . . . sas . . . sin . . .

(She collapses. Ex falls to his knees, exhausted. Pause. CASPER appears at one of the doors. He is wearing one of PEARL's long silk dresses, which of course is too big for him. In his hands, he carries the makeup case as if it were an offering. He slowly goes over to Ex, smiling timidly.)

Ex: Is that it?

CASPER: Yes.

Ex: They were tough.

CASPER: They were used to all this.

(Pause. CASPER opens the case and begins to put makeup on Ex's face.)

Ex: No witnesses?

CASPER: Not a one.

Ex: We'll have to keep this our secret.

CASPER: Nobody'll know.

(Pause. PEARL and LOLLY surreptitiously get up and survey the situation with sarcastic expressions on their faces.)

Ex: Then, that world, that strange and terrible world, I've lost it?

CASPER: Yes.

Ex: And death? I've lost that, too?

CASPER: That, too. But now we're kings.

Ex: Yeah, kings.

(Brief pause. CASPER suddenly stops making Ex up and pays attention to something he appears to have heard.)

Ex: Casper, what's going on?

(CASPER gestures to Ex to keep quiet and goes over to one of the doors, which he opens abruptly as if he wanted to surprise someone. He then repeats this action with all the doors but finds no one. He looks around, bewildered. Then, he stealthily goes over to the large entry door of the

apartment and attempts to open it quickly, like he did with the other doors. But this door will not open. CASPER then looks through the keyhole, lets out a scream, and jumps away from the opening.)

Ex: Casper, what's out there?

(CASPER, with his back to the door and his face distorted, makes big gestures toward the door.)

CASPER *(whispering):* There's someone at the door!

Ex: What?

CASPER *(louder):* Someone is watching us!

Ex: Were you expecting a visitor?

CASPER: No.

Ex: Then?

CASPER: I don't know. I saw him!

Ex: What could he want?

CASPER: I'm scared.

Ex: Come on, Casper, let's pretend he's not there.

CASPER: And what if he wants to come in?

Ex: He can't get in. The door is locked, and the windows are shut tight.

CASPER: And what if he manages to get in?

Ex: If he manages to get in. *(Pause.)* We'll at least have lived an instant of imagination.

Silence. PEARL and LOLLY have remained motionless, like huge, lifeless dolls. CASPER and EX wait. For a few seconds, the stage becomes more and more brightly lit until all the stage machinery can be seen, the falseness of the decor, the illusion of the staging . . . Sudden BLACKOUT.

TRANSLATOR'S NOTES

1. In the original text, reference is made to Prilidiano Pueyrredón, the nineteenth-century artist noted for his paintings of the Argentinean pampa and rural life.

2. Lolly refers here to the 1899–1902 war between the British and the Dutch Boers in present-day South Africa.

3. Casper recites the phrase, "And yet it does move," allegedly uttered by Galileo under his breath as he was formally recanting to the Inquisition his belief in a sun-centered universe.

Marrathon

Marathón premiered on 13 June 1980 in the Teatros de San Telmo, Buenos Aires.

Original Cast

ANIMADOR [EMCEE]	Arturo Maly
GUARDAESPALDAS [BOUNCER]	Jorge Fornes
HOMERO ESTRELLA [HOMER STARR]	Miguel Guerberoff
ELENA GARCÍA [HELEN GARCÍA]	Lidia Catalano
TOM MIX	Carlos Sturze
ANA D [ANNA D]	Marian Smibiansky
HÉCTOR EXPÓSITO [HECTOR MOSES]	Jean Pierre Reguerraz
EMA EXPÓSITO [EMMA MOSES]	Felisa Yeny
NN [MR. X]	Oscar Boccia
PIPA [CHARITY]	Rita Cortese
PEDRO VESPUCCI [PETER VESPUCCI]	Armando Capó
ASUNCIÓN VESPUCCI	Norma Ibarra
HERMANA [WOMAN]	Mónica Galán
HERMANO [MAN]	Leal Rey
Music	Sergio Aschero
Set design	Tito Egurza
Costume design	Graciela Galán
Lighting design and Direction	Jaime Kogan

Author's Note: The music heard and danced to comes from old recordings of tangos and milongas, as well as the occasional fox-trot, from the 1930s. The record player should be placed somewhere on the Emcee's platform.

Translator's Note: This translation is based on the published version of *Marathón* as well as recent revisions made by the author.

Scene One

A dance hall in the working-class outskirts of Buenos Aires. Five couples are moving on the dance floor; their movements are minimal, automatic, as if they were lifeless dolls covered in dust and cobwebs. Standing on a platform, in front of a microphone, is the Emcee. He is a man with slick-backed hair stuck to his head and wears a dark suit with shiny lapels. His face is powdered, his eyes are hidden under black eyelashes, and his lips are painted. The Bouncer moves among the dancing couples; he is ever alert and vigilant, furtive like a watchdog. The rasping of the old recordings of tangos and milongas from the 1930s constantly blasts out from the loudspeakers. The Emcee speaks into the microphone and addresses the audience.

EMCEE: Come on in, ladies and gentlemen! Make yourselves at home. There's room for everyone! If it's a little hidey-hole you're looking for, it's waiting for you right here. Right here. Come on in, ladies and gentlemen! We're thrilled you can be with us tonight, the twenty-third of June 19 . . . uhhh?

BOUNCER: 1933, sir.

EMCEE: Some of you weren't sure about coming here tonight. It's cold outside, you're short on cash, and life—who can deny it?—is a little bit uncertain these days. But I had a feeling that these folks here wouldn't be left all alone. Because without you, our audience, without the few coins you leave at the door, how could these folks go on? And believe me, ladies and gents, you're not throwing away your money. This marathon is first-rate. And not only because of all the time they've been dancing . . . No, ladies and gentlemen, I'm talking about the quality of our dancers. It's not that they're superhuman, they're just regular folks. So what is the difference, you might ask? Well, I'll tell you, confidentially speaking and jumping a bit ahead in our program: they're desperate. Come on in, ladies and gentlemen! Take back the night! In this light-filled spot you'll see the passage of: time, time, time! You'll be sheltered by the dark. During the next couple of hours, death won't touch you, not even the wear and tear that's eating away at our heroes! Come on in, ladies and gentlemen, you're about to get more than your money's worth!

(The Emcee takes a break to get a sip of water and dry his sweaty hands on a towel that's sitting on a small table. At the same time, the Bouncer discreetly distributes a few small blows to the contestants.)

BOUNCER *(in a low voice):* Come on, no sleeping.

(The Emcee resumes his place at the microphone, with a professional air.)

EMCEE: Last call! We don't want to leave anyone out on the curb! Look at these people, please. See for yourselves their battle wounds. They're exhausted, in pain. How long have they been dancing? They've lost count of the hours. *(The EMCEE pretends to have heard a question.)* What's the prize? I'm sorry, but I can't respond even to such legitimate curiosity because, in this marathon, ladies and gentlemen, the prize is a surprise. That's right, ladies and gents, these people don't know why they're dancing! It's faith that's keeping them going! They're dancing on faith! Blindly, they go marching toward their end, toward the thrill of victory or the agony of defeat. I ask you, ladies and gentlemen, who understands mankind? I wouldn't even presume to try to answer. But there they are, they stir, they move, they die ... They ferociously destroy themselves. And then they're reborn, reborn, like mayflies. But nevertheless, fighting against indifference and nothingness even unto death, they build their fragile works, preparing themselves for eternity. Ladies and gentlemen, if this weren't so ridiculous, it would be a tragedy. On with the contest! Homer Starr!

HOMER: Yes, sir?

EMCEE: All of you of course have heard of our little lark from the wrong side of the tracks.[1] How does this old guy manage to stay on his feet? Maybe poets do know the secret of eternal youth.

HOMER: Thank you, sir.

EMCEE: And your dance partner, Miss Helen García.

(Brief automatic applause from the EMCEE. Under pressure from the BOUNCER, some of the dancers imitate him even though they look as if they're about to faint.)

And at the other end of life's delicate thread, two sweet young things: Tom Mix and Anna D.!

ANNA D. *(as if she were in grade school):* Present!

(Slight scattered applause.)

EMCEE *(speaking confidentially):* I don't know why these two kids want to keep their true identities a secret. Oh well, marathon rules don't say anything about that. But it'll be hard to ... Hector Moses!

HECTOR: AWOL! *(HECTOR takes a few exaggerated dance steps. Some giggling is heard, but at the EMCEE's nonreaction, it quickly turns into a deathly silence.)*

EMCEE: This ... funny guy is Hector Moses, blue-collar worker, currently unemployed. His wife, Emma Moses. Hey, Moses, here's a piece of advice, don't wear yourself out yet, you've got a long ways to go.

HECTOR: Hey, as long as my body can take it ...

EMCEE: It's not just your body, my friend, not just your body. Mr. X!

MR. X: Present, sir!

EMCEE: Another incognito couple, ladies and gentlemen! The "gentleman" prefers to remain anonymous, and the "lady" ... is a specialist in anonymity.

(Derisive laughter from the DANCERS.)

I mean, just in case you didn't catch my drift, this lady toils away in obscurity, in the dark, well, she is a lady of the night . . . Mr. X and Sweeeet Charity! Confidentially, this gentleman was very wealthy up until a few days ago, the owner of I don't know which important corporation. An unexpected . . . Ruined overnight. Let's give him a great big hand!

(Some tepid applause from the other DANCERS, which MR. X pathetically acknowledges.)

MR. X: Thank you, thank you so much.

EMCEE: And last but not least, our marathon's purebred, the noble beast Peter Vespucci!

VESPUCCI: Here, sir!

EMCEE: A bricklayer by profession! His lovely wife, Asunción Vespucci! That's right, ladies and gentlemen, our marathon offers something for everyone! You won't go away disappointed! I have absolutely no idea what's going to happen tonight, because every evening here is different, but if your expectations aren't too high, you'll get the necessary quota of passion, love, hate—and maybe, if everything goes according to plan, maybe even a crime—and why not, a little drop of soul . . .

(Some DANCERS begin applauding.)

One moment please!

(Pause.)

Mr. X, I saw that, and it's against the rules.

MR. X *(smiling, confused)*: Excuse me, sir?

EMCEE: Are you going to deny that you stopped dancing for a moment so you could furtively scratch a part of your anatomy that I won't mention? The rules are very clear: you cannot stop moving. You lose an hour.

MR. X: Sir, I swear that I never . . .

EMCEE: Two hours docked. For arguing with the emcee.

(The other DANCERS applaud.)

ASUNCIÓN: He had it coming.

EMCEE: Silence, please.

BOUNCER: Silence!

EMCEE: But since it's your first offense, and just to show you how generous I am, if you'll tell us what part of your body you were scratching, I'll give you back half an hour. How about it, gent?

MR. X: Yes, sir . . .

(MR. X hesitantly laughs. The rest look at him in expectation.)

EMCEE: We're waiting . . .

MR. X: Sir, I was scratching my . . .

(Giggles from the DANCERS.)

EMCEE: Your what . . . ?

Mr. X: My . . .

(Mr. X murmurs something unintelligible.)

Emcee: Speak up, Mr. X!

Mr. X *(quickly):* My ass, sir!

(Derisive laughter from everyone except the Emcee. The laughter stops.)

Emcee: And just why were you scratching your . . . that, Mr. X?

(Mr. X swallows hard.)

Mr. X: Because . . . well, sweat builds up . . . and . . .

Emcee *(implacable):* And just where exactly does that sweat build up?

Mr. X: In your . . . *(He hesitates.)*

Emcee *(feigning condescension):* Very well . . . So you mean to say that sweat makes you itch?

Mr. X: Yes, sir.

Emcee: No, sir.

Mr. X: No?

Emcee *(imperative):* That's not why you itch!

Mr. X: I don't know . . .

(Mr. X hesitates. The other Dancers urge him on, subtly, feverishly.)

It must be . . . dirty down there, sir.

(A few laughs from the Dancers.)

Emcee: Thank you, Mr. X, for your brave confession. *(Brief pause.)* So much so that we'll give you back your two hours, because, of course, this has all been an innocent joke . . . But, wait a minute, we'll have to dock you ten minutes for vulgarity . . .

Mr. X: But if it was all just a joke . . .

Emcee: No, no, sir . . . not even joking around . . . You didn't have to say that word . . . It wouldn't be fair for some to enjoy certain privileges while others don't . . . *(To the audience.)* That's how it is, ladies and gents, that's how we pass the time away in the . . . , one great big happy family where we all love each other. A little bit of healthy fun mixed with a little bit of sadness, and sometimes a little bit of well-meaning, fatherly severity to keep the peace, and most important of all, fair play! On with the dance!

(The Emcee takes a sip of water from a glass and dries his sweaty palms with the towel. At the same time, the Bouncer gives Hector a swift punch to the stomach. Hector lets out a groan, doubles over, and falls down. A stifled exclamation from his wife, Emma. It all happens very quickly. Blackout.

SCENE TWO

A cold moonlight fills the space. The Dancers are asleep on their feet, each rooted to one place, swaying in slight automatic movements, each body supported on the other. The Bouncer, seated on the tall platform in front of

the microphone, keeps watch of the dance floor. His eyes glow in the semi-darkness, and every so often he takes a long drag on his cigarette, which causes it to glow briefly. The EMCEE has disappeared. The murmur of a tango can be heard over the loudspeakers. Suddenly, convulsive sobbing.
BOUNCER *(over the microphone):* What's going on over there?
(HECTOR softly shakes his dance partner.)
HECTOR: Nothing, sir. Just a bad dream.
BOUNCER: Well, calm her down, okay?
EMMA: He's dead.
HECTOR: Easy there, honey, wake up.
EMMA: He's dead! Don't you see him? Doesn't anybody else see him?
(Some of the DANCERS wake up, complaining sleepily. The BOUNCER, uneasy, tosses his cigarette and gets up.)
BOUNCER: Well, make her stop.
EMMA continues to sob. HECTOR shakes her and finally slaps her. EMMA's sobs are abruptly cut off. She looks at HECTOR as if she had just awakened, but just as quickly she falls onto his shoulder, with gradually weakening sobs, and goes back to sleep. The BOUNCER returns to his seat and lights another cigarette. BLACKOUT.

SCENE THREE

EMCEE: Ladies and gentlemen of the audience, I have nothing but admiration for your wisdom. You didn't bother to show up during the first few days, when a formless mob was shaking it up on the dance floor. No, with noble curiosity, you held out for the opportune moment. Because it is just this moment, after exhaustion has reduced the body to a handful of numb, sore fibers, when the human condition subtly comes into focus. Let's look at an example . . . I'm going to choose someone at random . . .
(The DANCERS avoid his eyes as they vainly try to hide from him. The BOUNCER scours the dance floor like a bulldog. Someone coughs.)
Him. The one who coughed.
(The BOUNCER immediately finds that person. Unyielding, he goes over to VESPUCCI and with a single shove separates him from his partner. VESPUCCI weakly tries to resist.)
VESPUCCI: Hey, not me . . . Why me?
(ASUNCIÓN nervously pushes him.)
ASUNCIÓN: Come on . . . What a picky man! *(She tries to justify his behavior to the others.)* He's always been like that.
(Relieved giggling.)
HECTOR: Give it to him, wop.
VESPUCCI *(to the BOUNCER):* It's okay, hey, you don't have to push . . .

EMCEE *(to the BOUNCER):* Leave him alone if he's willing to come up on his own . . . Stay with his wife . . .

(VESPUCCI casts a nervous glance at ASUNCIÓN.)

VESPUCCI: No . . . why? She can keep dancing by herself . . .

(Laughter from the other DANCERS. The BOUNCER goes over to ASUNCIÓN; he has a deliberately lewd expression on his face.)

EMCEE: Now, don't be afraid, man! They're not dogs, they won't do it here, in public!

MR. X *(in a falsetto voice):* Cuckold!

(The BOUNCER clutches ASUNCIÓN and pinches her rear. ASUNCIÓN lets out a little yelp. VESPUCCI stops in his tracks.)

VESPUCCI: Hey!

(But the EMCEE has already taken VESPUCCI by the hand and now drags him over to the microphone.)

EMCEE: Don't pay any attention to them. *(He drops VESPUCCI's hand, disgusted.)* Why is your hand so hot . . . and clammy? *(He examines VESPUCCI's hand.)* This man is drenched in sweat . . . and he has a fever . . . *(He returns to the microphone.)* Yes, ladies and gentlemen, our hero of the day has a fever . . . He's dancing with a fever of at least 102 degrees. A big round of applause!

(Some of the DANCERS applaud.)

Come over here to the microphone, Vespucci. Give us a few words.

VESPUCCI *(smiling feverishly):* What should I say?

(The EMCEE takes a sniff.)

EMCEE: And the smell, ladies and gentlemen! Who would've ever thought that the spirit smelled like this? Because this man, just as you see him here, there's nothing left of this man but his soul . . . Don't you believe me?

(VESPUCCI has a coughing attack.)

What's the matter with you, Vespucci? All choked up?

VESPUCCI: No, sir. It's the air . . . it's bad for my health . . .

EMCEE: Oh, the air is bad for his health! What do you think, ladies and gents? This air is bad for his health! Is this air bad for anyone else's health?

BOUNCER: No, sir, nobody else.

EMCEE: No, of course, it isn't. Air can't be bad for your health, air is what keeps you alive . . . But, nevertheless, the air is killing this man. *(To VESPUCCI.)* Go on, get back to dancing, you've rested long enough.

(VESPUCCI starts to leave.)

No, stay up here. *(To the audience.)* In everyone else's lungs, air nurtures life, but deep inside this mass of muscles the center is rotten . . . Watch this beautiful brick of a body dance, covered in sweat and stink, held up only by fever and the fleeting images that his brain continues to produce . . . Let us study this body, with our own noble human and scientific curiosity . . .

Continue dancing, please . . . Ladies and gentlemen, I ask you (and not without a certain amount of anguish), where is this body headed, covered in its own mist, in a frenetic and final flutter of its own muscles? Say!

VESPUCCI: What?

EMCEE: Come over here.

(VESPUCCI goes over to the microphone but continues to dance, moving in an automatic fashion.)

Why are you dancing?

VESPUCCI: We've got to dance, right?

EMCEE: Well, you could also leave . . .

VESPUCCI: But, I don't . . .

EMCEE: Don't what?

VESPUCCI: I want to win . . .

EMCEE: Why?

(VESPUCCI has a coughing fit, he starts to lose his balance and grabs on to the microphone for support. The BOUNCER quickly moves toward him. The EMCEE signals to the BOUNCER, indicating that he doesn't have to intervene yet.)

EMCEE *(between VESPUCCI's coughs):* When was the last time you were in the hospital?

VESPUCCI: I'm healthy.

EMCEE: Well, then, why are you coughing?

VESPUCCI: I'm worn-out . . .

(VESPUCCI starts coughing again. The EMCEE signals again to the BOUNCER, who immediately leaps onto the platform, a handkerchief in his hand. With professional brusqueness, he holds VESPUCCI from behind in a vice-grip while he uses the other hand to cover VESPUCCI's mouth with the handkerchief, as if it were a gag. VESPUCCI has a few more weak convulsions and then calms down.)

EMCEE *(to the audience):* Nothing to fear, ladies and gentlemen, this is science . . .

(The BOUNCER lets go of VESPUCCI, who teeters a bit, pale but relieved and smiling.)

(To the BOUNCER.) Show us the handkerchief.

(The BOUNCER unfolds the handkerchief; there's the stain of fresh blood. ASUNCIÓN anxiously bursts out.)

ASUNCIÓN: It's nothing . . . He must have bitten his tongue when he coughed . . . It's happened before . . . many times . . .

(VESPUCCI continues to dance, lost in his own world. Relaxed, detached, happy.)

EMCEE *(to the BOUNCER):* Show the handkerchief to the audience. We want them to see that we're on the up and up . . .

(The BOUNCER leaves the stand and goes up and down the rows of specta-
tors, giving them a close look at the handkerchief.)
That's life, ladies and gents, blood . . . human blood. Gaze upon this banner
. . . without disgust . . . It's what holds our seams together . . . This fragile
hem of mortal threads . . . It lightly holds us together . . . And this man, our
hero of the day, he's going to spill it out to the last drop . . . this man you see
dancing here before you . . . *(The EMCEE takes VESPUCCI by the arm and says*
to him.) Take a break, you deserve one . . . *(Sweetly.)* Now tell us . . . why
are you dancing?
VESPUCCI *(softly, docile):* I want the prize.
EMCEE *(with affected surprise):* What prize? Is there a prize here?
(The DANCERS giggle along with VESPUCCI, thinking that the EMCEE is jok-
ing.)
(Condescending.) Well, let's just suppose that there is a prize.
ASUNCIÓN: We want our house.
(The EMCEE acts annoyed by ASUNCIÓN's interruption. The BOUNCER, ever on
guard, goes over to her and forces her to dance.)
VESPUCCI: Yes, the house.
EMCEE *(still affecting surprise):* What do you mean? The prize is a house?
VESPUCCI *(feverishly):* No, my house . . . I have a house, it's my house . . .
EMCEE: Well, then, why do you want another one?
VESPUCCI: I built it myself, you see? *(VESPUCCI shows the EMCEE his hands,*
as if they were explanation enough.) I built it myself . . . brick by brick . . .
I'm a bricklayer, see?
EMCEE: A round of applause for our bricklayer!
(Applause.)
ASUNCIÓN *(while everyone is still applauding, unable to contain herself):*
We had to mortgage it!
EMCEE *(to the BOUNCER):* Get her to put a lid on it, would you? Pray con-
tinue, Vespucci . . .
(From this point on, the BOUNCER will focus his efforts on groping ASUNCIÓN.
VESPUCCI observes what is going on, alert despite his feverish state.)
BOUNCER *(to ASUNCIÓN):* Dance. Don't you know how to dance?
VESPUCCI: A house, kids . . . That's not too much to ask for, is it? The kids
never showed up. And the house, well . . . Hey, what's he doing? Why can't
he leave her alone?
EMCEE *(to the BOUNCER):* Hey, don't take advantage, you're supposed to get
her to dance, that's all. And as for you, Vespucci, don't get so worked up.
You know that everything we do here is just for show. Nobody's serious.
Please, go on.
VESPUCCI: A man without his own house, without his own kids, what is he?
A pariah, a bum, a dead man. He doesn't exist. On the other hand, if you

have a house . . . Everything's alright . . . Winter, summer . . . You come
home at night, you see it there, all lit up in the dark . . . you smell your
plants . . . and you think: everything's alright. Everything's A-okay.
(VESPUCCI has another coughing attack. Pause.)
EMCEE: That's enough of that. You may leave.
VESPUCCI: What?
EMCEE: Leave.
VESPUCCI: I can go back?
EMCEE: Yes, we're done here. Go back.
VESPUCCI: Thank you.
EMCEE: You're welcome.
(Pause. There's a silence as VESPUCCI begins to descend the platform steps.)
EMCEE *(whispering close into the microphone):* He begins to go down the
stairs, he sways, and on the last step he will fall.
On the last step, VESPUCCI collapses. BLACKOUT.

SCENE FOUR

MYTH I

*The music abruptly stops. A pale luminescence slowly covers the hall. On
the dance floor, VESPUCCI, the other DANCERS, and the BOUNCER have already
collapsed, frozen in the places where they were at the blackout. Only the
EMCEE moves, standing in front of the microphone, smiling and mysterious.*
EMCEE *(speaking softly into the microphone):* Come on in, ladies and gentlemen, welcome to our theater of events. Take your bodies for a spin across
and around the golden ring of our world circus. Don't leave any holes un-
explored. Let the halo of animal heat enfold our heroes and melt away the
chill that's knocked the wind out of them. Because they've danced so hard
that only their bones are left, their bodies melting away into death and the
few memories they leave behind. Come on in, ladies and gents. Grateful to
be here with us on this August evening in the year fifteen hundred and . . .[2]
(The EMCEE slowly backs upstage until he disappears into the darkness.)
VESPUCCI: Help, please help me . . . Is there a doctor . . . My lungs are
cracking open . . .and there's pus coming out of my sores . . . Isn't anyone
else left onboard? Won't anyone take pity on me? Can't anyone release me
from my body, this body, this bundle of pain?
*(An almost imperceptible murmur rises up out of the mass of fallen bodies,
a murmur that will continue throughout the scene: "Custodi nos, Domine.
Sub umbra alarum tuarum, protege nos.")* [3]
God, how I long to be with you! Be my doctor! End this voyage, this savage sea. Let me make it to the land you promised me. It was YOU who

promised me, my Lord, and don't you forget it. You, on the lookout, what do you see?

EMCEE: Nothing, Admiral sir, only the sea.

ANOTHER MALE VOICE: The prow, alert and on guard!

VESPUCCI: Lord, lift up the weight of this terrifying night. Let the Islands of Blessedness burst forth in your dawn.[4]

FEMALE VOICES: Blessèd be the light
                 and the One True Cross
                 and the Lord of all Truth
                 and the Holy Trinity;
                 blessèd be the dawn,
                 and the lord who leads us on,
                 blessèd be the day
                 and our Lord who sends us on our way.

(They continue their litany, almost imperceptibly.)

MALE VOICE: Our lord the admiral is almost dead.

MALE VOICE: He was already dead when he came on board.

MALE VOICE: Where will we end up if our only guide is a corpse?

VESPUCCI: My bones are breaking, my skin's on fire. Doctor, if you can't relieve me of all this, at least give my suffering a name.

EMCEE: Egyptian mange. The French disease. Syphilis, my lord.

(ANNA D., still asleep, leaps up with a shriek.)

ANNA D.: Don't you remember me, my lord? I'm the Roman whore! Don't you remember that night, your night of splendor and strength? Don't you remember the fires and the screams? Pillager! Rome's conqueror! Drunk on power! Remember me, my lord! You were soaked with sweat, blackened by the smoke from the fires, your hair burnt to the roots, your skin shining from other men's blood. You were immense that night in Rome! You bit into life so ferociously! And I was the body you despoiled! The body that ended up destroying your soldier's might! Remember me, my lord, because your triumph was your defeat; because you had only what was taken away from you; because at the height of your life, you were already dead! Remember me, my lord, now when I no longer exist, remember me! *(She falls back down.)*

VESPUCCI: Won't this sea ever purify me? Lookout, what do you see?

EMCEE: Nothing, my Admiral sir. Only the sea.

VESPUCCI: I, lord of Argüeso, of Campotejar, of Jayena, gentleman-in-waiting, knight of Santiago, I would give up all of that in exchange for just a piece of the land that was promised me. That my Lord the King and, through him, God promised me. Everything, I would give up everything to have that land rise up from the sea. My land, my house, my *home.*

BLACKOUT.

Scene Five

A few moments go by. The Dancers are scattered around the dance floor. Asunción tries to get the Bouncer's attention by raising her hand like a schoolchild.

Asunción: I have to go to the bathroom, sir.

Bouncer *(curt):* You'll have to wait your turn. Someone else is using it.

(Tom Mix, dancing by himself, starts to stretch. The Bouncer goes over by him and gives him a slight blow to the ribs.)

Bouncer: Watch it.

Tom Mix: Watch what?

Bouncer: Dance.

Charity *(lost in her own world):* Rude people.

Mr. X: What did you say, Charity?

Charity *(brusquely):* I wasn't talking to you.

Hector: What's the matter, Emma?

(Emma is trying to take off one of her shoes as she continues to dance.)

Emma: My feet hurt.

(Hector casts a furtive look around the hall.)

Hector: They're going to disqualify us.

Emma: I'm still dancing, aren't I? *(She takes off her other shoe.)*

Hector *(trying to control his anger):* Emma . . .

Emma *(defiant):* What?

(Pause.)

Hector: You've got holes in your socks.

(Emma pretends to be astonished. She lets out a hysterical giggle.)

Emma: So what?

Hector: Put your shoes back on, come on, do me that one favor.

(Emma laughs again.)

Emma: And so what if my socks are worn-out?

Hector: Lower your voice.

Emma: Just where do you think we are? Hey, everybody, listen up!

Hector: Emma . . .

(But Emma's already on a roll and speaks between hysterical giggles.)

Emma: Did you hear that? I've got worn-out socks! Oh my, but what will people think? Such an elegant gathering! Charity, be sure to hold your nose!

Charity *(mustering up as much dignity as she can):* What does her problem have to do with me?

Mr. X *(with an enthusiastic giggle):* She's got holes in her socks.

Emma: A word of advice, Helen. Don't ever get married. Men are a mystery. Take my husband . . . it's been months since we've even seen a penny! We live on credit, we live in someone else's house, tiptoeing around, putting up with my sister's contempt! But it's my old worn-out socks that embarrass him . . .

MR. X *(enjoying himself):* He must have very high standards.

EMMA: Oh, yes, very high. He won't put up with just any old thing or take just any old job. No. He's a very delicate guy.

HECTOR: Okay, that's enough, Emma.

EMMA: Or, maybe he's sick? *(To ASUNCIÓN.)* He must be sick, isn't that so, ma'am?

ASUNCIÓN: I wouldn't know . . .

EMMA: Sometimes he spends the entire day in bed, lying still, like a rock, like he's dead, pale, scruffy, his eyes staring at the ceiling, his dry, sunken eyes . . . He doesn't listen, he doesn't talk, doesn't even move! And it scares me! Hector, Hector . . . Is he dead? Nope, he's still breathing . . . He's alive. But cold as a corpse.

HECTOR: That's enough, Emma, please.

EMMA: And other times he acts like a cockroach.

MR. X *(singing stupidly):* "La cucaracha, la cucaracha . . . ya no puede caminar . . ."

(TOM MIX gives HECTOR a shove.)

TOM MIX: Do something, ya fool!

EMMA: Yes, ma'am, like a roach! He sneaks around the house, sliding along the walls! Just so my sister won't see him! So she won't sweep him out of the house with her broom! So she won't yell, "Get the hell outta here, you two bums. Give me my room back so I can have somewhere to store my old junk!"

(EMMA appears to have unburdened herself. Pause. Everyone else looks at HECTOR. HECTOR, pale, takes a few steps back but never takes his eyes off his wife's. Then, with deliberate slowness, he takes off his belt and begins to unbutton his pants. Giggles and nervous movement from the DANCERS; they are surprised at HECTOR's response. The BOUNCER looks questioningly at the EMCEE, who does not respond. Not knowing what to do, the BOUNCER goes over to HECTOR.)

BOUNCER: Hey, hold on a second.

HECTOR: I was going to show them my underwear.

BOUNCER *(unsure):* Okay, but not here.

HECTOR: You're right. I would just be making a pathetic spectacle of myself. My marriage's dirty laundry. Socks, underwear . . . Disgusting intimate stuff. But that's where it all is. All the marks. You want to see contempt? That's contempt. Abandonment, hatred, the misery of everyday life . . . filth, ladies and gentlemen! Because my underwear makes her sick. And all of you gotta know that if she can't touch my underwear, there's no way she's . . .

CHARITY *(severely):* Stop it! Afterwards I'm the one who has to put up with these guys!

BOUNCER: So what's she complaining about?

EMMA *(justifying herself in front of the others):* I have the right to live my life in peace, don't I? What more does he want from me? I'm worn-out. Did he fulfill his obligations? No. He's a pathetic excuse for a man, a failure. So he better not expect anything from me.

HECTOR *(in a pathetic outburst of histrionics):* Listen up, everybody! Why did I even marry this woman? Today, and only today, I'm going to let you in on that secret! You think I married her for her beauty? *(He pauses sarcastically and then points to EMMA. EMMA, feeling harassed, looks around. A few laughs.)* Could it possibly have been for her intelligence? Hey, she was always stupid. Maybe because she was rich?

EMMA *(with her teeth clenched):* You ate up all my savings.

HECTOR: You hear that? The pathetic savings of a spinster, a few pitiful dollars snatched away just in the nick of time to make way for a nice, bitter old age. No, sir, friends! If I didn't marry her for her beauty or her intelligence or her wealth, well then, why then? I'll tell you why. *(He pauses deliberately, to build the suspense.)* Just for fun!

(Some of the DANCERS laugh. EMMA glances around, tears in her eyes.)

Yep, that's right, friends. Just for the hell of it! When I came along, she'd given up, she was already resigned to her ugliness, her stupidity, to her miserable spinster's greed. It was just too big a temptation for me to resist. What do you want? That's my weakness. I can never resist a joke. So I proposed to her. And her carefully organized life just fell apart. She accepted my proposal, but she hated me for it! Of course, she didn't have any choice . . . Because it's one thing to be fate's victim and quite another thing to be responsible for that fate. And she was too much of a coward to say no. *(Brief pause.)* So that's the secret, friends, behind this . . . ridiculous marriage.

(A painful silence. HECTOR appears empty, depressed. EMMA, powerless, looks at him through her tears.)

ASUNCIÓN: Sir . . . the bathroom.

(EMMA silently begins to put her shoes back on. HECTOR goes over to her.)

HECTOR: Do you need any help?

EMMA: Don't touch me!

(HECTOR holds up his hands.)

HECTOR: Okay . . . what're you gonna do?

EMMA: I'm leaving.

(An exclamation runs through the DANCERS. Great anticipation. The BOUNCER is doubly on guard. He moves around the couples in an agitated manner.)

EMCEE *(whispering into the microphone):* Pay close attention, ladies and gents, this doesn't happen every day . . .

HECTOR: Emma . . . I . . . was only joking.

EMCEE: As you can see, it's not only physical resilience that counts here . . .

(HECTOR grabs EMMA's arm.)

EMMA: Let go of me!

(HECTOR lets go.)

HECTOR: Emma, we've already suffered so much for this. How can we just leave it all like that? So close to . . . ? Think about all we could lose.

EMMA: That doesn't matter to me anymore.

HECTOR: But do you believe what I said? I was . . . joking. You know me, Emma. Please, forgive me.

(EMMA remains unchanged even as she continues to dance, albeit in a rudimentary fashion.)

HELEN *(ferociously):* Don't forgive him! Emma, don't you forgive him! He doesn't deserve your forgiveness! He's a selfish pig just like all men!

VESPUCCI *(with feverish impatience):* So? Let's go! What are you waiting for?

HECTOR: Emma, this is our big chance . . . our last . . . everything could change.

HELEN: Don't you believe him! He just wants to use you! Like he's always done before!

VESPUCCI *(exasperated):* Come on! You disgusting bitch! Let's go!

(EMMA hesitates at the edge of the dance floor.)

HECTOR *(with one final, heartbreaking cry):* Emma, please don't leave me!

(Pause. Suddenly, EMMA turns around with a giggle.)

EMMA: No, you're not going to be the one who decides when this is over. I'll decide when I'm going to leave! And it's going to be at just the right moment! Right when it'll hurt you the most!

(VESPUCCI, exploding, tries to throw himself on top of EMMA.)

VESPUCCI: I'm gonna kill her!

(The BOUNCER goes over to break it up. But no intervention is required because VESPUCCI has another coughing fit. ASUNCIÓN runs to help her husband while she speaks to the EMCEE.)

ASUNCIÓN: Please, sir! Can I go to the bathroom? I'm about to faint!

EMCEE *(annoyed, to the BOUNCER):* Who's in the bathroom?

BOUNCER: The girl.

EMCEE: Go see what's taking her so long.

(Pause. An enormous exhaustion has overtaken the DANCERS. They seem even more tired, deadened, shut down.)

CHARITY *(still lost in her own world):* Yeah, those are the respectable couples. The ones that look down on me. Squeaky clean on the outside but full of crap on the inside. I've seen the shorts of more than one of those. I'm . . .

I'm proud of who I am. *(Unyielding, unconquerable, and magnificent.)*
I'm proud of who I am!
(As she says those words, the BOUNCER *comes running back with an expression of alarm on his face.)*
BOUNCER: Sir!
BLACKOUT.

SCENE SIX

Night. Even in the darkness we begin to hear the occasional sigh, scratch, giggle, or mumbling coming from the sleeping DANCERS. *The* BOUNCER *is nodding off at the foot of the platform. The* EMCEE *is seated in front of a table on top of the platform. He is motionless, his face in profile to the dance floor, a deck of cards in one hand.* HOMER *is awake but lost in thought. A little giggle from* CHARITY *grabs his attention. He goes over to her, being careful to drag his dance partner along with him.* HELEN *stirs and grumbles.*
HOMER *(whispering):* Charity?
*(*CHARITY'S *eyes are strangely open.)*
CHARITY: What?
HOMER: What are you laughing at?
CHARITY *(chuckling to herself):* At these flies. They have no respect!
*(*HOMER, *intrigued, observes her. He then snaps his fingers in front of her face.* CHARITY *laughs.* HOMER *sighs, disappointed. Pause.)*
EMMA *(abruptly, in the middle of a dream):* No! No! He's dead! I don't want to!
HECTOR *(automatically, without waking up):* It's okay, calm down. It's all over.
(Pause. The EMCEE *speaks to* HOMER. *He does this without moving his head, staying in the same position throughout the exchange.)*
EMCEE: Poor woman, always the same bad dream.
*(*HOMER *looks at him with curiosity.)*
HOMER: Yes . . .
EMCEE: And what's going on with you? Can't you sleep?
HOMER: No, sir, I sleep very little.
EMCEE: Do you like the nighttime?
HOMER: I keep watch.
(Pause. The EMCEE *whistles.)*
You understand what I mean, right?
EMCEE: No.
HOMER: Don't you hear it?
EMCEE: Hear what?
HOMER: The creaking. *(Pause. With an almost sinister giggle.)* You can

always hear it at night . . . You have to have good hearing and pay a little attention . . . But you must have heard . . .

(The EMCEE whistles through his teeth. HOMER decides to keep going.)

Because you don't sleep much either, do you? I've seen you up there a lot, not moving, just shuffling that deck of cards . . . Excuse me, sir, but there's something I've been meaning to ask you for a long time . . .

EMCEE: Yes?

HOMER: What game are you playing?

EMCEE: I just make it up as I . . .

VESPUCCI *(suddenly, still asleep):* Come on, you monkeys, you devils, scum! Wind to port! All ashore, you scum! The ship's going down! *(He suddenly opens his eyes and his mouth, gasping in an exaggerated fashion as if he can't get any air.)* Asunción . . . I'm drowning . . .

(VESPUCCI starts to lose his balance. ASUNCIÓN wakes up with a start and tries to hold her husband up.)

ASUNCIÓN: Help!

BLACKOUT.

SCENE SEVEN

The sound of a milonga⁵ is heard.

EMCEE: Let's go, ladies and gents! Get moving! I want to see you dancing around as fresh as you were when we started! Chests out! Eyes on fire! The future is ours! What's wrong with you? Are you dead? Well, come back to life! Get that blood boiling! Change partners!

(On the dance floor, the BOUNCER carries out the EMCEE's orders.)

Change partners! Change! Change! Change!

(The DANCERS go from inertia to a state of perverse excitation. When the EMCEE stops urging them on, the following tableau is set up: MR. X is dancing with HELEN; VESPUCCI is pawing ANNA D.; CHARITY, EMMA, and ASUNCIÓN are jokingly fighting over TOM MIX; and HOMER and HECTOR have been left on their own to observe the scene.)

VESPUCCI *(panting, feverish):* You like me, don't you? I'm big . . . and strong . . . Isn't that right, you little slut?

(At the EMCEE's signal, the BOUNCER frees TOM MIX from the women's siege.)

BOUNCER *(pushing them apart):* Okay, ladies, that's enough.

(One by one the women leave TOM MIX alone and go their separate ways, rearranging their clothing as if nothing had happened. ASUNCIÓN takes her husband away from ANNA D. and tries to calm him down. In the middle of the dance floor stands TOM MIX, his clothing in complete disarray, his pants half-undone. Pause.)

EMCEE: Young Tom Mix.

Tom Mix: Yassir?

Emcee: Button up your pants.

(Giggles from the women.)

Tom Mix *(with a wink):* Yassir, mister.

Vespucci *(referring to Asunción):* Look at this body! What a woman! What tits! How many kids do you think she could feed with these things?

(Asunción tries to calm him down. Pause.)

Emcee: Young Tom Mix.

Tom Mix: Mister?

Emcee: What scent do you give off, my dear young man? I'm talking about the ladies. They're all over you like flies.

Tom Mix *(laughing):* Yep, one of these days they're gonna be the death of me. *(Brief pause.)* Do I hafta stay here?

Emcee: Yes. *(Pause. To the audience, over the microphone, with a confidential tone in his voice.)* Ladies and gentlemen, look at this young masked man. He appears shy, almost submissive. But notice how his lips tighten up, how his eyes . . . want to eat us up. Who is he? A predatory animal? Young Tom Mix.

Tom Mix: Mister, sir?

Emcee: What are you doing here?

Tom Mix: I'm here to dance, mister.

Emcee *(harshly):* I'm asking why you're here and not somewhere else.

Tom Mix: Like where, mister?

Emcee: There are many places for a young man of your supposed age. The classroom, the fields, a garage . . .

Hector: A jail.

(Some giggles, cut short by the Emcee's icy glare.)

Tom Mix *(smiling):* Me, I'm nobody, mister.

Emcee *(violently):* I didn't ask you who you are but where you are. Where you stand. Do you follow me?

Tom Mix: Yassir, mister. I'm barely standing, mister. I'm just about to fall down.

Emcee *(to the audience):* He's defiant. I like that. Young man!

Tom Mix: Yassir?

Emcee: I suppose you have the usual goals. Build yourself a future, set up a home, have children.

Tom Mix: Nope, mister.

Emcee: Well, then, what is it you want? Just to have some fun? Son, life is not just one long dance . . . We let you in here on faith. We didn't ask where you came from, not even how old you were . . . And that despite police regulations. But neither do we wish to forget our pedagogical function here. And besides, you're not alone . . . That young lady who's here with you . . . I suppose that there's something more between you two than just a simple dancing acquaintance . . . *(He stops, waiting for a reply.)*

TOM MIX: I dunno who she is.

EMCEE: What?

TOM MIX: I don't know who she is. I ran across her somewhere, I don't remember. She just stuck to me.

(Pause. The EMCEE affects a look of professional surprise.)

EMCEE: She just . . . stuck to you! *(He pauses for effect.)* And you, my child?

ANNA D.: Yes.

EMCEE: Yes? Yes what? Oh, these people wear me out! They make me so mad! Dear, do you always say yes?

ANNA D.: Yes.

EMCEE: And I suppose that you don't know who he is either. You just stuck to him.

ANNA D.: Yes.

EMCEE *(with increasing "indignation")*: They just stuck to each other. They simply got stuck to each other, in the street, like a couple of animals, or insects. Because of a certain . . . sticky substance their bodies secrete. *(Brief pause.)* Young man!

(TOM MIX clicks his heels together, imitating a military salute.)

TOM MIX: Sir, yassir!

EMCEE: You are not totally free!

TOM MIX *(with a click of his heels)*: Sir, no sir!

(The EMCEE signals to the BOUNCER.)

EMCEE: There's Nature . . .

TOM MIX *(clicking his heels)*: Sir, yas . . . !

(The BOUNCER swiftly grabs one of TOM MIX's arms and twists it behind his back, the whole time smiling to the audience as if it were all a joke. The young man lets out a slight groan.)

EMCEE *(as if nothing strange is happening)*: Look, Nature is—how shall I put it?—fatalistic and emotional. It's not interested in anything but reproducing itself, according to some mysterious order. And you, my dear, don't you ever think about maintaining that biological order? *(Pause.)* Answer my question please.

(The BOUNCER twists the young man's arms mercilessly.)

CHARITY: Let go of him!

TOM MIX *(overcoming his pain)*: It's better if . . . you don't count on me . . . mister, sir.

(The BOUNCER lets go of TOM MIX. Pause. VESPUCCI points to his wife and to himself.)

VESPUCCI: A couple of strong, healthy bodies. Look at my hands . . . How many kids could they feed . . . ? Look at my wife . . . look at those hips . . . ? Is that fair, I ask you?

(ASUNCIÓN *tries to make* VESPUCCI *be quiet; he keeps jabbering. The* EMCEE, *absorbed, continues to contemplate* TOM MIX's *face, as if it were a problem in need of a solution. Pause.*)

EMCEE: Very well, young Tom Mix, principles are principles. I have a very open mind. But I warn you, there are certain lines that must not be crossed. It's one thing to be an irresponsible young man, and quite another . . . Anyway, on with the dance. *(He turns away, as if putting an end to the subject.)*

TOM MIX: I'm nobody, mister. I'm . . . *(He laughs. Brief pause.)* Hey, I'm not even here. Ya see? I'm on my way out.

EMCEE: Don't you want the prize?

TOM MIX: What prize?

EMCEE *(quickly):* I can't tell you that.

(Brief pause.)

TOM MIX: I don't want nothin'.

EMCEE *(to the audience, confidential):* Believe me, ladies and gentlemen, if this young man only knew what the prize was, he wouldn't be here. And not because it's not an important prize, no, but because even the greatest of prizes for him would be insignificant. Very well, young Tom Mix, your minute of grace is over. Do you have anything else to say?

(Pause.)

TOM MIX: Nope, nothin', mister.

EMCEE: Well, then, on with the dance.

BLACKOUT.

SCENE EIGHT

MYTH II

The music has stopped. In the center of the dance floor a halo of light encircles young TOM MIX.

TOM MIX: This darkness. This constant, deafening noise. And my body, numbed by the exhaustion of centuries. Walking, among the tattered, defeated masses. But toward what? Without looking back. Captives. The sword hanging over our heads. Blind from terror and hunger. Toward the slaughter. And then in my mind, in the middle of the night, a brief, intense lightning bolt. A memory of that lost light.

EMCEE: The year of Our Lord eighteen hundred and . . . ![6]

TOM MIX: South Americans!

(A sudden silence. Young TOM MIX then goes on to speak, his voice vibrant.)
Some foreigners have blamed the discontented masses for the recent upris-
ings in our America, basing themselves on the Spanish laws' admirable
wisdom and gentleness. But is it so wise and so gentle to have condemned
millions of inhabitants to vegetate in poverty and to subject them to the
viceroy's martial, despotic law, they who hold in their hands our neighbors' lives, property, and honor? Is it so wise and so gentle to have condemned the Indian to the condition of the Spanish Crown's tributary, to
wrench away from that unhappy race the fruit of their labors, watered by
their own blood in the mines? The tyrants have tried to justify this practice
by saying that only natives are strong enough to handle these jobs. But
since the Spanish have never had any personal experience in such matters,
it is wise to suspect that this is only an arbitrary assumption. The owners of
the mines, or those that enjoy their products without having to work in
them, dearly love their own lives; African slaves are the property of their
masters, it has cost them money to acquire them; therefore, only the Indians
are indifferent beings who must scorn death in the pursuit of others' gains.[7]
(Pause.)
FEMALE VOICE *(singing):*

> Cielo, cielito que sí,
> cielo lejano y celeste,
> si es que no puedo ser libre,
> mejor que me libre la muerte.[8]

TOM MIX: South Americans, it was not this aching and humiliated territory,
impregnated by generations of suffering, that the lightning bolt of my dream
illuminated. It was a land different from this one, one already hardened by
pain, already sterile. Because behind this sea of iniquity, America still rises
up, silent in her splendor, infinite. On her beaches, smiling, immortal children wait for us. That is the land of my dream, the land God has safe-
guarded for us, His promised land.
(TOM MIX falls down as if executed by a firing squad.)
FEMALE VOICE *(singing):*

> Cielo, cielito que sí,
> cielo lejano y celeste,
> If in this life I can't be free,
> let my noble death unfetter me.

BLACKOUT.

Scene Nine

Night. Dim lights and soft music. The couples sleep. Their dreaming voices accumulate, coming together like a chorus, until suddenly they form one brief outcry.[9]

HECTOR: We're crossing the border. The land is rocky, brown. The light soft, watery, and bright. We're nearing the city.

CHARITY: Flies, green, fat as fingers. Dear, dear flies. My little ones.

TOM MIX: Sand, sand. And pools of clean water, springing up out of the sand.

HELEN: Water. Water, please. My lips are burning.

HOMER: Words. I need words.

CHARITY: There they go, down my legs. They're tickling me.

ANNA D.: I'm running through the field. I'm barefoot. I'm running through the water.

EMMA: The shed is dark, it's dusty. It smells like rotten wood. Creaks. Rats. He's going to appear. I'm afraid. I have to stay.

HELEN: Water.

MR. X: A dark hole. Bang! Right on the head.

HECTOR: An ancient, uninhabited city. Ancestral walls of polished stone.

CHARITY: Flies in my hair, like a crown of emeralds.

TOM MIX: And children, children. Naked. Laughing. They jump over the pools of water. They throw handfuls of sand into the wind.

ASUNCIÓN: My breasts are full of milk. He sucks me dry. This man!

EMMA: First, a soft light in back. Way in the back of the shed. Fear. No. Go hold him.

CHARITY: Flies inside me. Moving around. They're all over. Filling me up.

HELEN: Water. So thirsty. I'm drying up.

ANNA D.: I'm running through the wind.

HECTOR: And there's an ancient drawing on every stone. Colors spring up out of the rock.

CHARITY: Flies all around me like clouds of smoke. Then the yellow cat leaps out! He scares them away! They fly away! My little ones, come back! Darlings!

MR. X: Bang! Right on the head.

HELEN: Water! I'm on fire! I'm drying up!

HOMER: Words! Words!

VESPUCCI: The ship's going down!

TOM MIX: And they're jumping! And laughing! And shouting! Free! Free!

EMMA: Way in the back of the shed. Phosphorescent. Wrapped in his white shroud. He's smiling at me! His little hands reach out for me! But he's dead! My God, he's dead!

BLACKOUT.

Scene Ten

Light. Activity. It is daytime.

Emcee *(speaking to the audience):* Life would be unbearable without our dreams. But our dreams, without poets, would also be unbearable. And even in our marathon, ladies and gents, our mirror of life, there has to be a poet. A man who will sing someday—and why not?—of this heroic and anonymous deed. Of course, you already know who I mean. The common man's interpreter, the illustrious Mr. Homer Starr! *(He applauds into the microphone. The Dancers applaud as well.)* Come on up, Homer. Do us the honor.

(Homer feigns modesty. Helen, ecstatic, applauds and pulls him over to the platform. She helps him up the steps, even though he does not need any assistance, and leans into the microphone.)

Helen *(speaking into the microphone):* I know it's hard to believe, but he's really as shy as a little boy. *(She gestures for Homer to come to the microphone.)*

Emcee: A pity we don't have any laurels for a crown . . .

Helen: Yes, a pity.

Emcee: But look here, our assistant . . . has repaired the oversight . . . and since we don't have any laurels . . . *(The Emcee takes the handkerchief that the Bouncer has held out to him. Each corner of the handkerchief is knotted. The Emcee raises it over Homer's head, with a wink to the audience.)* Gloria artistae![10]

(Helen joins in on the coronation.)

Helen: To poetry!

Homer: Thank you. I accept this humble . . .

Emcee: Venerated master!

Homer: Sir?

Emcee: You owe us a confidence.

Homer: At your service, sir. As long as it doesn't compromise my word, nor place a friend in peril, nor stain a lady's honor.

Charity *(admiringly):* I'm so excited I could pee!

Helen: Shhh!

Emcee: Of course, of course . . . We don't wish to snoop around in the bedroom nor estrange you from your lady friend here . . .

Homer: But not to worry, my friend. Miss Helen is only a . . . *(ambiguous)* a friend, here to console me in my old age, a . . .

Helen: In reality, and just so there aren't any misunderstandings, so nobody gets the wrong impression, I wish to make it perfectly clear that our relationship is based exclusively on mutual admiration. I perform a worthy cultural service. I champion new ideas in my role as librarian at the Society for the Strengthening of the Soul. It was there that we met and began our friendship, which has never extended beyond the limits of poetry.

HOMER: Helen has stayed up entire nights typing my unworthy poems.

HELEN: His interminable poems, I might add. But not only that. I soon realized that Homie . . . I mean, Homer, possessed huge cultural lacunae. And I resolved myself to remaking this man. I created a course of systematic readings for him. Since then, his poetry has improved notably. Also, when I type his poems, I often polish a little image here, fix a minor error there . . . They're right when they say that behind every man there's a great woman.

(The EMCEE moves her away from the microphone.)

EMCEE: But to tell the truth, maestro, my question had to do with, well, considering your age, your merit, your fame . . . That is, your presence here is a mystery . . .

HOMER: Yes, it is. But one would have to say that our presence in general is a mystery, is it not? Look, I've been breathing this air and looking at this sky for almost seventy years, and I still don't pretend to comprehend it.

HELEN *(grabbing the microphone):* I don't know if you understand . . .

EMCEE *(moving her to one side):* Yes, yes . . . But what I don't quite get, Homer, is what motivated you to participate . . .

HOMER: It was not greed, sir.

HELEN: Although he is pretty tight with his money.

HOMER: Helen's joking.

HELEN: No, no, he's a tightwad. He's really cheap. Nobody else knows that he keeps this bank account . . .

HOMER: Helen exaggerates, of course. When I was born, my parents were very old. They had already amassed a lifetime's worth of labor. And they left me some things, a few things . . . Their memory, which I revere; a large, old house in which I was born and where I still reside; and the metallic fruits of their lives' efforts . . . A small amount of capital that, with much penury and care, allows me to dedicate my life to pure inspiration . . .

EMCEE: And I suppose it allows you to pay this poor woman to type your poems.

(HELEN laughs sarcastically.)

HOMER *(nearly startled):* Excuse me, sir, but that would have been, begging the pardon of all the ladies present, like paying a prostitute. Let me make it perfectly clear, of course, that I mean no disregard to those unlucky nocturnal flowers . . . whose friendship I have enjoyed and with whom I've spent many a night. And, I say this with the utmost respect, together we've worshiped at the cult of Venus . . . But, let me make it perfectly clear, never for money.

(Everyone looks malevolently at CHARITY.)

CHARITY *(sourly):* If it had been with me, old man, I'd have cured you of any desire of getting it for free.

EMCEE: So, Homer, why are you participating?

HELEN: In reality, it was all my idea. I have only one goal in this life and that is to see the publication of the complete works of Homer Starr.

(HOMER surreptitiously makes the sign of the devil toward the floor.)

As you surely must understand, such an enterprise requires money. And I am willing to make any sacrifice to obtain the necessary funding.

CHARITY: *Any* sacrifice, honey?

(Laughter from the dancers.)

HELEN: There are people who enjoy staining the purest of causes. Dirty people . . .

CHARITY: Publish his complete works! All she wants to do is fill herself up with cash and play the widow.

HELEN: Shut up, you piece of dirt! Whore!

CHARITY: Old maid!

(The BOUNCER intervenes.)

BOUNCER: Quiet down there, Charity . . .

CHARITY: Well, don't come running to me! *(She continues to grumble.)*

EMCEE: So, maestro, it's Art that has led you here?

HOMER: I suppose one could say so . . . although, in reality, it was all a whim of Helen's . . . At my age, I have no lofty ambitions . . . But what can one do? I never could say no to the pleas of a lady. With the exception of not giving in to the matrimonial yoke, I have never let a lady down . . . As long as one drop of the juice of life remains in my body . . . But in everything else, I've always been humble. Only once in my life did I have any great ambition . . .

EMCEE: Pray tell us.

HOMER: To publish a poem in the literary supplement of the *Times*.[11] Now I can die content. That dream has been fulfilled.

EMCEE: A round of applause for Mr. Homer Starr, whose poetry has appeared in the *Times*!

(A few disheartened claps from the dancers. HOMER, his hand trembling, takes a piece of paper out of his pocket. He hands the paper over to the EMCEE, who takes a quick look at it and then gives it to the BOUNCER. The BOUNCER works his way through the audience, showing the paper to the spectators.)

HOMER *(speaking as these activities are going on):* Do you see? There are many ways of making one's dream come true. I spent years sending out the humble products of my wit. And without one single bite. But then I thought, Aren't I a poet? Isn't my only reality the dreamworld? Well, let's give reality a hand. With a bit of cunning and innocence. Do you remember the

Gospel of Matthew? "So be wise as serpents and innocent as doves."[12] Well, sir, I chose my most recognized poem, I took up scissors and paste, and every weekend I clipped each of the words I needed from the Sunday supplement . . . And don't think that it was easy, oh no. When everything was almost ready, I was still missing a word. One word, a single word, I pursued it over months, years . . . Torture, torment . . . One word separated me from fame and immortality. I began to hate that word, I despaired, I would have committed suicide over that word . . . But it was all in vain, there it was, an empty space in the middle of my poem. Humiliating me. What could I do? Fake it? No, no, one ought to be consistent with one's invention . . . That is the first law of poetics. Change the word? God knows that that would have spelled the defeat of poetry. And nevertheless, I was just about to . . . I was going to do it, when it appeared. My word appeared, my beloved, hated word from which the thread of my life hung suspended. And I published my poem in the *Times*. I was saved. I could die a happy man.

(Pause.)

EMCEE: Thank you, distinguished maestro. Thanks to you, a gust of spirit has passed through our humble marathon. And once the spirit has passed through, the flesh is welcome. Charity, pluck up your courage and come up onto our historic stage.

(Laughter from the other DANCERS motivates CHARITY's refusal.)

CHARITY *(bitter, strident):* No, sir, I'll pass. I don't have any history. I'm only a body here.

BLACKOUT.

SCENE ELEVEN

It is dawn. Most of the DANCERS are dozing; the rest have just awakened or haven't gone to sleep. On the platform, the EMCEE washes his hands in a washbasin that the BOUNCER, from down on the dance floor, is holding up in front of the EMCEE. This long scene transpires in silence. Suddenly, the EMCEE shoots a look at a single point, near the entrance. The BOUNCER follows suit. A WOMAN has just entered the hall: she is elegant, beautiful, fragile; her long evening gown displays her perfect, lightly tanned shoulders. The WOMAN enters languidly, slowly, the train of her dress and her white fur stole dragging behind. She holds an unlit cigarette between her gloved fingers. As the BOUNCER and the awake dancers look on in amazement, she advances to the center of the dance floor, like some vague apparition. She silently looks around. Finally, the BOUNCER reacts and goes over to her. He's obsequious.

BOUNCER: May I get you a seat, madam?

(After a pause, the WOMAN *speaks but does not look at him.)*
WOMAN: Give me a light.
(The BOUNCER *clumsily rummages through his pockets. The* EMCEE *looks once more toward the entrance. The* BOUNCER *takes out a box of matches and lights one. He holds the match in front of the* WOMAN, *who remains impassive. The* BOUNCER *now looks at the entrance. A* MAN *is entering, slowly, weakly, unsteady on his feet. He is wearing a tuxedo with a white cravat draped around his neck. He goes over to the* WOMAN.)*
MAN: Ma sœur, let's go, my dear, on nous attends.[13]
(Silence. The WOMAN *does not answer. Instead, she stares at the couples as if she were trying to distinguish between dream and reality.)*
WOMAN: Mon frère[14] . . . what are they doing?
(Unsteady, the MAN *looks around him.)*
MAN: I think they're . . . dancing.
WOMAN: Dancing? There's dancing . . . in Hell?
(The WOMAN *laughs, slowly. Then she closes her eyes, a bit unsteady. The* MAN *helps support her body.)*
MAN: Let's go, darling, on nous attends.
(The WOMAN's *head is resting on her brother's shoulder.)*
WOMAN: But why do they . . . dance?
MAN: I have no idea, sister dear. It's late.
WOMAN: Mon frère, these people . . . dancing here in the dawn . . . I don't understand why . . .
(She lets out a cutting, acidic laugh.) It's positively sinister.
MAN: Not everything has an explanation, ma sœur.
WOMAN: No, no . . . I insist upon an explanation. I must have an explanation.
MAN: Et voilá[15] . . . *(He goes toward the platform, turning slowly in an unsteady, ghostly dance and singing softly.)*

> "London Bridge is falling down,
> falling down, falling down . . .
> London Bridge is falling down,
> my fair lady . . ."

(The MAN *speaks with the* EMCEE *in a low voice. Meanwhile,* CHARITY, *a hypnotized expression on her face, goes over to the* WOMAN *and points at her.)*
CHARITY: Madam, a fly. You have fly in your ear.
(The MAN, *softly singing, returns to the* WOMAN's *side.)*
MAN: Ma sœur, they'll continue to dance until . . . something . . . Je ne sais pas[16] . . . It's something rather like a . . . competition . . . I don't know why . . . There's apparently a prize of some sort . . .

WOMAN: I want to dance.

MAN: Darling, we're all done in . . . We've been out all evening . . .

WOMAN: I want to dance. There's a prize, isn't there? I want that prize.

MAN: Your dress. You'll ruin it on this floor.

WOMAN: I'll tie my dress up, just like a laundry-woman.

MAN: Ma sœur, je t'en prie,[17] they're calling us, can't you hear the horn? We'll be left behind. And we don't even know where we are.

WOMAN: That doesn't matter. Anyway, we're going to be here for a long time. *(The MAN smiles smoothly, singing softly.)*

MAN: "London Bridge is falling down . . ." *(To the EMCEE.)* You heard her, monsieur, we're staying . . . My sister is very headstrong. It will be impossible to change her mind.

EMCEE: I'm sorry, sir, but to add anyone at this point . . . except unofficially, of course . . .

(The MAN looks questioningly at his sister.)

WOMAN: I want to dance . . . officially.

(The MAN laughs once more, smoothly.)

MAN: You heard her.

EMCEE: Yes, yes, but please understand . . . These people have been dancing for a long time . . . You would have too great of an advantage . . .

WOMAN *(laughing):* But we can barely stand up.

MAN: Very well, I suppose that if we have to pay . . . something along the lines of an entry fee. Not a problem . . . "London Bridge is falling down . . ." *(Softly singing and dancing unsteadily, the MAN goes toward the platform. He takes out his billfold and discreetly offers some bills to the EMCEE. The EMCEE quickly puts the money away and, with an expression of professional surprise, goes over to the microphone and speaks intimately to the dancers.)*

EMCEE: Ladies and gents . . . wake up . . . Something unexpected . . .

(The BOUNCER claps his hands and distributes various punches and shoves.)

BOUNCER: Wake up! Let's go! Wake up!

EMCEE *(with the same tone as before):* Forgive me, ladies and gents . . . Something has come up that wasn't in our original plans . . . At this unearthly hour . . . These distinguished folks ask . . . ladies and gents, friends, the secret of the prize precludes my revealing this gentleman's offer . . . But you must surely be able to tell from my face that it is something truly exceptional. *(He points at his own face and its histrionic expression.)* But it is ultimately you who must . . . the decision is in your hands . . .

(The EMCEE's words resound like sarcasm compared to the dancers' numb stupor as the group becomes more and more like an exhausted herd. A herd that the BOUNCER amuses himself with as he trips and movies them around by force, shouting out like a cowpoke. Suddenly, like a cow making a break

from the herd, CHARITY begins to run around the new couple.)
CHARITY: Madam . . . ! Madam . . . ! There's a fly in your ear!
BLACKOUT.

SCENE TWELVE

MYTH III

*In a continuation of the previous scene, in the darkness we hear the scuffled
running, interjections, and whistles associated with driving a herd of cattle.
A grayish light comes up and reveals the DANCERS, moving like cattle circling the new couple, slowly dancing. On the platform, the EMCEE plays
solitaire, whistling through his teeth. Every so often, he casts a glance at
the action on the dance floor.*[18]
WOMAN: Mon frère, what a nightmare . . . Don't these beasts ever stop?
They're making me dizzy.
MAN: I told you, darling sister, that this wasn't the show for you. But never
fear. It's not difficult to stop them. You follow them on horseback, and
then, with a steel loop on the end of a pole . . . One sharp, quick tug on the
back leg . . . and there it is, hamstrung, thrown down in the field. After that,
you slice its throat. And then you remove the hide, which is the most valu-
able part, the horns, the fat . . . and with the meat, if there's time, jerky . . .
WOMAN: They're stirring up so much dust, dirt.
MAN: Yes, lots of dirt in the air. And acres of land. Everywhere you look!
Earth and sky! So much free-roaming cattle, so much windswept land, it
makes one dizzy. "Horror vacui."[19] Sister, we have to tame this endless
wild land, tame it like a wild mustang. Mount it, give it a good spurring in
the flanks. Fence it in.
WOMAN: I can't even begin to understand your business. Just leave me
alone in my world of domesticities: my Italian tapestries, my English por-
celains, our French carved-mahogany bed . . .
MAN: Sister, a dream. The land was calm. All of America, one motionless,
thick, grimy mass of land. An immense, pregnant woman. Ceaselessly giving birth to sheep, cows, horses . . . Sister, a dream. The earth bleeds.
America: one enormous slaughterhouse. Cattle stretched out in the mud, a
swarm of Negresses huddled over the entrails, and, in the middle, the butcher,
his chaps, shirt and face smeared with blood, a knife in his hand. And above
the gulls were flying about, hovering over the smell of flesh and shit, while
down below, the skinners flayed the hide. They hoisted the carcass onto the
moving belt. They gutted it, cut off its head and tail. They split it in half
with an electric saw. And then they buried it in niches, in enormous holes

in the ice. And that's how that sad flesh finally met the end of its hard travails. *(Brief pause. Solemn, in a Roman salute.)* All praise be to refrigeration![20]
BLACKOUT.

SCENE THIRTEEN

EMCEE *(stretching in front of the microphone):* Well, my little ones, we're going to lower the lights. Have a nice rest.
(An air of strange restlessness floats among the DANCERS. A vague tension is in their alert, feverish eyes, as if something were just about to happen, particularly something coming from outside the dance hall.)
EMMA: Sir . . .
EMCEE: Yes?
EMMA: No . . . well, it's just that I'm not really sleepy yet . . . But if everyone else . . .
ASUNCIÓN: I'm not sleepy either.
MR. X: If you could leave the lights on for just a little longer. *(He looks over at CHARITY for her approval.)* Well, if it's alright with everyone else.
CHARITY *(curtly):* Yes.
(Everyone else agrees.)
TOM MIX *(to the EMCEE):* Say, listen, mister. Why were we here all alone today?
(The EMCEE laughs, rubbing his hands together.)
EMCEE: I don't know. The cold scares people away.
BOUNCER *(following the EMCEE's lead):* Do you know how cold it is outside? Below freezing. Great little night out there, eh! You're all very lucky to be in here, nice and warm, well fed, able to move. Just think about the poor folks out there. How about getting disqualified now? If I was you, I wouldn't even sleep, just to keep my place . . . Below freezing!
CHARITY: Somebody must be frozen out there.
HECTOR: And you complain, Charity. Look, if I had to walk those streets . . .
CHARITY: I'm not complaining.
VESPUCCI: I'm hot.
ASUNCIÓN *(with exaggerated enthusiasm):* What a live wire! With a body like that! How could he ever be cold!
VESPUCCI *(naïvely):* Sometimes I'm cold, too.
ASUNCIÓN: That's because you never wear a coat! What a man! Sometimes I'll see him in the middle of winter in just a thin shirt, and it gives me goose bumps. "Put something on," I tell him. "I'm not cold," he tells me.
ANNA D. *(laughing):* In the country we'd have to walk to school in the mornings. One mile. Our slippers would get soaked by the dew and they'd

freeze. So we'd take them off and hide them in the grass. Then we'd walk around barefoot.

(Pause.)

EMCEE: Well, lights out.

EMMA: No, just a bit longer, please.

EMCEE *(laughing):* What's the matter with all of you tonight? Are you afraid?

ASUNCIÓN: Sir, could we . . . lie down on the floor . . . just for a little while?

EMCEE *(sweetly):* No, that can't be done.

ASUNCIÓN: Why not? No one will see us.

EMCEE: No, it's impossible. It wouldn't be moral.

HECTOR *(laughing mockingly):* Moral?

EMCEE *(paying no attention to HECTOR):* And anyway, it's not to your advantage. If someone lies down, who can assure me that he'll get back up? Plus, you would lose any incentive to go on. Resting will be the consolation prize for the losers.

HECTOR *(mocking):* Wearing yourself out just so you can rest. So that's all there is to this?

BOUNCER *(to the EMCEE):* Turn out the lights, sir?

(The DANCERS protest.)

EMCEE *(laughing):* Homer, why don't you give us one of your poems, maybe that'll put them to sleep.

HOMER: My poems are that boring, sir?

EMCEE *(laughing):* I didn't say that. *(Slightly ironic.)* I only meant that, on a night like this, when dawn seems so uncertain and far away, and the herd is wandering around lost . . . the immortal voice of the poet . . . Come on, give us a poem.

HOMER *(ceremoniously):* Very well. If everyone's in agreement . . .

(The DANCERS approve.)

"The Wedding."

HELEN *(annoyed):* Oh, everyone already knows that one!

HOMER: I didn't realize that you disliked it so.

HELEN: It's not that I don't like it. It's just that it's too well known.

HOMER: Well . . . I don't know . . . It's the only one I can remember all of . . .

HELEN *(suggesting):* "Rose of Fire."

CHARITY: No! No! "The Wedding!" What does she know about poetry anyway?

(Calls for "The Wedding" rise up from the DANCERS.)

HOMER: Helen, my public demands . . .

HELEN *(brusquely):* Recite whatever you want.

HOMER: At your request . . .

(Applause and exclamations of approval. HOMER pauses momentarily and then begins to recite in a solemn voice.)

She was a beautiful white dove,
the town's most fragrant flower.
As she walked down the bower,
along the path sprang up words of love.

She never responded a single time
to such virile attentions.
Neither desire nor love's mentions
could soften her heart of stony lime.

But one day a stranger came to town,
a man of looks roughly hewn,
and won her untouched soul with a tune,
merely by singing, "I love you," aloud.

And he at last asked her in secrét
all her idle hours to cast away
in preparation for her wedding day
which for the following year was set.

And then her gentleman went away.
Yet pausing not, nay, with great care,
her white trousseau she did prepare,
while overcome with love she did stay.

But as the waiting time drew to an end,
after she had passed the entire year,
her sweet smile extending ear to ear,
illness laid her low, her body it did offend.

Yet even on her virginal bed of pain
she wiped away her mother's tear,
as she calmly awaited another more dear,
the one who her heart had gained.

And finally one sad Friday came, unplanned,
when finally her gentleman appeared.
He gazed into her eyes so clear;
he held her in his large, strong hands.

With a slight smile, near a state of grace,
she said, "Here I am, here is my arm."

And without fear she gave herself still warm
to the eternal chill of death's embrace.

(Long pause. CHARITY begins to cry disconsolately.)
CHARITY: Why is life so sad?
(HECTOR steps away from EMMA and opens his arms wide.)
HECTOR *(mockingly solemn):* Come, my belovèd, come to my arms!
(All look on with malice. But surprisingly, EMMA, in one dry and convulsive sob, nestles herself on HECTOR's chest. HECTOR, surprised and anguished, continues to stand with his arms straight out, like a cross. He then slowly brings them down around EMMA.)
MAN: Have you had enough, darling? Shall we go?
WOMAN *(laughing):* No, mon frère, not until the bitter end.
BLACKOUT.

SCENE FOURTEEN

Lights on full. Strident music.
EMCEE: Come on in, ladies and gents, come on in! Our marathon is still in progress, indefinitely. It's March of . . . ?
BOUNCER: 1932, sir![21]
EMCEE: No one's giving up. But the critical moment is drawing near. They're only bodies, after all! Come on in, ladies and gents! Tomorrow will be too late! Don't wait too long!
BLACKOUT.

SCENE FIFTEEN

An idle moment in the late afternoon. The EMCEE is on the platform, smoking and lost in his thoughts. CHARITY gives a sudden start.
CHARITY: What the . . . ? My watch stopped! What time is it?
(MR. X blinks his eyes at her, afraid.)
MR. X: I-I don't know, Charity . . .
CHARITY: Does anybody know what time it is?
(Brief pause. No one responds.)
Elephants! Nobody here knows what time it is?
EMCEE *(over the microphone):* It's 6:15, Charity.
CHARITY *(to MR. X, harshly):* Listen, you owe me for five.
MR. X: For five what?
CHARITY: Five hours, honey.
MR. X *(smoothly):* It hasn't been five hours, Charity.
CHARITY: What do you mean it hasn't been five hours? It's after six!

Mr. X: Yes, and you'll get paid at eight . . .

Charity: No, no. You don't understand. The other hours . . .

Mr. X *(pale):* What others?

Charity *(furious):* Five . . . the other five from before these that are up at seven!

(Mr. X is becoming desperate.)

Mr. X: At eight, Charity.

Charity: No, no. I'm not talking about these hours. I'm talking about the ones you already owe me for!

Mr. X *(trying to put a stop to the discussion):* Charity, I'm all paid up with you. I don't owe you anything.

(Charity vehemently moves away from Mr. X, but she continues to dance.)

Charity: What? You think I majored in bullshit? I'm here just for the hell of it? Because I like to dance? Did we have a deal, yes or no? Answer me!

(Mr. X is so angry that he cannot speak.)

So much money every five hours or a fraction thereof! Everything you win or think you might win or lose with me here, that thing about the prize, well, that's your business. You want to use me in this way instead of that? Fine, I don't get involved in your dealings. What I charge is time, whether I'm horizontal or vertical, it's services rendered. So my time's of some service to you? You think you can do something with it? Fine. But let's keep our accounts clean! That's all that's missing here, for you to exploit me! Just like you do those poor people who work in your factory! No, sir! My body is sacred! If you want to enjoy yourself . . . here I am, my legs are wide open, there's my pretty little hole, sir: But pay up!

(Mr. X, very upset, finally explodes. His voice is sharp, and he's stammering with fury.)

Mr. X: You! You . . . took advantage of me! You took advantage of my needs!

Charity: Really! Well, I'm not going to take advantage of my own needs? *(She takes a look around, with an air of satisfaction, seeking the others' approval.)* I'm not going to take advantage of *my own* needs! *(To Mr. X.)* We women don't have that kind of need, honey. It's men who impose it on us.

Mr. X *(confused, stomping):* No, no, no! It's you . . . ! Bloodsuckers!

Charity: How dare you!

Mr. X: You take advantage of a man when he's down! All of you! Usurers! You wait until he trips! A minor debt! A mountain! Ruin! What do you want? Huh? You want me to blow my brains out? *(Ferociously, really worked up because he's finally found the right words.)* Is that what you want? For me to blow my brains out?

Charity: As far as I'm concerned, you can blow whatever you like. If you feel like blowing your brains out, fine . . . But not at my expense!

MR. X *(exasperated, impotent)*: Bloodsucker! Bloodsucker!

EMCEE: Well, that's enough, Mr. X. Calm down. And as for you, Charity! Look at this man, he's a wreck. Show him a little bit of understanding, for God's sake.

CHARITY: Don't make me laugh. Understanding for who? For this . . . creature? I know him really well, mister. He's an old client. And if he's broke, it's his own fault. Because he's an idiot.

MR. X: It's not my fault! No, sir! I . . . was thrown by the death of my brother!

CHARITY: Who was the one who kept the business running.

MR. X: That's not true! *I* was the one who kept it all running! He was the one who made it fun, wild. He had the supporting role! I was the workhorse. He . . . was in charge of the financial part . . . He reeled in half the world. He knew how to . . . strike a balance. With him it was all in . . . fun. They were afraid of us. And he would always laugh! He needed me. We could communicate with just a look! And I . . . I loved him . . . so much . . .

CHARITY: How touching, but he left his widow without a cent.

MR. X *(as if he'd just been punched)*: Who told you that?

CHARITY: Who else? You, honey.

MR. X: They weren't married! She didn't have any rights! She was his mistress!

CHARITY: And so their two kids didn't have any right to his money either?

MR. X: She was his mistress! He . . . liked women . . . He was a Romeo!

CHARITY *(moving)*: Not even half a buck! Not even their house! That poor woman . . . with two kids . . . out on the street!

MR. X: There weren't any contracts! There wasn't anything! She wasn't family! Why should I give her anything? Did they ever give me anything? He always said, "You can't get rich on love." No one else ever spared anyone's life, so why should I have to? . . . Anyway, I . . . He's the one who died! He went and dumped it all on me! He could have played the generous one! *(He suddenly interrupts himself. Long pause.)* Sir, I'm not feeling so good. I want to go to the bathroom.

EMCEE: No.

MR. X: I want to . . . get out of here . . . I've got a loaded gun. Bang. Right through the brains. In the bathroom. *(He laughs.)* I'm not going to wait until the end. Did you want a pool of blood? Bang, right through the brains. *(He laughs.)*

EMCEE *(smooth, whispering into the microphone)*: The prize, Mr. X.

MR. X: A dark hole, a little blood. An empty head. The prize? Yes . . . It's a matter of time. Striking the right balance. Covering the hole.

CHARITY: That's fine, honey. But the only hole that matters to me is this one. You owe me two-fifty.[22]

Mr. X *(weakly):* You . . . I . . . don't owe you anything.
Charity: Is that your final word?
Mr. X: Yes.
Charity: Well, this is over with. *(She makes as if to leave.)* How do I get
out of here? *(She hesitatingly heads over to one side of the dance floor.
Pause.)*
Mr. X: Charity!
(She slowly turns around.)
Charity: What do you want?
(Mr. X takes out his billfold, his hand shaking.)
Mr. X: Keep dancing.
Blackout.

Scene Sixteen

Myth IV

*A cone of light shines down over Mr. X. Behind him, in the semidarkness,
the Dancers form an imprecise line. Mr. X, in his sleep, sings and dances a
fox-trot, his voice and movements disjointed. The dancers reproduce the
melody in off-key voices and imitate Mr. X's steps, but with the gestures of
exhausted puppets. A ghostly revue.*
Mr. X *(singing):*

> Believe me when I say I was a good man,
> I had the cleanest of intentions,
> I was an honest, good businessman.
> In good faith, made my great inventions.
>
> One day I dreamed that our land,
> Oh, America,
> was covered in a great steel band,
> Oh, America.
>
> Chimneys and petroleum,
> rivers of electricity,
> and mountains of tall ovens
> against the gray sky of industry.
>
> It was a dream of machines,
> Oh, America.

A dream of machines it was,
Oh, America.

Oh, then why did my dream fail?
Did luck run away from me?
Or was it all a big mistake
that left me behind to grieve?

One day I dreamt that the land,
Oh, America,
was covered in a great steel band,
Oh, America.

There's not left even a memory
of the world of my invention,
and so ends the short history
of this honest, good businessman.

It was a dream of machines,
Oh, my America.
A dream of machines it was,
Oh, my America.

BLACKOUT.

Scene Seventeen

EMMA is on the platform, in front of the microphone, a wild look in her eyes. The EMCEE is at her side. On the dance floor, the DANCERS continue to move, but they're indifferent, dull. The BOUNCER is holding HECTOR back.

EMMA: Sir, he keeps coming back out of the darkness. My little boy, sir. He's holding his little white hands out to me. And he's looking at me, with his dark, quiet eyes. He was with me! It's not a dream. He was alive . . . in a hole, in my arms . . . His heart beating . . .

HECTOR: That's enough, Emma . . .

EMMA: I held him . . . He was warm. Believe me, sir.

EMCEE: Yes, Emma.

EMMA: Two months, that's all. He was the only happiness I've ever known in this life . . . And it lasted . . . only two months! My little boy, sir! So warm . . . in my arms . . . so trusting. I couldn't! I couldn't hold on to him! He slipped away . . . just like air . . . His life, sir, it slipped away, as if he'd never . . . He was crying, sir, as if he was saying to me, "Don't leave me,

don't let go of me, don't let this strange thing . . . happen to me . . . !" He
was suffering, sir . . . And I would have ripped out even the last piece of my
own life with my fingernails so I could give it to him!
HECTOR: Emma!
EMMA: It's not fair, sir! It's just not fair! Two months! And I have to put up
with . . . all the rest? With this trash? No, sir! If it's true that there's something else . . . If it's true that after death . . . If anyone is going to judge me,
well, when they call me, sir, I'm going to spit in their face and say, how
dare you? I was alive for only two months! I'm not responsible for the rest!
I'm not to blame! Nobody has any right to accuse me of anything! I'm
innocent! Innocent! Innocent!
EMCEE: Thank you, Emma Moses, for that delicate and moving moment.
Yet more proof that here we don't hold anything back. Would someone
please escort the lady to the dance floor. And on with the dance, ladies and
gents, on with the dance!
BLACKOUT.

SCENE EIGHTEEN

Night. The degradation has achieved an almost unreal level.
HELEN: You make me sick.
HOMER: Helen, my dear friend, I didn't realize . . .
HELEN: You-make-me-sick! How can I get that through your head?
HOMER: Helen . . . I think you've reached the end of your rope and . . .
HELEN: You make me sick!
HOMER: Helen, this is . . . a stain upon our friendship . . .
HELEN *(completely hysterical):* You make me sick! You make me sick!
BLACKOUT.

SCENE NINETEEN

Only the EMCEE is clearly lit. Frenzied music.
EMCEE: Ladies and gents, ours is a curious world and our decade, sublime.
It is a decade of inventions. Penicillin, for example—well, not for you,
Vespucci, sorry—. That is, inventions of ways of not dying, and the best
ways to make it happen. Take Spain, for example.[23] Or Berlin, with the
little chancellor.[24] And in our own little southern corner of the universe, an
Australopithecus.[25] From Wall Street, a specter is haunting the world.[26] And
in 1933, here in Buenos Aires—the city without hope, Le Corbusier[27] called
it—a wave of suicides. Le Roi du Tango triumphs in Paris only later to
meet his most serious defeat in Colombia.[28] Mussolini in Abyssinia,[29] the
obelisk.[30] Joliot-Curie,[31] the Kid Cabeza.[32] And Guernica.[33] And a serrated

cross, waving on black banners, covers the sky.[34] And in Berlin, ein kleiner Kanzler![35]
BLACKOUT.

SCENE TWENTY

MYTH V

Following quickly on the previous scene, the lights come up on the dance floor, where the DANCERS have formed a closed circle.
ALL *(cutting off the EMCEE's last words):* Heil!
(All the DANCERS collapse as if struck by lightning. From the center of the circle, the BOUNCER emerges, holding up his revolver. The EMCEE is on the platform, playing solitaire and whistling the tune from the previous scene.)
BOUNCER *(moving among the dancers' bodies, like an elated sleepwalker):* Victory is order. This land is rotten. We have to cauterize her wounds. America rears her head, we must rein her in. I dream a dream of stillness, a vast cemetery. This territory that our race conquered four hundred years ago, are we going to give it up now to these masses that come from across the sea? To their half-breed accomplices? To this riffraff majority, this sad bunch of rabble-rousers from the big cities? It doesn't matter if right is on our side, the only thing that matters is winning. History is written by the victors. And execution must be brutal and indiscriminate. Anyone who's ever thought about bringing order to this world knows that it can only happen by the success of those who know best how to use their force.[36]
BLACKOUT.

SCENE TWENTY-ONE

MAN *(singing in the darkness):*

> "London Bridge is falling down,
> falling down, falling down.
> London Bridge is falling down,
> my fair lady . . ."

(A tango purrs over the loudspeakers. The exhaustion is complete. Long pause. We hear only the monotonous, maddening voice of VESPUCCI.)
VESPUCCI: No one wants to leave, eh? You keep biting, until you kill or are killed . . . Crows, you're waiting for your carcass . . . Just flying in circles above the weak, sick man . . . What're you looking at, eh? What're you waiting for? For me to fall, right? For me to die. No, I'm not going to give

you that pleasure. Even if I don't have any air or blood left in me. I'll keep on dancing, without my blood. *(He laughs quietly.)* Like a ghost.

EMMA *(bursting out):* Make him shut up! My God! He's driving me crazy!

ASUNCIÓN: Mind your own business, lady. Be still, Peter, you have to save your breath . . .

MAN: Ma sœur, let's get out of here.

WOMAN: Impossible, mon frère.

MAN: Mais pourquoi?[37]

WOMAN *(with a giggle):* Because we're trapped. Don't you see our bodies there, in front of us? They're dancing. And where would we go without our bodies?

(Brief pause.)

VESPUCCI: Dung flies . . . Nothing frightens you . . . You could be dying and you'd still go on, go on . . . You don't look around, you don't look back . . . don't look at the guy who's falling down, or the one in need or the one that's suffering . . . No, what does that matter to you? . . . You circle around, robbing, killing, going on . . .

(MR. X staggers over to VESPUCCI. He confronts him.)

MR. X: How dare you? You're the one here who's . . . making the air rotten. Taking space away from the living! You're a dead man! *(He slaps VESPUCCI in the face. There's a commotion among the DANCERS.)* You've got tuberculosis! You're a dead man!

VESPUCCI: Lice! Lice! *(Exasperated, VESPUCCI spits indiscriminately around him. CHARITY shrieks. An abrupt silence.)*

CHARITY *(paralyzed with terror):* He spit on me! He's got tuberculosis and . . . he spit on me! *(She tries to clean herself. She starts yelling again.)*

VESPUCCI: Lice, everywhere, lice! *(He continues to spit around him indiscriminately.)* The grave!

(Lots of cries and confusion. All the DANCERS are trying to save themselves.)

HELEN: Homer, what's the matter with you? Let go of me! Help, he's killing me!

(Silence. Everyone looks at HOMER. The old man looks mad, rigid, pale, his eyes staring, vacant; his hands are clinging to HELEN's arms, and she's yelling like a madwoman. Suddenly, HOMER collapses and almost drags HELEN down with him. She finally frees herself. Everyone else is motionless for a few seconds while HOMER lies on the floor, gently shaking. Everyone, paralyzed, has stopped dancing. HECTOR runs over to HOMER.)

HECTOR: Take it easy, old man. Are you alright?

HOMER: I need . . . words . . .

EMCEE: What's going on down there?

HECTOR: I don't know.

HOMER: Confession! *(He laughs.)* Give me some . . . words . . .

HECTOR: Calm down there, old guy.
(HOMER tries to stand up.)
HOMER: A new poem . . .

> And finally that sad Friday came, unplanned,
> and finally the Lord his Father appeared.
> He gazed into his eyes so clear,
> He held him in his large, strong hands.
>
> With a slight smile, near the state of grace,
> He said, "Here I am, this is my arm."
> And without fear he gave himself still warm
> to the eternal chill of death's embrace.

(He dies. Silence.)
EMCEE: Mr. Moses, could you please tell us what is going on down there?
HECTOR: I believe that . . .
(Pause.)
EMCEE: Yes?
HECTOR: I believe that . . . he's dead.
VESPUCCI: One down.
(Pause.)
EMCEE *(to HECTOR):* You're not sure?
HECTOR: No.
(The EMCEE signals to the BOUNCER, who goes over to HOMER. His verdict is quick, professional.)
BOUNCER: He's dead.
(A nervous movement among the DANCERS. Almost everyone goes over to the corpse. HELEN bursts out sobbing, in a release of tension.)
CHARITY: He recited the same poem as always! And he thought it was new!
(Indignant, almost in tears.) It's just not . . . fair!
HELEN *(between sobs):* His memory let him down . . . He didn't know any others.
EMCEE: Ladies and gents, this man has already won his prize.
HECTOR *(heatedly):* This was his prize?
EMCEE: Of course not. It's a metaphor. I mean that this man gave everything he had, he didn't back down . . . *(To the BOUNCER.)* Call an ambulance. And he gave us his very best, the last moments of his worthy existence. And that is his prize: the part of him that remains behind with us, in our eternal memory. This man lives! He lives on in his works! He lives on in us! He has not died!
CHARITY: You're right! Who doesn't remember his poem? "And finally that sad Friday came, unplanned . . ."

VESPUCCI: Friday? Why Friday? It could've been a Thursday or a Wednesday.
MR. X: Today's Friday?
CHARITY: Oh, shut up, idiot. It was a Friday and that's that. That sad Friday, I remember it perfectly, and her gentleman . . .
ASUNCIÓN: Her lord.
ANNA D.: *The* Lord.
CHARITY: A gentleman! It was a gentleman! Do you want to drive me crazy? Are you happy now? I've forgotten! Great! How did it go on? Hmmm? How did it go?
(Brief, tense silence.)
EMMA: Helen must surely remember!
HELEN: I . . .
VESPUCCI: Death was embracing him.
MR. X: Embraced him.
EMMA: He smiled.
ASUNCIÓN: There was something about hands.
CHARITY: Oh, God!
EMCEE: Ladies and gents, I beg you . . . We have to stay calm. We're confused, perplexed. Death has treacherously, savagely, claimed one of our own . . . We have to close ranks . . . Right now. We're a small community. And so we have to respond in an organized fashion to this challenge. We must take some concrete steps . . . Helen, will you take charge?
HELEN: What? No, no . . . I . . . Look, I'm an unmarried woman . . . It would compromise my . . . Anyway, I must be going . . . *(She looks at her hands as if they felt empty.)* I . . . it seems that I brought something . . . a purse . . . and a jacket . . .
EMCEE: Yes, they're at the coat check.
HELEN: Oh, thank you. *(She leaves.)*
EMCEE: Please, if you would be so kind . . . I don't think this should be part of the show . . . Under the platform you'll find a sheet.
(HECTOR goes to look. When he returns with the sheet, VESPUCCI takes it out of his hands.)
VESPUCCI: Let me have it . . .
(ASUNCIÓN intervenes.)
ASUNCIÓN: No, give it to me . . .
VESPUCCI *(furious, he rips the sheet away from her and stammers)*: No . . . I want to be the one . . . *(He kneels and slowly, almost lovingly, covers HOMER's corpse with the sheet.)*
EMCEE: Now, if you would be so kind . . . a couple of volunteers . . . could you move him next to the platform?
(VESPUCCI and HECTOR volunteer to perform the task. ASUNCIÓN, in distress, tries to move her husband away.)

ASUNCIÓN: You're going to hurt yourself!

(*VESPUCCI, in desperation, hits ASUNCIÓN and with a shove pushes her away. They carry the corpse to one side of the platform. HELEN returns with her jacket over her shoulders, carrying her handbag.*)

HELEN: Well, there's nothing left for me to do here . . . May I say good-bye?

EMCEE: Yes, of course.

HELEN: Well, good-bye, everyone. It's a pity that so much effort . . . well, it's always the same thing . . . I'm so tired . . . (*She goes around shaking hands good-bye.*)

ASUNCIÓN: My condolences.

HELEN: It's alright. Thank you. Sorry for the bother.

SOME DANCERS: Good-bye.

HELEN: Where's the exit?

BOUNCER: This way. Come, I'll escort you out.

HELEN: No, no, never mind . . . I've figured it out . . . It's just that I'm a bit dizzy. (*She teeters at the dance floor's edge as if she were about to faint. Pause. Distressed.*) Can I rest here a little before I leave? (*HELEN stays and will participate in all the action that follows.*)

EMCEE: What is man, ladies and gents? The memory of himself. A dead man is a memory forever sealed off from the curiosity of the rest. A dead man is a fleeting show. Let us then give a last glance at this memory that no longer belongs to us; and then return this cold disguise of the intangible back to the universe whence it came. For reasons beyond their control, this couple is now disqualified. You, survivors, keep dancing.

(*The DANCERS return to dancing. Slowly we become aware that TOM MIX is no longer dancing. He has remained motionless, lost in himself. In front of him, ANNA D. looks at him, uncomprehending but waiting obediently. The BOUNCER consults with the EMCEE, speaking in hushed tones.*)

EMCEE (*smoothly*): What's the matter, son? Why aren't you dancing? You're losing your place . . .

(*The BOUNCER goes over to TOM MIX. He slaps him on the back.*)

BOUNCER: Come on, kid, you've gotta dance . . .

EMCEE: Young Tom Mix, I can understand your feelings, but I'm obligated to tell you that your time is being docked.

BOUNCER: Don't be a fool, what do you gain by being so bullheaded? Look, everyone else is dancing, but you . . .

EMCEE: Listen, Tom Mix . . . I'm very sorry, but I'm going to give you one more minute to change your attitude, and that's it. If you don't, my friend, your partner will be disqualified.

(*The BOUNCER pushes TOM MIX.*)

BOUNCER: Move it, kid . . .

(*HECTOR unexpectedly goes over to the record player, takes off the record, and breaks it. Rapidly the* BOUNCER *turns toward him, pointing his revolver.* HECTOR *raises his hands. There's some scurrying and women's cries.)*

EMCEE *(to the* BOUNCER*):* Don't move! *(Tense pause. Then mildly.)* Mr. Moses, why did you do that?

HECTOR *(his hands still raised high):* Sir . . . he could still shoot me.

EMCEE *(with a condescending giggle):* Alright. Lower your weapon.

(The BOUNCER *does so, but he does not put the gun away.)*

EMCEE: Is that better, Mr. Moses?

HECTOR: Yes.

EMCEE: Now could you explain yourself?

HECTOR: Yes, sir . . . It was a stupid mistake. This kid . . . I want to know what's going on with him, that's all.

EMCEE: Well, it wasn't necessary to be so extreme. Ask him.

HECTOR: Can I?

EMCEE: Of course.

(Brief pause.)

HECTOR *(TO* TOM MIX*):* Son . . .

(Pause.)

TOM MIX: What am I doing here . . . dancing . . . on enemy soil? What am I doing . . . in this place? Lost among all of you . . . and all of you lost . . . Scratching . . . scratching the earth with our nails . . . Scratching out a hole where we can lie down and rest . . . Finally, rest . . . in this foreign land . . . What am I doing here? Outside myself? If there's another place. Every night, in my dreams . . . An endless beach. There are children . . . immortal . . . They're running naked through the water and laughing . . . beautiful, free . . . That's life . . .

(Pause.)

EMMA *(bursting out sobbing):* There's my son . . . he's coming from over there . . . every night, he comes . . . And I'm not afraid!

(Pause.)

EMCEE: Satisfied, Mr. Moses? What did you accomplish? You paralyzed the herd . . . When our purpose here is exactly the opposite. We want to maintain the momentum.

HECTOR: But didn't you . . .

EMCEE: What?

HECTOR: What he said . . .

EMCEE: It doesn't move me. Every man has dreamt of immortality. Mr. Moses, this is our world, it's not perfect, but it took great effort to build. Let's keep it going.

HECTOR: Keep this world going? Why?

EMCEE: Do you know any others?

HECTOR: No.

EMCEE: Well, then?

HECTOR: But it's possible, isn't it?

EMCEE: And how would it be different?

HECTOR: It would be . . . right, fair, just.

EMCEE: Mr. Moses, look around you . . . Do you think justice matters one bit to these desperate beings? These voracious, starving creatures, besieged by death? These animals in flight? Justice, in the middle of panic? If we could remove death from men's hearts—but then they wouldn't be what they are—yes, in that case, it would be easy to imagine a just world . . .

HECTOR: So for you, there aren't any just men?

EMCEE: Yes, the victims. We could say that the victimized are certainly more just than their victimizers. Someone once said that it's preferable to suffer an injustice than to commit it. So you see, if the only way of being just is to suffer injustice, then justice is only a form of passivity.

HECTOR *(stubbornly):* No, justice is possible.

EMCEE: You have the gift of obstinacy.

HECTOR: And what else is left to us, sir? Maybe justice is nothing more than a form of blind obstinacy.

EMCEE: Maybe . . . But this has gotten a bit too talky, and people came here to see a show. Ladies and gents, down to business. Shall we continue dancing?

HECTOR: Sir?

EMCEE: Yes?

(Brief pause.)

HECTOR: What's the prize?

(Brief pause.)

EMCEE *(mildly):* Mr. Moses, there are rules to the game. You accepted those rules. By your presence here at this very moment, you're accepting them.

HECTOR: Rules can be changed.

EMCEE: Not during this game.

HECTOR: Who made them up?

EMCEE: I did. And understand, sir, that while you're here, I'm the one who dictates the rules. And if you don't want to accept them, you run the risk of being disqualified. In that case, yes, sir, we would be equal, because then I wouldn't have any power over you, but you wouldn't have anything to do with me or with this, nor would you receive any prize, of course. I am no one and everyone. In a certain way, I don't even exist; one might say I'm inside you. I possess you because you possess me. It's your own desire that gives me my power. From this side, I'm everything to you; from the other side, I'm just some vague dream. Those are the terms of our alliance.

(Pause.)

HECTOR: All I want to know is, is there even a prize?

EMCEE: Mr. Vespucci, why are you dancing?

VESPUCCI: I want to . . . pay off the mortgage on my house.

EMCEE: And you, Mr. X?

MR. X: I want to . . . save myself from bankruptcy.

EMCEE *(to HECTOR):* So you see, the prize does exist.

HECTOR: I want to know if there's a *real* prize!

EMCEE: Mr. Moses, you must accept the conventions!

HECTOR: That man is dead! Is that a convention?

EMCEE: That is outside my jurisdiction!

HECTOR: So you're saying that . . . that all of this could be a trick, an illusion?

EMCEE: Decide for yourself. *(Brief pause.)* Those of you who wish to remain in our marathon, please keep dancing. Those who do not will be disqualified.

(Tense pause. Suddenly, the following actions take place in rapid succession: Young TOM MIX throws himself onto the BOUNCER and takes his revolver from him. VESPUCCI then pounces on TOM MIX and knocks the revolver out of his hand. In the middle of confused cries, VESPUCCI runs to the edge of the dance floor, hesitates for an instant, and then, as if not knowing what else to do with the weapon, raises it to his own head. ASUNCIÓN cries out, runs over to her husband, and attempts to take the revolver away from him. There's a struggle and then the sound of one shot. The BOUNCER falls to his knees.)

VESPUCCI: I want to die! I want to die!

BOUNCER: I didn't have anything to do with this! I was just following orders! That's my job! It's a paying job! I have a family! Children! I didn't know anything! Please, believe me . . . I'm . . . completely innocent . . .

(But no one's paying any attention to the BOUNCER, still on his knees, whimpering. All the DANCERS, in a mad rush, hurl themselves toward the platform, crying out "Thief!" "Swindler!" etc. The EMCEE barely has time to exclaim.)

EMCEE: You mob of lunatics! This is a show, a device, a game!

(The DANCERS all climb up onto the platform; there's great confusion. They encircle the EMCEE and begin to hit him, spit on him, and knock him around; finally they push him down to the dance floor. They remove his jacket and rub off his makeup. This happens very quickly and confusedly. The EMCEE tries to run away, but he falls down at the dance floor's edge. His appearance is pathetic: his hair a mess, his makeup running, his shirt torn off of him [he's left with only his shirtfront and cuffs], his undershirt ripped, a shoe missing, and one of his socks is ruined. Once the EMCEE is down, the BOUNCER springs on top of him. He's holding his revolver again.)

BOUNCER *(worked up):* Let's kill him! Like a dog!

(The BOUNCER savagely grabs the EMCEE by his hair and points the revolver to his temple. When the DANCERS see this, they freeze where they are, behind the EMCEE and the BOUNCER. A "click" is heard. The BOUNCER looks at his gun.) Did it go off?

(The EMCEE is left on the floor, curled up in a ball. It's impossible to tell if his convulsions are produced by laughter or sobbing. Silence.)

EMCEE: Murderers . . . mob of lunatics . . . I'm a human being . . . *(He sits up on the floor, complaining and crying. The DANCERS and the BOUNCER look on in silence, stupefied.)* What do you want? Blood? To destroy me? Kicking me like I'm a dog . . . a rabid dog? *(He whimpers.)* You've ruined my jacket . . . and it was the only one I had . . . Cowards . . . A defenseless man . . . So you like to tear up the other guy's hide, huh? You wanted to see what I'm made of? . . . Beat, rip, smash. Murderers . . . Go ahead, shoot me . . . Don't make a martyr of me . . . Who am I anyway? Who do you think I am? You think I'm going to get rich off of you bunch? Fools! How much do you think it's worth to have you here destroying me so that they can laugh at you! Less than for some chimpanzees in a zoo, morons! A couple of pennies, that's what it's worth, a couple of filthy pennies, barely enough to pay for some grimy room in a cheap boardinghouse! *(He whimpers.)* And on top of that, you ruined my jacket . . . so go ahead, shoot me! I'd be much obliged! *(He moans in pain.)* What trash! Yeah, I'm a thief . . . as if you had anything for me to steal . . . ! Thief of miseries . . . That's right: I've made a fortune in miseries . . . So you want to know what my life's like? Who's the loneliest, the sickest, the poorest . . . ? *(He laughs.)* The prize! Yes, ladies and gents . . . Sure, why not, my pleasure . . . I'll tell you what the prize is . . .

(VESPUCCI pounces on him and gives him a ferocious kick.)

VESPUCCI: Shut up!

(HECTOR struggles with VESPUCCI.)

HECTOR: Enough!

VESPUCCI: He just wants to keep it all for himself! Starving piece of crap!

(In the meantime, MR. X slaps the EMCEE.)

MR. X: The prize! Where's the prize?

(TOM MIX separates MR. X from the EMCEE.)

TOM MIX: Let him . . . ! Let him speak!

(MR. X, furious, confronts TOM MIX.)

MR. X: There's nothing more to know here! We're here to win! That's all! Each one of us knows exactly what we need to know! What we can win and what we can lose! I'm not here slogging away just so some snot-nosed kid can tell me what I need to know!

TOM MIX *(so angry he's stuttering)*: You . . . coward! You fat old pig!

CHARITY: Hey, kid, a little respect for your elders!

TOM MIX: You're a bunch of worn-out bodies! Rotten flesh!
(A wall of protest goes up around TOM MIX. The BOUNCER overpowers him.)
BOUNCER: Put a lid on it, son, okay?
TOM MIX *(extremely violent):* Take your hands off me, you sack of shit!
BOUNCER: So now the gloves come off, yeah? Now the gloves are off.
(TOM MIX spits on him. The BOUNCER coldly raises his revolver and points it to TOM MIX's head, his arm stretched out straight.)
TOM MIX: Go ahead! Go ahead and shoot me, you son of a bitch!
(An instant of silence. The music unexpectedly starts to play: the MAN has put on a record.)
MAN: Please, s'il vous plaît . . . Time marches on. And my sister has a migraine. Let's get this over with, shall we? Ma sœur . . .
(The MAN and the WOMAN begin to dance. VESPUCCI also begins to move, automatically.)
VESPUCCI *(delirious):* What is a man without his house, his wife, his kids . . . ? If I lose my house, where am I going to store this body, eh? I'm not a bum . . . I'm a man . . .
MR. X: Shall we dance, Charity?
CHARITY *(laughing):* I'm just a girl who can't say no. You owe me five more hours . . .
(MR. X, resigned, sighs.)
MR. X: Already? *(He takes out his billfold and pays her.)*
HELEN: Well, I guess it's time . . .
(Contrary to what her words might suggest, HELEN continues to move around the dance floor. In the meantime, the BOUNCER is still pointing his gun at TOM MIX. Each looks at the other, tense, motionless. HECTOR, EMMA, and ANNA D., all three paralyzed, are watching the two men. The EMCEE, still on the floor, tries to readjust his clothing.)
EMCEE: Someone give me a hand here, please.
(Brief pause. The previously described scene continues; no one moves. Finally.)
BOUNCER: Bang. *(He laughs and puts his revolver away. He goes over to help the EMCEE.)* Are you alright, sir?
(The BOUNCER escorts the EMCEE over to the platform. The BOUNCER is obedient. He brushes off the EMCEE's clothing, etc. Pause. TOM MIX appears to have shattered inside. He laughs convulsively as tears run down his face. Then, on an impulse, he heads toward the exit. ANNA D. follows him. Before he leaves, TOM MIX stops and turns toward HECTOR. Brief pause. They look at each other.)
TOM MIX: Hector . . . are you going to stay?
(HECTOR looks at EMMA.)
HECTOR: Emma?

(HECTOR and TOM MIX look at EMMA, who returns their gaze as if she were waking from a dream. Imperceptibly, automatically, she begins to dance.)

EMMA: Me? *(Pause.)* There are so many things . . . that I never had . . . I always . . . was taking care of everybody else. I want to have servants! I've . . . never been out of this dirty, filthy city . . . I want to see the ocean! I want to see islands! I want to . . . feel a mink coat against my skin! I want to go to California, Bengal! *(Brief pause.)* No. I'm staying.

(EMMA dances. HECTOR, without taking his eyes off TOM MIX, begins to move as well.)

HECTOR *(to TOM MIX):* You see . . .

TOM MIX: Good-bye.

HECTOR: Hold on, why're you going?

TOM MIX: Because I'm dying . . . of a broken heart. And you, why're you staying?

HECTOR *(laughing):* I must like to suffer . . . Now who'd say that I . . . don't love this poor unlucky woman.

(TOM MIX begins to go.)

Young Tom Mix! Don't judge us too harshly . . . Your dream someday just might . . .

(TOM MIX is by now very close to the door.)

TOM MIX *(laughing):* Let me know if that day ever comes! And if I'm already dead, bring me back to life! Even if that's all it is: because I've dreamt it so many times . . .

(He leaves with ANNA D. following behind).

EMCEE *(once again behind the microphone):* Ladies and gentlemen, I'm pleased to see that the dance is still going on. Our marathon has survived a minor crisis. It will soon be forgotten. Growing pains, perhaps. Happens in every living body. Of course, we lost a few on the way. But when, under what circumstances, is there never at least someone lost on the way? What's important is for everything to continue. Keep the big picture going, keep the flow going. On with the show. *(Changing his tone, he speaks to the audience.)* Come on in, ladies and gents, take a look at our heroes. How long have they been dancing? They've already lost track . . . Blindly they head toward the end, toward the thrill of victory or the agony of defeat. Ladies and gents, who among us understands human beings? They stir, they move, they die . . . They ferociously destroy themselves . . . and then they're reborn, reborn like mayflies. Yet nevertheless, in the life-and-death struggle against indifference and oblivion, they construct their fragile works, preparing themselves for all eternity. Ladies and gents, if this weren't so ridiculous, it would be a tragedy. On with the dance, ladies and gentlemen, on with the dance![38]

The music grows louder. BLACKOUT.

Translator's Notes

1. In the original text, the poet Homero Estrella is from Almagro, a working-class neighborhood of Buenos Aires.

2. The play constantly focuses our attention on historic dates but just as constantly omits, or falsifies, important details surrounding said dates. Here the text alludes to the date of the first founding of Buenos Aires, in 1536, by the Spanish conquistador Pedro de Mendoza. The author's notes credit the information presented in this scene to Enrique de Gandía's contemporary biography of Mendoza.

3. Latin: "Take care of us, our Lord. Shelter us under your wings."

4. In the original text, they are the mythical "islas de la Bienaventuranza."

5. A milonga is a musical composition as well as a dance in simple 2/4 time; it has a lively and clear rhythm.

6. The original text alludes to the year 1810, when Buenos Aires (in the name of Ferdinand VII) declared its independence from the Cádiz government in Spain. Argentines consider 25 May 1810 to be their Independence Day.

7. According to the original text's "author's note," Tom Mix's "revolutionary" speech is based on the writings of Manuel Moreno (1781–1857), the brother and biographer of the Argentine patriot Mariano Moreno.

8. The song evokes the early gaucho poems of Bartolomé Hidalgo (1788–1822), whose "cielos"—so classified because of their repetition of the chorus "cielo, cielito, cielo"— are identified with Argentina's independence struggle. "Sky, little sky, I tell you, / distant sky, celestial blue. / If in this life I can't be free, / let my noble death unfetter me."

9. The lines spoken by Anna D., Asunción, Homer, and Mr. X do not appear in this scene's original text. They have been added by the author to a newly revised version.

10. Latin, "Glory to the artist."

11. In the original text, it is *La Nación,* perhaps Argentina's most powerful daily newspaper, founded in 1870 by Bartolomé Mitre. Its Sunday literary supplement is widely respected and distributed.

12. Matthew 10:16.

13. French, "My sister" . . . "they're waiting for us."

14. French, "My brother."

15. French, "And there it is."

16. French, "I don't know."

17. French, "I beg of you."

18. The scene that follows (and especially the Man's description) appears to have been inspired by the Argentinean poet, essayist, and fiction writer Esteban Echeverría (1805– 51) and his short story "El matadero" [The slaughterhouse], most likely written in 1838. Echeverría makes his opposition to the dictatorship of General Juan Manuel de Rosas violently clear in his quasi-fictional allegory. Angel Flores's English translation of the Argentine story may be found in *The Borzoi Anthology of Latin American Literature,* edited by Emir Rodríguez Monegal (New York: Knopf, 1977).

19. Latin, "The dread of emptiness."

20. In the original text, the Man says, "¡Gloria a Tellier y al 'chilled beef'!" Charles Tellier was the French engineer who adapted the principle of refrigeration for shipping. In 1877 refrigerated meat was first shipped from the Southern Cone to Europe.

21. Remember that, in the first scene, the Emcee and the Bouncer give the date as 23 June 1932. Time appears to be receding.

22. In the original text, Pipa (Charity) demands to be paid four pesos. This is about

$US2.50, based on the 1932 exchange rate of 1.00 U.S. dollar to 1.71 Argentinean gold pesos but rounded up from $2.34.

23. The text refers to the military dictatorship of Miguel Primo de Rivera from 1923 until early 1930. Primo de Rivera's nationalistic concept of *hispanidad* set the stage for Franco's fascism.

24. The reference is to Adolph Hitler.

25. Latin, lit. "Southern ape." It is a reference to the Argentine general José Félix Uriburu, who headed a coup in September 1930. This was the first of the army-led coups in twentieth-century Argentina, and thus the derisive term can be applied to all leaders of Argentine military dictatorships.

26. Wall Street "fell" in 1929; the U.S. stock market crash preceded a global economic crisis that gravely affected Argentina.

27. The renowned French architect Charles Eduard Jeanneret (known as Le Corbusier) visited Argentina in 1929.

28. The "King of Tango" was the singer Carlos Gardel, who died in a plane accident in Medellín, Colombia, in 1935.

29. The Italian fascist dictator Benito Mussolini invaded Abyssinia in 1934.

30. The obelisk, perhaps Buenos Aires's best-known physical landmark, was inaugurated in 1936.

31. Irène Curie (daughter of Marie and Pierre Curie) and her husband Frédéric Joliot discovered artificial radioactivity in 1934; they won the Nobel Prize for Physics the following year.

32. The infamous Argentine bandit "El Pibe Cabeza" was killed in a shoot-out with the police in 1937.

33. The Emcee refers to Guernica, the northern Spanish city destroyed by the Nationalists in 1937 during the Spanish Civil War. That same year it would become the subject of one of Pablo Picasso's most famous paintings.

34. The reference is to the Nazi swastika.

35. German, "A little chancellor."

36. According to the author's notes in the published text, these lines were inspired by the writings of Leopoldo Lugones (1874–1938), the Argentinean *modernista* poet and prose writer, whose racist interpretation of social Darwinism was not atypical of certain early-twentieth-century Latin American intellectuals.

37. French, "But why?"

38. According to the original play-text's "author's note," certain passages from this scene refer to the works of Vladimir Mayakovsky (1893–1930), the Russian poet and playwright known as "the very embodiment of the Revolution." Although the passages are not specified, Tom Mix's final words recall the character Mayakovsky's monologue that concludes the Russian dramatist's *Vladimir Mayakovsky, A Tragedy*; and the Emcee's final comments are not unlike the Director's remarks regarding the "insect" Prisypkin in Mayakovsky's best-known play, *The Bedbug*.

The Beaded Curtain

La cortina de abalorios premiered in September 1981 in the Teatro del Picadero as part of the Teatro Abierto festival.

Original Cast

Mozo [Servant]	Patricio Contreras
Mamá [Mama]	Cipe Lincovsky
Pezuela	Juan Manuel Tenuta
Popham	Miguel Guerberof
Costumes	Mené Arnó
Music	Rodolfo Mederos
Set Design	Jorge Sarudiansky
Assistant Direction	Carlos Sturze
Direction	Juan Cosín

ONE ACT

A ghostly and dusty brothel from the late nineteenth century. Upstage, a beaded curtain. Tables covered in moth-eaten cloths, rickety Viennese chairs. A large freestanding mirror, with an oval frame. A cow's skull.

Collapsed on one of the chairs, the Servant *sleeps. He's a small, sad, tense figure. His serving tray begins to slide off his lap. Just as the tray is about to fall off, he grabs it back, without waking up, ever alert even when sleeping.* Mama *pulls the curtain back abruptly. She is an aged, large madam. Her makeup-caked face suggests a sinister mask.*

Mama: Aha, so you're here! You lazy good-for-rien! Allez! *(She gives the* Servant *a blow to the head and then quickly goes over to the mirror. She carefully studies her face, her wrinkles, while continuing to give the* Servant *orders. Madam's blow brings the* Servant *to his feet in one jump, and he moves around in an automatic and senseless fashion, his eyes wide open.)*

185

Our master's coming! Qu'est que tu fait? Look at the mirror. Tout filthy!
This is a high-class whorehouse! Des boires! Lumière! Le master vient!
Ne comprends pas! Well, c'est assez! I told you to assez, imbecile, enough.
(The SERVANT stops abruptly, as if some internal mechanism suddenly broke.)
Why do I even bother to speak to you in French if you don't understand a
damn word? *(She collapses onto a chair.)* Absinthe! *(The SERVANT disappears quickly behind the curtain. Brief pause.)* Whatever will I do here,
mon Dieu . . . In this sordid place, a place je deteste . . . Among uncouth
barbarians . . . Stuck in these plains *(She scratches her head.)* devoured by
lice . . . This desert that smells like shit . . . Oh, how tedious, mon Dieu!
*(She throws a furtive glance at the mirror. Brief, languid pause. Studying
her gestures in the mirror, MAMA takes out a long cigarette holder and cigarette from her décolletage. The SERVANT quickly appears from behind the
curtain. He's carrying a tray with a bottle and a goblet. MAMA points to the
cigarette.)* Feu! *(The SERVANT leaves his tray on the table and lights the
cigarette. MAMA inhales deeply. The SERVANT begins to serve her a drink,
but the bottle is obviously empty. Despite all his efforts, he manages to get
out only a single drop. MAMA looks at him with growing annoyance until
she finally grabs the goblet in an explosion of impatience. She avidly swallows the droplet and licks the glass; she is not satisfied. She studies her
dissatisfaction in the mirror.)* "The flesh is sad, Alas! and I've read all the
books."[1] *(Brief pause. She holds the goblet out to the SERVANT.)* Mallarmé.
(The SERVANT once more tries to fill the glass.) Empty! Devoured! I who
have seen my petits pieds embalmed in satin slipping across the marble's
opaque brilliance . . . Suspended in the light tumult of sighs . . . My excited
white breasts, fluttering in the salons . . . *(Abrupt transition.)* Run down by
dogs! Yes, run down by dogs! Their teeth bared at me! In the middle of the
night! *(Pathetically, to the SERVANT.)* The bowwows, comprenez-vous? A
fugitive of the French Revolution! Émigrée! *(Like a tragic curse.)* Merde!
I, who on the best stages of Europe have chiseled out the sonorous lines of
Cor . . . *(She vacillates.)* of Cor . . . Cor . . . Corkspeare! *(She makes an
imperative, imperial gesture to the SERVANT.)* À genoux! *(The SERVANT slowly
falls on his knees.)* I am going to reveal to you my true identity . . . *(She
spreads her legs and points to her crotch.)* Do you know what this is?
(Brief pause.) A museum. Let's call it a museum of the imagination . . .
Observe carefully, not just anyone looks at himself in this mirror. Here you
could thumb through the most brilliant pages of world history . . . You're
standing before an open book . . . Here is the substance . . . Le tout . . .
The absolute . . . Do I make myself clear? Another example: a stage. The
folds of the curtain separate, the protagonists leap onto the stage, a pirou-
ette, they disappear into the shadows, curtain; the folds draw back once
again, and so on, forever . . . Do I make myself clear? A blink of the eye,

poof, good Richelieu appears; another blink, poof, all the Louis, the First, the Second, the Third . . . poof! Do you get it now? *(Pause. She studies the* SERVANT'*s expressionless face. She concludes.)* No. *(Abrupt transition.)* I have inspired the great! Le plus grandes de l'Histoire! And you are too, too small to be there, in front of me, enjoying the privilege of looking at me . . . Eyes down! *(The* SERVANT *obeys.)* Lesson Two, come here . . . *(The* SERVANT *attempts to stand up.)* On your knees! *(The* SERVANT *attempts to move closer, on his knees.)* There! *(Pause. She looks at him, panting.)* Do you know what shines deep down inside? A diamond . . . Not a common diamond, non. You would not be able to look at it, half-breed, because it would burn your eyes. After that there's nothing left. La vie eternelle . . . Everything you've ever desired, infinite pleasure . . . *(Brief pause. By thumping the* SERVANT *on the chin,* MAMA *forces him to raise his head. She looks at him with curiosity.)* Aren't you ever going to say anything? Not even when I order you to? I order you to desire me, damn it! *(Pause.)* And what if I were to kill you? *(She reaches out to his neck with her scrawny, white, twitching hands, fingers covered in rings, her nails pointed, long, painted. A ferocious grimace disfigures her face. She whispers.)* Swarthy flesh, it would be so easy for me to split you . . . *(She smoothly draws her finger across the* SERVANT'*s neck. She pants.)* Would you let me? *(Brief pause. She grabs him by the hair.)* Oh, tu m'enerves! *(Her free hand goes over to the* SERVANT'*s face.)* With the point of your tongue, the tips of my fingers! *(He brushes the point of his tongue across her fingertips. As soon as he's done so, she slaps his face.)* Assez! *(She wipes off her fingertips.)* You're damp, disgusting, damp and hot! How disgusting! If I could die, I would . . . *(Pause. Panting.)* Would you lick me? *(She shivers in disgust at the mere thought.)* Oh, how can I . . . Regarde moi! Who are you? There you are, dreaming flesh, waiting . . . waiting for what? What do you desire? Regarde moi! I don't exist, do I? I'm dead. And you knew it, you dog! That's why you're here, unafraid? Full? Regarde moi! My face, now! My eyes! They're empty, aren't they? My wrinkles! My veins! They're dried up, aren't they? And don't look at me like that! Don't look at me like that! *(Brief pause. Break.)* Lesson Three, what is this? *(With a slow, contained fury, she places the heel of her shoe on the* SERVANT'*s face. After a brief pause, she drives it in with a sharp blow. The* SERVANT *falls backward.* MAMA *appears to have achieved some sudden relief.)* That's the way it is, my child, heaven becomes hell. That's who I am. *(She gets up, indifferent.)* Did I hurt you? *(The* SERVANT'*s face is bloody.)* Well, well, he turned out to be something of a wimp . . . Let's have a look . . . *(She takes a handkerchief out her décolletage and climbs on top of the* SERVANT'*s body as if he were a horse.)* Stay still . . . Am I heavy? *(With a point of the handkerchief, she barely touches the blood. She suddenly looks at the handkerchief with attention,*

she sniffs it, she tastes it.) Yes, it's blood . . . But, my dear, it wasn't that big of a deal!
(MAMA plays at reining in the SERVANT's limp body. She tickles him. Finally, she begins to undo his pants.)
PEZUELA *(from offstage):* Hail, Mary, full of grace!
MAMA *(letting out a cry and bringing a hand to her mouth):* Ah, mon mari! *(Responding automatically, in a falsetto voice.)* Conceived without sin! *(She gets up and gives the SERVANT a swift kick.)* Your boss is here!
(The SERVANT pulls himself together quickly. PEZUELA enters. He is wearing a soaking wet jacket; his muddy boots bear the stains of dried blood. MAMA goes over to him, smiling, with both arms extended toward him, with all the dignity of a great lady.)
MAMA: Mon cher ami! Is it raining outside?
PEZUELA: Blood.
(PEZUELA does not respond to MAMA's reception; instead, he goes over to the mirror.)
MAMA: Out butchering?
PEZUELA: Indians.
(He takes from his jacket an object wrapped in a handkerchief and throws it at MAMA. MAMA catches the bundle in midair and looks at it.)
MAMA: Erect?
PEZUELA: Rigor mortis.
(MAMA hides the object away in her décolletage.)
PEZUELA *(dryly, to the SERVANT):* My boots. *(He collapses into a chair. The SERVANT races over to his feet and begins to take off his boots. PEZUELA to MAMA, with a wink.)* You should have been there.
MAMA: Ah, non, je m'excuse. Those emotions are too strong for a lady.
(PEZUELA lifts up the SERVANT's head with his foot.)
PEZUELA *(referring to the blood on the SERVANT's face):* What's this? Rouge stains?
MAMA *(nervously):* A drink, mon cher ami?
PEZUELA: Thank you, Mama. *(He bends over suddenly and sniffs at the SERVANT.)* Does this man use perfume?
MAMA *(bringing a goblet over to him):* How can you even think that, mon cher ami? It must be me.
(She bends over him, suggestively, her robe slightly open.)
PEZUELA: There's nothing like the smell of the country, my darling; the city makes one queasy.
MAMA: Relax and let your cares go, my friend, rest your head back here between my breasts. You've had a long day.
PEZUELA: Thank you.

MAMA *(with PEZUELA's hair so near her nose, she can't resist sniffing it):* Pomade? *(She looks at her posture in the mirror.)*
(PEZUELA hands the goblet over to the SERVANT.)
PEZUELA: I don't like this. Gin.
(MAMA snaps her fingers. The SERVANT leaves in a flash. PEZUELA spins MAMA quickly around and seats her on his knees.)
PEZUELA: I need your help, Mama.
MAMA: But, Bébé, it's not the end of the month yet . . . Anyway, the clients always barter. Il n'y a pas d'argent!
PEZUELA: I'm not asking you for money. Do you know the Englishman?
MAMA: Oh, what disagreeable people!
(PEZUELA gestures that they have money.)
PEZUELA: Pounds.
MAMA *(fully aware of the situation):* Hmm. *(Reacting to the SERVANT, who enters.)* En garde, mon ami!
(MAMA quickly gets up, as if trying to dissemble, and goes over to the mirror. PEZUELA collapses back into his chair. The SERVANT has a bottle of gin and a glass. He begins to pour the drink, but, no matter how hard he tries, only a single drop comes out.)
PEZUELA *(in the meantime, to MAMA):* There's no way you can imagine the spectacle of it all. You have to feel the cold air, at a gallop . . . So much dust is stirred up that you think it's night . . . the ground shudders . . . and in the darkness, in the middle of the tumult, the yelling and the neighing, you begin to understand what hell is like. *(Pause. PEZUELA looks silently at the SERVANT, who hands him the glass. PEZUELA suddenly yells out.)* The least you could do is button your fly, animal!
(The SERVANT makes a valiant effort to button his fly, with his one free hand.)
PEZUELA *(to MAMA):* Do you know how many leagues I've traveled this month? *(Without any transition.)* Please forgive the indiscretion, madam, but, has this man taken advantage of your good will?
MAMA *(affectedly prudish):* I'm quite afraid that he has, mon cher ami.
PEZUELA *(while standing up, mundane):* Do you know how it feels, madam, to have the land we walk on be ours? I mean to say, when we ride over the land all the way to the horizon, it's ours. It makes one drunk, madam. Something like immortality . . .
(During his speech, PEZUELA has very delicately taken the glass the SERVANT was holding out to him. And after speaking, with a lightning-speed move, he takes a knife from his side and stabs the SERVANT. After one moment of immobility and surprise, the SERVANT leans forward and grabs the knife, holding on to it with a blind fury. PEZUELA is forced to make a great effort to withdraw the blade, taking care at the same time not to spill the contents of

the glass he still has in his other hand. Finally, the SERVANT *staggers and falls.* PEZUELA *is left with the bloody knife in his hand.)*

PEZUELA *(his face still tense from the fight, worn-out):* Rough . . . *(He drinks avidly.)*

MAMA *(with a tone of amiable reproach):* But, mon cher ami, we're so short on help!

(The following actions are very quick. MAMA *drags the body by one foot toward the curtain. Both she and* PEZUELA *have a furtive air about them, as if they wanted to erase quickly the traces of something very obscene.)*

PEZUELA: Handkerchief.

*(*MAMA *takes a handkerchief from her décolletage, hands it to him, and continues on with her work.)*

MAMA: Ah, mon Dieu, these beasts weigh so much!

*(*PEZUELA *hands her back the handkerchief, after he's cleaned the knife with it.)*

PEZUELA: Cards.

*(*MAMA *lets out an impatient sigh, takes a deck of cards from her décolletage, and hands it to him. She exits, dragging the* SERVANT's *body.* PEZUELA *carefully studies the deck.* MAMA *returns. They look at each other in silence, accomplices. They calm down.)*

MAMA: Is that a full deck?

PEZUELA *(giving her a wink):* Now?

MAMA *(thrown):* What? . . . No, no, I'm still upset.

PEZUELA: Tonight?

MAMA *(laughing):* How much?

PEZUELA: That depends on how much I take from the Englishman.

MAMA: It's a risky proposition.

PEZUELA: Not with this deck. Look, I have a fever. My eyes are burning. I smell death. Now.

MAMA: Cette nuit.

PEZUELA: Huh?

MAMA: Tonight.

PEZUELA: It might be late. Look, I'm covered in sweat.

MAMA: Cette nuit, cette nuit légère.

PEZUELA: Huh?

MAMA: Tonight . . . "I bring you the fruit of an Idumaean night . . ."[2]

PEZUELA *(showing her a card):* Look, this one's not marked.

(A violent tremor throws them to the ground. The cards go flying, and a thick puff of smoke comes through the curtain. MAMA *is on all fours.* POPHAM *enters immediately; he tries to dissipate the smoke by waving his hands lightly in the air.* POPHAM *is dressed like an official in the British navy, circa eighteenth century.)*

POPHAM: Beg your pardon. Forgive me, forgive me, please. It was an accident. The guard's artillery. Careless man. Lit his pipe. Leaning on the cannon. Disintegrated. Same thing happened in China. *(He comes to a full stop at MAMA's rear end, disconcerted.)* Excuse me, milady, but haven't we met somewhere else before?

MAMA *(her face covered by her robe):* Maybe so, but help me get up.

POPHAM: Yes, of course . . .

(POPHAM helps her get up, an action that requires great effort from MAMA, because the blow has apparently discombobulated her.)

MAMA: Are you always so violent, darling?

POPHAM: Oh, no, no . . . I'm a peace-loving man . . .

MAMA: Help me up.

POPHAM: Weren't you in Ceylon?

MAMA *(sensually):* Peut-être.

POPHAM: Paris!

MAMA: You threw my hip out.

POPHAM: Your hip?

(MAMA suggestively shows him her hip. POPHAM caresses it and closes his eyes as if he were remembering something.)

POPHAM: Let me see . . . Bengal?

MAMA: Perhaps . . .

POPHAM: Buckingham Palace?

MAMA: But of course. I've been in so many places.

POPHAM: South Africa?

MAMA: The world is so large, my dear friend . . .

POPHAM: It's not all that large, madam . . . Look.

(He takes a few steps forward and extends an arm with an arrogant gesture, his palm open.)

MAMA *(limping over to his side, with a greedy air):* What is it?

POPHAM: The world. *(He closes his fist in a ferocious gesture of triumph.)* In the name of Her Majesty, the Queen of England.

MAMA: Daring navigator.

(POPHAM, "daringly" embraces MAMA, grabbing her buttocks. MAMA lets out a yelp of surprise, and PEZUELA clears his throat.)

POPHAM: Oh, Mr. Pezuela. Allow me to help you up . . .

(He extends his hand. PEZUELA throws him an icy look.)

PEZUELA: In Her Majesty's name?

POPHAM *(with British pride):* Of course.

(PEZUELA gets up, with POPHAM's help. MAMA, standing near the curtain, claps her hands several times.)

MAMA *(to POPHAM):* Is this trunk yours?

POPHAM: Why, yes, it is.

(Popham goes over to the curtain and returns, dragging a trunk behind him. Mama and Pezuela follow over, curious.)

Pezuela: A lovely artifact.

Popham: Uh-hmmm.

(Popham kneels next to the trunk. He puts on a pair of metal-framed glasses that give him a stingy, mean look. He takes a key out of one of his pockets and opens the trunk, but doesn't open the lid all the way. He looks for something inside.)

Pezuela *(at the same time):* British-made?

Popham: Uh-hmmm.

(Mama has crouched down in order to sniff around the trunk.)

Mama: What's that shining in there?

Popham *(slamming the trunk lid shut):* Here it is.

(Mama has let out a shout. Popham has a file of papers in his hand.)

Popham: Pardon me, madam. Did I hurt you?

Mama: No, darling, but you almost took my nose off.

Popham: So sorry, privileged documents. *(He sits down on top of the trunk.)* Sit down, Mr. Pezuela. We have many things to speak about . . . *(Slapping the file.)* First of all, the small matter of the loan . . .

Pezuela: Oh, yes, that blessèd little loan . . . Look, the drinks have arrived. *(The same Servant reenters with a tray filled with bottles.)* A drink, Mr. Popham?

Popham: What have you got?

Pezuela: Whatever you want.

(Mama takes a bottle of brandy from the tray and shows it to Popham.)

Mama: You'll surely like this one.

(Popham's eyes light up. He gets up to examine the label.)

Popham: An old, noble brandy . . . *(Winking at Mama.)* You know my weaknesses, eh?

Mama: Knowing a man's weaknesses is part of my job.

Popham *(referring to the papers):* Well, perhaps this could wait.

Pezuela: Brandy for everyone!

Popham: Just a few drops for me; I don't drink when I'm on duty. *(He throws the papers on top of the trunk. He takes off his glasses and looks around. Laughs.)* Odd place for a business meeting . . .

(Pezuela has sat down and now stretches out and relaxes. Meanwhile, the Servant has begun his determined effort to wring something out of the bottle of brandy. Every so often, the others throw him an annoyed look.)

Pezuela *(stretching):* On the contrary, Mr. Popham . . . This is the ideal place for a profit . . . Here I air out the most delicate matters, the ones that require my greatest mental concentration, because here, you see? . . . *(He*

snaps his fingers at MAMA.) . . . you can loosen up, nothing gets in the way
. . .

(MAMA *goes to stand behind* PEZUELA *and begins to massage him.*)

MAMA: This is my chéri's home away from home . . .

PEZUELA: You're wrong, darling, this is my home . . . The other is only a bureaucratic detail . . . over there, on the other side . . . *(He lets out a sigh of pleasure.)*

(MAMA, *hearing* PEZUELA's *words, lowers her eyes and smiles modestly, like a chaste housewife.*)

MAMA: Don't pay any attention to him, Mr. Popham. Bébé spoils me too much . . . It's true that I have done all I can to make this a refuge from the torments of life . . . You won't hear anything but the most discreet voices here . . . Ah, non, monsieur! Tranquility and prudence! That's how I've trained my girls . . .

POPHAM *(scratching his crotch):* Do you have many girls?

MAMA: Nine.

POPHAM: What a prolific family!

MAMA: The product of our austere habits.

POPHAM: And they all enjoy good health?

MAMA: All healthy, sir, thank God . . . normal development . . . of course, one can't ask for everything . . . Last year, one of the darlings left us . . . Syphilis . . . How we cried over her, yes, yes . . . *(She dabs up a furtive tear and goes on massaging* PEZUELA.*)* But why talk about such sad things. The Royal Family, are they well?

POPHAM: Yes, very well, thank God . . . The Prince of Wales caught quite the cold this winter . . .

MAMA: For a cold, there's nothing like a nice hot cup of milk with honey and cognac, a couple of pats on the rump and off to bed . . .

POPHAM: And that's exactly what we did.

(A brief, bothersome pause. The SERVANT *is still trying to pour some liquid in the glasses.* MAMA *abruptly strikes out at him.)*

MAMA: Idiot! *(She pushes him off, beating him about the head.)* Get out! *(She begins to serve the drinks herself.)* As if we could wait for eternity!

PEZUELA *(with the lost look of a tragic puppet):* That's the problem: eternity.

*(*PEZUELA *remains motionless.* MAMA *goes over to* POPHAM, *suggestively holding two goblets at the level of her breasts.*)*

MAMA: Choose one.

POPHAM *(throwing himself at* MAMA*):* I want it all!

MAMA: No! No! Careful there! Mr. Popham, mind your manners! *(Ticklings and scandalous laughter that* MAMA *tries to repress in* PEZUELA's *presence.*

Finally, MAMA manages to push POPHAM into a chair and holds him there with a severe look and a motion of her head in PEZUELA's direction.) There, sitting pretty just like an English gentleman. Let me serve you!

(She hands him a goblet. POPHAM grabs her hand and pulls her toward him.)

POPHAM: Let's go to another room!

MAMA: No, no, I'm all flustered . . . Cette nuit.

POPHAM: Beg your pardon.

MAMA: What?

POPHAM: I didn't understand you.

MAMA: Nor I you.

POPHAM *(impatient)*: When?

MAMA: Ah, tonight . . . Cette nuit . . . Cette nuit légère . . . *(She rather awkwardly gets away from POPHAM. She then goes over to PEZUELA and indifferently hands him the other goblet, without looking at him.)* Drink.

(PEZUELA does not move.)

PEZUELA *(slowly, without looking at her)*: I saw everything.

MAMA: Please, chéri, no scenes! *(She leaves the goblet in PEZUELA's hands and, with a gesture of bad mood, goes over to the table, takes a goblet, and raises it to toast.)* To us! To a night of pleasure and good business!

(ALL THREE gulp their drinks down but remain unsatisfied. POPHAM puts his glasses back on and picks up the papers.)

POPHAM: Mr. Pezuela, about the loan . . .

PEZUELA: I'm all yours, Mr. Popham.

POPHAM: More than you think, my distinguished friend . . . let's see . . .

(POPHAM begins to thumb through the papers. PEZUELA winks at MAMA, directing her attention to the Englishman. MAMA responds with an understanding, complicitous gesture. A brief silent scene ensues in which MAMA performs a series of actions designed to distract POPHAM, such as rubbing her breasts against him, or picking something up off the floor so that she can show off her buttocks. As a last resort, she tosses a card, the ace of diamonds, on top of POPHAM's papers. He slowly picks up the card.)

POPHAM: Diamonds.

MAMA *(with a sigh of relief)*: Diamonds, yes. Apparently the only thing that can move an Englishman.

(She calls the SERVANT, clapping her hands. When he enters, MAMA signals for him to pick up the cards from the floor.)

POPHAM: Mr. Pezuela, do you play?

PEZUELA: Of course I do . . . well, I'm just an amateur, in reality . . . a Sunday player . . .

(Pause. POPHAM and PEZUELA size each other up.)

POPHAM: And what do you like to play?

PEZUELA: Oh, anything . . . well, let's just say that I don't have any favorites . . . it doesn't matter to me . . . Hearts?

POPHAM: A stupid game . . . I mean, I don't know how to play it very well . . . is that what you play around here?

PEZUELA: Yes, in the country. But you can suggest another game, if you like.

POPHAM: I'm not suggesting anything. *(He lets out a slightly villainous chuckle.)* It's quite all right . . . but, please, don't make fun of me if I . . .

PEZUELA: Don't worry on my account. I've only seen it played.

POPHAM: Now, playing just for the sake of playing . . .

PEZUELA *(with a roguish laugh):* I'll play you for the loan . . .

POPHAM *(catching on to the joke):* A bit much, don't you think? With so many years of interest accumulated . . . No. How about thirty thousand pounds to start with?

PEZUELA *(with a little giggle):* Not bad.

POPHAM: And you, Mr. Pezuela, you'll wager . . . ?

PEZUELA: Well, you know that I have a problem with my liquid assets.

POPHAM: I can give you credit for your lands.

PEZUELA *(shocked):* My lands, no! *(Then changing his attitude and chuckling a little.)* But we'll work something out. I have some friends in government. Do you mind public lands?

POPHAM *(shrugging his shoulders):* As long as you guarantee me them in writing.

PEZUELA: Of course.

POPHAM: Done!

(The SERVANT has been at POPHAM's feet for several moments, trying to retrieve a card from under one of the Englishman's feet. POPHAM now pushes the SERVANT away, slowly bends over, and picks up the card. He looks at it carefully as the others stand by in tense anxiety. He brushes his fingertips across it.)

POPHAM: What a pity, it's marked!

(POPHAM quickly takes a step back, pulls out his pistol, and shoots the SERVANT. A very tense pause. The SERVANT takes a few wavering steps toward POPHAM and falls down. Relief.)

MAMA *(looking at the corpse, makes a resigned gesture):* Bon . . . *(POPHAM puts his gun away.)*

POPHAM *(looking intensely at PEZUELA):* I can't stomach a cheat.

PEZUELA *(weakly):* Outrageous! You can't trust anyone . . . And now what will we do?

POPHAM: Now we'll play, Mr. Pezuela.

PEZUELA: I'd be delighted to, but . . .

POPHAM: Don't worry.

(POPHAM goes over to the trunk and looks inside it for something. MAMA goes over to the corpse.)
MAMA: Right into the cœur . . . Magnificent marksmanship! Isn't death just fascinating?
(POPHAM removes something from the trunk.)
PEZUELA: Don't tell me you have a deck of cards?
POPHAM: First-rate.
PEZUELA *(ambiguous):* Stupendous.
(PEZUELA starts to reach for the deck.)
POPHAM: Three pence.
PEZUELA: What?
POPHAM: So sorry, but they're not my property . . . I only carry them for sale . . . three pence . . .
PEZUELA: Yes, of course . . . forgive me . . . three pence, now that would be . . .
POPHAM: Fifty cents.
PEZUELA *(searching in his pockets):* That's a shame, I don't seem to have any change on me . . . *(To MAMA.)* Do you, madam?
MAMA *(greed has distorted her face):* What?
PEZUELA: Lend me fifty cents . . .
MAMA: Ah, it's unlikely that I have . . . Anyway, I'll go look . . . *(She looks inside her décolletage.)* Just as I said, I only have thirty-five . . .
PEZUELA *(happy to have gotten out of playing):* What, so we're going to lose thirty thousand pounds because of thirty-five cents! Isn't that ironic?
MAMA *(greedily):* How can we belittle such a sum of money! After all, someone has to take charge of those fifty cents . . . *(Pointing to the SERVANT.)* Since he's the one responsible for the incident, let's dock his pay.
POPHAM *(to PEZUELA):* Do you agree?
(PEZUELA makes a gesture of resignation. POPHAM takes out the cards and begins to shuffle them with enormous skill.)
POPHAM *(to MAMA):* Of course, madam, you too shall play.
MAMA: Ah, non, je m'excuse. I will remain an impartial spectator.
PEZUELA *(vengeful):* No, no, no, there are no spectators here. Mr. Popham, you sit here . . .
MAMA: But, Bébé, I don't have any cash . . .
PEZUELA: What? You don't have thirty-five cents?
POPHAM *(shuffling):* Come on, madam!
MAMA: Well, si vous insistez . . . But my participation is purely symbolic . . . I'm not used to games of chance . . .
(ALL THREE take their seats around the table.)
POPHAM: The king of diamonds. Milady and gentleman, I'll be the bank! Ante up, please!

PEZUELA: I'll open with one hundred pounds.

MAMA: I bet ten cents . . . *(She vacillates.)* No, no, it's better to be prudent . . . five cents.

POPHAM: The betting is closed. Five of clubs, seven of diamonds, six of spades. You lose, Mr. Pezuela.

MAMA *(clapping her hands):* I won! I won! Pay me my five cents.

PEZUELA: Be patient.

(POPHAM shuffles with great velocity.)

POPHAM: Place your bets, milady and gentleman.

(The lights begin to grow darker, and the three actors are cloaked in a tenuous semidarkness. The game continues, but the movements become slow and unreal, and the sounds are inaudible murmurs. A soft light comes up over the SERVANT's corpse. The SERVANT gets up, with great difficulty. He has a huge bloodstain on his shirt, over his heart.)

SERVANT: They didn't even save you the trouble . . . of having to bury yourself . . . Let's go, brother corpse. Come with me. *(He leaves, staggering, through the curtain. The lights come up once again. There has been a jump forward in time.)*

POPHAM: The gentleman loses once again.

(PEZUELA, upset, jumps up, pounding on the table.)

PEZUELA *(his voice mellow):* What are you saying? What the hell are you saying?

MAMA *(very nervous):* We've all lost here! Tout le monde! C'est incroyable! Thirty cents! Je ne comprend pas!

POPHAM *(to PEZUELA, still shuffling the cards):* Please sit down. No need to become violent. Just the luck of the draw. Place your bets!

PEZUELA *(without sitting down, exasperated):* My last fifteen cents!

MAMA: Five cents and nothing more!

(POPHAM starts dealing the cards, face up. To each of his movements, MAMA reacts with a yell: the first one is a cry of stupefaction, and the last one the hysterical screech of a tantrum.)

POPHAM: So sorry, milady and gentleman, you've lost again.

MAMA: Plucked clean!

(PEZUELA throws a blind punch at POPHAM's face from across the table, but POPHAM avoids the blow.)

POPHAM: What is this?

MAMA *(out of control because of her tantrum, to PEZUELA):* Swine! Swine! Lost my precious coins! And all because you made me do it! My savings!

(MAMA goes after PEZUELA with her nails. PEZUELA throws himself on top of MAMA.)

PEZUELA: I'll strangle you, you old hen!

MAMA: M'aidez! Mayday!

PEZUELA *(shaking her by the throat):* Meddling whore! Thirty thousand pounds down the drain because of you!

POPHAM: I'm afraid I cannot allow you to insult a lady in my presence! *(He knocks PEZUELA down and hurls himself on top of him.)*

MAMA *(to POPHAM):* Who asked you to get involved in this? *(She begins to beat him around his head.)* Maudit, maudit, maudit! Damned cheat!

POPHAM *(to MAMA):* You bloody, filthy hag! *(He gets to his feet and begins to attack MAMA.)*

MAMA: Mayday! Mayday!

PEZUELA: How dare you lay your hands on her!

(PEZUELA attacks POPHAM from behind. POPHAM turns around quickly and knocks PEZUELA down. Then he sits on him and begins to beat him viciously.)

POPHAM: I'm going to rip your bloody guts right through your bloody teeth!

PEZUELA: Oh! Oh!

(MAMA lets out cries of desperation. She attempts to separate the two men and then goes over to the curtain, clapping furiously.)

MAMA: Enough! Enough! Assez! They're killing each other! *(The same SERVANT reappears.)* Get them apart, they're killing each other!

(The SERVANT doesn't know what to do, but then takes a bottle by the neck and is about to break it over POPHAM.)

PEZUELA: Leave me alone, damn it, I'm going to throw up!

POPHAM: Oh God, disgusting!

(He lets go quickly, with a gesture of repugnance.)

MAMA *(disgusted and reproachful):* But, chéri . . .

PEZUELA *(trying to keep it in):* I'm sorry, but I have a very delicate stomach . . .

MAMA *(to the SERVANT):* Help him . . .

(The SERVANT takes PEZUELA away. POPHAM goes over to the mirror, swaying. MAMA follows him.)

MAMA *(to POPHAM, furtively, pinching him):* I'll always be yours.

(POPHAM leans on the mirror.)

POPHAM: I'm going to retch.

MAMA: Oh dear, you too?

POPHAM: I could never tolerate . . . vomiting . . . What could he have eaten? Ah . . . *(His stomach turns just thinking about it.)* I feel sick . . .

(MAMA draws away, skeptical.)

MAMA: The ruling class, tsk . . . Quel temps!

(She serves herself a drop of liquor and licks it, absently, disillusioned.)

POPHAM: Lower the mizzen and the mainsail! The ship is going down! Bloody hell, I feel sick!

MAMA: It was so much easier before . . . The kings were born under the crown, as they say . . . But these people, fighting each other for power, when they get there they're done for . . .

(PEZUELA returns, pale and shaky, aided by the SERVANT. He collapses into a chair.)

PEZUELA: I've just looked death in the eye.

MAMA: Sacre cœur, what a dreary man!

PEZUELA: She had old, icy hands, covered in rings, and she smiled lasciviously at me. Her face was wasted by razor blades, covered in rice powder, and she had two blotches of rouge on her cheekbones. The empty holes of her eyes were like wells of stinking water, and when she opened her lips lined with red paste, out came black cigarette smoke that smelled like vomit . . .

POPHAM: Oh, not again . . .

MAMA *(guffawing):* I know that old whore: she's my mother. But calm down, Bébé, nobody's going to die here. I'm very close to the old woman. And if she shows up, I'll say to her: "Dear Mother Death, why are you going about frightening these dignified gentlemen, the crème de la crème of our society?" And she'll say: "Forgive me, I didn't know who you were. I was just fooling around." And then she'll go away.

PEZUELA: But she'll come back. She always does.

MAMA: In that case, we'll play a lovely dirty little trick on her . . . Let's hide in the armoire and disguise ourselves, alright? And when Mama Death gets here, she'll wonder, "Now where have those children gotten to?," and when she opens the armoire she won't even recognize us . . . To the armoire, quick, before she shows up! *(She opens the trunk with a bang, as if it were the armoire. Overwhelmed.)* Oh . . . what delicious bijouterie, Mr. Popham! And feathers! I just adore feathers! May I do a little rummaging? *(She begins to go through the trunk's contents.)* A choker! Look at this beautiful woolen cloth, Bébé! *(PEZUELA begins to pay attention.)* And this little container, what's it for? And all these papers?

POPHAM: Careful, madam, those are business documents, stocks . . .

PEZUELA: What kind of stocks?

POPHAM: Well, there's a little bit of everything. Mines, railroads, banks . . .

(MAMA has decked herself out in the huge feathers and jewelry of a starlet.)

MAMA: How do I look?

POPHAM: Please, madam. Everything has its price.

PEZUELA: And what might that price be?

POPHAM: Mr. Pezuela, you're completely in debt, you don't have a copper in your pocket, and you're still asking me the price.

(MAMA continues digging about in the trunk.)

MAMA: Marmalade!

PEZUELA *(in a huff):* Look here, no, but allow me to . . . what are you trying to say? I may not have any cash, but you know very well that my credit is . . . My lands, 125,000 acres . . .

MAMA: He even has the gaucho balls to prove it!

POPHAM: Yes, yes, land . . . I can't deny you that, that's wealth . . . Now, lands can't reproduce . . . I can make loans, Mr. Pezuela, I have no problem with that . . . It just saddens me so to see people suffer . . . But I wouldn't want to leave you out on the street should you not be able to . . . Well, it just isn't enough to have wealth, you must have something that can reproduce itself, do you both understand me?

PEZUELA: I understand you perfectly. Mama!

MAMA: Yes, mon cher ami?

PEZUELA: Come here a moment, please. *(MAMA goes over to him, swinging her hips. PEZUELA takes her by the arm and leads her over to POPHAM. MAMA lets him do so; she, all in feathers, an enchantress, smiles at POPHAM.)* Very well, Mr. Popham, she can be touched, she's tangible, real. With a little bit of care and the help of God, she'll reproduce herself from here to eternity . . . This is my product: flesh . . .

POPHAM: I'm sorry, Mr. Pezuela, but in England we too produce a great deal of whores.

MAMA *(offended):* What does that mean?

PEZUELA: You did not understand me, Mr. Popham; not human flesh, ugh, or whatever you may think she is, but rather edible, juicy, nutritious . . . *(To MAMA.)* Please, my dear, help me out here, could you get down on all fours . . .

MAMA *(dignified, but willing to do what PEZUELA has just requested):* Je dois dire que ce que vous me demandez is just a teeny bit extravagant . . . I'll do it just the same, in the name of our long friendship, but not without protest, given that this, well, en fin . . . *(Grumbling in this way, she gets down on all fours.)*

PEZUELA: Please observe, Mr. Popham, this poem so rich in protein . . . observe her forequarters and her hindquarters . . . !

(He lifts up MAMA's robe.)

MAMA *(laughing):* Don't go too far!

POPHAM *(laughing):* I understand completely, Mr. Pezuela. *(He feels MAMA up.)*

PEZUELA *(enthusiastic):* And not only fresh meat, Mr. Popham . . . but also milk, fresh, creamy, frothy . . . squeeze her, go ahead, give her a good milking . . .

POPHAM: May I?

PEZUELA: Pretend that I'm not even here.

(He closes his eyes. POPHAM fondles MAMA's breasts.)

MAMA *(laughing scandalously):* Cut that out, you're tickling me!

PEZUELA: Well, Mr. Popham?

POPHAM *(with a wink to PEZUELA):* Excellent quality.

PEZUELA: And there are millions more just like her . . . Regiments of cows, an entire layer of them covering my lands, fucking like bunnies . . .

POPHAM *(trying to stand up, wiping his hands on a handkerchief):* Very well, very well . . . Naturally, I knew that . . . I've thought about this . . . Help me up, please . . . *(PEZUELA helps him stand up.)* My knee . . . possibly a touch of gout . . . Of course I knew that . . . But it's not so easy . . . You have the raw material . . . Very well . . . And it would go bad. But how to get it to Europe? It's just not that easy. Transportation, refrigeration, ports, ships . . . Ahhhhhh!

PEZUELA: You have the funds required, Mr. Popham.

MAMA *(still down on the ground):* Excuse me, are you finished here?

PEZUELA: Oh, sorry, madam.

(He helps her to her feet.)

MAMA: Mon Dieu, I think after all that I deserve a little drink.

(She goes to serve herself one. POPHAM waits for PEZUELA and smiles slyly at him.)

POPHAM *(tapping PEZUELA's head with his finger):* Yes, I have the funds required. And so what? Why throw away money on trains or ports that others are going to use? I'm a generous man, but I'm not stupid, right? Anyone can use the sea, and it's filled with pirates . . . the French, the Dutch . . . so . . . I need for you to guarantee me certain privileges, shall we call them . . . tariff-free importation of my goods, customs exemptions . . . In a word, Mr. Pezuela, free trade . . .

PEZUELA: We can do that . . . There will be some protests . . . you know, the local producers . . . But I see no reason for me to protect someone else's interests if they're not mine . . . Is that all?

POPHAM: The price, Mr. Pezuela . . . We need to come to an agreement . . .

PEZUELA: Well now, that's another issue.

POPHAM: I can guarantee you, hmmm . . . *(He writes down an amount on a small piece of paper, which he then shows to PEZUELA.)*

PEZUELA *(reading the number):* But . . . allow me an indiscreet question, Mr. Popham: how much do you get for a ton in London?

POPHAM *(laughing):* Well, it's none of your business, but I'll answer you anyway. The bottom line. *(He writes down another amount.)*

PEZUELA *(reading, shocked):* But, Mr. Popham, I refuse to believe that . . . such a small commitment on your part . . . Especially if we keep in mind that for your products you . . .

POPHAM: Mr. Pezuela, international division of labor . . . Selling is not what's important; what's important is what you sell. Anyone can sell selling. But what are you selling, and what am I selling? I, Mr. Pezuela, I sell . . . textiles, jewels, railways, artifacts, I sell money, just imagine, money! Yes, Mr. Pezuela, I sell items that in a certain sense are superfluous but long-lasting. Don't let the word escape your attention: long-lasting, I mean, they contain time. And you, my friend, what is it that you sell? Meat. Common meat, short-lived, corruptible. And dead meat, that is, only an edible step away from rot. In short, pieces of death and rot. *(Solemn.)* I sell things that last, what proud humanity has wrested away from time. And what is it you sell? Instincts, blind force, destructible basics. I sell civilization, and you sell nature, barbarity. So, Mr. Pezuela, choose: civilization or barbarity.

MAMA: Civilization, darling, obviously.

POPHAM: Believe me, Mr. Pezuela, in time we'll arrive at the ideal exchange: flesh for spirit.

PEZUELA *(with a little giggle):* Mr. Popham, who needs your product?

POPHAM: Not you, my friend, because you already have the power. But look at him . . . *(He points to the SERVANT.)* What is that? *(The SERVANT looks at him.)* A monkey . . . A poor, unpredictable beast. We must give him morality.

PEZUELA: I think you're exaggerating.

POPHAM: Certainly not. And I'll prove it to you. *(He goes over to the trunk and begins to take out a series of horrible, unrecognizable medical instruments.)* In order to inoculate the subject with a sense of duty . . . sacrifice and productivity . . . domestication . . . discipline . . . Christian resignation . . . respect for order and hierarchy . . . awareness of his own insignificance . . . in short, all the regalia of the honorable worker . . . Ready! *(He has finished arranging his instruments on top of the trunk.)* You, sir and madam, have every right to ask what these instruments have to do with high moral precepts . . . And I will respond to you that, milady and gentleman, I am a progressive man . . . *(He puts on a pair of rubber gloves. Indicating them.)* The latest in science . . . derived from rubber, complete coverage, also for sale . . .

PEZUELA *(dictates to MAMA):* Make a note: rubber.

POPHAM: Milady and gentleman, experimental psychology has made some surprising discoveries: behavior modification. The human body's responses to different stimuli have been minutely classified. If I, milady and gentleman, for example . . . I have in my hand a delicate product of our steel mills, a sewing needle . . . Observe, Mr. Pezuela, its noble alloy . . .

(He shows him the needle. PEZUELA looks at it briefly.)

PEZUELA *(to MAMA):* Make a note: needles.

POPHAM: Very well, sir and madam, automatic response . . . If I go over to our experimental subject with this British-made sewing needle, and if I poke . . .

(He pokes the SERVANT and receives an immediate response: the SERVANT delivers a colossal punch that throws POPHAM several meters across the floor. Stupefied pause. MAMA runs over to POPHAM.)

MAMA: Mon cher ami, did he hurt you?

POPHAM *(getting up with MAMA's help):* No, no, I'm fine, forgive me. Experimental psychology is still a young science . . . There are responses that still have not been classified . . . That was an anomaly, very easily corrected . . .

(He takes out his pistol.)

MAMA: Please, my dear friend, I suggest that we leave that experiment for later . . .

(POPHAM goes over to the SERVANT with his pistol in one hand and the needle in the other.)

POPHAM: If I, sir and madam, poke . . . *(He threatens to do so, but the SERVANT jumps on top of him and grabs him by the throat. A shot is heard. MAMA and PEZUELA manage to grab on to the SERVANT's arms, who resists desperately. POPHAM yells to MAMA.)* The scalpel! Scalpel!

(MAMA finds the scalpel, takes it in her two hands, lifts it up over her head, and plants it with one blow into the SERVANT's chest. A small splash of blood lands on her face. With a disgusted expression, MAMA rapidly wipes herself clean. The other two men let go of the SERVANT's body.)

POPHAM *(to MAMA):* Would you like a handkerchief?

MAMA: No, that's all right, I have one. *(She cleans herself.)* How disagreeable!

POPHAM: His state of barbarity was much greater than I had thought.

MAMA *(with a touch of reproach):* It was you, darling, you got him too worked up. Are you harmed?

POPHAM: I'm broken, milady.

MAMA: Let's have a drink and put this ugly incident behind us. Bébé . . .

(POPHAM and MAMA go over to a table where MAMA begins to serve everyone a drink. POPHAM collapses into a chair. He is absolutely worn-out. PEZUELA has remained by the corpse, observing it. MAMA looks at him.)

MAMA: Chéri, darling, do you feel ill?

PEZUELA: No, darling, I was just thinking . . . *(Indicating the SERVANT.)* This makes me think . . . To die like that in public . . . When you feel like peeing, my dear . . .

MAMA *(with a disgusted gesture):* Oh . . .

PEZUELA: No, no, allow me . . . It's not disgusting, it's a biological act . . . When you feel like peeing, you have to hide it, don't you? You go to the bathroom. Now, a man's most private act, the supreme act of biological necessity, one . . . I know something of animals, right?

MAMA: But of course.

PEZUELA: When an animal senses that it is about to die, it draws away from the herd . . . and nevertheless . . . think about the deaths of our great men, surrounded by indiscreet eyes, ears intent on catching their last words . . .

How obscene! And afterwards, they write it down, they publish it . . . No, no, it's better to do it in the bathroom.

POPHAM *(waking up):* Speak of the devil . . .

PEZUELA *(raising his glass):* To a solitary death.

POPHAM: To England.

PEZUELA *(with a wink):* And to the newest pearl in her crown.

(PEZUELA and POPHAM drink.)

MAMA *(solemnly):* And what could I possibly add to this picture, it strikes my innermost chord . . . *(A scoundrel's laugh from POPHAM.)* Darling, don't be disgusting . . . *(She continues on, solemnly.)* Perhaps in the fullness of time . . . keep your hands to yourself . . . in the fullness of time . . . when the snow of the years . . . *(Giggles from the other two, their hands working under the table. MAMA defends herself, tapping on the table.)* When the years' snow has frosted my hair . . . no, not my garter! . . . I'll remember this fucking-around . . . *(She begins to laugh, raucously.)* Not my garter, it's a family heirloom!

(The other two pull her down onto the floor. MAMA disappears under the table. A big ruckus.)

MAMA *(clapping each time she appears from under the table):* Service! Service, I say!

(In order to escape, she begins to sing "God Save the King." After a few instants, she emerges, completely disheveled, and makes her way, staggering, over to the mirror. The other two emerge, singing, and they can barely stand up. POPHAM wears MAMA's garter, with one of her feathers, around his head like a headband.)

MAMA: I can't keep up that pace anymore.

(POPHAM drags himself over to the trunk.)

POPHAM: Well, I believe it is time to go to the lavatory . . . What did you call him, "Baby"? To the loo . . . I'm taking the pearl with me, "Baby."

(He begins to drag the trunk toward the curtain, but he can barely move it. He's wrung out. He sits down on the trunk, panting, breathless. PEZUELA, meanwhile, staggers over toward MAMA.)

PEZUELA: Mama . . . I'm on fire . . . Please . . . just this once . . . before night falls . . . I want to cool off . . .

(He is about to touch MAMA, but she abruptly moves away.)

MAMA *(hysterical, her eyes bathed in tears):* Touche pas!

PEZUELA: What's the matter?

MAMA: It's no use, I'm just not made for these times! I miss the monarchy!

PEZUELA: But I'm the king here!

MAMA: A king without a crown. A spear-carrier.

(PEZUELA picks up the cow's skull and raises it solemnly over his head.)

PEZUELA: I crown myself king. Per saecula saeculorum.[3]

(He pulls the skull on over his head.)
POPHAM *(laughing):* Ha, ha, ha, the cuckolded king.
PEZUELA: I can't see a thing.
MAMA *(to PEZUELA):* Take it off, darling, you look ridiculous . . .
(PEZUELA tries to take the skull off, his entire head covered.)
PEZUELA: It's not coming off.
(MAMA halfheartedly claps her hands.)
MAMA: Service!
(POPHAM erupts in sidesplitting laughter.)
POPHAM: Well, at least it was entertaining.
PEZUELA: Mama, help me . . .
MAMA: Bend over.
(PEZUELA bends over, and MAMA begins to tug on the cow-skull, with no luck.)
MAMA: Does it hurt?
PEZUELA: I'm in pain.
(In one of her tugs, MAMA loses her grip, and both MAMA and PEZUELA fall backwards onto the floor. Brief pause.)
MAMA: Shall we try again?
PEZUELA: No, that's alright, it's my fate. I had a feeling something horrible was coming my way . . . Mama, are you still there?
MAMA: I'm already on the other side, darling. I'm barely able to stand.
PEZUELA: I can't see you.
MAMA: So much the better.
(PEZUELA stands up and takes some tentative steps.)
PEZUELA: Mama . . .
MAMA *(clapping her hands):* Service!
(PEZUELA stumbles upon the SERVANT's corpse. PEZUELA bends over and touches it.)
PEZUELA: Mama?
POPHAM *(laughing so hard he can barely speak):* My dear, I'm hardly in any condition to do it even if I cared to . . .
MAMA: Service! Why doesn't anyone come? Service!
PEZUELA *(disoriented):* Mama? *(PEZUELA goes toward the mirror.)*
POPHAM: Hmmm, I'd best be popping off . . .
(POPHAM starts dragging his trunk toward the curtain. By this time, PEZUELA has gotten to the mirror and begins to caress it.)
PEZUELA *(with a sigh, as if he'd found MAMA):* Mama . . .
(POPHAM sees him and nearly chokes laughing.)
POPHAM *(pointing his arm at PEZUELA):* You kill me, sir . . . well, anyway it was terribly fun . . . Madam, be sure to clean the mirror afterward! Ah!
(Suddenly serious.) Trafalgar![4]

(He collapses on top of the trunk. PEZUELA continues to caress the mirror.)
PEZUELA: Mama, you're cold as the grave . . .
MAMA: Mr. Popham, what's the matter? Service! *(She goes over to the table and takes the last glass. She collapses slowly on top of the table.)* What an evening. *(Weakly.)* Service . . .
The stage begins to go dark. Finally, only PEZUELA's pantings can be heard, punctuated every so often by MAMA's increasingly weaker voice calling out: "Service. Service."

TRANSLATOR'S NOTES

1. Mama quotes the opening lines of French symbolist poet Stéphane Mallarmé's poem "Brise Marine." The original reads: "La chair est triste, hélas! et j'ai lu tous les livres."
2. Mama once again attempts to quote Mallarmé, this time the first line of his poem "Don du poëme." The original reads: "Je t'apporte l'enfant d'une nuit d'Idumée!"
3. A Latin liturgical phrase, "Through all the ages of ages."
4. A cape on southern Spain's Atlantic coast, Trafalgar was the site of Nelson's 1805 victory over the Spanish and French fleets.

A South American Passion Play

(A Mystery Cycle in One Act)

to Teresita

Una pasión sudamericana premiered on 9 November 1989 in the Martín Coronado Theater of the Teatro Municipal General San Martín, Buenos Aires.

Original Cast

SAN BENITO [SAINT BENEDICT]	Luis Campos
FARFARELLO	Miguel Moyano
ESTANISLAO [STANISLAV]	Iván Moschner
MURAT	Osvaldo Santoro
BIGUÁ	Derli Prada
BRIGADIER	Arturo Maly
EDECÁN [AIDE-DE-CAMP]	Jorge Petraglia
ESCRIBIENTES [CLERKS]	Pedro Cano, Manuel Cruz
BARRABÁS [BARABBAS]	Augusto Kretschmar
CANNING	Jorge Baza de Candia
MUSICIANS	Jorge Valcarcel, Mariano Cossa
Lights	Roberto Traferri
Music	Jorge Valcarcel
Costumes	María Julia Bertotto
Set design	Jorge Sarudiansky
Direction	Ricardo Monti

Translator's note: At the author's request, the present translation is based on an unpublished, revised version of *Una pasión sudamericana*, from which several characters and sections of the original, published text have been omitted.

Characters

BRIGADIER: Rough complexion; tanned, tough skin; dark, curly hair; and most importantly, dark, burning eyes. The authority emanating from him is inarguable and paralyzing. Everything about him reflects a fanatical austerity. He dresses simply, like someone from the country. He wears a poncho.

AIDE-DE-CAMP: A tall, thin, wasted old man. Taciturn and formal, he is the confluence of goodness and resigned skepticism. Serene, even in the midst of chaos. He wears a worn-out uniform, and his arm bears a slight wound from a recent skirmish.

The CLERK: A wan moth, with long, straight hair and a pale face. Dressed in a frock coat.

The BUFFOONS (or CRAZIES):

FARFARELLO: Popular Neapolitan street musician. Bright, dark eyes, curly hair, a hoop in one ear, wearing lipstick and rouge. Loudmouthed, strident, a charlatan, lewd and mysterious.

SAINT BENEDICT: A lean mystic, a feverish visionary. He wears a threadbare habit and always carries with him an old, weighty Bible.

PRINCE MURAT: A small, nervous man with dark skin and small, shifty eyes like those of a viper. He wears discarded, bloodstained military gear that is too large for him, and carries a toy saber made of brass.

STANISLAV, THE FOUNDLING: Thin, dried-out blond hair and childlike, enormous, luminous blue eyes.

PROLOGUE

The hall of what remains of a ranch, located on the plains outside Buenos Aires. The ranch is of a colonial construction that would already be old at the time of the play's action, i.e., the middle of the nineteenth century. Thick walls, barely whitewashed; very high ceilings held up by wooden beams; brick floors. The shutters of the windows are hermetically sealed. With the exception of one table and two or three chairs, there is no furniture. There are two large doors, one each right and left.

A rough winter night. It has been raining for several days. The hall is closed up and in complete darkness. The only sounds are the wind outside and the murmurs of an army that is camped beyond the ruins: horses neighing, voices commanding, and the sounds of guns. After a few seconds, the merry tinkling of a mandolin is heard as it comes nearer. Finally, the stage-

right door opens with a crash, and a curious company bursts into the hall. They are the BUFFOONS, *wet and muddy.* SAINT BENEDICT *is the first to enter, carrying an oil-lamp in one hand and, in the other, his heavy Bible.*
SAINT BENEDICT *(as he enters):* Lux in tenebris![1]
*(*STANISLAV *follows, whirling in place as if in a trance, and then* PRINCE MURAT, *sniffing out the room suspiciously and brandishing his saber.* FARFARELLO *circles the group as he plays his mandolin. The group, coiling around itself, crosses the hall and disappears through the stage-left door. Little by little, as the voices grow more distant, the shadows return to hang over the scene. Darkness and silence, except for the sound of the wind and the murmurs of the army.)*

ONE ACT

Another wavering light begins to take shape through the stage-right door, left open by the CRAZIES. *A few seconds later the* BRIGADIER *and his* AIDE-DE-CAMP *enter, followed by the* CLERK, *who carries a candle and a mountain of files, papers, dossiers, and writing instruments. Like the* BUFFOONS, *all are muddy and wet.·In the center of the hall, the* BRIGADIER *stops and takes in the room. The other two maintain a respectful distance, a few steps behind him.*
AIDE-DE-CAMP *(to the* BRIGADIER*):* Is this alright, sir?
BRIGADIER: Yes.
(The AIDE-DE-CAMP *signals to the* CLERK *by snapping his fingers; in turn, the diligent* CLERK *puts his things on top of the table. Meanwhile, the* BRIGADIER *collapses into a chair. He is motionless for a second, his eyes closed. The* AIDE-DE-CAMP *stands at his side, waiting, expressionless.)*
BRIGADIER *(without opening his eyes):* How long until dawn?
AIDE-DE-CAMP: A couple of hours, sir.
BRIGADIER: There will be battle.
AIDE-DE-CAMP: Who knows, sir? The enemy has done nothing but sneak away from us.
BRIGADIER: So they're still moving?
AIDE-DE-CAMP: They seem to be leaving.
BRIGADIER: Dodges, feints. But they're avoiding the fight. What has happened to the Madman? Why won't he fight? He came to devour the world, and now he wants to dance a minuet?
AIDE-DE-CAMP: That's how they are, sir. Guts of smoke.
BRIGADIER: Who knows? Since it's been raining for so long . . . They probably don't like to fight in the mud. They're clean people.
AIDE-DE-CAMP *(smiling):* Yes, sir.
BRIGADIER: It's cold.

AIDE-DE-CAMP: Yes, sir. Shall I send for a brazier?

BRIGADIER: Is the wound deep?

AIDE-DE-CAMP: No, sir. Just a scratch.

BRIGADIER: Let me see.

(The AIDE-DE-CAMP draws near. The BRIGADIER, without looking, touches the wound. Afterward, he examines his own bloodstained fingers.)

BRIGADIER (smiling): Old man's blood.

AIDE-DE-CAMP: Yes, sir.

BRIGADIER (teasing): Watered-down.

AIDE-DE-CAMP: Not as vigorous as it once was.

(Pause.)

BRIGADIER (absentmindedly rubbing the blood between his fingers): How long has it been since I've slept?

AIDE-DE-CAMP: Two nights, sir.

BRIGADIER: I'm running a fever.

AIDE-DE-CAMP: Shall I send for a doctor, sir?

(Pause.)

BRIGADIER: This country . . . always in darkness. Like a sleeping animal. Nothing but mud, blood, and fever. And these people who come here with their topographical charts, with dreams of waging war just like in Europe. Broken-down butts. They wander like madmen in the desert, pursuing a factory of mirages. They don't deserve anything but disdain; nevertheless, here we are, sniffing around in the night. And at dawn, if God is served, we'll split each other's skin right open. (Pause. Referring to the CLERK.) Why is the moth sleeping?

AIDE-DE-CAMP: He's awake, sir.

BRIGADIER: Don't you know this louse yet? He's figured out how to sleep with his eyes open. Hit him.

(The AIDE-DE-CAMP crosses over to the CLERK and gives him a cuff on the head. The CLERK jumps up like a spring. Pause.)

BRIGADIER: You must write everything down. Don't skip a single word.

(The CLERK automatically sits down and begins to write. The scratching of his quill on paper is heard.)

BRIGADIER: Whose ranch is this?

AIDE-DE-CAMP: Enemies, sir. They grabbed everything and went over to the Madman's army.

BRIGADIER: When we go, set fire to the place. Leave me now.

AIDE-DE-CAMP: Sir . . .

BRIGADIER: Oh, and send in the fools.

AIDE-DE-CAMP: Sir . . .

BRIGADIER: What is it?

AIDE-DE-CAMP: The girl, sir . . .

BRIGADIER *(smiling):* What girl?

AIDE-DE-CAMP: The one they found. She's here.

(Pause.)

BRIGADIER *(smiling):* She who was once lost and now is found? Why is she here?

AIDE-DE-CAMP: His Excellency's orders. Don't you remember?

BRIGADIER: No.

AIDE-DE-CAMP: His Excellency ordered that the prisoners be brought back in covered wagons with bars . . . The girl and that priest who seduced her . . .

(Pause.)

BRIGADIER *(exploding):* But what do I have to do with that mess? Do I look like a playwright? The plot's too thick for me . . . Come on, don't get upset, I'll take care of it later.

AIDE-DE-CAMP: Sir.

BRIGADIER: What?

AIDE-DE-CAMP: The girl . . .

(He makes a gesture over his abdomen indicating that the woman is pregnant.)

BRIGADIER: That so?

AIDE-DE-CAMP: This cries out to heaven. It's a shame.

BRIGADIER: Don't worry, man. We're not monsters. It's only to set an example. It'll soon be over. Go on, send in my fools.

(The AIDE-DE-CAMP exits stage left. The BRIGADIER begins to pace around the room.)

BRIGADIER: Moth, are you awake?

CLERK: Yes, sir.

BRIGADIER: Sure?

CLERK: Yes, sir.

BRIGADIER: I know you're trying to fool me. And even if I were to rip open your throat, you wouldn't wake up. You would bleed to death in dreamland. The blood would float in the air, like smoke. I'm not sure if I'm even awake. But no matter if you're in dreamland, moth, write.

(Like electricity, the CLERK opens his inkwell, dips his quill, and waits, crouched over his paper like a hunting-dog. After a brief pause, the BRIGADIER begins to dictate.)

BRIGADIER: "To the Commander in Chief of the Northern Provinces, General Flores. My friend . . ."

(The BUFFOONS suddenly burst in through the stage-left door. FARFARELLO throws himself at the BRIGADIER's feet and embraces his legs. The BUFFOONS all fall down on their knees. The BRIGADIER remains absolutely motionless, like an ice sculpture.)

FARFARELLO: Signore! Signore!

BUFFOONS (*excited and amused*): Sir! Sir! He's means "sir"!

FARFARELLO: When will I be libero? Signore!

BRIGADIER (*motionless*): Speak in our language, dago.

FARFARELLO: Libero! Libero!

BUFFOONS: Free! Free!

(*The* BRIGADIER *lets out a chilling laugh and suddenly grabs* FARFARELLO *by the hair. The Italian moans. Pause.*)

BRIGADIER: Why do you want to be free, dago? So you can go over to the Madman's army?

FARFARELLO: Per carità, signore, no!

BRIGADIER: Are you on the Madman's payroll?

FARFARELLO: No, no, signore! Ti giuro!

BRIGADIER: So then why did they find you snooping around the camp?

FARFARELLO: I got perduto!

BUFFOONS: He got lost! Lost!

FARFARELLO: Perduto al buio!

BUFFOONS: Lost in the night! The night!

BRIGADIER: Well, you got lost in the wrong place, dago. I think you're an enemy spy.

FARFARELLO: Nemico, me? Ma cosa dice, signore? Me straniero.

BUFFOONS: Foreigner! He's a foreigner!

FARFARELLO: Me no capisco never di tutta questa cosa americana, questa war! Tutti contro tutti!

BUFFOONS: Everybody fighting each other!

FARFARELLO: Tutti ammazzandosi!

BUFFOONS: Everybody killing each other!

FARFARELLO: Me, sono neutrale!

BUFFOONS: He's neutral! Neutral!

BRIGADIER: No one's neutral here. If you're not with me, you're against me.

(*He lets go of* FARFARELLO, *who remains kneeling on the floor, trying to regain his balance, moaning histrionically, and rubbing his head. The* BUFFOONS *disperse to different areas of the room.*)

FARFARELLO: Dio, oh Dio, when will this nightmare end, this dream of the assassini? When will I wake up, in my sunny terra? Al sole, ayyyy, l'Italia mia, clean, civilizzata. Napoli, Napoli.

(*Long pause. The* BUFFOONS *are scattered around on the floor and beginning to doze off. The* BRIGADIER *does not move.* FARFARELLO *strums his mandolin.* SAINT BENEDICT *murmurs a psalm in Latin, the old Bible open on his lap. His head begins to nod as he falls asleep. The* CLERK *looks in the* BRIGADIER's *direction with empty eyes.*)

BRIGADIER: Moth, are you awake?

CLERK: Yes, sir.

(The BRIGADIER snaps his fingers. The CLERK grabs his paper and begins to read.)
CLERK: "General Flores: My friend . . ."
(The BRIGADIER interrupts him by snapping his fingers. The CLERK grabs another page.)
CLERK *(reading):* "sentenced to die at the hands of the firing squad . . ."
(The BRIGADIER snaps his fingers. The CLERK grabs another sheet of paper.)
CLERK *(reading):* "I have ordered that you be sent the following, without delay . . ."
(Another snap of the BRIGADIER's fingers.)
CLERK *(reading):* "Declaration regarding the theft of several ranches . . ."
(The BRIGADIER snaps his fingers once more, impatiently. The CLERK is terrified.)
CLERK *(reading in a faltering voice, trembling):* "Brigadier, Sir: I appeal to you, with a trembling hand, oppressed by and bewildered at this atrocity, never heard of before in the land, this terrible tragedy that has swept down upon my house and me in my old age . . ." *(He sneaks a look at the BRIGADIER and sees that he has chosen the right document; his voice becomes stronger, taking on a pathetic and indignant tone.)* ". . . at the hands of my very own daughter and an immoral, unworthy, wicked priest, a vile renegade, who, taking advantage of his position as cleric, managed to worm his way into the sacred enclosure of my home and seduce this evil child, whom I no longer call my daughter, rendering her accomplice to his villainous lust and throwing her headlong into a world of vice . . ."
(FARFARELLO, who up until now has been softly strumming his mandolin, interrupts the reading with brusque chords, and lets out a strident guffaw. His laughter is not spontaneous but rather histrionic, feigned, and therefore joking, obscene, with a hint of the sinister and disgusting. The BUFFOONS twitch uncomfortably in their sleep. The BRIGADIER looks at FARFARELLO with repulsion. Time seems to freeze.)
BRIGADIER *(smoothly):* What are you laughing at?
FARFARELLO: At the madness of love, signore. I'm laughing at it so it doesn't laugh at me. *(He laughs.)* Love is too much for one poor man. È troppo, troppo. A curse, a thing of the devil. We must protect ourselves. And the laughter, it can protect us. And if it does not . . . *(Mysteriously.)* There's a formula that never fails. Even the pope knows it. Because if not the pope, then who? He's a man. *(Formal.)* Does the signore wish to learn it?
BRIGADIER: Why do I need to learn to cast spells?
FARFARELLO: The signore is a leader of men, powerful. Love weakens and arrives unexpected, just like death. One must be on his guard. The signore makes the war. The signore knows. When the troops sleep, do not the sentinels always keep the watch?

BRIGADIER: I hardly ever sleep.

FARFARELLO: Yes, but Nature always works on the side of sleep. And the minute a man falls asleep, love takes him over. A man who sleeps is a man in love. Because love, signore, love is a figliol' . . .

PRINCE MURAT *(in his sleep):* A child, he means to say.

FARFARELLO: . . . of the darkness and of sleep. When the body frees itself from the luce . . .

SAINT BENEDICT *(in his sleep):* The light, he means to say.

FARFARELLO *(closing his eyes and pointing to them):* See? When the skin covers the eyes, and the light of God cannot enter the body per gli occhi, through the eyes, then the body returns to its former darkness and becomes one with love. And then, the sogni . . .

STANISLAV *(in his sleep):* Dreams, he means to say.

FARFARELLO: . . . those tricky dreams burst open like bubbles on the surface of stagnant water. And where do they come from, all stirred up like that? From the rotting of the più deep down, the darkness. Because il corpo, signore, the body, the darkness, the dream, and love are all the same thing, the same substance in different states. Even these poor fools, they dream about love. Look at how they twitch, how they suffer. That's why I don't sleep. But at any moment, even this poor fool, one day . . . In the meantime, I laugh. See, signore? Rido.

(FARFARELLO points to his face, which becomes transformed into a horrible laughing mask. He laughs. The BRIGADIER cannot avoid a shudder of repulsion.)

BRIGADIER *(to the CLERK):* Make this disgusting thing shut up.

(The CLERK gets up and lightly beats FARFARELLO, who transforms his laughter into a histrionic howl of pain.)

BRIGADIER *(laughing):* It hurts that bad, eh, dago?

FARFARELLO: No, signore. I'm pretending. If I pretend, it doesn't really hurt me at all. Vede? Ow, ow, ow.

(The BUFFOONS turn over while sleeping, affected by FARFARELLO's "suffering.")

BUFFOONS: Ow, ow, ow.

(The BRIGADIER stomps once, ordering them to be silent.)

FARFARELLO *(a laughing mask, with a histrionic gesture):* Il pain si sfuma. *(He laughs, sarcastically.)* Theater is such a comfort. *(The CLERK hits him.)*

BRIGADIER *(laughing):* Alright, moth. That's enough.

(The CLERK returns to the table, worn-out. The BUFFOONS moan in their sleep.)

FARFARELLO: Hey, signore, let them get some relief, too. Mi fanno pietà. Poor devils. Let them perform for you, how about it, signore? Without waking them up . . . let them perform in their sleep, so they can find some relief from love.

BRIGADIER: Why do I keep fools around if not to have them perform? They get their benefit out of it and I get mine.

FARFARELLO: Ruling is a heavy load. Even the great leaders need some entertainment now and then.

BRIGADIER: And if it's good entertainment, it always carries a lesson with it. Avanti, illustrious Italian, you may create your theater of dreams. How does the comedy begin?

FARFARELLO: In *Inferno*, that's how it should be.

BRIGADIER: Inferno is a good place to start.

(FARFARELLO gets up and begins to walk among the BUFFOONS, playing his mandolin.)

FARFARELLO: Fratelli pazzi, fools, actors! Voi che sapete, from the depths of sleep, what happened to that girl?

(The BUFFOONS respond in their sleep.)

PRINCE MURAT: To the maiden?

FARFARELLO: Yes.

SAINT BENEDICT: The maiden that tempted Evil?

FARFARELLO: Yes.

STANISLAV: The maiden transfixed by love?

FARFARELLO: Yes.

PRINCE MURAT *(laughing in his sleep):* In the holy place we see the trace of a cloven hoof.

FARFARELLO *(singing):*

> What did the maid see that day,
> that first time?

(The BUFFOONS sing and dance, like sleepwalkers.)

BUFFOONS *(singing):*

	What happened?
	What happened?
SAINT BENEDICT:	She saw a priest blessing a font
	and hastened quick to be next it;
	and since she knew it naught,
	the priest for her he did wet it.
BUFFOONS:	The priest for her he did wet it.

BRIGADIER: What disgusting crap!

FARFARELLO: It comes out the way it comes out.

BRIGADIER: Let's see if you can do any better.

FARFARELLO:	What did the maid do then, that day,
	that first time?
PRINCE MURAT:	She looked at it so sweet and calm,
	and sighing, she moistened her palm,
	her little fingers holy water did toss,
	e dopo she made the sign of the cross.
BUFFOONS:	E dopo she made the sign of the cross.

(The BRIGADIER shifts uncomfortably in his seat. The CLERK stifles his puerile giggles.)
BRIGADIER: Well, I never expected this.
FARFARELLO: What's that, signore?
BRIGADIER: Obscene little verses, children's dirty jokes.
FARFARELLO: That's what Hell is like. Ma scusi, signore, may we continue?
BRIGADIER: Let's see where your buffoons end up, Italian.
FARFARELLO: Thank you, signore. *(He sings.)*

	What did the maid say that day,
	that first time?
STANISLAV:	She said: smooth brother, dear lad,
	No one in this world has ever had
	within their hand's reach
	a mystery so very deep
	nor as Communion host to follow
	something so very hard to swallow.
BUFFOONS:	So very hard to swallow.

BRIGADIER *(gloomy):* That one alone's worth an excommunication.
FARFARELLO: They're just some poor fools, signore, spirits of evil, and anyway, it's only a dream.
BRIGADIER: A sinner's dream.
FARFARELLO: Just like all dreams.
BRIGADIER: This had better not go beyond these walls.
FARFARELLO: Don't worry, signore, these are things that live in secret.
PRINCE MURAT *(interrupts them by singing):*

	And what did the priest say that day,
	that first time?
SAINT BENEDICT:	Belovèd child, look and see,
	three are one and one is three.
	Count, my child, with great care,
	two hang down and one's in the air,

                the truth is always a mystery:
                the Holy Trinity.
BUFFOONS: The Holy Trinity.

BRIGADIER: Enough! Blasphemous spirits! Devil's legion! Get out of this house! To the wilderness!
STANISLAV *(singing):*

                I fear, my father, it does me harm,
                this truth, so large and so very warm.

(At a sign from the BRIGADIER, the CLERK jumps on top of STANISLAV and beats him, but SAINT BENEDICT takes up the song.)

SAINT BENEDICT: Oh, my child, what is the chance
                   that pain is worse than ignorance?

(The CLERK now throws himself on top of SAINT BENEDICT.)

STANISLAV: Oh, my father, it is your will:
                with your kindness please do me fill.

(The CLERK, like a stirred-up fly, tosses blows around without rhyme or reason.)

PRINCE MURAT: And thus the two bodies one flesh did become.
                That's how the will of God is done.

(Without leaving his chair, the BRIGADIER slaps and kicks at the BUFFOONS as they come nearer to him. In reality, he appears to be laughing while doing this.)

BUFFOONS: That's how the will of God is done.

(In the midst of this reigning confusion, the stage-right door flies open and the AIDE-DE-CAMP appears. The BUFFOONS collapse, in deep sleep, and FARFARELLO stops playing the mandolin. There is a heavy silence, during which the BRIGADIER and the AIDE-DE-CAMP look at each other.)
BRIGADIER: Knock before you enter!
AIDE-DE-CAMP: Sorry, sir. I heard music.
(He makes a gesture to leave, but the BRIGADIER stops him with a gesture of his own.)

BRIGADIER: It's alright, the show's over. What is it?

AIDE-DE-CAMP: A report on developments and a letter from General Flores. *(The BRIGADIER motions for him to come closer. As the AIDE-DE-CAMP passes by FARFARELLO, he gives the fool a kick. The BRIGADIER takes the papers out of the AIDE-DE-CAMP's hand and throws them onto the table, where the CLERK, already seated in his chair, grabs them in mid-flight.)*

BRIGADIER: Classify these.

(The CLERK goes to work immediately.)

BRIGADIER *(to the AIDE-DE-CAMP):* What's going on outside?

AIDE-DE-CAMP: It's raining heavily, sir.

BRIGADIER: It's not letting up, eh?

AIDE-DE-CAMP: No, sir.

BRIGADIER: A regular New World downpour.

AIDE-DE-CAMP: Yes, sir. To flood out the Madman, who's below us.

BRIGADIER: And the artillery's been deployed?

AIDE-DE-CAMP: Yes, sir. Among the troops, as the brigadier ordered.

BRIGADIER: Are we going to see battle?

AIDE-DE-CAMP: It's still not certain, sir. The Madman's movements still aren't very clear. We'll probably have to wait until daylight . . .

BRIGADIER: Yes, when it clears up . . .

(Pause. The only sound is that of FARFARELLO strumming his mandolin lightly.)

FARFARELLO: Che bello spectacle the war, eh, signore!

BRIGADIER *(absentmindedly, to the CLERK):* The letter, give it to me.

(The CLERK hands it to him. The BRIGADIER breaks the seal and begins to read. In a rapture of inspiration, FARFARELLO stands up and adopts the puffed-up breath and stance of a neoclassical actor, as he begins to recite.)

FARFARELLO: Che bello è when finally at dawn . . .!

(The AIDE-DE-CAMP goes quickly over and slaps him.)

AIDE-DE-CAMP: Don't bother the brigadier!

BRIGADIER *(without looking up):* Leave him be, he's not bothering anybody. He's an artist.

FARFARELLO *(with a bow):* Grazie, signore. *(He returns to his previous stance.)*

> Che bello è when fin'lly at dawn
> the young warriors are unleashèd
> from women's sleep and the pillow's yawn!
>
> And their eyes recover from the glass
> the virgin's clarity, the remote light,
> and the dark shades ultimately pass.

And the sun, the battle's sun buds out
from the earth's breast, in all its glow,
the singular light of vict'ry or rout.

Phoebus Apollo, light that ne'er will quake,
dissolve into flames nocturnal scoria,
and the air in all its splendors shake.

BRIGADIER *(still reading):* How very neoclassical.
AIDE-DE-CAMP: Shall I make him be quiet, sir?
BRIGADIER: Man! What do you have against the theater?
AIDE-DE-CAMP: Nothing, sir. But it's not very serious.
BRIGADIER: Well, aren't you the solemn one. Go on, Farfarello.
FARFARELLO: Grazie.

Let the drums roll and the playful cub,
white, freed from memory, rush out,
to glory's plain down the slope, to rub.

See, signore, they've become lions now.
Seriously they play the sacred game,
in the face of furious cannons' howl.

How it doth stir the ruffled breast!
How the virile blood streams forth,
its purple mirth in the golden air blest!

BRIGADIER *(still reading):* Not bad.
FARFARELLO *(with a slight bow):* Here comes your part, signore.

And trembling, on the hill, awaits
a vile, loutish, but astute herd,
the end of such youthful debate;

Because he knows, Gaia's realm within,
within the earth so silent, so black,
there are fruits deaf to the outside din.

And the mystical bird of war
hovers over the anguished fields . . .

AIDE-DE-CAMP: What anguish!

(FARFARELLO throws him a brief but severe glance and continues.)

FARFARELLO: spies upon the weak, seizing once more

the fleshy off'ring this artifice yields.
The spirit triumphs, the gods look on,
satisfied at such vain sacrifice it wields.

And then, desdegnosi, they are gone.
The shades return, the sounds concealed,
the corpses now one, their breathing done.

And deliv'ring to one sole oblivion all,
like a cold, indiff'rent spouse, spurned,
the night dissolves into senseless pall
what had so sensibly in broad daylight burned.

(Pause. FARFARELLO takes two long bows and throws himself back down to the floor. The AIDE-DE-CAMP looks at him with cold hostility. The BUFFOONS sleep. The sound of the CLERK's quill on the papers is heard. The BRIGADIER folds the letter.)

BRIGADIER: Yes, dago, but that's Europe. Here we wage war differently. Always under the cover of darkness, even in broad daylight. In rain, in mud. In the hand-to-hand you don't know who's who. There aren't any flashy uniforms, and the only thing that glows is fever. Mud, blood, and fever, all mixed together. Here, dago, God never stopped giving breath. Genesis is still in the making. *(Pause. He gives the folded letter to the AIDE-DE-CAMP, who drops it onto the CLERK's table.)* Letter to Flores. "Friend: Unhappy are the moments of destruction, when politics shows itself in its crudest form. How I would have liked to have lived in gentler times! I answer each movement of that assassin, that Madman, with one of my own, just like in a mirror. Because now we see through the glass, darkly . . ." Delete that last phrase. "And when I see my own assassin's face in that looking glass, behind that stony mask, I see only the grimaces of anguish and remorse." Delete that last phrase. "And compassion. But I am my own will. And I am multitude. A peaceful multitude that, in my hands, becomes sharp and hard like the edge of a knife. In order to rip open a place in history. In order to become one people." Delete "peaceful." "But how long, my friend, will I be able to sustain the general will? When will the spell be broken? When will I see only myself standing in front of the mirror? I await that moment with fear." Delete. "With impatience." Delete. "That moment with concern. The moment when history will let me be and I will

finally recover my own true face . . ." *(Brief pause.)* Delete all that. "How I would have liked to have lived in gentler times! But here is where the times have placed me, and I would never let foreign nations, no matter how virile, plunder my land, as if it were a no-man's land." Delete "no matter how virile." "That's why I'm here, dear Flores, riding high on time, weapon in hand, on the lookout for whatever there may be. In order to open the way. To God: the true center of everything."
(Pause.)

BRIGADIER *(to the AIDE-DE-CAMP):* Now you may leave.

(The AIDE-DE-CAMP clicks his heels and goes toward the door, where he vacillates, turning toward the BRIGADIER .)

AIDE-DE-CAMP *(imploring):* Sir . . .

BRIGADIER: Yes?

AIDE-DE-CAMP: Allow me to remind you of the girl . . .

BRIGADIER: Yes, yes . . . And I'm going to resolve it. Now get out of here, and close the door behind you.

(The AIDE-DE-CAMP leaves. The door slams shut with a large echo. The BUF-FOONS shiver. The silence reinforces the sensation of enclosure. The only sound is that of the CLERK's quill scratching across the paper, and the occasional sigh of one of the BUFFOONS. The BRIGADIER paces around the room, in deep thought, his hands interlaced behind his back. FARFARELLO begins to softly play his mandolin.)

BRIGADIER *(with an amused expression):* Farfarello.

FARFARELLO: Signore?

BRIGADIER: You know something of these things. Why do you suppose that a young woman from a good family . . . ? *(He laughs briefly.)* I'm not asking about the priest, because I'm no kid easily shocked by church scandal. But she . . . It's a mystery, don't you think?

FARFARELLO: You should ask the buffoons, signore.

BRIGADIER: Them? What can they possibly know?

FARFARELLO: Oh, they know, signore. *(Mysteriously.)* If one scratches a fool's heart . . . Everything's in there, locked up.

BRIGADIER: And how do you get it out into the open?

FARFARELLO: It's an art. *(Professorial.)* Civilization, signore, she has been studied up and down, the laws that govern the stars and the darkest secrets of the human heart . . .

BRIGADIER *(sarcastic):* So you're also a phrenologist?

FARFARELLO: Un po', signore. Sono a modern spirit. I know a little . . . about everything. *(Getting down to business, with an expert look around.)* Ebbene, only women can talk about women. We need a woman.

BRIGADIER: No women here.

FARFARELLO *(laughing):* There are always women. *(Joking.)* Eh, signore, you're not very moderno! You don't capisce! Things are not as they would seem! That's the first law of modernità! *(Laughing, he points at the* BRIGA-DIER *and says to the others.)* He doesn't believe me!

BRIGADIER: Watch it, dago.

FARFARELLO *(circumspect):* With all due rispetto, signore, inside every man, it's possible to find a woman.

BRIGADIER: Watch it, dago.

FARFARELLO: Don't fear, signore. It's only a piccolo scientific esperimento. With your permission. *(While playing his mandolin, he begins to circle around the other* BUFFOONS, *who twitch and stir in anguished dreaming whenever* FARFARELLO *approaches.* FARFARELLO *sings enigmatically.)*

> If impurity is found in the pure,
> if softness resides in all that endures,
> if in clarity is found the obscure,
> let it all be cleansed by what I now conjure.

*(*FARFARELLO *abruptly stops in front of* STANISLAV *and breaks off his song. He squats in front of the* BUFFOON *and observes him with a cold and penetrating stare. He then lets out an amused guffaw, roguish and childlike.)*

FARFARELLO: Behold the lady! Ecco la donna!

*(*STANISLAV *shoves him away.)*

STANISLAV: Get thee back, Satan!

(He stays curled up in a ball on the floor, trembling.)

FARFARELLO: Open your eyes, buffoons! *(He shoves the* BUFFOONS *with his foot as he plays a happy melody on his mandolin.)* Come on, wake up! Aprite gli occhi!

(The BUFFOONS *begin to wake up; they rub their eyes, yawn, and stretch.)*

FARFARELLO: There's someone here among us, a brother who has a secret.

PRINCE MURAT *(laughing softly):* We all have secrets, mister. There's a reason they say we're crazy.

FARFARELLO: But this one is covering up a dreadful crime. *(He points to the* BRIGADIER.*)* And the signore wants to know about it.

SAINT BENEDICT *(laughing):* The Foundling, a crime? But he's innocent! We're worse than he is.

PRINCE MURAT *(proudly):* Much worse. We're real murderers. I've slit the throats of dogs, parrots, hens. My hands are stained with blood. I've slaughtered all kinds of animals.

SAINT BENEDICT: Sir, I've pissed on an altar. That's why they locked me up.

PRINCE MURAT: And I, sir, contracted matrimony with a she-goat. We, yes, *we* are guilty. But that fool, sir, the only thing he does is look at himself in the mirror, at his reflection in the water. There's nothing wrong with that.

FARFARELLO *(continuing to play his mandolin):* Water, water is the worst. It's deceiving, and it's full of dreams. Water è molto dangerous. Buffoons, help me get our brother to reveal what it is he dreams of in the water.

SAINT BENEDICT: And what do we have to do?

FARFARELLO: You know.

(PRINCE MURAT gets up and lumbers over to STANISLAV. Without any enthusiasm but with a ferocious automatism, he gives him a kick.)

PRINCE MURAT: Speak! *(STANISLAV curls up even more. To FARFARELLO.)* He doesn't want to talk.

(Throughout this scene, FARFARELLO has not stopped playing his mandolin in monotonous, obsessive, ritualistic chords.)

FARFARELLO: Andiam', pazzi! It's not easy getting the water to reveal its secrets.

(PRINCE MURAT, his hands on his hips, looks disconcertedly at STANISLAV.)

PRINCE MURAT: We're going to have to slice his throat.

(SAINT BENEDICT goes over to STANISLAV, sits down on the floor in front of him and opens his Bible.)

SAINT BENEDICT *(reading):* "Nigra sum, sed formosa, filiae Ierusalem . . ."[2]

PRINCE MURAT *(to FARFARELLO):* Shall I hurry him along?

FARFARELLO *(making a quick sign of the cross in the air):* In nomine Patris . . .[3]

(PRINCE MURAT straddles STANISLAV and grabs him by the hair.)

PRINCE MURAT: Speak! What do you see in the water?

STANISLAV: My mother.

PRINCE MURAT *(to FARFARELLO):* He says his mother.

SAINT BENEDICT: "Filii matris meae pugnaverunt contra me . . ."[4]

PRINCE MURAT *(triumphantly):* This one's not a man! He smells like a bitch in heat. *(He beats STANISLAV on the head.)* You were keeping it to yourself, weren't you? *(To FARFARELLO.)* Can I slice his throat now?

FARFARELLO: Lascialo, fool! He's trying to tell us something. Let him get up.

(PRINCE MURAT jumps up and gives STANISLAV a kick.)

PRINCE MURAT: Get up!

(STANISLAV slowly gets up. SAINT BENEDICT also rises, his Bible still open in his hands.)

STANISLAV: My mother rises up from the depths of the water.

FARFARELLO: Eccola qua!

SAINT BENEDICT: "Una est matris suae . . ."[5]

STANISLAV: My mother, sweetly . . .

PRINCE MURAT *(exulting):* They slit her throat, his mother's throat! And then his father's! Because they were enemies!

FARFARELLO: Zitto, Murat!

PRINCE MURAT *(ordering):* Zitto!
STANISLAV: My mother moistens her breasts in the water . . .
PRINCE MURAT: He saw his own mother, naked.
STANISLAV: She sinks down and then returns, trembling.
FARFARELLO: Eccola qua!
STANISLAV: I give her a kiss, in the water as it falls apart.
SAINT BENEDICT: "Osculetur me osculo oris sui . . ."[6]
STANISLAV: And in the water's kiss, we are one. I am the water she plays in. She comes up from my depths and appears in my lips and my eyes. She looks out from my eyes, she is full of smiles. She kisses me in the water with my lips. I look at myself in the water and I am she. I am she. *(Pause.)*
SAINT BENEDICT: "Ecce tu pulchra es, amica mea . . . Oculi tui columbarum."[7] *(He closes his Bible. Pause.)*
PRINCE MURAT: We should slice his throat. That's all I have to say. *(Pause.)*
FARFARELLO: Behold, signore, this transfigured man. Under his rough skin, there's another, softer. Other eyes look out from behind his eyes. Behold, signore, how the two forms fight, with a fever's brilliance. Behold him, crowned in roses.
PRINCE MURAT *(ordering):* Bring in the roses!
BRIGADIER: There aren't any roses here.
FARFARELLO: There are always roses. *(Brief pause. Formal.)* But the experiment's over. If our master would care to interrogate him . . .
BRIGADIER: I see no change in him.
FARFARELLO *(laughing):* Oh, ye of little faith!
(The stage-right door suddenly opens, and the AIDE-DE-CAMP appears in the doorway.)
AIDE-DE-CAMP: Sir!
BRIGADIER: Get out!
(The door slams shut. Pause. FARFARELLO holds a crown of roses over STANISLAV's head. They're transparent, pale in color, and wave in the air as if they were flames just about to go out.)
BRIGADIER: And where did these roses . . .?
FARFARELLO: Silence, signore . . . They're the roses of dreams.
(He slowly crowns STANISLAV with the wreath. Trickles of blood begin to run down the fool's temples. Pause.)
STANISLAV: I am she.
SAINT BENEDICT: I'm the priest.
PRINCE MURAT: And I'm her manly father.
FARFARELLO *(to the BRIGADIER):* We're ready, signore.

BRIGADIER: And where does this comedy take place?
FARFARELLO: In the World.
BRIGADIER: First Hell, now the World, a logical move. It has a certain order.
(*FARFARELLO begins to pluck his mandolin and to circle around STANISLAV and SAINT BENEDICT. STANISLAV and SAINT BENEDICT are standing, separated, each in a hieratic attitude. They are looking at each other, but it is clear that they are transfigured. During the course of this scene, the two will direct their voices to each other with chords that grow deeper and deeper. Their bodies will gradually gravitate to each other in a sleepwalker's attraction.*)
FARFARELLO *(singing):*

> How insidious is love!
> How it does play and plot
> the whirling demon dove,
> always naked, e'er hot!
>
> Sworn enemy of the chaste,
> no sanctuary enjoys its respect,
> as it swoops down in haste,
> e'en in the tombs it may resurrect.
>
> Spreading to all corners
> its ancient, golden flame;
> in the agèd, slow burner,
> mere sparks in a childish game.
>
> As for the young, ah, my lord,
> they are consumed in a trice;
> brighter than the solar orb,
> love in their veins bleeds its price.
>
> Upon the maid, let's turn our eyes,
> she, secretive, etern'ly hidden;
> so if her father's vigil dies,
> mother leaps to the watch unbidden.
>
> Thus from the familial cave
> to the grotto of our Lord,
> pris'ner of their shrouds she's made
> so only her voice may soar.

PRINCE MURAT *(singing):*

> The voice is the first to sin,
> its lustful tone beckons in.
> And thus silent she remains,
> mute, with her gaze restrained.

FARFARELLO *(singing):*

> Ah, there is one o'erlooked:
> her father confessor
> in the confessional booked.
> Love, thou art transgressor!

STANISLAV: Your voice, dark sir, undoes clarity. It comes in shadow, eroding light. And it contains, within, a night of recently forged steel, and inside that night, a rough and jagged diamond.

SAINT BENEDICT: Your voice, dark lady, arrives drenched in clear liquids. Your voice is open, astonished. Like a bird at dusk, slowly unfolding its dark wings, burnished by water.

STANISLAV: Whence comes your voice, so dark? The light, the clarity that enveloped me was too fragile a protection from your deep sigh that spread throughout me, that filled me forever with darkness. Because, even though I cannot see you, dark sir, your voice is too deep, too penetrating to be any other color . . .

SAINT BENEDICT: Your voice conquered me, gentle lady, my blood's been raised. But only my blind voice can reach you. What is my blood doing inside me, gentle lady? How can my impassive skin hold back such abundance?

PRINCE MURAT *(singing):*

> First the voice commits the sin,
> to be followed by the eyes.
> From this man shut yourself in,
> do not let him enter nigh.
>
> Yet once a damsel pure and young
> her own gaze she doth unfurl,
> she too is soon to be stung
> and not even paid like a whorish girl.

STANISLAV: Dark sir, I have found out your eyes, because there in that corner, there was a blackness so thick that it devoured the surrounding shadows. Because your eyes are so dark, they breed clarity.

SAINT BENEDICT: Gentle lady, I discovered your eyes, because there where they were, the darkness palpitated and drew apart and made itself so clear that the night of my own eyes could enter and fill you up.

STANISLAV: Dark one, I have marked your rapid and black trace in the shadows: it is one, only one, of your brows.

SAINT BENEDICT: And I could see, dark lady, a vertigo of matte brilliance slipping in the shadows: is it your polished forehead?

STANISLAV: And I could see a smooth and burning slope: is it the line of your lips?

PRINCE MURAT (singing):

> The eyes, over the skin,
> sinfully they slide;
> clothing serves to hinder sin,
> a maidenhood it must hide.

> Child, cover yourself just so,
> in thickest robes ensheathe,
> in crinolines, in fine picot,
> and four slips underneath.

SAINT BENEDICT: Why should the world wrap you up and shatter you, keep you secret from me? Those luxurious rags that shelter you? Those heavy rags, that bejeweled shroud with which the dead of the earth tried to rip your live flesh for me?

STANISLAV: What is this black velvet that roughly scrapes your delicate, hidden flesh? This incomprehensible banner?

SAINT BENEDICT: I see you only in fragments.

STANISLAV: And I would desire to envelop you and slip through the smallest folds of your skin, and, in order to give you breath, I kiss you, entering you through your mouth and your throat finally to the depths of your body, unto the limits of your blood, and nestle there, rocked by your heartbeats, sleeping forever, like a forgotten breath.

PRINCE MURAT (singing):

> All darkness is obscene;
> in ebon and secret skin,
> jet eyes with lustful sheen,
> black hair in nocturnal sin.

SAINT BENEDICT: I love only the tenuous colors of your darkness. The rest are abominable, bitter, harsh, the horrifying colors of the empty multitude. Their faces caked with paint, their flaccid white cheeks, flaps of bitter cream, their disgusting blond tresses, of rotten burlap, their watery blue eyes, like cloudy glass.

PRINCE MURAT *(singing):*

> And must yourself in paint cover,
> cover your face in powders white,
> lighten your hair in vinegar,
> and make your lips carmine-bright.

STANISLAV: I am very dark, my brother, but comely. I carry within my shadows secret perfumes. I bear within me precious, transparent liquids.

BRIGADIER *(with a hard look, withdrawn):* Enough.

(FARFARELLO automatically stops playing. The BUFFOONS remain motionless, waiting.)

FARFARELLO: Did you say something, signore?

BRIGADIER *(as before):* I said that was enough.

(FARFARELLO, with rapid and furtive gestures, indicates to the BUFFOONS that their sleepwalking performance is at an end.)

FARFARELLO: Eh, pazzi, pazzi . . .

(The BUFFOONS change their attitude immediately, immersing themselves once again in their isolation, indifference, and sleep. Pause. FARFARELLO carefully observes the BRIGADIER.)

BRIGADIER *(without changing his manner, in a paused fashion):* Where are you going with this, Italian?

FARFARELLO: Me, signore? Nowhere. I'm lost, remember?

BRIGADIER: Who are you working for?

FARFARELLO: For nobody, signore. I'm unemployed.

BRIGADIER: What's the purpose of your mission?

FARFARELLO: But . . .

BRIGADIER: To weaken our soldiers? To insinuate a woman's malice into their hearts?

FARFARELLO: It is not my fault. The signore asked me to.

(The BRIGADIER stands up and approaches FARFARELLO in a menacing fashion.)

BRIGADIER: Do you know the Madman?

FARFARELLO: I know lots of madmen.

(The BRIGADIER lets out a short laugh.)

BRIGADIER *(calmly, to the CLERK):* Get me a whip.

(The CLERK gets it for him, quickly. The BUFFOONS and FARFARELLO cluster together in a corner; they are trembling. The BRIGADIER goes over to them.)

FARFARELLO *(trying to maintain a modicum of dignity)*: Signore, we are artists. You yourself said so.

(The BRIGADIER begins to whip them.)

BRIGADIER: Get out! Get out!

(The BUFFOONS and FARFARELLO disappear through the stage-left door. Pause.)

BRIGADIER: You could suffocate in this place. *(To the CLERK.)* Open the door, hey. Let some of the cold air of war in.

(The CLERK races to the stage-right door and opens it. In the doorway stands the AIDE-DE-CAMP.)

BRIGADIER: So you were spying on us?

AIDE-DE-CAMP: No, sir. I was just waiting next to the door.

(Pause.)

BRIGADIER: Any news?

AIDE-DE-CAMP: The plenipotentiary minister of the British Realm has arrived from the city.

BRIGADIER: What could England want at this hour?

AIDE-DE-CAMP: I don't know, sir.

BRIGADIER: Is he hungry?

AIDE-DE-CAMP: Yes, and cold, sir. Frozen to the bone.

(Pause.)

BRIGADIER: Let him wait. But you, come on in, man. What are you doing there, rooted like the guardian of some tomb?

(The AIDE-DE-CAMP enters.)

AIDE-DE-CAMP: It's very stuffy in here, sir. Shall I throw back the shutters?

BRIGADIER: No. Is it still raining?

AIDE-DE-CAMP: No, sir. The rain and the wind have stopped.

BRIGADIER: No one's heard any movement from the Madman?

AIDE-DE-CAMP: Nothing, sir. No reports.

BRIGADIER: He must be waiting for light. *(Pause.)* I can picture the Madman. I can see him now in his tent, wide awake, with his Madman's eyes. *(Pause.)* What does he want? Why is he fighting me?

AIDE-DE-CAMP: He's a savage, sir, a traitor.

BRIGADIER: Yes, of course. *(Brief pause.)* But there he is in his tent, in the candlelight, with his shining eyes wide open. He's feverish and dreaming. What is he dreaming about?

AIDE-DE-CAMP: Who knows?

BRIGADIER *(with a slight laugh, pointing to the CLERK)*: He knows. *(The CLERK drops his quill, paralyzed with panic.)* Isn't that true, louse? You know.

CLERK *(terrified)*: I don't know anything, sir.

BRIGADIER *(laughing)*: Come on, louse, who do you think you're fooling?

You're a man of learning, cultured. A man of letters. Your dreams are just like his.

CLERK: No, sir, I never dream.

BRIGADIER: You read his proclamations on the sly.

CLERK: Only when you yourself order me to read them, sir.

BRIGADIER: But you understand them.

CLERK: No, sir, not a word.

BRIGADIER: I'm surrounded by malice, secrets, plots, conspiracies!

CLERK: Sir, I am completely loyal to Your Excellency!

BRIGADIER: Completely?

CLERK: With all my soul.

BRIGADIER: Then you're a traitor. Because, moth, you don't even have a soul.

CLERK: No, sir.

BRIGADIER: You have nothing where you should have a soul.

CLERK: Yes, sir. But that's where you are, sir.

BRIGADIER: Me?

CLERK: Yes, sir. Right there in my soul's hole.

(Brief pause. The BRIGADIER, sarcastic, motions with his finger for the CLERK to approach. The CLERK takes a few steps toward him. The BRIGADIER makes a clicking sound with his tongue and shakes his head.)

BRIGADIER: Not that way. Not like a man. On your knees.

(The CLERK drops to his knees and goes over to the BRIGADIER, who takes him by the chin and looks deep into his eyes.)

BRIGADIER: No, no. I know when I see myself in a mirror. And I'm not there. *(His hand locks onto the CLERK's face.)* Have you forgotten, louse, that I am who I am because I can read more than papers and books? For example, here, inside this place, everything's empty, it gives me the chills to look at it, a blank page, endless . . . But how? Over there, in that corner, there's a little black spot . . . No one would even notice it . . . It's barely noticeable. But I have perfect vision. I was raised in the country, my friend, with an eye always on the horizon. And what is that little spot? Let's have a look. Aha, it's a letter. And I recognize the handwriting. How many times have I had this handwriting before my eyes? It's from the pen of the Madman. *(The CLERK stirs. The BRIGADIER tightens his grip as if he were reining in a horse.)* Shhh, whoa there, whoa . . . Let me see what this handwriting has to say . . . It's becoming clearer . . . Come on, friend, speak up, call out. *(The CLERK looks at him, pale.)* Oho, you don't want to? *(The BRIGADIER steps away and indicates with his finger for the AIDE-DE-CAMP to approach.)* Corvalán, you read it. The ink's still wet . . .

(The AIDE-DE-CAMP goes over to the BRIGADIER.)

AIDE-DE-CAMP *(to the BRIGADIER):* With your permission.

BRIGADIER: By all means.

(The AIDE-DE-CAMP kneels before the CLERK and, with a furrowed brow, fixes his eyes on the CLERK's, as if he were reading his mind.)

BRIGADIER: Can you read it?

AIDE-DE-CAMP: Yes, sir.

BRIGADIER: Go on.

AIDE-DE-CAMP: Here it says: "Our South American man must be prepared to defeat the great and exhausting enemy of our progress: the desert, backwardness materialized, and the brutish and primitive nature that is our continent."[8]

(Pause. The BRIGADIER rubs his eyes.)

BRIGADIER: Yes, that's what the Madman says. What else?

AIDE-DE-CAMP *("reading" the CLERK's eyes):* "What do we call good taste, if not all that is European? When we say *confortable*, convenient, *bien, comme il faut*, are we talking about all things indigenous?"

(Pause.)

BRIGADIER: Poor fool. Yes, I can see him in his tent right now, by the light of a wax candle, in mud up to his ears, shivering with cold and fever, and dreaming of golden cities in the desert, his countrymen in their frock coats, speaking in French, *comme il faut*. Poor fool, a shopkeeper dreaming about his retail trade.

(He snaps his fingers.)

AIDE-DE-CAMP *(returning to his "reading"):* "Let every cove be a port, so that the same flags from all points of the world shine together in our rivers, the same flags that cheer the waters of the Thames, the river of England and the Universe."

(The BRIGADIER lets loose a sonorous guffaw.)

BRIGADIER *(to the AIDE-DE-CAMP):* Say, Corvalán, have you ever taken a bath in the river of the Universe?

AIDE-DE-CAMP *(standing up):* No, sir. I've never left this land.

BRIGADIER: How uncouth, my dear compatriot! You mean you've never been to the Jordan of shopkeepers? You've never been baptized?

AIDE-DE-CAMP *(catching on to the joke):* Yes, sir, but not in those waters.

BRIGADIER: Of course not. *(Pause.)* This Madman, he'd be disgusting if it weren't for the dignity of his madness. Using the rivers to open up the country to foreigners ... *(Pause.)* I've never trusted rivers, Corvalán. They're nature's traitors. One would think that they run, innocently, sweetly, taking the land to meet the sea. And it's just the opposite. They bring the intruding sea far inland. And the sea is our worst enemy. It doesn't belong to anyone. Not even to men. It has no nationality, no history, no one's ever been born there. It exists only to be crossed by daring, savage men, who have left behind forever the homes of their elders, the land of their dead. We should dry up the rivers, Corvalán, chain them up for being traitors to the father-land.

AIDE-DE-CAMP *(standing at attention):* Yes, sir.

BRIGADIER: Letter to Flores! *(The CLERK jumps up and flies over to the table.)* Go on, Corvalán. Tell them to prepare a mixed grill for England, and tell him to wait.

AIDE-DE-CAMP: Yes, sir. *(He heads toward the stage-right door and opens it, but, as he is about to exit, he stops, doubting.)* Sir . . .

(At the same moment, the stage-left door opens, and FARFARELLO's head appears.)

FARFARELLO: Eh, signore . . .

BRIGADIER: What is it?

AIDE-DE-CAMP: That poor young woman, sir . . . all chained up . . .

FARFARELLO *(whining):* I pazzi, signore . . . They're cold and hungry . . . They're crying . . .

AIDE-DE-CAMP: Sir, just one word from you . . .

FARFARELLO: Signore, forgive them . . . They're weak in spirit.

(The BRIGADIER remains deep in thought. FARFARELLO takes a few steps forward, cautiously, followed by the other BUFFOONS.)

AIDE-DE-CAMP: Sir, these sinners aren't worth the attention.

FARFARELLO: They're sinners, but they're simple people . . . And all of us have un po' of the sinner in us, right, signore?

AIDE-DE-CAMP: Sir, let them go . . .

FARFARELLO: Signore, let them entrare . . .

AIDE-DE-CAMP: Sir . . .

FARFARELLO: Signore . . .

(Pause.)

BRIGADIER: I'll do justice to them.

AIDE-DE-CAMP: Yes, sir.

FARFARELLO: Grazie, signore . . . Because it is not fair for these poor things to be at the mercy of the elements.

(He motions for the BUFFOONS to come in. The AIDE-DE-CAMP closes the stage-right door behind him, at the same time as SAINT BENEDICT closes the stage-left door. The slamming shut of both doors simultaneously produces a strange echo, like that of a stone slab closing a crypt. The lights flicker, and a shiver runs through the characters. There's a long silence. Without anyone asking, the CLERK picks up a piece of paper and begins to read, in a monotonous and somnambulant voice.)

CLERK: "The undersigned has the honor of informing Your Lordship that the two notorious criminals who have scandalized the country, the Priest and his concubine, arrived on the twelfth of this month at our district; given the late hour, the two spent the night in a nearby arbor . . ."

(Pause. FARFARELLO begins to strum his mandolin softly.)
FARFARELLO: From Inferno to the World. And from the World, where to next, signore?
BRIGADIER: It's your game, Italian.
FARFARELLO: Well then, on to *Purgatory*.
(The BUFFOONS collapse, as if overcome by sleep. FARFARELLO circles around them, always playing the same obsessive chords on his mandolin.)
CLERK: ". . . and the accused priest, recently shaved, was seen riding a roan, with a harness and some saddlebags . . ."
(The BUFFOONS talk in their sleep, half-hidden in the shadows.)
SAINT BENEDICT: I see you, my sister, stretched out on the ground, your loose hair misted by the dew. Your eyes are two dark wells, full of trembling water, expectant.
CLERK: ". . . and she rode sidesaddle, with a velvet cap and an English cape . . ."
STANISLAV: I see you, my brother, standing in front of me. Your assassin's eyes shine, dark and hard. My eyes tremble and fill up. And my blood flees deep inside me.
PRINCE MURAT: This is the mystery of the flesh. The eyes slide over the surface, but it's inside, deep inside . . .
SAINT BENEDICT: This is the mystery of the flesh. Only slightly more solid than air, its form slips away and takes flight once again, or it descends in a slow rush into hidden corners. But the form is wispy, changing. It's something else that I seek, my sister: something viscous that lies inside, the darkness within, motionless, that which never changes.
STANISLAV: And nevertheless, stretched out on the ground, I await your dark lion's leap, the wounding rub of your cheeks, your fingers sinking into my flesh like claws, your mouth devouring me in a single bite.
PRINCE MURAT: I hunt you, my wife, like I would an enemy. Impatient to rip open your smooth skin, to pierce your surface, to annihilate the form that covers and cloaks you.
SAINT BENEDICT: Dissolved in fear, only blind fate binds together my blood and my hair, my nerves, my skin, and my bones. Because I was created to wait. In order to be unmade at your hands.
STANISLAV: And in any case, my sister, how could I ever destroy the thing that so sweetly contains you? How could I disfigure such a beautiful thing merely because it contains you? I am inside my body, torn from yours, and I contemplate you and I caress you, with an endless desire for what is deep down inside. And I know that what I desire is beauty. And I protect you from myself because I am self-absorbed and greedy, in love with my own excitement brought on by the scent of your unattainable flesh.
PRINCE MURAT: I was made of dark crevices, of ravenous cavities. I was

made to envelop and swallow. Peaceful and slight, like the dark night opening up its lips to the impetuous light and then, almost unnoticed, once again closing them. Not even my bones will resist your campaign, my brother. Elastic and fragile, they will dismantle their own unnecessary structure. Inside, deep down inside myself, I wait for you, softer and softer.

SAINT BENEDICT: I travel around your body, my sister, with the ointment of my fingers and the secret softness of my tongue. I breathe, drunk, in the hollow of your neck and your shoulder, and for me, the night watchman, your armpits open, there where the ever-damp moss grows.

STANISLAV: Righteous warrior, my arms will not raise up to cover myself, nor to stop this war against me, but instead they encircle your tense back, your arched waist . . .

PRINCE MURAT: And I rest my head between your breasts, that coo like two doves. And my lips linger at your nipples, wrinkled and ripe.

SAINT BENEDICT: My fingers sink into your hair, my beloved, caressing the stubborn crook of your neck, my fingers are like a laurel wreath anticipating your victory.

STANISLAV: And in the dwindling light of your womb, I become undone in shadows that slither around until they fill up the small chalice that is your navel.

SAINT BENEDICT: Your arms, my beloved, enclose me and suffocate me. Your chest weighs like a mountain on top of me.

STANISLAV: What a wide expanse your back is, my sister!

PRINCE MURAT: What a beauty your taut belly is, my brother!

SAINT BENEDICT: And what smooth, shining, and abundant haunches you have, my mysterious mare! They burst forth quivering, in their round fullness, they raise up, voluptuous, and suddenly split open the depths of your body.

STANISLAV: What deep and brutal grooves there are in your flanks as you rear up, my colt! With what energy they descend from your hips to meet in hiding, like violent rivers in a primitive jungle! What lofty columns your haunches are, sculpted in the solid night!

PRINCE MURAT: And from what fantastic animal did your legs come, my sister, from what sacred gazelle, so agile, so firm, set upon such delicate ankles?

STANISLAV: And there, my brother, in the very center of your darkness, upon black crags there rises up a dense shower of resplendent blood. So dense this blood that gleams, vermilion! Upright blood! Your most sacred insignia!

SAINT BENEDICT: And in the very center of your darkness, my sister, other lips barely open, under the shade of nocturnal laces, and the true, pink flower shyly peeks out, the Mystic Rose, living flesh, blood's most fragile borderline, hidden even from me, so that it can be broken, so that I can enter bleeding and we become one flesh in the communion of blood.

CLERK: ". . . and the undersigned individual, having received descriptions of both the accused criminals, swears as to their identity . . ."

SAINT BENEDICT: Because if we have to tolerate the horror of being two bodies and not one . . .

STANISLAV: Because if even the smallest drop of air is not exhaled directly from your mouth, it is unbearable . . .

PRINCE MURAT: The only possibility, my beloved, is for us to devour each other and drink each other up . . .

STANISLAV: So you can quench your thirst with my essences: my saliva, my sweat, my urine . . .

SAINT BENEDICT: So you can nourish yourself with my feces . . .

STANISLAV: With my semen . . .

BRIGADIER: This must stop.

(With some effort, he gets up and, vacillating, goes over to the shadows, where the BUFFOONS stroll about, sleepwalking. There, the BRIGADIER tries to stop the BUFFOONS, hitting them, but they all continue moving with an exasperating slowness and ease, as if trapped in a dreamlike, unreal zone.)

PRINCE MURAT: With your viscous, white semen . . .

STANISLAV: With your cunt's sealike juices . . .

SAINT BENEDICT: So I can sniff your rump, like a bitch . . .

PRINCE MURAT: So I can squeeze your hard breasts until your transparent milk leaps out . . .

STANISLAV: So I can shove my fingers up into the orifice of your ass . . .

PRINCE MURAT: So I can dilate each one of your holes and penetrate each one of your pores . . .

SAINT BENEDICT: So I can mount you, like some fabulous animal with a thousand pricks, and riddle your body until all the blood's run out . . .

STANISLAV: So I can bite into your balls and suck out all your fresh semen . . .

(A heavy silence suddenly descends upon everything. There is a whirling in the shadows, and when it opens, we see the BRIGADIER, standing, with a crown of blazing red roses on his head. Trickles of blood run down his forehead and cheeks. A long silence, abruptly interrupted by several loud knocks at the door. FARFARELLO takes the crown from the BRIGADIER's head, and the BUFFOONS crumble, fall away, plunged into a deep sleep. Pause.)

BRIGADIER *(his voice weak)*: Enter.

(The AIDE-DE-CAMP enters.)

BRIGADIER: Why did you knock so hard?

AIDE-DE-CAMP: Sir, I've been knocking for quite some time.

(Brief pause.)

BRIGADIER: What do you want?

AIDE-DE-CAMP: Sir, did you hurt yourself?

BRIGADIER: No, my friend. *(Smiling.)* It's only the blood of sleep. What do you want?

AIDE-DE-CAMP: The Englishman. He insists on seeing Your Excellency.

BRIGADIER *(singing softly):* "Britannia, Britannia rules the waves . . ." *(Pause.)* Corvalán, tell me about these youngsters.

AIDE-DE-CAMP: The accused?

BRIGADIER: Yes, the accused. You've met them before, haven't you?

AIDE-DE-CAMP: Once or twice, yes, sir, our paths crossed . . .

BRIGADIER: And what impression did they make on you?

AIDE-DE-CAMP: Nothing out of the ordinary.

BRIGADIER: Tell me what they're like.

AIDE-DE-CAMP: Well, he is young, rather short. He appears to be strong but has delicate manners. Black, curly hair. His skin is dark, and he has very lively eyes. Overall, very nice. I don't know if Your Excellency remembers that the young man was recommended to you and to Father Palacio by the governor of Tucumán.

BRIGADIER: Yes, I remember. And what about her?

AIDE-DE-CAMP: Well, she . . . *(His look takes on an intense inner concentration.)* She has dark eyes, with long lashes . . . and her hair is black and full . . . *(Brief pause.)* She walked with so much ease and grace. Well, she's in irons at the moment.

BRIGADIER: You've seen them . . . recently?

AIDE-DE-CAMP: Yes, of course. Both of them.

(Pause.)

BRIGADIER: And how did they meet?

AIDE-DE-CAMP: Well, at confession.

BRIGADIER: At confession?

AIDE-DE-CAMP: At confession.

(The two men look at each other, tentatively, and then suddenly burst out laughing heartily.)

BRIGADIER: What a cheeky pair! A couple of rascals!

AIDE-DE-CAMP *(still laughing):* It appears that he began to visit her every day. At her home.

BRIGADIER *(splitting his sides):* Right under her father's nose!

AIDE-DE-CAMP *(also dissolved in laughter):* Right under the entire world's nose! And she would go to meet him at church.

BRIGADIER *(pointing his thumb up):* Right under the Lord's nose!

(Both split their sides laughing. They calm down. Pause.)

AIDE-DE-CAMP: Well, and then finally they eloped.

BRIGADIER *(admiringly)*: They eloped!

AIDE-DE-CAMP: They eloped.

BRIGADIER: Just like that?

AIDE-DE-CAMP: Just like that.

BRIGADIER *(severely):* Did they steal anything?

AIDE-DE-CAMP *(quickly):* No, sir. They left everything behind.

(Pause.)

BRIGADIER: Why wasn't I informed of this?

AIDE-DE-CAMP: Everyone was terrified. They kept thinking they'd return.

BRIGADIER: They thought they'd return?

AIDE-DE-CAMP: Yes, sir. Until her father finally sent a letter to Your Excellency.

BRIGADIER: Which I read. What a weakling.

AIDE-DE-CAMP: And then the vicar-general wrote you.

BRIGADIER: Yes. He called it a "horrid occurrence."

AIDE-DE-CAMP: And then His Grace, the bishop of the diocese.

BRIGADIER: Another asshole.

AIDE-DE-CAMP: And then Your Excellency's usual enemies . . . Well, you know, sir. They hold Your Excellency responsible for all this immorality.

BRIGADIER: Hah, these people will take advantage of anything to attack me. And the youngsters?

AIDE-DE-CAMP: It appears that they were heading for Entre Ríos.[9]

BRIGADIER: Entre Ríos?

AIDE-DE-CAMP: Yes . . . *(Pause.)* Who knows why?

BRIGADIER: And did they make it?

AIDE-DE-CAMP: Yes. But a curate recognized the accused priest. And he turned him in to the authorities.

BRIGADIER: He did his duty.

AIDE-DE-CAMP: The rest of it, Your Lordship surely recalls.

BRIGADIER: No.

AIDE-DE-CAMP: They brought them in in covered wagons. In chains.

(Pause.)

BRIGADIER: And now, how are they?

AIDE-DE-CAMP: Calm.

BRIGADIER: They're brave.

(Pause.)

BRIGADIER *(softly):* Old man . . .

AIDE-DE-CAMP *(surprised):* Yes, sir?

BRIGADIER: Don't you ever rest, old man? What's your secret, old age? Does this blood ever become thinner?

AIDE-DE-CAMP: Sir, as it gradually becomes thinner, yes, it becomes light itself, but with a light that never stops giving off heat.

BRIGADIER: Do our passions ever grow old?

AIDE-DE-CAMP: I don't know, sir, if our passions grow old, or if it's just the memory of old passions that keeps us alive, or if old age itself has its own weak passion.

BRIGADIER: And just what kind of passion might you have, old man?

AIDE-DE-CAMP: To become light itself.

BRIGADIER: Oh, yes? And how might you go about doing that?

AIDE-DE-CAMP: By cleansing myself of even the smallest stain of desire. But that in itself is a desire. And so we go on, always in the dark, we travel through this earth, hungry for light. Yes, sir, I ache, I long to be pure light. And that is what still makes me burn. And it is my longing to extinguish myself that fans the fire. But don't think that it's a docile, kind fire. Sometimes in the morning, I go out riding through the countryside, and the light jumps up and smiles in my direction; and I smile back and I say: I'm going to make it; I'm going to make it.

(Pause.)

BRIGADIER *(astounded):* I didn't know that you were so crazy, too. So you really do that? Talk to the light?

AIDE-DE-CAMP *(smiling, his eyes lit up with a sweet dementia):* Yes, sir. Sometimes this madness is very strong. And I become furious with impatience, because of this little patch of darkness and fear that separates me from . . . all that light that just hovers there . . . huge, unyielding . . . over the earth. Then my thoughts take me into the future. And I see the moment in which my veins, my lips, rapidly burst into repugnant bubbles. But that will not be more than just a . . . an instant of indignity, of disgust . . . My bones will stay behind to reestablish my respectability . . . Clean, dry, free from all that filthy liquid . . . They will grow old and gray, respectably, growing whiter and clearer all the while . . . All the while more porous to the light . . . Until they're nothing more than illuminated dust. And then not even that. Nothing but light.

BRIGADIER: What a crazy old man! And God?

AIDE-DE-CAMP: Well, that's God, isn't it? That's heaven.

(Pause.)

BRIGADIER: But right now everything is so dark.

AIDE-DE-CAMP: Yes, sir.

BRIGADIER: It's so difficult to get one's bearings in this darkness, to find one's way, and, on top of that, lead this pack of fools.

AIDE-DE-CAMP: Yes, sir.

BRIGADIER: And to be just!

AIDE-DE-CAMP: Yes, sir.

BRIGADIER: Corvalán, for that, one would need to live thousands of years, because it's only out of world-weariness that justice is born. *(Pause.)* How much longer till dawn?

AIDE-DE-CAMP: Not long, sir.

(Pause.)

BRIGADIER: Did you hear that?

AIDE-DE-CAMP: I heard nothing, sir.

BRIGADIER: The Madman, he's beginning to stir. He's getting ready to fight.

AIDE-DE-CAMP: I don't hear anything, sir.

(Pause. FARFARELLO begins to play his mandolin, softly. They're very strange chords that become increasingly intense.)

BRIGADIER: And you don't smell anything?

AIDE-DE-CAMP: No, sir.

BRIGADIER: I do. I smell battle. Soon everything will begin, the blood, fever . . . Look out, everything's about to happen. We don't want the Madman taking us by surprise. *(He goes over, frantic, to the table and grabs a handful of papers.)* Take these, convey my orders.

AIDE-DE-CAMP: Sir, what orders?

BRIGADIER: You already know. Everyone on the alert! Get out! Get out! Out!

(He pushes the AIDE-DE-CAMP out the door and slams it hard behind him. FARFARELLO's music abruptly halts. The BRIGADIER leans against the door, agitated. In the profound silence, the lighting begins to change. It becomes golden, strange, resplendent. FARFARELLO slowly rises; he goes to the center of the stage and solemnly announces.)

FARFARELLO: Paradise, signore!

(He bows and moves away. The BUFFOONS very slowly stand up, still asleep.)

SAINT BENEDICT: One afternoon we were in our full flight
                  by an old and lum'nous river delayed.

PRINCE MURAT: "Look, sister dear," said I, "The tree of life
                  across the river grows beauteous and straight.
                  Go you alone, or does your path join mine?"

STANISLAV: "Brother," I replied, "I go with my mate,
                  our roads will run together ever right."
                  Thus our feet as one broke the river's light.

SAINT BENEDICT: And sinking down into the clarity great
                  of the waters, we were two impostor fish,
                  already cleansed of mortal rust's plate,
                  as clothes the river had stripped,
                  and with them went all our shifts
                  and days and the world. We did wake
                  all polished and naked; afloat, adrift
                  on the opposite shore, our eyes on each other lit.

PRINCE MURAT: How strangely our soft, milky skin did shine
                  in the silent, silver air of a grand,
                  lush, eternal dawn! It rained and rained light.

STANISLAV: And the nearby sun was all golden sand,
we never knew if it chose to decline
or rise up . . .

SAINT BENEDICT: Nor knew we what divine hand
placed it there forever, e'er unrestrained
from time, keeping our tender sun enchained.

PRINCE MURAT: Our eyes burning, aflame from our innocence
and pure astonishment, we wandered lonely
into a virgin jungle. No insistence,
our voices forgotten, now listening only
to the limpid sounds. A strange, unknown science
guided us in our footsteps. When forlornly
the air moved, its sigh carried us along;
once calm in the light, it calmed us, too, strong.

STANISLAV: Peace-drunk animals still meandering
brushed up against our skin, in love, lovesick.

SAINT BENEDICT: We saw tigers satisfy their hungering
in the soft, snowy combs of honey stick.

STANISLAV: We saw both lambs and jackals in a clearing,
dwelling together, blessed, heaven's pick.

PRINCE MURAT: And we dreamt a dream of a venom'd serpent,
cradling a child, the viper's skin transparent.

STANISLAV: Each shining, each resplendent stone unveiled
the clear path to the center, still, mysterious.

SAINT BENEDICT: And the translucent, glitt'ring earth displayed
her veins of metal . . .

PRINCE MURAT: In a wide, rigorous
labyrinth of light we slowly made way
to the last tree. I saw its fronds, luxurious,
glory's outburst, the corn's great tasseling picket,
grace's crown residing there in the thicket.

STANISLAV: As I lie down at his feet, on a bower
of eternity, under sacred wood,
he falls over me, falls like a shower,
this severe owner o'erpower me should,
o'er my being he has absolute power,
he falls like mist, a cloak, a dream, a hood.
And I am he, we are one and the same,
there's no other, no borders, nothing unnamed.

SAINT BENEDICT: And I am she. My annihilated skin
sets loose the juicy dizziness, uproarious.
Finally freed from my delicate, thin

jail, I die and I am reborn victorious,
in our own transparent blood, illumin'd.
I am, and in her, my own body glorious.
Dissolved in the brilliance of a lover's fire,
I am time unfettered, timeless desire.

STANISLAV: Words have run away from us, each one flees,
their selfish pride no longer freely blows.

PRINCE MURAT: Nothing mars aged wisdom, swollen on dreams.
Of the exploit of flight, like the bird knows,
of the thunder of pounding, churning steeds,
of the spider's ritual as its fan grows.

SAINT BENEDICT: Immortal home of every dawn and animal,
of all games shared, and of all games perpetual.

STANISLAV: In slow spirals, we go down, disembark
the tree's sleep . . .

PRINCE MURAT: And in the tenacious center
of its mystery, we become the night's dark.
Where the heartbeat is born, we deeply enter,
submerged in sap, we become the tree's bark.

SAINT BENEDICT: Fruit and flower nuptials, amorous presenter,
encounter of petals and lips; the wood
made flesh, the mane in full flowering brood.

STANISLAV: And in the primal mud, in dust, in clay,
our bodies are unborn . . .

PRINCE MURAT: To him the sigh
returns, He who first gave it, He, the days'
Seed. And at peace, each element alive
renews its dream of earth . . .

SAINT BENEDICT: The dry shine plays
on metal, lightness floats in the wind's eye.

STANISLAV: All wetness returns to live water's weft[10]
and woof, all hot things to the flame are left.

PRINCE MURAT: And in shadows, at the end of the feast,
the awful face of God, seeing and seen,
surrounded by both the Lamb and the Beast.
And the knots come untied, of all that's been
wrought from the last day back to the first, least.

SAINT BENEDICT: We're the remains, Genesis undone, green.

STANISLAV: Fragments of water and light.

SAINT BENEDICT: Shadow, frothing.

PRINCE MURAT: Even less than its remains.

STANISLAV: Nothing, nothing.

(Pause. The light gradually returns to normal. The BUFFOONS have thrown themselves on the ground throughout the space, and the BRIGADIER is seated with a tranquil expression on his face, facing stage left. The stage-right door opens by itself, slowly, and the AIDE-DE-CAMP appears in the doorway. Pause.)

BRIGADIER: Come in, man. Don't just stand there in the doorway.

(The AIDE-DE-CAMP slowly, calmly, enters.)

BRIGADIER: What's going on outside?

AIDE-DE-CAMP: Everything's quiet.

BRIGADIER: But I know that the Madman is out there, crouching.

AIDE-DE-CAMP: Yes, sir. There will surely be battle. I feel it, too, now.

(The BRIGADIER expels all the air out of his mouth, slowly, and sags into the chair. Pause.)

BRIGADIER: What peace! What enormous and simple peace! Now everything has its order. *(He stretches.)* Let me rest, will you? It's been a very long night.

(Pause. The AIDE-DE-CAMP vacillates.)

AIDE-DE-CAMP: Sir . . . now that battle is certain . . . and it's only a little while until dawn, and Your Lordship said . . . Forgive me for reminding you that you have to make a decision about that irritating matter. But it's just that having those youngsters here is a nuisance. And furthermore, if it gets rough, they'll be in danger.

(Brief pause.)

BRIGADIER: It is an irritating matter.

AIDE-DE-CAMP: Yes, sir.

BRIGADIER: And what do you recommend?

AIDE-DE-CAMP *(smiling):* And how should I know, sir? I'm long past affairs of the heart . . .

BRIGADIER: Then why do I have you on my staff, man? Venture some advice.

AIDE-DE-CAMP *(coming to attention):* Yes, sir. I believe, sir, that they should be punished.

BRIGADIER: Aha.

AIDE-DE-CAMP: They have much offended and scandalized society with their crime.

BRIGADIER: Aha.

AIDE-DE-CAMP: So I would advise Your Excellency to be strong.

BRIGADIER: And what would you do?

AIDE-DE-CAMP: I would stick the renegade priest in jail for a while, until the dust settles, and then I would hand him over to the Holy Church and let them decide what he has coming to him.

BRIGADIER: And as for her?

AIDE-DE-CAMP *(vacillating):* Well, sir, given her delicate condition and her dishonor, I think she's already been punished enough . . . Anyway, her parents will know what to do with her . . .

(Pause. The BRIGADIER gets up, laughing.)

BRIGADIER: The Madman has finally decided! I was getting tired of looking at myself in the mirror, darkly . . . Now we'll see each other face to face. What's the morning like?

AIDE-DE-CAMP: It started drizzling again.

BRIGADIER *(laughing):* Always the same old mud. Won't it ever dry up? What does God want from us?

AIDE-DE-CAMP: We'll know soon enough.

BRIGADIER: Right, soon enough.

(Pause.)

AIDE-DE-CAMP: And, sir? Have you made a decision?

BRIGADIER: Shoot them.

(The AIDE-DE-CAMP looks at him in astonishment. The BUFFOONS wake up with a start; they sit up and remain paralyzed, with their eyes wide open.)

AIDE-DE-CAMP *(reacting):* No, sir, I meant those crazy-headed youngsters.

BRIGADIER: Yes, shoot them.

(The AIDE-DE-CAMP, pale and terrified, looks at him.)

BRIGADIER *(exploding):* What's wrong with you? Don't you understand?

(He suddenly leaps over to the AIDE-DE-CAMP, and, with a savage unleashing of passion, blind and desperate, with all the violence he has kept contained up until now, he shakes the AIDE-DE-CAMP by his clothes.)

BRIGADIER: Moron! You've always been a moron! Puppet! What do you think they expect of me, waiting over there, so immense, so calm? How could you possibly think that I wouldn't give a response worthy of their bravery? They're the ones I love! But I have to create a world! Don't you get it? Don't you get it?

(He slaps him several times, then lets him go. Pause.)

BRIGADIER *(calmer):* Look at them all: how they ran away to their homes, afraid, trembling, when that stain appeared. It's a scandal, yes. Because any enormous passion like that scandalizes the world. Because it turns it upside down and disintegrates it. Because the world is nothing more than an infinite web of petty cowardices. And here the web broke. *(Brief pause.)* What irony, Flores, that I in all my bravery would be the representative of all that cowardice! That I would commit this atrocious act so that tomorrow that bunch of sheep might breathe easy and send their daughters to mass without any fear of a priest following them behind the altar with his dick in his hand. So that tomorrow all that rabble, all that riffraff whose only desire is to live *confortable, comme il faut,* that wouldn't risk their skin for any freedom, because freedom terrifies them, so they can whimper about freedom . . . So that these dishonorable types, that shit their pants out of fear for love's fury and disorder, so that they can slobber over love massacred, and write sentimental little verses and let drop a little tear for the poor, star-crossed lovers. I cannot deal with these people all by myself, Flores. It weighs too heavily on me. *(Pause. Calmer.)* But let's not be so unfair. It's preferable to dream about love than suffer through it. And it's from these nightmares that dreams are born.

AIDE-DE-CAMP: But, sir . . . what about compassion?

FARFARELLO: "Qui vive la pietà quand' è ben morta . . ."[11]

BRIGADIER: They were . . . too close to nature. And if we're here, Flores, trying to create a world it's because Someone, sometime, split Nature in two . . . Because we were expelled forever from Paradise . . . And because on the road we're on, even though we don't know where we're going, we can't go back.

AIDE-DE-CAMP: But a world without compassion, sir?

BRIGADIER: Wherever they are, that's where I'll be. Wherever I am, that's where they'll be. This way the Madman will know that I too am a civilizer . . .

AIDE-DE-CAMP: Without compassion, sir?

BRIGADIER: Now go.

AIDE-DE-CAMP: Without compassion?

BRIGADIER: Do as I ordered.

AIDE-DE-CAMP: Sir!

BRIGADIER: Do it.

AIDE-DE-CAMP: Sir!

BRIGADIER: That's an order.

AIDE-DE-CAMP *(with a howl of heartbreaking anguish):* Sir!

(There is no answer. A pause. The AIDE-DE-CAMP leaves. When the door has shut, STANISLAV leaps up.)

STANISLAV: Brothers, verily I say unto you that all this is hollow shell and paint! All this is not real. Reality, resplendent, eternal, lies behind this painted world!

(The BRIGADIER leaps onto STANISLAV, takes him by the neck with his arm, and drags him toward one of the walls.)

BRIGADIER: And here, what's painted here?

STANISLAV: A rough, white wall. The wall of a tomb.

(The BRIGADIER brutally slams STANISLAV's head against the wall. He lets go, and the fool falls down on his knees, stunned and bleeding.)

BRIGADIER: And now?

STANISLAV: Forgive me, sir . . . it's still a painting of a wall. *(He runs his fingers through the blood on his face.)* And this is painted blood.

(The BUFFOONS begin to throw themselves against the walls like blind birds.)

BRIGADIER *(to the CLERK):* Help me!

(With the CLERK's help, the BRIGADIER tries to stop the BUFFOONS. The discharge of rifles outside is heard. A violent death rattle shakes the BUFFOONS, and they fall down, asleep. The CLERK, broken, goes over to the table, sits down, and also collapses, face-down, onto his papers, struck down by sleep. Only the BRIGADIER and FARFARELLO are still awake. The BRIGADIER, exhausted, stands center stage, and FARFARELLO, smiling, has not moved from his corner.)

BRIGADIER *(noticing FARFARELLO):* And you, Farfarello, why are you so quiet?

FARFARELLO *(smiling):* The director's forgotten me, signore. I'm no longer needed. Arrivederci.

(He throws kisses into the air with his fingers and falls asleep. Pause.)

BRIGADIER *(to himself):* Time. I need time.

(The cry of a child is heard, coming closer. The AIDE-DE-CAMP enters, carrying in his outstretched arms, like an offering, a newborn child, still bloody, that writhes about in his awkward hands.)

AIDE-DE-CAMP: It's the woman's son. I don't know how to carry him. I think he's cold.

(Without looking, the BRIGADIER hands him his poncho.)

BRIGADIER: Wrap him up.

(While the AIDE-DE-CAMP dresses the child, cannon fire is heard.)

BRIGADIER: What's that thundering?

AIDE-DE-CAMP: Battle.

TRANSLATOR'S NOTES

1. "The light shines in the darkness."
2. "I am black but lovely, daughters of Jerusalem" (Song of Sol. 1:5 [New Jerusalem Bible]).
3. "In the name of the Father."
4. "My mother's sons turned their anger on me" (Song of Sol. 1:6 [NJB]).
5. "She is of her mother" (Song of Sol. 6:9 [NJB].
6. "Let him kiss me with the kisses of his mouth" (Song of Sol. 1:2 [NJB]).
7. "How beautiful you are, my love . . . Your eyes are doves" (Song of Sol. 1:15 [NJB]).
8. Scattered throughout the Madman's letter are paraphrases of texts by Argentinean "generation of '37" intellectuals, including Juan Bautista Alberdi and Domingo Faustino Sarmiento.
9. The northern Argentine province of Entre Ríos [Between rivers] is so named for its location between the Paraná and Uruguay Rivers. It is the "purple land" of W. H. Hudson's 1885 book.
10. Here "live" rhymes with "five."
11. Literally, "Pity/piety should live when it is good and dead." Farfarello quotes from the *Inferno,* specifically, Virgil's protest when Dante expresses pity for the diviners.

Asunción

The mystical delirium, passion, and death of
Doña Blanca, who, once the concubine of Don Pedro de Mendoza
and now ill with syphilis, agonizes in the still
Paraguayan night, while at her side, Asunción,
an Indian girl, gives birth to the land's first mestizo,
in the Year of Our Lord 1537

Asunción premiered on 2 November 1992 as part of the series "Voces con la misma sangre" [Voices with the same blood] in the Alvear Municipal Theater, Buenos Aires.

Original Cast

DOÑA BLANCA	Patricia Gilmore
ASUNCIÓN	Alejandra Pita
IRALA	Héctor Bidonde
Set design	Tito Vilar
Direction	Laura Yusem

Translator's note: Prior to the play's action, Doña Blanca allied herself with Pedro de Mendoza, Buenos Aires's first founding father, only to take up later with the less-known conquistador Domingo de Irala. By 1537 (*Asunción*'s historical moment), Mendoza had died of syphilis, a disease he most probably passed on to the dying Doña Blanca. Irala would spend some thirty years in Paraguay.

I have chosen to keep the original Spanish title *Asunción* to retain its semantic richness. Asunción here refers to the assumption of a throne or of power, the Virgin Mary's Assumption, and the indigenous woman's Spanish slave-name. The reader might also bear in mind that the city of Asunción is the present-day capital of Paraguay and that the English translation of Doña Blanca would be "Mistress [or Lady] White."

ONE ACT

The middle of the night in a miserable building constructed out of mud and straw, stripped of everything except for two or three transplanted objects whose sumptuousness seems out of place. An enormous baroque crucifix and an armchair made of worked wood, both of the same period. In the armchair sits DOÑA BLANCA. *Hers is a spectral image: her head is quite likely bald, and her face, daubed with makeup, is a mask of white lead, with rouge stains on her cheeks and crimson lips. Her gowns display all the satin, brocade, and pomp Europe had to offer. A seemingly infinite number of jewels cover her. Her hands have disappeared under her rings, her neck barely emerges from the necklaces that encircle it, and all sorts of earrings hang from her ears. She can barely move because of her illness as well as all the ornaments under which she attempts to dress and conceal her state. In a corner, on top of some blankets that have been thrown onto the dirt floor, we see* ASUNCIÓN, *a pubescent girl in the throes of childbirth. Like an animal in a wooded glade, the Indian girl does not scream out the pain of giving birth; rather she moans and murmurs: a continuous, imperceptible Guaraní prayer. The lighting is uncertain, like that of candles or candlesticks.* DOÑA BLANCA *has a dagger in her hand.*

DOÑA BLANCA: I will follow you,
                      my love,
                      by the riverbank . . .

(Pause. ASUNCIÓN *moans.)*

                      Asunción,
                      Asunción,
                      stop your moaning,
                      now, dark one.
                      Must you take it all?
                      Even my moaning?
                      Let me moan.
                      I ache more than you,
                      and I have lost
                      much more.
                      And I will lose.
                      You, on the other hand,
                      what you lose now
                      will soon be pure gains.
                      You moan
                      because you give birth,
                      because light is opening a path,
                      through you,

clawing right through you,
and you do not know
that what you sow
is your own illumination.
I, on the other hand,
look at me,
pregnant with shadows,
what else can I give birth to
but the night?

(Short pause.)

I will follow you,
my love,
by the riverbank . . .

(A sudden pain rips her in two.)

It hurts so much,
this body of mine,
it grinds so grudgingly
to leave itself!
Explode, once and for all!
Explode into shadows,
finally!
Mater Dolorosa,
Our Lady of Sorrows,
succor me!

(Pause. ASUNCIÓN murmurs something in Guaraní.)

Asunción,
Asunción,
does it hurt
you, too?
Here we are,
you and I in the night,
both with our labor pains,
yet how different are the things
to which we are giving birth!
I birth my shroud,
you the morning that you will see
when I am
already dissolved.
I will follow you,
my love,
by the riverbank . . .
The night is so heavy

here,
in this land!
Felt drapes,
smooth and suffocating . . .
Why am I
here,
in this night that never ends?
I, Doña Blanca,
concubine to Don Pedro,
the Admiral of the Sea
and all its Islands,
I,
the favorite,
beloved
of my Magnificent Lord.
What am I doing here
in the dark-beating heart
of this unknown
land?
I will follow you,
my love,
by the riverbank . . .
Don Pedro, sir,
Admiral of the Sea,
how your ship groaned
in all that ocean,
and your body groaned, too,
in the ship's groaning,
Admiral of the Sea . . .
Poor little one,
I lulled you to sleep
between my breasts,
as if you were a son,
ill-kempt,
ill-bred . . .
They treated you ill,
those ship's doctors,
who were brought together
over your half-corpse
and joined together their fetid breaths
to curse you:
the French disease,

Siphilidis . . .
Rocked by the sea
I rocked you,
Admiral,
in my health.
You must have forgiven me,
you never lacked a cradle
in me.
Because the weak woman
kept herself strong
for you.
Even among strong men
who became seasick,
whose gums exploded
blackness
and whose eyes cried
blood,
I stayed strong,
for my own misfortune.
You, my lord,
you were splitting in two,
your bones ground
more than ship's timbers,
you burned and shivered at the same time,
and I,
healthy,
I warmed you
and I cooled you
with my own body . . .
Oh, ocean's vessel,
cradle of my illness,
you carried in your breast,
hidden,
the serpent
that punctured my health
and filled it with the venom
that is killing me!
Because all it required,
Asunción,
was that I set foot
on the riverbank
and my composed

flesh began
to decompose
and explode
into pale fires,
and terrible,
carnal red
sores . . .
Where to hide my corpse
in this wasteland?
There, where the buzzards
meet,
there will be my body.
They met, above me,
the buzzard-doctors,
they pecked at me,
and on my flesh they inscribed
the same
fateful word:
syphilis . . .
Yet they did not know
that, if I exploded,
it was out of love.
I will follow you by the riverbank,
upstream,
downstream . . .
Because on that ship,
first fruit of my sorrows,
Asunción,
I met your lord . . .

ASUNCIÓN: Yourlord, yourlord,
yourlady . . .

DOÑA BLANCA: Yes, your lord,
and lord, too,
of your lady,
Don Pedro's concubine,
the great whore of Babylon,
the slut of the Oceanic Sea,
she who on the wild seas
loved unto frenzy
your lord,
Irala's lord . . .

(Short pause.)

Irala,
Irala,
son of all ire,
son of a bitch . . .
Why did you look at me,
wild man?
Why did you inject in me
the frenzy
of your black eyes,
there on the sea?
Why did you empty me
with a single glance,
only later
to refuse
to fill me up again?
Son of all ire,
Son of a bitch,
rich Irala . . .
You were so cold
and calculated your life so well,
second-born son!
Because you knew
that if on shipboard
you touched
the one who offered herself to you,
your life
would be worth nothing
in the hands of the Magnificent Lord
who kept me.
And was your life worth more
than mine,
coward?
What man is
he, who can,
calculating,
shut off like that
his passion,
and disdain
a mare such as I?
That man is worth nothing!
And look at me,
Asunción,

How I am dying,
because of this nothing,
my life runs away
in such pain!
You never wanted to touch me
on that sea,
cold man.
You refused to risk
your life
for me.
You kept yourself
for something else,
and I gave myself away,
entirely.
But, shut up,
bitch-hound!
stop your moaning!
I cannot bear it!

(In exasperation, Doña Blanca stabs her own palm with her dagger. She feels better.)

Flow, flow,
blood . . .
You've been so still,
stopped up . . .
But now everything begins
to flow;
the night runs,
the river flows . . .
I will follow you,
my love . . .
Do you hear it,
Asunción,
the sweet flowing
of the river?
And when it feeds
into the salty sea,
so much sorrow.
This river suffers,
Asunción,
the night suffers.
The humid breeze suffers,
wounding the tree,

and do you hear the cry
of that wounded tree?
You and I,
we suffer,
everything suffers,
Asunción,
all Creation
suffers birth pains . . .
Holy Mary,
intercede for us . . .
Look at me,
our Lady,
in eternal night,
look at this body that loved,
now shattered,
and pick it up,
raise it up to you,
our Lady,
raise it up in your own Assumption,
in your fingers
of delicate light.
Raise up
this body,
our Lady,
let it not disgust you.
Look at your Son,
how they bruised Him,
and even so
you raised Him up to You,
and You healed Him.
How could You not heal
this body,
my bruised body?

(Pause.)

Asunción,
my slave,
when I
rise up,
will you go with me,
will you leave behind
your son,
on the riverbank of the night,

next to that river
that never stops flowing
and will flow forever?

(Pause.)

I left my lord behind,
agonizing,
in that village,
I fled,
and I followed your lord
upstream . . .
Surreptitiously,
I followed behind him,
followed his scent,
like a she-wolf,
starving,
upstream,
and downstream,
and upstream,
until here . . .
And here
I stopped
to die . . .
Because even when
I could offer myself to him,
my body free,
free of any risk to him,
even then
he would not touch me,
now out of disgust
and fear
of my sores . . .

(She laughs.)

Brave man!

(Pause.)

If I were you,
if you were
the rotting one,
I,
I would follow you,
my love,
by the riverbank,
I would follow you,

upstream,
downstream,
I would follow you
like a she-wolf,
starving,
sniffing the warm body
carried by the water,
I would follow you, my love,
by the riverbank,
and when I found you,
when the water
let you rest
on the riverbank,
when I found you
among the waving rushes,
I would devour you,
gradually,
in the moonlight,
I would devour,
enjoying,
slowly,
your fading corpse . . .

(Short pause.)

But you,
a coward wedded
to power and to life,
you first feared the pomp
of my Magnificent Lord,
and then
you consecrated yourself
to a foreign body,
made of smoke that shone,
aloof and trembling . . .
That was you,
Asunción,
budding fruit,
wild,
more desirable than I,
old fruit . . .
Oh, Asunción,
Asunción,
child of the land,

if only
you spoke my language!
Each word
that you spoke
would be a salve
for so much desire,
so much wounding!
Tell me,
for example,
when he throws himself
on top of you,
like the dusk,
do his nocturnal eyes
flash like lightning?
Tell me,
does his most secret skin
beat darkly?
what does he smell like?
how do his thighs burn?
Tell me,
is his hair,
there,
black and thick?
And there,
where a man's blood
becomes hard,
how burnished is it?
Tell me,
what does his tongue taste like,
his saliva?
And when he enters you,
is it like the night
entering?
Does he flood you,
slow,
serious,
motionless,
invincible?
First
in deep thrusts
and then
like a swoon of darkness

that closes you up
that drowns in you
even the most tenuous
of glimmerings?
Do you tremble?
Do you fear?
Speak!
Do not keep it all
to yourself!
Give birth to
the word!

(Pause.)

I will die
without ever knowing.
You will keep
the secret
forever,
in your incomprehensible murmurs,
in your earthly perfume,
you,
you do not move away
from the rain,
the dew,
the grass,
the wind . . .
I only know
that he scattered
his juice
in you,
a child with breasts
barely sketched out.
He entered you,
making you bleed.
He preferred you
to me.
You were afraid,
I know you were afraid
of his brutal embrace,
of his burning thorn
that made you bleed.
And to his war
in turn you'll give back,

like an offering
of peace,
a chunk of warm flesh
that you've gathered together
patiently
in some corner
of yourself.
But I know that you'll give back
also
a mystery
that will praise him
or condemn him.
What will come forth?

(Pause.)

Raise yourself up,
child!
What are you doing there,
cast down
before your lady,
the palace whore,
the concubine
of our Magnificent Lord?
Do not moan,
lump of clay!
Speak!
Come to me
since I cannot move!
Come!
Let me kill you,
and his child
you carry!
Come!

(Furious, she stabs her other palm with the dagger. Pause.)

Flow, flow,
blood . . .
Take me to the river,
take me to the sea,
flee this world,
lost.
What were you pursuing,
fool?
What tracks?

Return to the midday
sun!
I followed you,
my love,
by the riverbank,
I did not find you . . .
Did I try to kill you,
Asunción?
Never fear,
child . . .
why should you?
He will take others like you,
from all the clay there is here . . .
Your lord
does not require more than holes
in order to water his seed,
and this land is porous,
full of starving
holes.
And I,
look,
my face does not even exist,
I would never recognize it
under all this paint.
My body
bleeds to death,
and my breasts,
dry,
they will never suckle
the children I never had.
My nipples
cry out in suffering,
because now there will never be
any little teeth
to bite them.
My flower
has withered.
Here,
under all my gowns,
I keep for myself
a dark, withered
flower.

Will you accept it,
our Lady,
this flower that never bore fruit?
You,
who gave so much fruit
to the world.
Holy Mary,
intercede for us . . .
Look at me
in eternal night,
look at this body
that once loved,
now shattered,
and pick it up,
raise it up to you,
our Lady,
raise it up in your Assumption,
in your fingers
of delicate light.
Raise it up,
our Lady,
raise up this body,
this handful of sorrows.
Let it not disgust you,
our Lady . . .
Look,
Asunción,
my blood is dripping out,
finally . . .
Soon
I will be transparent,
I will have no weight . . .
I am already floating
in the darkness . . .
delicate and blue,
like a flame
that is about to die . . .
Cleansed of blood,
empty . . .
And even this flame,
this last flame,
will go out . . .

I give myself to the night,
because the night
does not rise up . . .
I will follow you,
my love,
by the riverbank . . .
Asunción,
Asunción,
when you return to the light
with our lord,
will you remember
me?
Will you remember
this thief
of grace?

(She lets her dagger fall as she dies. From the shadows emerges IRALA, slowly.)

IRALA: Doña Blanca, lady . . . *(He goes over to DOÑA BLANCA and picks up the knife.)* Are you finally at rest? *(ASUNCIÓN moans. IRALA goes over to her.)* And you, are you going to have it or not? *(Pause. Coldly curious.)* What will it be?

The Obscurity of Reason

A Play in a Prologue and Three Acts

La oscuridad de la razón premiered on 8 September 1993 in the Payró Theater, Buenos Aires.

Original Cast

MARIANO	Leonardo Sbaraglia
ALMA	Virginia Innocenti
MARÍA	Rita Cortese
DALMACIO	Miguel Guerberoff
PADRE [FATHER]	Aldo Braga
MUJER [WOMAN]	Felisa Yeny
LACRIMOSAS/CORO DE LA MUJER	
[WEEPING WOMEN/WOMEN'S CHORUS]	Dana Basso
	Silvina Katz
	Graciela Paola
	Graciela Peralta López
GALERUDOS/PARTIDA	
[TOP HATS/MEN'S CHORUS]	Horacio Acosta
	Carlos Kaspar
	Javier Niklison
	Marcelo Pozzi
MUSICIANS	Chango Farías Gómez
	Rubén Mono Izaurrualde
Original Music	Chango Farías Gómez
Lighting Design	Alfredo Morelli and
	Jaime Kogan
Set Design	Tito Egurza
Costume Design	Marlene Lievendag
Direction	Jaime Kogan

265

*The play's action takes place in the heart of South America sometime around
1830.*

Translator's note: La oscuridad de la razón/The Obscurity of Reason glosses
many sources, among them the *Oresteia*, the writings of Esteban Echeverría
and Jean Racine, and the New Testament (especially Revelation). In keeping with the original published text, these sources are not specifically noted
but rather have been incorporated into the translated version. A translation
of the play's French dialogue follows the play-text.

The original Spanish names of the characters have been retained. However, the reader should bear in mind that the word *alma* is not only a proper
name but denotes soul or spirit and, figuratively, heart. Note also that Alma's
name is contained in Dalmacio's. The name of Mariano brings to mind the
nineteenth-century Argentinean independence hero Mariano Moreno. Finally, María's name resonates with Christian intensity even as the character herself seems to contradict some of her biblical namesake's defining
characteristics.

PROLOGUE

*A building under either construction or demolition. Scaffolding, wooden
wheelbarrows, mountains of debris. And rising up from all of this, in a
monstrous grab bag of styles, are walls finished in baroque ornamentation,
neoclassical colonnades, stairs that lead nowhere. Taken as a whole, it is
absurd, the product of some mad architect's dream or delirium. We can just
make out, in dusk's shadows, a young, almost adolescent* WOMAN. *She is
seated among the debris, lost in thought.* MARIANO *enters. With the expression of a sleepwalker, he slowly makes his way over to the* WOMAN.

MARIANO: Femme,
          es-tu d'ici?

(Silence.)

          Réponds-moi:
          suis-je arrivé?

(Silence.)

          Es-tu réelle?

*(*MARIANO *draws near to touch the* WOMAN.*)*

WOMAN: Don't touch me,
          Mariano.

MARIANO: Mariano, yes . . .
          Me connais-tu?
          Alors éclaire-moi

tout à fait.
Vois, je suis perdu.

WOMAN: You're home,
Mariano.
This is your house.

MARIANO: This?
My house?
My childhood home?
This land that's falling apart?
Alors,
from what rêve
—vers que rêve—
suis-je revenu?
Or am I never going to wake again?
Always the stranger,
thirsting for reality,
and banished to the desert?
Toujours le mirage?
I thought it was solid earth,
the land that sheltered me
and supported me.
But the sea wasn't
that wide
nor that deep,
and my terrible father's
last, dying breath
crossed the waters.
His cold breath
liquefied the Frankish earth,
it made me tremble
—and I'm still trembling.
He swept my sleep away,
I sank down,
and of the lands where I grew up
there was left only one word:
France, la France,
whose fragrance drifts further and further away,
drunken nights and hungover days
on this thirsty man's dried lips.
Dancing about
on the crest of the choppy sea,
I almost died of longing

for the terra firma of my childhood.
And now I've returned only to stumble over debris?
What terrible force
has demolished my homeland?

WOMAN: This is your destiny,
castaway.

MARIANO: Quelle incertaine plage,
Madame!
Dazed,
tossed about by the sea,
I threw my body on course,
without any holy thought for myself.
Shaken by days,
sleepless nights,
my dust-covered wagon
dragged on by
bolting horses,
I searched for my home.
And once the dust had settled,
there was only scaffolding and debris
that had risen up,
my house pulled down
in lofty demolition,
my fatherland
a simulacrum,
lying in ruins.

WOMAN: But you have come home, traveler,
you can rest.

MARIANO: It was a long journey,
madame,
si je suis arrivé
mais je ne me retrouve pas.

WOMAN: I will seek you out.

MARIANO: Pourras-tu déchiffrer l'enigme,
my lady?

WOMAN: I know who you are,
Mariano.

MARIANO: If you know who I am,
my lady,
même si je ne te connais pas,
je t'en supplie,
please lead me to myself.

WOMAN: I will lead you.
MARIANO: Dessille mes yeux,
            enlighten me.
WOMAN: I will enlighten you.
            Come.
The WOMAN *and* MARIANO *disappear into the debris.*

ACT ONE

SCENE ONE

The same place. The WEEPING WOMEN *enter, surrounding* ALMA.
WOMEN: Pale lady,
            struck dumb,
            terrified . . .
ALMA: Struck dumb, yes,
            like this land . . .
            Terrified, also,
            both of us disturbed:
            my father's land,
            once so solid,
            now crumbling away
            into fragile debris.
            When we buried the man,
            darkness rose up,
            the headstrong mare
            uncinched herself
            and tossed the manes of those she carried.
            Reality departed with my father,
            and like tenuous specters,
            those of us above
            began to tremble.
WOMEN: Let the dead lie,
            pale lady,
            struck dumb,
            let them rest,
            and let your dry eyes
            and your disheveled hair
            rest.
ALMA: Leave me in peace, you madwomen!
            Don't I deserve some solitude?

(ALMA shoves the WOMEN away, throwing pieces of debris after them. The WOMEN flee, with strangled cries, and they hide among the debris, spying.)

ALMA: Where can I find you, dead father?
So strong was your exit,
like some colossal slam
that knocked the door out of its frame,
the universe has come unhinged.
Where can I find you now, dead father?

(The WOMEN begin to appear among the debris.)

WOMEN: Calm your fury,
oh furious,
unhinged girl.
Fill yourself with patience,
oh impatient girl . . .
Something will happen,
order will return,
disordered girl.

ALMA: So much out of order,
only a greater disorder
could order it out.
A disorder so great
that we would long
for this one,
pale in comparison.

WOMEN: What do you seek, madwoman?
More scandal?

ALMA: There will always be scandals . . .

WOMEN: But woe to him
through whom such scandals
come into this world.

ALMA: The world does not turn
'round because old words
are dusted off.
When the foundations give
—and my father was one—,
when the entire building
loses its balance,
isn't it better
if it all comes tumbling down
and finds peace in its own rubble?

WOMEN: And what if it tumbles down
on your own head,
unbalanced girl?

ALMA: Then I would lose
my head,
but what a relief
to lose it!

WOMEN *(to themselves)*:
Cassandra,
madwoman . . .

ALMA: If my own head
finally spun 'round
away from me,
with its feverish brow,
its sleep-deprived eyes,
its bloody visions,
then, women,
it would finally
come to rest
on my ruins.

WOMEN: It is unworthy of the young
to desire death
without having first borne the world their fruit.

(Pause.)

ALMA *(sinister)*:
No,
I won't die
without bearing my fruit.

WOMEN: How should we interpret
her words?
Are they sane
or insane?
Must we intone
a funereal hymn
for this selfish girl
who shuts herself up,
gathering shadows,
as if it were a gulf of death?
Or a joyful canticle
for she who undertakes

to open her body
and receive life
in order to give it?

ALMA: I will answer
            if you respond to me.
WOMEN: Ask away.
ALMA: Could a woman
            give life
            to her own father?
WOMEN: Disgusting!
            What a repulsive idea
            from such a dying head!
            Wild woman!
ALMA: Then,
            if I cannot return his life to him,
            I will become his delighted tomb.
            No,
            I will not open my body
            to anything.
            I will not let life or light
            into where my father,
            nestled in eternal night,
            like a cub
            licks
            his mortal wounds.
            I will be his watchdog.
            If women are the ones who give light,
            we can also take it away.
            If we can give life,
            we can keep death.
WOMEN: Your father's death
            had nothing to do with women.
            It was men's doing.
ALMA *(sarcastic):*
            Women's as well.
WOMEN: —What does she mean?
            —We won't listen to her.
            —Wasn't your father wounded in battle?
            —There weren't any women there.
            —What do we know about war?
            —Other than nighttime wars
            and battles of love . . . ?

ALMA: Wasn't it a love battle
         in whose embrace my father
         found death?
WOMEN: It was the war in which he lived,
         the war he embraced
         and loved
         more than life.
ALMA: Life that gave him death.
WOMEN: Yes, war kills.
ALMA: We're not talking about the same thing.
WOMEN: We don't know what you're talking about.
ALMA: You don't know?
         But even these stones do,
         and soon they'll scream out.
WOMEN: Then we'll be quiet
         and let the stones speak.
         Silence
         is better
         for women.
         Or talking about nothing.
         A woman needs to listen inside,
         to the murmur of her body,
         the slow ripening of her fruit,
         until the time is right
         and her opulent seed
         offers itself up
         and falls to earth
         —Mother Earth—
         in sacred dissolution.
         Let us leave the world to men.
         We will support it.
ALMA *(pensive)*:
         Like mothers who watch over
         their children playing games?
WOMEN: Yes.
ALMA: Who watch them frolic,
         filled with melancholy
         even as they smile?
WOMEN: Yes.
ALMA: Even if the game is rough,
         even if it's deadly,
         like war?

WOMEN: Yes, you've understood.
ALMA: How I wish
          it had been like that!
          We would be equals, fellow women.
          But here there was another game,
          and it did not happen in the daylight.
          It was a secret,
          obscene game,
          of silenced cries,
          muzzled by the night,
          a criminal game.

(Brief pause.)

          My father must be avenged.
WOMEN: Yes, but not by women.
          Let men
          have vengeance on men.
          Let the dead
          bury their dead.
          Each to his own.
          Why cry so much,
          annoying girl,
          for a man who found his destiny?
          Dry your tears
          and seek out your own.
ALMA: My own destiny?
WOMEN: Your own man, stupid girl.
          We women don't have a "destiny."
ALMA: I'm getting tired of this.
WOMEN: And so are we.
          Why cry so much
          over your father?
          If he had been your intended,
          we would understand,
          we would cry with you.
          But your father,
          he was already dead to you.
          Or did he maybe embrace you
          in the privacy of your bedroom?
          Children are not conceived
          by public, paternal
          embraces!
          Cry for the sons and daughters

you have yet to raise,
barren girl,
not for the father
who could never give them to you!
The man who's gone
was not for you.
Cry
for the one yet to arrive.

(ALMA, stupefied, looks at them and then explodes in anger.)

ALMA: What wretched,
dirty,
disgusting and dirty,
foulmouthed vultures!
Get away from me,
leave!

She begins throwing stones at them. The WOMEN flee, crying as they climb onto the debris. ALMA's last cries mix with the WOMEN's first exclamations of discovery, spoken from up above.

SCENE TWO

WOMEN: A man!
A man!
An unknown man!
A stranger!
Look how he plays among the debris,
holding his little brass saber
like a boy!

ALMA: Who is he?
Who are you talking about?

(Pause. MARIANO appears from out of the debris, his eyes feverish. The WOMEN are stirred up. Carrying a little toy saber, MARIANO goes slowly over to ALMA.)

MARIANO: Mon âme,
ma sœur,
j'ai trouvé
ce sabre de laiton,
oxydé parmi les décombres,
avec lequel enfant je jouai,
et le passé tout entier
s'abattit sur moi,
fossoyeur.

Je tombai à genoux,
écrasé par le poids sacré
de l'enfance.

ALMA *(with a strange serenity):*
Don't come near me,
stranger,
don't walk toward me
brandishing your brass weapon.
Don't threaten me
with pretend toys,
because I have a real weapon
in my belt,
and I could do more with it
than threaten you.

MARIANO: Ma sœur,
mon âme,
comme j'étais vide sans toi,
mon âme,
et tellement incomplet!
Quelle creux
dans l'ombre de mon corps!

ALMA *(pulling a real knife from her belt):*
Don't come any closer,
stranger,
jabbering away
in your barbaric gibberish.

MARIANO: Je me croyais plein,
entier,
et je n'étais que la moitié de moi-même!

ALMA: Don't come any closer,
specter,
to someone who's barely
holding on to her reality.

MARIANO: Quelle marionette agitée,
sans histoire,
j'ai été!

ALMA: And I'm telling you
that one has to be very brave
to keep a hold on this reality!

MARIANO: Quel homme sans vérité!
Quel furtif habitant

	de ce qui est à autrui!
ALMA:	Keep coming closer,
	stranger,
	don't stop.
	And if you have any blood, specter,
	give it up
	to my father's thirsty
	knife.
MARIANO:	Même si je meurs,
	mon âme
	—car tu es trop vraie
	pour tant de mensonge— . . .
ALMA:	If your bravery only consists
	of your having no fear of death,
	stranger,
	don't stop.
MARIANO:	. . . même si en nous unissant
	je te dévore,
	et tu me dévores,
	et mon corps
	et son âme,
	éclatent en morceaux,
	now, yes, I can say it,
	my destiny:
	Alma,
	sister,
	It's Mariano.

(Pause.)

ALMA:	What?
MARIANO:	Alma,
	It's Mariano.

(Long pause. ALMA and MARIANO stare at each other, soaking in the suspense. Suddenly, with an unexpected, abrupt, and furious gesture, ALMA tries to stab MARIANO. Instinctively, MARIANO raises his little saber in self-defense and is wounded. The saber falls.)

WOMEN:	Oh!

(Pause. They look at each other. MARIANO's hand is bleeding. Finally, ALMA drops her knife and impetuously leaps over to her brother, taking his hand and passionately kissing the wound.)

ALMA:	Your blood,
	your real blood!

MARIANO: Finally,
            my blood!
ALMA: Your blood,
            so precious to me!
MARIANO: Falling on the ruins
            of our childhood.
ALMA: On me.
MARIANO: On the land
            of our dead.
ALMA: On me.
MARIANO: On our father's
            grave.
ALMA: On me.
MARIANO: It has finally left me,
            this blood
            that was drowning me,
            it has finally fled my dreams,
            and I'm real.
ALMA: Your dear blood,
            selfish brother,
            that you kept to yourself,
            so far away.
MARIANO: I'm here now.
ALMA: Let it return to the earth,
            drop by drop,
            and flow back to me!

(Ecstatic pause. The WOMEN, *paralyzed in amazement, have been following the action and now begin to react.)*

WOMEN: Children,
            children,
            children . . .
            What are you doing?
            This boy's
            bleeding to death!
            How could you throw away
            such precious material?
            What a waste!
            We must help
            the beautiful
            wounded boy!
ALMA *(as if waking up):*
            Wounded?

WOMEN: Can't you see it?
(ALMA sees the wound.)
ALMA (frightened):
            Who did this to you,
            Mariano?
WOMEN (secretly):
            Stark raving mad woman.
ALMA (getting up):
            A bandage, women,
            a handkerchief,
            something to hold back
            all this blood!
(The WOMEN stir. One of them rips up a handkerchief, which ALMA uses to
bandage MARIANO's wound. NOTE: From here on out, MARIANO will always
wear this bloodied bandage.)
WOMEN: The wound is already bound.
            Let us now be discreet.
            Let blood recognize blood,
            without witnesses.
            Brother traveler
            who has returned from distant lands,
            and homebound sister
            who has been waiting.
(The WOMEN pretend to leave, but they stay in the area, spying. Pause.)
ALMA: Mariano,
            son,
            brother,
            father,
            let me look at you.
MARIANO: Alma,
            daughter,
            sister,
            mother,
            let me gaze upon you.
WOMEN (secretly):
            Madness runs in the family.
ALMA: Must I look up?
MARIANO: Must I look down?
ALMA: There's violence in my eyes
            because inside me you are one,
            fragile, small,

	but before me another,
	solid, lithe.
WOMEN:	No argument there,
	this young man's a looker.
MARIANO:	And what do I do with
	my older, luminous sister,
	whom I always looked up to
	with astonished eyes?
	How can I look at her now,
	smaller,
	withdrawn,
	and dark?
WOMEN:	She is consumed
	by fury and bitterness.
ALMA:	Brother,
	you take up the light and the air
	of my brother.
	How did the sickly little boy
	turn into
	such a good-looking and virile
	man?
MARIANO:	Sister of the shadows,
	once so lofty
	and full of light,
	how did you
	turn into
	such a dark and diminished
	little girl?
ALMA:	Untiring time
	stretched out your dimensions.
MARIANO:	Who devoured your heights,
	time's squeezed-dry victim?
ALMA:	Did you come here
	to reestablish proportions?
MARIANO:	Because I'm here,
	the disproportionate will level out.
ALMA:	Was truth always that close?
MARIANO:	My presence here is enough
	for the lies to end.
ALMA:	Well, then, welcome,
	injustice's
	blessèd annihilator.

WOMEN: Welcome,
            son, brother, and father
            of peace!
            Welcome!
MARIANO: Now truth will explode!
            Now trembling and fevers
            will end!
            All passion's been drowned in you,
            still waters.
            Child,
            I will recover calm in your eyes.
ALMA: But there is no calm.
MARIANO: Now everything will return
            to childhood's motionless breast.
ALMA: Why do you threaten me
            with childhood,
            stranger?
            There aren't any children here.
MARIANO: But there were, once . . .
ALMA: A long time ago,
            I don't even remember them.
MARIANO: Let the children
            come to us,
            sister,
            in all the innocence and peace
            of their games.
ALMA: But there is no peace.
            And there never was any innocence
            in their games.
            There never were any rounds,
            or jacks,
            or hide-and-seek,
            or playing with dolls.
MARIANO: I was your doll,
            your child.
            You dressed me
            and undressed me.
            Don't you remember?
            You submerged me
            —you and our mother—
            bathed me in the tub.
            Don't you remember?

ALMA: What strange memories?
                How could such a young man . . . ?
                No, stranger, I don't remember.
(MARIANO picks up his toy saber.)
MARIANO: Look at this piece of our childhood,
                this leftover from the shipwreck.
                Isn't it a mystery
                and a sign
                that the sea that grabbed it away
                returned it to the very beach
                that I have also returned to?
ALMA: That merely shows
                we were children
                once.
                Yes, I remember it.
                Our game was war.
                With that saber
                you disarmed traps;
                you subjected
                countless armies to your rule.
                I was your troop, Mariano.
                Because the game
                determines the child's destiny.
                Already little warriors,
                that was the way we learned
                what our father
                had to teach us.
                Ancestral dominion
                by the sword;
                how easily
                we learned
                to kill
                and to die.
(Brief pause.)
                I'm still faithful,
                I'm still playing that game.
(ALMA picks up her knife from the ground.)
                Do you remember this?
                With this blade's reality,
                our father sliced open
                the world we live in.

MARIANO: Still faithful to your condition,
             you use real things for your games.
ALMA: And you, Mariano, you still believe
             that your games are real.
MARIANO: This little brass saber,
             already rusted, I'm sure
             caused great loss of life,
             but it only spilled
             the blood of dreams.
ALMA: But this butcher's knife,
             in our father's grip,
             spilled oceans of living blood,
             even his own . . .
MARIANO *(interrupting her)*:
             And what would you say, sister, if I told you
             that during my years in exile
             I too learned of the bravery
             in gripping a toy saber?
(Brief pause.)
ALMA: I would say, stranger, that time
             turns innocence into cowardice.
             But will you listen to me?
             Or aren't you brave enough
             to listen?
(Brief pause.)
MARIANO: Speak.
(The WOMEN stir, restless.)
WOMEN: It's better if we give warning.
             When the furious girl begins,
             you never know
             where she may end up.
ALMA: Tell me, Frenchman,
             our father's last
             dying breath,
             that crossed the seas,
             what did it whisper?
             Does your language
             have words that differentiate
             between crime and death?
MARIANO: All death is criminal.
ALMA: Let me be clearer:
             did he die, or was he murdered?

MARIANO: Every death murders
             someone more valuable than death itself.
ALMA: Are you blind?
MARIANO: No, dazzled
             by the incandescent dawn
             of childhood.
ALMA: You don't want to see!
MARIANO: Why not?
             If I see what I love.

SCENE THREE

MARÍA bursts onto the scene; she is exuberant. DALMACIO and the MEN'S CHORUS follow behind; circumspect, they maintain their distance.
MARÍA: Mariano!
             My little boy!
             Is it true?
MARIANO: Mother!
(*MARIANO throws himself at her feet and embraces her knees. MARÍA holds tightly to his head, drawing it to her breast. MARÍA laughs voluptuously.*)
MARÍA: My little boy, yes,
             back inside me,
             like this,
             at my breast.
             Breathe deep,
             yes,
             breathe in deep
             your mother's scent.
             How long has it been?
             Twenty years!
             And you were only five!
             They ripped you out of my arms,
             and you were only a boy!
             And now he's returned, ladies,
             and he's a beautiful man!
(*MARÍA buries her hands sensually in his hair.*)
             Your hair's so dark!
             So curly!
             But I haven't seen
             your face yet!
(*MARÍA raises MARIANO's head and laughs.*)
             Beardless!

	And such dark eyes!
	How they shine!
ALMA *(bitterly, to herself)*:	
	Shameless.
MARÍA:	Like a dark colt.
ALMA:	Like a rutting mare,
	she sees a small colt, sniffs
	the air, and shudders all about.
MARÍA:	How I love
	your murderer's eyes.

(Brief pause.)

	Ladies, a chair!
	I want to feel
	his weight on my lap!
MARIANO:	Mother, no.
MARÍA:	He's ashamed!
	And there's still a drop
	of mother's milk clinging to his lips!

(MARÍA laughs. The WOMEN bring her a chair.)

	Come here!
	One last time,
	your weight
	on my lap!
MARIANO:	Mother . . .
DALMACIO:	My dear lady . . .
ALMA:	Lusty old mare.
MEN:	Ahem! Ahem!

(MARÍA sits down on the chair and obliges MARIANO to sit on her lap. The WOMAN from the prologue stands behind MARIANO, caressing his hair.)

MARÍA *(irritated, to the WOMAN)*:

	What are you doing?
	Get away from him,
	he's mine!
WOMAN:	He is yours today, mother.
	Who can take him away from you?
	Mariano, now
	you're to be delivered to the night.
	And I will not return
	until the dawn.
MARÍA:	Alright,
	leave.
DALMACIO:	Too many women

for only one man.
A bit of modesty, ladies,
don't crush him.

(The WOMAN has disappeared.)

MARÍA: Good, all mine.
All your weight
on me.

(MARÍA laughs voluptuously.)

But what fiery thighs,
young lad!

MARIANO: Madam . . .

MARÍA: Madam,
that's what you call your mother!

(MARÍA laughs again, now joined by the WOMEN'S CHORUS.)

ALMA *(with secret admiration)*:

How she loves flesh . . .
Hot blood
makes her drunk.

MARÍA: What are you muttering about,
bitter girl?

ALMA: Nothing,
my lips are sealed.

DALMACIO: Please, my lady,
let the boy go.

MARÍA: Already? So soon?
What's the rush?

(MARÍA passionately hugs MARIANO.)

Why do they always
take you away from me?
Ladies,
why do men always take him away?

WOMEN: Enjoy your son,
without modesty,
without hurry,
mother;
delay his exit,
we'll hide you.

(The WOMEN form a semicircle around MARÍA and MARIANO.)

MARÍA: Now,
Mariano,
once
and for all,

	fall asleep on me, fall asleep, little one.
WOMEN:	Sleep, Mariano, return to your mother's eternal breast.
ALMA:	Wake up, Mariano.
MARÍA:	Let the eternal instant prolong my fire in you, before your own fire rejects mine and you pull away forever, in your eternal search to cool yourself. Let us be one warm body, before you're swallowed up by the cold universe, never to return.
WOMEN:	Sleep, Mariano, return to your mother's eternal breast.
ALMA:	Wake up, Mariano.
DALMACIO:	Women, enough! This is not dignified, there are men present. Get up, young man!

(MARIANO leaps up off of MARÍA's lap.)

MARIANO: Forgive me, sir.

(The WOMEN break the semicircle. MARÍA grabs MARIANO's hand and pulls him toward her.)

MARÍA: Absolutely not!

(MARÍA notices that his hand is bandaged. She speaks the next lines lightly.)

> You're wounded.
> Why do men get the pleasure
> of wounding themselves?
> But come back,
> I am not done having found you.
> And you, Dalmacio,
> don't meddle.
> You don't try so hard

    to get away

    when I have you on my lap.

MEN: Ahem, ahem!

DALMACIO *(taking a few steps back):*

    Impossible

    to fight women

    on their own turf.

ALMA: Just to feel a man

    between her legs,

    she'll lay her hands on

    even her own son.

MARÍA: Enough, moron,

    enough grumbling

    against your own mother.

    Come here, too,

    look at him,

    it's your brother,

    go on, touch him.

(MARÍA unbuttons MARIANO's shirt and caresses his chest.)

    Such a smooth chest . . .

(MARÍA runs her lips over his body.)

    The scent of his skin,

    so taut . . .

(MARIANO starts to move, trying to get up.)

    Be still,

    my skittish little colt.

    You'll be out of the corral soon enough,

    and then you'll be able

    to run around the lands,

    unfettered.

(MARÍA runs her cheek over his chest.)

    Your scent makes me drunk,

    my frightened little colt!

    Come, my Alma,

    come touch life.

    Because he was once gone

    and now he's returned,

    he was dead

    and now he's come back to life,

    and he's alive,

    and he's beautiful.

    Take it in, my Alma,

the scent of life.
Do you remember, my dear,
when you used to help me bathe him
in the tub?

(The MEN start beating their top hats; they're confused and upset.)

DALMACIO: My lady,
I beg you . . .

MARÍA *(to ALMA):*

Come, my dark one,
you make me sad,
you're always in death's shadows,
and life is this fleeting,
dull sheen
that ends.
One moment you see it,
you're looking at it,
and the next,
you look away,
and it goes out
forever.
Don't let the moment
get away.
Do you remember the tub?
How he jumped about,
like a little fawn,
all glistening soap?

ALMA: He'd slip away from us.

MARÍA: Yes, and we both
ended up
soaking wet!

ALMA: And then,
his damp hair . . .

MARÍA: Drunk with sleep,
covered in the cloud
of his nightshirt . . .

ALMA: We'd submerge him
in crisp, white
sheets . . .

MARÍA: Nestled between us,
we'd caress him
until he fell asleep.
Didn't you like it, Alma,

	being his mother, too?
	Sharing at least that bed
	with me?
ALMA:	Yes . . .
MARÍA:	You see?
	I always gave you
	whatever place was mine to give.
ALMA:	If it weren't, Mother,
	for what you took away from me . . .
MARÍA:	What are you dwelling on?
	Gloomy once more?
	Run away from death,
	she's an old, stinking
	bitch.
	Remember life!
	Remember the little fawn
	in the tub,
	all glistening soap!
ALMA *(sadder):*	
	He slipped away from us.
MARÍA:	And we both
	ended up
	soaking wet!
ALMA:	He was savage,
	frightened.
MARÍA:	Like a little deer
	just caught
	in the hills!
ALMA:	Slippery
	and clever.
MARÍA:	Lean meat,
	elastic.
ALMA:	Stubborn
	and proud.
MARÍA:	Do you remember when you saw him
	naked
	for the first time?
	You couldn't shake off your astonishment.
	What?
	The world wasn't flat?
	There was another?
	Different, pointed, sharp?

ALMA *(smiling):* Shameless.
(MARIANO has managed to free himself from his mother and leaves her, going over toward the MEN.)

MARÍA: He was ours,
             and now look at the traveler,
             how he runs away
             from us,
             now distrusting,
             after his indecency
             in the tub,
             entrusting us
             with his body
             and his proud little bud.

ALMA: That bud is surely now a branch.
MARÍA: A shiny trunk.
ALMA: The glorious boast of men.
MARÍA: The hopeful desire of women.

(ALMA and MARÍA burst out guffawing, accompanied by the WOMEN'S CHORUS and the indignant muttering of the MEN'S CHORUS. DALMACIO picks up a piece of wood from among the debris and brandishes it menacingly.)

DALMACIO: Ladies,
             that's enough!
             Do I have to use this stick?

(MARÍA and ALMA look at him for a moment in silence and then break out laughing, even more shamelessly than before, once again accompanied by the WOMEN'S CHORUS.)

DALMACIO: Par Dieu,
             ladies!
             Let's end this indecent comedy.
             Go to the kitchen,
             prepare something
             to welcome our recent arrival!
             It's time for some gravity,
             there are serious things
             to discuss
             just among us men.

MARÍA/ALMA:
             We're going, we're going,
             before the master
             takes the stick
             to us.

(María and Alma exit guffawing, pushing each other, accompanied by the joyful Women's Chorus.)

WOMEN: Thanks to the stranger,
            peace and happiness
            has been restored
            to this house!

SCENE FOUR

DALMACIO *(to the Men):*
            Let's be seated,
            citizens.

(The Men set rigid chairs in a semicircle and sit; in the middle of the semi-circle, Mariano and Dalmacio sit in two chairs facing each other.)

MEN: What a terrible time!
            What must our young man,
            so cultured and foreign,
            be saying about
            our brazen local girls?

DALMACIO: You must forgive your mother,
            Mariano.

MARIANO: Oui, mon père.

DALMACIO: What, Nephew?

MARIANO: Mustn't I call you Father now?

(Dalmacio springs up.)

DALMACIO: I loved your father!

MARIANO: As much as my mother?

DALMACIO: Nephew,
            Son,
            Mariano,
            it was a necessary step.
            When battle
            sank its teeth
            into your father, my brother's flesh,
            it was rabid,
            like a dog that refuses to let go
            of its prey;
            it followed him
            to his own house,
            where he threw himself down
            to die
            —because that's how long and cruel

was his fight
to live—,
and when that happened,
the foundations of the fatherland
shook.
The land's stupor and agony,
and the enemy's haughtiness,
were such that,
the anarchy so ferocious that,
there was no choice but
to close in the flesh
what had been opened in the flesh.
What you see here
is a scar,
not a marriage.
That is,
the family,
in order to survive,
had to close its ranks.

MARIANO:　And the embrace was so close
that it made you
both
my father and my uncle!
But whoever you may be,
I assure you that
you don't have me to fear.

DALMACIO:　I'm not afraid.

MEN:　A scar,
not a marriage.

MARIANO:　I didn't come here
from the other side of the ocean
to pick over the corpses
like a vulture.
If the smell of death
was what brought me,
it wasn't so that I could feed upon it.
Exhaustion and sadness
muddle my words,
but I did not come to judge.

DALMACIO:　Nor then to be judged.
Prudence in such a young man
is admirable.

	And your plans, Nephew?
	What ambitions
	nest in your generous heart?
MARIANO:	Sleep, Uncle.
DALMACIO:	But, Son . . . !
MARIANO:	Ever since the terrible news
	reached me
	in France,
	a sleeplessness as immense as my father
	has slept in me,
	to the point
	that when I think I'm asleep,
	I am awake,
	and when I think I'm awake,
	I am dreaming.
DALMACIO:	Don't worry,
	Nephew,
	in the country
	your nerves will yawn,
	the women
	will make you
	the softest bed,
	with pillows of lightest feathers,
	the crispest, whitest sheets,
	and you will sleep.
MARIANO:	And when I awake,
	will I find my real home,
	or will I continue to see
	this absurd construction?
DALMACIO:	Oh, this . . . ?
MEN:	In the country
	your nerves will yawn.
DALMACIO:	I wanted to erect a building to reason,
	a temple
	where Greece and Rome
	would cohabit,
	in this uncultured
	and primitive land.
MARIANO:	And what happened, Uncle?
DALMACIO:	The clever architect tricked me.
	He claimed to know
	the laws of symmetry

	and perfect order,
	but confusion was his science.
	I had him beheaded,
	as my tribute to reason.
MARIANO:	Quel barbare!
DALMACIO:	It would have been more barbaric
	to have pardoned his life.
MARIANO:	And what did you have against the first house,
	Uncle?
DALMACIO:	Old-fashioned Spanishism.
	How could one live inside those walls
	that were nothing but
	ignorance and error
	hardened by the centuries?
	If they fell,
	old habits collapsed with them.
MARIANO:	My father
	did not think the same way.
DALMACIO:	I have to admit he thought the opposite.
MEN:	How could one live inside those walls?
DALMACIO:	But it was necessary
	for everything to change.
	For the old dictator,
	war was his lady
	of lands and souls.
	Industry agonized,
	science was dead.
MARIANO:	But, as I walk around,
	all I see
	are lands laid waste by war.
DALMACIO:	Yes, there is still war,
	but everything is different.
	Before, they fought on sown land,
	and now they sow
	in the battlefield.
MARIANO:	And what's the difference?
DALMACIO:	Before, there was peace in war,
	now, there is war in peace.
MARIANO:	I'm still in the dark.
DALMACIO:	So too
	was your father,
	my beloved brother in error.

But I was there,
like a small flame,
burning in the dictator's night.
Son,
you need to know something.
It was I,
who, in order to perpetuate
what had been born in me
—the desire for enlightenment—,
I who prodded your father
to send you
to the fountain of light,
to France.

MARIANO: Have you ever been to France,
mon oncle?

DALMACIO: Only in spirit
—and you've seen it
face to face—,
I in spirit,
but so intensely
that I'm not fooling myself
if I say
that I'm not only a native son
but also French,
mon fils.

MARIANO: Then you're my spiritual father?

DALMACIO: So be it.

MARIANO: But don't you know
that every son's
destiny
is to kill his father?

DALMACIO: What do you mean, Nephew?

MARIANO: Not literally, Uncle.
I mean that we are
on opposite roads,
and if you sent me
to France
in order to perpetuate your thinking,
whatever thought France imbued in me
contradicts yours.

DALMACIO: Why, Nephew?

MARIANO: Those walls you knocked down

<pre>
                from the fatherland,
                those centuries you sought
                to demolish,
                are the sap
                and root
                of the new era.
                In the land of history,
                the further away the root drifts
                from the tree,
                the lusher the treetop
                and the tastier the fruit.
DALMACIO: That's what they're saying today
                in France?
                But it's the return
                of barbarism!
                You must have gotten it wrong,
                Nephew.
MEN: Wrong nephew.
DALMACIO: Tell me,
                in all these years,
                what activity,
                what industry,
                what science
                kept you up nights?
                What did you study?
                What have you been?
MARIANO: A poet.
DALMACIO: Ah.
                So.
                Poetry is the mother
                of all industry
                and science.
                I too,
                more than governor,
                unfortunate successor to my brother,
                your father,
                moi aussi,
                je suis poète.
MEN: Moi aussi,
                je suis poète.
DALMACIO: So what are they writing today
                in France?
</pre>

MARIANO: "Éclaire ma parole, dissipe Dieu ma brume;
            De ton rêve remplis le sang chaud de ma plume."
DALMACIO: Strange, morbid poem.
            Doesn't France write like this anymore:
            "Des Dieux les plus sacrés j'invoquerai le nom:
            Mercure l'industrieux, l'auguste Apollon"?
MARIANO: Old-fashioned, ice-cold poet.
DALMACIO: Nephew,
            the lines are mine.
MARIANO: I'm sorry, sir.
DALMACIO: And I suppose that the other
            was yours.
MARIANO: That's right, Uncle.
DALMACIO: So tell me,
            is that the only "brume"
            exhaled by your "plume,"
            or are there others?
MARIANO: "When a tomb is the moon's light,
            how to hide the dead in the dark night?"
MEN: Why "moon,"
            such a common word,
            instead of "Selena"?
            And besides,
            why so much mystery
            and interest in death?
DALMACIO *(jumping to his feet, inflamed)*:
            "Now great Phaeton rises up and his steeds
            frighten all shadows with their lustrous sparks,
            painting light that e'en Appeles' exceeds!"
*(The MEN also stand up and show their approval by beating their top hats
with their knuckles.)*
MEN: An excellent tercet!
            How it radiates light
            to the entire world!
            How it inspires
            and blinds!
MARIANO: "Who am I? What is my pale fate?
            What uncertainties at my road's end await?"
MEN: Why so many questions?
            Aren't there enough enigmas
            already?

Someone with that many doubts
can never be
a good poet.

SCENE FIVE

The merry troop of ALMA, MARÍA, *and the* WOMEN *bursts onto the stage.* ALMA
and MARÍA *carry a laurel crown, raised in the air.*
ALMA/MARÍA/WOMEN:
      Enough, enough,
      it's clear who is victorious.
      We sisters,
      mothers,
      muses,
      we bestow upon him
      his victory.
*(*ALMA *and* MARÍA *raise the crown of laurels over* MARIANO's *head.)*
ALMA/MARÍA:
      We
      have woven you
      this crown of laurels,
      because you have vanquished,
      you have vanquished
      the sea,
      the highways,
      and death.
ALMA/MARÍA/WOMEN:
      It's clear
      who is victorious.
      We sisters,
      mothers,
      muses,
      pass judgment:
      we bestow upon him
      his victory
      and crown
      his head
      with laurels.
*(*ALMA *and* MARÍA *crown* MARIANO.*)*
DALMACIO *(shaking his head):*
      Ladies, ladies.

Alma/María/Women:
>> Glory be to our lost brother,
>> glory be to our found son,
>> to our pilgrim,
>> our stranger,
>> our hero,
>> glory.

ACT TWO

Scene One

Mariano's room, which bears the same characteristics as the rest of the house: a mix of projects under simultaneous construction and demolition. Mariano, reclining on his bed, is playing with the crown of laurels he holds in his hands.

Mariano *(softly singing)*:
>> "When a tomb is the moon's light,
>> how to hide the dead in the dark night?"

(Ironic.)

>> Enough, poet,
>> won't even victory
>> let you rest?
>> Sleep, little boy.
>> The moon has just come up,
>> the night is long.
>> Let sleep whisper
>> her secrets to you.

(Alma has secretly entered and watches Mariano. From now on, the mysterious white faces of the Women start popping up one by one from everywhere: from behind a chest, above a half-fallen wall, and even from underneath the bed.)

Alma: Why did you remove
>> your laurels,
>> Brother?

(Mariano, smiling, looks at her but doesn't move.)

Mariano: Lune, lune,
>> comment es-tu entrée
>> ainsi furtivement,
>> pour découvrant
>> les secrets de mon couche?

ALMA: Don't talk like that,
I want to understand you.
MARIANO: I've been waiting for you,
furtive moon,
my soul, my Alma.
I needed
your strange light
and your cold,
trembling body.

(ALMA runs to him; seated on the bed, ALMA and MARIANO hug and caress each other. ALMA picks up the crown.)

ALMA: Put it on.
I want to see you
always like this.

(ALMA softly places it on MARIANO's head.)

Your hair,
how I've wanted
to caress it!
How fine
and curly it is!
So dark.
Your curls
are night's
childhood.
If you had seen her . . .
MARIANO: Seen who?
ALMA: Did she caress you like this?
No,
she buried her hungry fingers
in your hair.
If you had seen her,
when we were weaving
the crown,
how she made fun of you.
MARIANO: My mother?
She made fun of me?
ALMA: Of everything.
Of your clothes.
She said they were extravagant,
that maybe they wore them in France,
but here . . .
MARIANO: She was always like that.

ALMA: So why do you dress like this?
MARIANO: What?
ALMA: This way . . .
                     so extravagantly.
MARIANO: It's the style in France,
                     it's normal.
ALMA: It doesn't seem very virile.
MARIANO: Don't you like it,
                     my Alma, my soul?
ALMA: Yes, yes . . .
                     She also said that you were still beardless,
                     and she laughed at you.
MARIANO: She laughed?
ALMA: Yes,
                     she said that only one hair
                     from our father's beard
                     would be enough to cover your entire body.

(ALMA laughs.)

                     What a joker!
                     Mariano, do you remember
                     our father's
                     beard?
                     It was like a wild mountain river,
                     thick and wavy;
                     it ran down off his head
                     and flooded his chest.
MARIANO: Yes, I remember it.
                     I don't know what frightened me more,
                     his ferocious eyes,
                     like lightning
                     in the night,
                     or his beard,
                     that when he leaned over me
                     swept down
                     like a storm.
                     That beard
                     could cover up daylight
                     with its macabre shadow.
ALMA: But it was oily,
                     when he had me on his knees
                     and I sank my little hand
                     into its tufts,

        and I got lost,
        a little girl, in its thickness.
(A sudden pain contorts ALMA's body.)
        Oh, Mariano,
        what visions of fear
        your poor sister
        holds on to!
        Those soft threads
        stuck together by black blood,
        puddled up in . . . !
        I can't breathe!

MARIANO: Calm yourself . . . !

ALMA: You didn't see
        his body torn open
        by stab wounds!
        Those obscene
        red mouths
        locked in a mortal kiss
        with his innocent
        white flesh!
        How carnal
        is death,
        Brother!
        The body's there,
        nothing hides it;
        not a gesture,
        not a light,
        not a word . . .
        And you discover
        that what you loved
        wasn't this body,
        but the movement
        that hid it.
        There's his body,
        in all its nakedness.
        I can see it,
        I can still see it.

MARIANO: Calm down!
        You'll explode
        from sorrow.

ALMA: Oh, Father . . .

	Oh, Mother . . .
	Oh, Father and Mother . . .
MARIANO:	Didn't you ever learn to bear
	the horrors of war?

(ALMA savagely moves away from MARIANO.)

ALMA:	War?
	War?
	How could war have done this
	to the one who was
	its owner?
	Our father
	played with war!
	It was the cub
	that entertained him,
	the apple of his eye!
	War licked his feet,
	nibbled at his heels,
	scratched at his knees!
	It wasn't war
	that brought him down like that;
	it wasn't war
	that hated him so much,
	wasn't war,
	Brother.
MARIANO:	What?
WOMEN:	Now it all begins.
	How to hold it back
	in the middle of the night
	when everyone is sleeping?
	We did what we could,
	we can't do anything more.
ALMA:	Do you remember how Father
	was always coming back?
MARIANO:	Yes,
	he'd return from war
	just like from hunting,
	but instead of a brace of animals,
	he bore gunpowder on his skin,
	dried blood.
ALMA:	His last night,
	he also
	came back, victorious

from battle.
His thoughts on home,
he left his army behind
and went ahead
with his band of faithful men
and Dalmacio.
Among his trophies
he claimed
a pair of slight wounds.
Those are
the cold facts.
But that very same night,
his thoughts on leaving
for I don't know what battle
or victory
or its celebration,
he climbed into bed
with his enemy
—I mean, death—
and that night it swallowed him
alive,
only to vomit him out dead
the next morning.
His bedmate's shrieks
deafened
the house.
She accused the poor, silent man
of having covered up
other injuries
out of pride,
grave, secret, fatal injuries.
The silent man could not speak
in his defense,
but there were other mouths
—so many, oh—
that did cry out
in his silent body,
and later
there were further cries,
the noise of jubilation
for an obscene wedding,
and if you've need

                      of even more cries,
                      the light cried forth
                      when it innocently,
                      shamelessly received
                      a marriage already consummated
                      in the shadows.
MARIANO: Why does all this
                      sound so dark and terrible?
                      Why don't you make
                      what you're saying clearer?
ALMA: The two of them killed him.
MARIANO: Who did?
(Brief pause.)
                      What are you insinuating?
                      What are you saying?
(Brief pause.)
                      What am I to make of this?
                      What a joker!
                      Isn't it possible,
                      Sister,
                      that you're putting me off this?
(Brief pause.)
                      Moon, are you that cold?
                      I'm freezing!
                      I'm drowning from the cold,
                      Alma,
                      I can't breathe!
ALMA: Go ahead, suffer,
                      just as I've suffered.
                      Those
                      are the cold facts.
MARIANO: Hold me,
                      show some mercy.
                      I didn't come here to . . .
                      I didn't come here,
                      I'm not here.
                      This isn't me,
                      these aren't my hands.
ALMA: Calm down.
MARIANO *(looking at his injured hand):*
                      Sister,
                      what a terrible wound!

ALMA: It will heal soon enough.
MARIANO: I have to go.
ALMA: What are you doing?
MARIANO: I never must have come here.
           I haven't even arrived,
           and now I'm leaving.
ALMA: You want to run away?
MARIANO: Je suis étranger!
ALMA: Don't talk that way,
           coward!
(ALMA slaps his face. Silence.)
MARIANO: Why do you hit me?
           What do you want from me?
ALMA: For you to fulfill your duty!
MARIANO: Which one?
ALMA: Don't you know?
MARIANO: You tell me.
ALMA: Don't you think I can?
MARIANO: Yes.
(Brief pause.)
ALMA: Take up your knife,
           Mariano,
           you're a man.
           Give yourself over
           to the pleasure of
           ripping into another man's flesh.
(ALMA howls.)
           Kill Dalmacio
           and that bitch in heat!
MARIANO: Dalmacio?
           How could a boy do that?
ALMA: What boy?
           Don't make me sick.
           All the children
           were murdered.
MARIANO: You want me to take up
           the criminal knife against him,
           sink it into his scornful chest?
ALMA: Yes, up to the handle, all the way
           into the center of his name,
           all the way until you find his proud soul,
           and kill him there,

there where he has it locked up.
Set me free, Mariano,
from this horrible man's prison.

(Pause.)

MARIANO: No,
            you don't understand.
            Who am I?
            Back in France
            I was one person,
            here I'm another.
            In barbaric,
            foreign lands,
            I felt virile,
            full, proud.
            And I was only
            a body,
            without a soul.
            Look at me now,
            all shaken up
            by you,
            by everything.
            Every breeze
            carries its own memory.
            I'm the leaf
            that trembles,
            childhood's bud
            barely holding on
            to memory's
            fragile stem.
            Be careful, storm,
            you might knock me off,
            and I'll fall.

ALMA: I didn't expect some trembling little boy;
            I ardently waited for my stranger,
            the bearded man,
            burned by the sun,
            salty and sore,
            the hardened barbarian.
            And, how ironic,
            I'm the already hardened one
            who's to soften the tough man?

	I spit on that little boy!
	I spit on childhood!
MARIANO:	Be careful, storm,
	you might knock me off,
	and I'll fall.
WOMEN:	What's going on with her?
	Look how fat
	the skinny girl's gotten!
	How the gloomy girl's
	beginning to shine!
	How burnished her
	clever, woman's flesh
	has become!
	She's carrying something
	in her hands!
ALMA:	Look, Mariano,
	I'm no longer
	the squalid,
	bony, skinny
	but strong little girl,
	the one who could throw stones
	farther,
	who would let you win
	in our games.
	The one who could climb
	up to the highest branch.
MARIANO:	You were like a little mother,
	faintly sketched,
	who held me
	between her skinny knees,
	when the turbulent mother
	made her way to another bed.
ALMA:	No,
	look at me.
	I'm no longer that girl
	that made you cry and then laughed at you;
	now I'm the one destined to cry
	and to be laughed at.
	Look at my chest
	that you used to blindly push.
	Look at its delicate
	slopes.

                Everything I am
                is a slope
                for some rough hand
                that trembles as it brushes against me,
                that slips
                and then falls
                on my soft breast.
                That's what I am.
MARIANO: Who are you?
ALMA: I'm the one who wants
                to wound herself
                by caressing
                your rough beard.
MARIANO: I have no beard.
ALMA: No,
                my hand would get hurt
                on your cheek.
                If it went near you
                like a shadow,
                it would bleed away
                in shiny drops.
                All of my self
                would dissolve
                in your day's fire.
                I could sate in me
                your thirst for darkness,
                thirsty, parched
                stranger.
                Full of juice, I
                would give in
                to your ember-embrace.
MARIANO: Sister . . .
ALMA: What?
                Didn't you long for me?
                Didn't you want to discover
                what I had hidden away?
                Didn't you snoop,
                without embarrassment,
                all about me?
MARIANO: I was just a child then.
ALMA: And so was I.
                And I longed for you.

<pre>
                I wanted for myself
                everything that you could
                so bravely unfurl
                to the light.
                And now,
                I want to cut
                my soft dough
                on your sharpest
                knife-blade flesh.
                Because I was hard
                and you were soft,
                and look:
                I've softened,
                and you've become hard!
                Come, Brother,
                life urges us on,
                it's run out of patience,
                and it wants to consummate
                this old longing,
                over the corpse of those children.
MARIANO: So
                life is
                this dream that sweeps over me
                and submerges me
                in dark waves,
                in deep beats?
                Will I finally sleep?
ALMA: Yes, you'll sleep.
MARIANO: Sister,
                is this right?
ALMA: It doesn't matter.
                Fall down,
                sleep in my arms.
MARIANO: Sister . . .
ALMA: Brother . . .
MARIANO: Will I wake up?
ALMA: Yes, to a shining,
                orderly world . . .
WOMEN: This is dark,
                secret,
                veiled . . .
                Let's veil ourselves, sisters,
</pre>

let's cover up
this criminal encounter
between brother and sister,
with the veil of night.

Scene Two

María and Dalmacio's bedroom. María is sitting up in bed. Dalmacio is sleeping beside her. He is naked or nearly so.

MARÍA: Sleepless
in the sinister night . . .

(María looks at Dalmacio.)
And you sleep,
my little one . . .
Yet how restlessly you sleep,
my poor little body!
Your muscles all alert,
your brow exuding,
in its worked-up fluid,
the visions that stir it up . . .
Is the peace I give you,
my little one,
so ephemeral?
Only in the instant
that you are undone in me,
in the waters
in which my fire is pacified?
And instantly
war comes back to steal you away
and with it
go your peace
and mine?

(Pause. To herself.)
What's keeping you awake,
woman?

(The bloody ghost of Mariano's Father appears, seated on one of the bed-room chairs.)
Oh, you're here . . .
I should have known . . .
What do you want from me
tonight?
You keep coming back, coming back . . .

	What do you want?
	To keep me from sleeping?
	To keep me from resting
	even in the comfort of nightmares?
FATHER:	Are you that tired,
	María?
MARÍA:	Yes, of you.
	Of your atrocious persistence,
	of the stubborn gift of your death
	every night,
	of spending my long,
	tedious, despicable days
	waiting with troubled longing
	but also
	with fear
	and anger,
	because I know you're here,
	walking round and round my bed,
	the bloody witness
	to my games of pleasure.
	Why do you keep coming back?
	What do you want from me?
FATHER:	I'm damned . . .
MARÍA:	You were already damned.
FATHER:	. . . to return.
MARÍA:	Why?
FATHER:	You call me back.
MARÍA:	Me?

(MARÍA laughs.)

	I tossed you
	out of life.
FATHER:	Yes, María,
	and I keep coming back
	to life,
	like a beaten dog
	who forgives his abusive master
	every time
	he is thrown out,
	until one time he doesn't return
	because he's died of a broken heart.
MARÍA:	And when will your heart break,
	damned dog?

FATHER:	I don't know.
MARÍA:	Well, I want to sleep!
FATHER:	You'll sleep soon enough,
	my soul mate.
MARÍA:	So that's
	what's keeping you around?
FATHER:	What?
	My soul?
MARÍA:	Not the one you never had.
	Another one . . .
FATHER:	No,
	it's you.
	You're the one keeping me here.
MARÍA:	You dirty,
	despicable
	dead man!
	Get out of here!
	I couldn't stand you when you were alive;
	I hate you even more
	now that you're rotting!
FATHER:	Why did you kill me,
	María?
MARÍA:	You got on my nerves.
	You were dirty.
	Your disgusting beard
	got stuck in my mouth;
	you suffocated me.
FATHER:	Was that enough of a reason
	to kill me?
MARÍA:	How else could I
	free myself?
	Besides,
	what did one more death matter,
	after so many others?
FATHER:	It was mine.
	And the way you did it,
	while I rested in your arms,
	trusting you . . . !
MARÍA:	Enough, enough!
	I can't take your reproaches!
	You come here,
	just after dark,

you thief of dreams!
I want to sleep!
I want to enjoy the day
and the night!
I need some peace . . .
Tell me,
what does your death
matter to you?
You lived like a knife,
sheathed in crime;
others' lives didn't matter to you.
So why should your own?

FATHER: I killed in order to have you.
When I would go out on a campaign,
as I went deeper into the desert,
with the cold already numbing me,
you would appear before me,
from a distance,
and my blood would once again
heat up.
All my savagery
was so I could return to you.
I measured the distance
by the bodies
that separated us.
Annihilating them was not a game;
it was the only way to eat up that distance.
I killed
like a growing fire.
As innocently as the fire.
I killed
like someone kills for his fatherland.

MARÍA: What a sad fatherland
you had!

FATHER: That's what he used to say.

MARÍA: I don't know what he used to say.
I never listened to him;
what I want from him
aren't words.
What do I care about politics!
Leave that to Alma, your soul mate.

FATHER:	Why are you so worried
	about souls?
	Are you worried about your own?
	You, too,
	are already damned.
MARÍA:	Yes,
	and my only regret
	is that I'll have to keep seeing you
	in hell.
FATHER:	Yes,
	along with my younger brother.

(A sudden stab of pain causes MARÍA *to double over.)*

MARÍA:	Leave him alone;
	you don't have him
	in your bloody mouth.
	I'll save him,
	I'll rescue him
	with my own blood.
FATHER:	How faithful
	you are!
	Why so faithful to him
	and not to the other one?
	Couldn't you be
	faithful to both
	in different ways?
MARÍA:	I love him;
	I don't love you.
FATHER:	What an abominable
	double betrayal!
	Deceiving one brother
	with the other!
MARÍA:	What did you want?
	To see me in the arms
	of a stranger?
	I didn't betray you,
	I stayed with your bloodline;
	look at it that way . . .
	Doesn't the Good Book say
	that the duty of a brother
	is to take his brother's widow
	to bed?
FATHER:	But, María,

          not when there's already an heir
          and a murder in between.

MARÍA: Details.
          Too many details
          make life unbearable.

FATHER *(laughing quietly)*:
          I always loved your shamelessness,
          your hunger for life above all else.
          You were the one I loved,
          Wife;
          you aren't
          what he loves.
          I know so well
          that cold man
          who keeps your bed warm.
          You were my end,
          and now you're his means?
          Does his ambition walk
          across the only thing
          I ever wanted?
          Don't you realize
          that?

MARÍA: Yes, I knew.
          I know.
          But what do you know
          about us women?
          Of the pleasure
          of letting the light shine through?
          My happiness resides in giving away
          something that doesn't matter to me.
          You only wanted to fall,
          and the farther into the world you went,
          the more the distance exacerbated you
          and the more urgent and rabid
          your falling
          on top of me.
          A brief, brutal jolt.
          But he,
          because he's about to leave,
          he holds back,
          and I,
          because he's already leaving,

I want to hold him back.
And the game
I play to postpone his departure
is one of agony
and anguished tenderness.

FATHER: But why are you telling me this?
As if I were still able to suffer.
I thought love was something that
swooped down like a bird of prey.
I thought you wanted
to be my catch.

MARÍA: How very natural,
but we women have
more than enough nature as it is.

(DALMACIO *wakes up. At this moment, the* MEN *begin to appear, just like the* WOMEN *in the last scene, popping out of all corners.*)

DALMACIO: Who are you talking to,
María?

MARÍA: Go back to sleep;
it's no one,
just an old dog
scratching at the door.

DALMACIO: Oh, it's you, Brother . . .

MARÍA: No, go back to sleep . . .

(*To the* FATHER.)
Why wake him up?
He did a lot today,
he's tired . . .

DALMACIO: What do you want,
Brother?

FATHER: How are you . . .
I should say:
my loyal minister,
my faithful brother?

DALMACIO: Don't mock me;
I loved you.

FATHER: Cover up your naked body
around me!
Why don't you try on my jacket?
Didn't you always want
to be in my shoes,
to wear my clothes?

Try my jacket on for size!
There are a few rips and tears,
but maybe the knife holes
will suit you.

(The FATHER laughs softly.)

MARÍA: Evil shadow,
go back to the shadows you came from.

FATHER: But tell me, Brother,
aren't you surprised?
Aren't you afraid?

DALMACIO: Why should I fear you
if I'm not really here?
The night is dark,
reason sleeps,
and its dream
engenders monsters.

MEN: Reason sleeps.

MARÍA *(to DALMACIO):*
Yes, you're asleep.
Close your eyes;
I'll cradle you in my arms.
It's only
a bad dream.

(To the FATHER.)
As for you, silly spook,
what are you looking for?
Vengeance?

FATHER: Justice.

MARÍA *(sarcastic):*
When did justice
ever matter
to you?

FATHER: We dead
are more fair-minded.

DALMACIO: I'll stand trial,
Brother.
No matter how high and severe
the jury,
there I'll be,
my body naked
and my soul clean.

FATHER: Prepare yourself for your soul,
             Brother.
             But I'll be your only jury:
             victim and judge.
             Speak.

MARÍA *(to DALMACIO):*
             Don't go along with this
             macabre farce.

DALMACIO: I plead innocence!

MARÍA: You are innocent!

DALMACIO: I, your little brother,
             I loved you!
             But what did love matter
             when it was reason
             that cried out
             for the justice of your death!

FATHER: Why, Brother?

MARÍA *(to DALMACIO):*
             Don't give him any reasons.
             Don't fall into his trap.

MEN: Reason cried out!

DALMACIO: I grew up in your shadow,
             and I admired you.

FATHER: I trusted you.

DALMACIO: I was such a child!
             But there was something in me,
             something godlike.
             A spark flew out
             from I don't know where,
             and the fire ended up
             devouring me.
             Light opened up in me,
             tearing its way out.
             My nurtured spirit
             gave form
             to all that enlightenment.

FATHER: You were a fox.
             I made you a minister.

DALMACIO: And I saw that you were
             dead wrong.

FATHER: I knew about your criticisms.

DALMACIO: The ones I dared
           to tell you about.
FATHER: The rest you kept hidden.
DALMACIO: Yes.
MARÍA *(to the FATHER):*
           Should he have exposed himself
           to your knife?
FATHER: No, I was the one exposed.
MEN: Dead wrong.
DALMACIO: I understood that it was useless,
           that the lights
           would not burn in our people
           until you were gone.
FATHER: What do you know about our people?
DALMACIO: Their thirst for freedom.
FATHER: Freedom for the people,
           and death to the family!
DALMACIO: By any means necessary.
FATHER: So you're freedom?
DALMACIO: Yes.
FATHER: The people hate you.
MEN: Dead wrong.
DALMACIO: Perhaps . . .
           They're still children,
           just like I was.
           I know they love you,
           just like I loved you,
           just like someone who hasn't seen the light
           loves the shadows,
           just like someone who's born chained up
           loves his chains.
FATHER: What arrogance, Brother!
           And that's why,
           for nothing,
           you betrayed me
           and our family?
           Or was it because I was the firstborn,
           our father's
           favorite?
DALMACIO: Just how far back do you think you can go?
           Look, we're parents now.

FATHER: You, a father?
DALMACIO: Your children
                  are mine as well.
MARÍA: Our children in common.
(To the FATHER.)
                  Die once and for all,
                  for them!
FATHER: You're the one who'll die
                  for them.
MARÍA: What do you mean?
FATHER: You're damned,
                  Dalmacio.
                  That's my sentence.
MARÍA: No, he's saved,
                  because he's mine!
FATHER: I'm your judge.
                  Come with me.
MARÍA: No!
FATHER: Are you afraid of me?
DALMACIO: No.
FATHER: Cover yourself up,
                  Brother!
MARÍA: His naked body is mine!
FATHER: Try on my jacket!
MARÍA: Your clothing reeks!
FATHER: If you love me so much,
                  come here, embrace me!
(MARÍA leaps to her feet.)
MARÍA: I'm the only one he'll embrace!
                  Get out of here, repugnant cadaver!
                  Go back to your worms!
                  Let them finish
                  eating you!
                  Let them finish
                  their savior's job!
FATHER: I'll go,
                  but I'll keep coming back.
(The FATHER disappears, laughing softly. Silence.)
MARÍA *(shuddering):*
                  What cold he left behind!
                  How thick and black it is!
                  He left,

                    dragging behind him
                    every single shadow,
                    but even that shadow
                    had more light
                    than this empty, freezing darkness.
DALMACIO: María, cover me up.
                    I'm cold.
MARÍA: Yes, my child . . .
(MARÍA *bundles him up.* DALMACIO *goes back to sleep.)*
MEN: What a thick,
                    terrible,
                    hollow
                    darkness.
MARÍA: Go back to sleep,
                    my little
                    frozen body.
(MARÍA *cradles* DALMACIO *in her arms.)*
                    It's so quiet!
                    The sound
                    of my own voice
                    frightens me.
                    Ladies!
                    Come help me!
                    Lights! Lights!
                    Let's light up
                    all this desolation!
WOMEN (*from offstage):*
                    Light! Lights!

SCENE THREE

The same place as in act 1. The WOMEN, *in groups, run through the debris.*
Lights—candlesticks, oil lamps, or torches—begin to appear. A moment
later the MEN *join in.*
WOMEN: Light! Lights!
                    The night is heavy!
                    It's weighing down like a tombstone!
                    It's asphyxiating!
                    The dead are waking up!
                    And crime is rolling around
                    in the hay!
                    Light! Lights!

MEN *(entering):*

              What an earthquake of silence!
              The house is shaking!
              And it's going to come down
              on us!

ALL: Light! Lights!
              Darkness hurts our sight!
              We're blind!
              Where are we going!
              We're lost in the debris!
              We hear cries!
              Dogs barking!
              Knives biting!
              Moans like one incestuous body
              biting into another!
              Light! Lights!
              No one's asleep!
              The house is shaking!
              The night's a tombstone!
              Light! Lights!

(MARIANO enters, agitated, followed by ALMA. The two CHORUSES make room for them and scale the mountains of debris. From up there, holding out their lights, the two CHORUSES will watch until the end of the scene.)

MARIANO: Light!

(To ALMA.)

              Leave me alone!
              Who are you?
              I had a terrible dream!
              Why are you following me?
              What do you want from me?
              Who are you,
              pale sphinx?
              You don't talk,
              you refuse to speak,
              so
              stop following me around,
              silent dog!

ALMA: No need for words,
              you're already mine.

MARIANO: Yours? Yours?
              Go ahead, take me,

if you can grab on to air,
capture sleeplessness,
sorrow,
anything of ungraspable substance,
but not a man of flesh and blood!

ALMA: Your flesh and blood
recently pressed against me.

MARIANO: Against a half-dead shadow,
against a dying flame,
against a nothing?

ALMA: Against a woman.

MARIANO: Against a terrible dream
just like so many others,
a sad and bitter dream
that's spat out at dawn.
Get away from me,
I don't want to see you,
I've already spat you out.

ALMA: Oh, yes, you spat into me!
What burning spit!

MARIANO: I feel sick.
I'm going to fall.

ALMA: You already fell
onto me.

CHORUS: Some things should be left
unspoken, and unseen.

MARIANO (staggering):
Light!

(MARÍA enters, followed by DALMACIO.)

MARÍA: Lights! Lights!
So much night
to come
is overwhelming!
Lights!

MARIANO: Light . . .

DALMACIO (to MARÍA):
Come here . . .
Why did you run away,
so terrified,
from our bed?

MARÍA: I want to sleep!
And I have every right to do so!

DALMACIO: Come here;
           this isn't
           where you'll find what you're looking for.
MARÍA: I want to sleep!
MARIANO: And I can't wake up.
           I'll trade you, Mother,
           my nightmare
           for your vigil.
MARÍA: Done!
           It can be the most pathetic charity,
           but let it be dreamy sleep.
           A little bit of sleep.
           Just a crumb.
MARIANO: Mother,
           give me refuge;
           I'll be your dream,
           if I can sleep in you.
MARÍA: Get away from me, annoying child!
           I don't have any more
           room left!
           No, my son,
           forgive me . . .
           Come here,
           darling . . .

(MARIANO and MARÍA go to embrace each other, but MARÍA rejects MARIANO.)

           What's that smell?
           You've lost your smell!
           I don't know who you are!
           Who are you?
           No, my son, come here . . .

(MARÍA attempts once more to embrace MARIANO, only to once again reject him brusquely.)

           But what do you smell of?
           I can't stand it!

(MARIANO guffaws bitterly.)

MARIANO: It's my soul
           that stinks.
MARÍA: Your soul, your soul!
           If only we could rip it out of you
           in one fell slash!
           Then you'd be only a body!

ALMA: Oh, if only I could rip myself
out of your body, Mother!
And out of your name,
Dalmacio!

(Pause.)

MARÍA: Is she there?
That girl,
is she there?
Come closer, darling . . .
It's so dark,
I can't see you.

(ALMA steps into the light.)

ALMA: Here I am,
Mother.

(MARÍA looks her over carefully. She smiles.)

MARÍA: Why are you shining?

(MARÍA laughs.)

Look how she glows,
men!
The night
wasn't so dark
for you.

ALMA: I lit it up.

MARIANO: And stole my light away.

MARÍA: Yours?
Why?

DALMACIO: Every question
has its price.
Come back to bed.

MARÍA *(to ALMA):*

Friend,
come nearer.
If I can smell on you
what I think I can,
then we're two of a kind.
Come nearer,
companion;
if I could find a trace
of that lost smell,
then we would be equals.
Then nothing,

                    nobody
                    could accuse me of anything.
CHORUS: Can it be that this unhappy night
                    will bear the fruit of reconciliation?
ALMA: You'll find nothing on me,
                    Mother,
                    that doesn't accuse you.
                    Not a single smell,
                    not even the finest lock of hair,
                    not a drop of lost blood
                    will you find that doesn't cry out:
                    my father's murderer!
MARÍA: The ravings of a madwoman!
ALMA: The murderer of my father!
MARÍA: They can hear you!
ALMA: My father's murderer!
DALMACIO *(turning on ALMA):*
                    How dare you,
                    ridiculous creature of the night!
ALMA: What?
                    Are you hurt
                    because I left you out?
                    Do you want to share
                    her bloody laurels?
                    There's room enough for you!
                    Which do you prefer,
                    being a murdering consort
                    or consorting with a murderer?
MARÍA: Rabid pest!
                    Grave-sniffing weasel!
ALMA: There's only one grave
                    that matters,
                    Mother.
DALMACIO: Sleepwalker!
                    You stir up the night,
                    feeding on suspicion
                    as if it were carrion.
ALMA: You're the carrion
                    that feeds my hate!
                    Baneful scarecrow,
                    criminal puppet!

DALMACIO: Niece,
        what horrible insults!
        Have you no respect for anything,
        little girl?
        Not even for your own blood kin?
        I'm your uncle.

ALMA: Uncle,
        forgive me . . .
        Give me back
        that blood kin
        I loved,
        and I swear to respect you
        forever;
        let that blood
        gather up once more,
        that blood you scattered
        —blood that you were supposed to
        care for but didn't—;
        let the red herd
        return to its corral,
        careless shepherd,
        and I swear to respect you
        forever.

DALMACIO: If only I could,
        but it's not in my hands.

ALMA: What, his blood
        is not on your hands?
        Then I am mad?
        What am I seeing then?

DALMACIO: You've said it.
        You're mad.

ALMA: Not only crimes,
        but lies, too!

DALMACIO: There have been crimes committed,
        yes,
        but in your head,
        nightwalker!
        You've killed restraint,
        you've slit light's throat,
        and worst of all, you've murdered
        your own reason!

MARÍA (*absently*):
>   Let her be;
>   don't waste your breath.
>   I know.
>   Even if she dares,
>   she can't accuse me anymore.
>   Here,
>   to each
>   her own crime.

MARIANO: And as for me,
>   Mother?

MARÍA: Might you be innocent?

MARIANO: I don't know,
>   Mother.
>   You're the only one
>   with the key to that chest.
>   What's inside?
>   If the first link
>   on this chain
>   that binds me
>   was a crime,
>   then I'm a criminal, too;
>   if it wasn't,
>   then everything has been
>   an unholy dream
>   and nothing else.
>   You're reality's keeper,
>   Mother;
>   your word
>   is my destiny.

ALMA (*to* MARIANO):
>   Don't ask her
>   about your dream,
>   coward.
>   Ask her about her own
>   and why she runs away from it.

MARIANO: What do you dream about,
>   Mother?

MARÍA (*with an absent tone*):
>   Yes, yes,
>   I dream about him,
>   so what?

          Does that make me guilty?
          He comes to me
          in the night;
          he seeks me out in my bed.
          He's always sought me out.
          He talks to me.
          He tells me of his sorrows
          from the other side.
          He accuses me . . .
          of things that a husband
          usually accuses his wife of.
          He's awful,
          jealous,
          he follows me . . .

DALMACIO: Be quiet, María . . .

MARÍA: He shows me his wounds
          and tells me:
          This is what you did to me . . .
          one day,
          don't you remember?
          You broke my heart in two
          with this one
          and that one;
          you plunged the knife in here
          and here and here . . .

DALMACIO: María, I beg you . . .

MARÍA: Normal stuff,
          sentimental
          games.

(The FATHER's ghost appears.)
          Quit following me,
          I tell him,
          we're all wounded.
          What do you want now?
          I ask him.
          Don't torment me,
          I tell him!
          Is it so cold
          there
          in hell
          that you still have to seek out
          my warm flesh?

                    Aren't there any whores
                    in hell?
                    Leave me in peace!
CHORUS: She's gone mad.
                    Who's she talking to?
MARÍA *(to the FATHER)*:
                    Tell me once and for all,
                    why do you keep coming back?
FATHER: To repeat my death.
DALMACIO: You enjoyed it that much?
FATHER: Why not?
                    It was in her arms . . .
                    don't you remember,
                    María?
MARÍA: Yes, I remember . . .
FATHER: I came in all worked up,
                    still burning
                    from the heat of battle,
                    in virile triumph,
                    full of gunpowder.
                    I needed to cool down in you.
                    I never thought
                    that the cold could go so far!
                    And there,
                    on our bed,
                    I took you.
                    My assault was
                    so pressing,
                    the victory I sought was
                    so rapid,
                    that I didn't even succeed
                    in taking off
                    my jacket.
                    I didn't enter you naked,
                    not even in death.
MARÍA: That's how
                    we'd planned it.
DALMACIO: We didn't want you
                    to suffer.
MARÍA: We didn't bear you
                    any rage.

DALMACIO: We loved you.
MARÍA: The plan was
          that once you dissolved
          inside me
          you'd leave life
          behind forever.
DALMACIO: One single ecstasy,
          of complete dissolution.
MARÍA: So you wouldn't feel
          any pain.
DALMACIO: Or see our betrayal.
MARÍA/DALMACIO:
          We loved you!
FATHER: And so we all knifed each other.
(Speaking ambiguously to MARIANO and ALMA, who watch, frozen.)
          The first stab
          was here . . .
          This open sore
          on my side.
          The blade passed through
          my kidney.
          I was still alive.
(Now MARÍA and DALMACIO address MARIANO and ALMA.)
MARÍA: He spun toward him,
          looking at him.
          He got free of me,
          he pulled himself away.
DALMACIO: I pulled the knife
          from his body.
          His wound
          was spitting out blood,
          his eyes spitting fire
          at me.
          I plunged the knife
          into his belly.
FATHER: Here,
          at my waist.
          The cold
          opened up
          my frightened guts.
          I was still alive.

DALMACIO: I pulled it out
             and attacked again,
             this time at his chest.
FATHER: My chest, Brother,
             that had sheltered you!
DALMACIO: I was looking for his heart,
             but I couldn't find it.
FATHER: He wounded me here,
             in my lungs.
             I was still alive.
DALMACIO: His heart,
             his heart kept beating!
             It thundered!
             I had to stop it!
MARÍA: His boiling heart!
DALMACIO: He wouldn't be quiet!
             He roared!
FATHER: I threw myself on him!
DALMACIO: And he stabbed himself
             on my knife!
MARÍA: Only he
             could silence his own heart!
FATHER: I had to end
             such horrible pain!
DALMACIO: And finally
             he burst!
MARÍA: What thunder
             shook the earth!
DALMACIO: What lightning,
             what light
             covered the earth
             when that heart
             of darkness
             died!
FATHER: I was dead.
DALMACIO: I was born.
FATHER: I was enslaved in death.
DALMACIO: I was freed in life.
MARÍA: And I was free and a slave,
             both at the same time.
FATHER: And he kept on stabbing

what was now nothing but a body.
As my soul moved away,
I saw
how she helped him.

MARÍA: When he was tired,
           I took the knife
           and continued the job.

DALMACIO: Each stab
           shored up
           freedom's building.

MARÍA: Each blow
           stitched up
           freedom's flag!

FATHER: A black banner,
           that flag!
           A ruin
           of a building!

(Long pause.)

ALMA: I've been knocked down.
           I've died.

MARIANO: They've buried me alive
           in my own debris.

ALMA: So much rage.

MARIANO: So much furor.

ALMA: So much hate.

MARÍA: No, it was love.

DALMACIO: It was light.
           It was an act
           of reason.

CHORUS: My God!
           Why must all this
           come to light?
           It should have died
           among the shadows,
           silenced.
           Who cares
           if the world
           turns like this,
           so long as it keeps turning?
           What a dangerous
           delay!

(Pause. ALMA slowly unsheathes the knife at her waist.)
ALMA *(to MARIANO):*

        Brother,
        Father,
        Husband,
        Son,
        do I have to do it?

(Her FATHER goes over to her.)
FATHER: Don't dirty
        your woman's hands.

(The FATHER takes the knife from her and offers it to MARIANO.)
        Mariano . . .
MARIANO: Yes, Father.
FATHER: Grab hold of me, Mariano.
        Hold me fast,
        without trembling,
        and plunge me into him.
MARIANO: Father,
        that's dreadful.
        I've never killed before.
FATHER: It must be done.
        You're a man,
        my son.

(The FATHER leaves the knife in MARIANO's hand and moves away.)
MARIANO *(with sadness and remorse):*

        Uncle . . .
DALMACIO *(absentmindedly):*

        Yes?

(MARIANO thrusts the knife once into DALMACIO's chest and pulls it out. Pause. DALMACIO grabs his chest, staggering.)
FATHER: One more dead,
        what a tedious
        and sad sight!
DALMACIO: What abominable
        fate is mine!
        To be forced to die
        at the hands
        of some detestable poet!
        Et voilà,
        there's always a glimmer
        of reason:

France gave me light,
and France is taking it away.

(DALMACIO falls.)

Au-re-voir . . .

(DALMACIO shudders a few times and then dies. Pause. ALL look at the cadaver, lost in their own dreams. MARIANO still holds the bloody knife.)

MARÍA: But can this be real?
Did what I see
really happen?
It's not a delusion?
Not some dirty little trick
played by insomnia?
He's lying there,
in the middle of the night,
and a dark,
sticky
pool
is bubbling out
of his chest . . .
Is this true?
Am I dreaming?
Is it real?
Move!

(MARÍA moves DALMACIO's body with her foot.)

Jump up to me!
Do I have to go down
to you?

(MARÍA falls on her knees next to DALMACIO's body. MARÍA touches his chest and looks at her bloody hand. MARÍA then let outs a long howl of pain, the wild howl of a dying animal.)

Owwwwwwwwww . . .

(Pause.)

Your juice
is spilling away.

(MARÍA tries frantically to collect the blood.)

Help me
collect his blood!
Help!
The bloody thief
is getting away!
Traitorous night!

She takes everything
with her!
Help!

(Suddenly MARÍA stops and lets the blood run over her lips.)

It's still hot.
Who said
you were cold?
Bundle me up,
darling,
because I'm the one
who's cold now!

(With a hungry, desperate passion, MARÍA begins to cover her face with blood and tear off her clothes in order to cover her body in blood.)

Give me your last heat,
agonizing ember!
We'll have so much time
as ashes
and the instant's so brief,
that there's barely time
for us to be warm together!
Give me your last heat,
agonizing ember!
Yes, my darling,
empty yourself out if you want,
if you can fill me up
and drench me!
Scrub yourself on me!
Like this . . . yes . . . yes!
More!
Give me your heat,
liquid ember!
Oh . . . !

(MARÍA stops. Pause.)

There it is.
You're almost cold.
And I'm warm, warm,
God's vomit.
Anyway, alive . . .
Will I never sleep again?
And he who loved daytime so,
he had to die like this
on a miserable night?

             Hmph,
             that's life.
             What else is there!

(MARÍA looks at MARIANO.)

             Son,
             why are you trembling?
             You were brave.
             Careful, boy,
             don't undo your work,
             don't tremble.

(MARÍA goes over to MARIANO.)

             What are you doing
             with this toy in your hands,
             child?
             You could hurt yourself.

(MARÍA gently takes the knife from him and goes over next to DALMACIO's body.)

             Look, Dalmacio,
             it was only a toy he wounded you with.
             It was a lie,
             a game.

(MARÍA turns violently back to MARIANO.)

             You were always so aggressive
             and bad!
             You always liked
             to play war!

ALMA: We both played it!

MARÍA: You don't matter.

ALMA: I don't matter?

MARÍA *(to MARIANO):*

             You always ran away from me;
             you admired your father!
             Your name suits you,
             Mariano!
             María . . . no,
             from all women denied,
             from even his own mother denied.

MARIANO *(babbling):*

             Mother,
             just because of this dried-out man . . . ?

MARÍA: This dried-out man
             was my life's juice!

Look how his juice
covers me!
Oh, Mariano!
María . . . no!
What terrifying negation!
What emptiness!
That is life.

(Pause.)

What can I do?

(Pause.)

As for you, Alma,
I forgive you.

ALMA: I beg you,
Mother,
don't forgive me!

MARÍA: You're condemned
to be a woman.

ALMA: Don't forgive me,
Mother!
Don't do it!

MARÍA: But as for him . . .

(MARÍA looks at MARIANO with hatred.)

the other one,
the beardless one,
the Frenchman,
the Frenchie,
the one who came
from dark lands
of disgrace,
the disgusting
sickly one,
that pathetic excuse
for a man,
effeminate
and ridiculous,
that insignificant
and cowardly doll,
who killed
a man
when he wasn't paying attention,
as for that one,
I curse him.

MARIANO: Mother . . .
MARÍA: Don't call me mother;
             I aborted you!
             Did you want to suck me dry,
             glutton?
             Not only my breasts
             but now my blood?
             You wanted my blood-food
             to come gushing forth?
MARIANO: What are you going to do,
             madwoman?
MARÍA: Look,
             I'll give you all of it!
             Go back to the sea,
             castaway,
             drown yourself in it,
             in this sea of blood!

(MARÍA *slices her own throat with lightning speed and in a single stroke.*
Silence. MARIANO *is completely motionless, like an ice sculpture, and will*
remain so for the rest of the act. The FATHER *goes over to* MARÍA's *dead*
body.)

FATHER: Love,
             poor dark love,
             poor darkness,
             poor undone flesh.
             Now I'm going
             to repeat my death
             and your death
             and all death
             until eternity.
ALMA (*in a dream*):
             Mariano,
             look how happy,
             how bright
             her blood was,
             like some red champagne
             from your beloved France.

(*The* FATHER *slowly begins to leave, over the mountain of debris. The* CHO-
RUSES *do not see him.*)

FATHER: Can I be different
             as a dead man,
             different from what I was when alive?

ALMA *(still distracted, to* MARÍA*):*
>You'll never again jump
>lightly for joy.

FATHER: Gestures
>repeated throughout eternity,
>an actor's routine.

ALMA: Your laughter will never again
>make us giddy.

FATHER: With less and less passion,
>fading more and more,
>until there's nothing
>left.

(The FATHER *disappears.)*

ALMA: Dancer,
>no more leaps?
>What do you want to do,
>clever one,
>make us feel sorrow?
>Or did life die
>with you?

*(*ALMA *goes over to* MARÍA*'s body; she kneels next to it and examines it carefully.)*

>Or maybe you're still alive?
>Look, Mariano,
>look how she's still holding on to the knife.

*(*ALMA *tries to take the knife away, but she cannot.)*

>Let go,
>let go.
>You have to hold it
>so tight?
>You want everything
>for yourself until the last minute?
>Let go of the knife;
>its job
>isn't done yet.
>Let go.

*(*ALMA *manages to take the knife away.* ALMA *stands up and, brandishing her weapon, turns toward* MARIANO*.)*

>Mariano . . .

CHORUS: Finally peace
>in the midst of horror.
>Now we,

the poor,
we will pay for the others.
But we have to put up with it.
The law is the law,
even if it kills us.

ACT THREE

The high altar of an ancient, abandoned church, which war has ravaged. The ruins of the magnificent baroque altarpiece dominate the space. But this will be seen only later, once dawn approaches. Now it is one dark, indiscernible, menacing mass. A closed darkness hovers over the place.

SCENE ONE

MARIANO is collapsed on the steps as if he'd been knocked down; he's a trembling rag.

MARIANO: Light . . . ?
              Is it dead?
              Forever?
              Is the light
              gone?
              Where are you, Mariano?
              Where have you
              gotten to?
              Why come back
              to yourself?
              Damn you,
              don't put your pieces
              back together.
              Let them float,
              drifting
              in eternal
              darkness.
              Turn yourself off
              once and for all.

(Brief pause. Singsong.)
              Morbleu,
              sacrebleu,
              Sacré-Cœur,
              sacré diable . . .

(He lets out a sinister laugh.)
        How a damned man's heart
        abounds
        in curses.
        Quiet, quiet,
        can't you turn yourself off
        yet?
        Isn't this darkness
        enough?
        Does it need to close in
        on itself even more?
(Brief pause.)
        Morbleu,
        sacrebleu,
        Sacré-Cœur,
        sacré diable . . .
(MARIANO laughs. Brief pause.)
        Can you still see, Mariano?
        Yes,
        but not outside,
        inside,
        inside yourself . . .
        Last light of reason,
        fragile little flame,
        go out once and for all,
        I can't stand to see
        what you've still lit . . .
(Brief pause.)
        Father, Father,
        why . . . ?
        Sacré diable . . .
(Brief pause.)
        Oh, Mother,
        what a terrible birth . . .
        How could you leave me
        abandoned like this
        in the cold . . . ?
        With no mercy.
(MARIANO sings brokenly, cradling himself.)
        "Fais dodo, Pierrot, mon p'tit frère;
        fais dodo, mon petit Pierrot . . .
        Maman est là haut,

qui fait des gateaux;
papa est sur l'eau,
qui fait des bateaux . . ."
Go to sleep, my little one,
the bogeyman will get you
if you don't watch out!
Mother!

(Brief pause.)

Off,
quiet . . .

(Brief pause.)

Enfant gâté,
spoiled rotten . . .
Go drown yourself
in the tub!
I'm slipping,
Mother!
I'm sinking!
Hold me,
quick!
Your hands
can't hold on to
my soapy body!
Sister!

(Brief pause.)

C'est toi
Madeleine?
In Paris, France
une petite putain,
une petite putain,
she had the longest legs . . .
Did you use to love me,
little one?
Oh, how I long for
your long legs now!

(Brief pause.)

So you don't want to die,
is that it, Mariano?
Crude life
is holding on
to you,
dangling

from between your legs?
Your fever
keeping you warm?
(Brief pause.)
Une petite putain,
une petite putain . . .
(Brief pause.)
Who's whispering over there?
Who's laughing?
"Maman est là haut . . .
Papa est sur l'eau . . ."
Falling,
falling . . .
Take me!
Hold me!
Don't leave me tossed
into this cold pool
of fear!
It's deep,
eternal . . .
(Brief pause.)
Can't you die?
Didn't you fulfill
your agony?
All the horrors
of death
but not death itself?
A Golgotha
without a cross?
Let this cup
pass me by . . .
Father,
Father!
Why have you forsaken me?
MARIANO *collapses on top of himself. Pause.*

SCENE TWO

ALMA *slowly enters. Following behind her, the* MEN'S CHORUS, *a group of throat-slitting butchers, a threadbare group of pale, sinister men, ferocious, armed specters. The* CHORUS *stays on the edges, without entering the area of the altar.* ALMA *goes over to* MARIANO.

ALMA: Are you asleep?
MARIANO: Non.
ALMA: Well, then,
          get up.
          Come with me.
MARIANO: Femme,
          qui es-tu?
          Viens-tu me consoler?
ALMA: Don't talk
          like that . . .
MARIANO: C'est toi Madeleine?
          Une petite putain,
          une petite putain . . .
          You had such very long legs,
          didn't you, Madeleine?
ALMA: I'm Alma,
          your sister,
          your mother . . .
MARIANO: I've no use for you.
          I need relief,
          shelter,
          it's cold.
          I've no use for you,
          I need a woman.
ALMA: I am a woman.
MARIANO: Quelle horreur!
          Death's down there below,
          go down,
          go down . . .
          Don't you want to go with me,
          Sister?
          Don't you want
          to be my death?
ALMA: I'm your life,
          and you're mine.
          Look at me,
          I carry life . . .
MARIANO: Yes,
          there's no peace . . .
          And peace
          is needed
          even in order to die . . .

                    Do I have to go
                    to the depths
                    of my soul?
ALMA: Yes,
                    to my depths.
MARIANO: Yes, Mother, yes . . .
(MARIANO nestles against ALMA.)
                    C'est toi Madeleine?
ALMA: I'm Alma,
                    your mother,
                    your sister.
(MARIANO pulls away.)
MARIANO: I've no use for you,
                    I need a woman.
ALMA: I'm your woman.
MARIANO: Yes.
(MARIANO nestles once more against ALMA.)
                    How deep does the soul
                    go?
ALMA: Here.
(MARIANO pulls away again.)
MARIANO: Quelle horreur!
                    Can't even death
                    forgive me?
                    I need to calm down
                    so that I can die . . .
ALMA: Come here,
                    poor cursed man . . .
                    Look at my full
                    breasts . . .
                    Cling to them,
                    you're starving . . .
                    Shelter yourself.
MARIANO: Yes.
(MARIANO presses his head against ALMA's chest.)
ALMA: Don't tremble like that!
                    Don't tremble like that!
                    Incorrigible,
                    why must I always have to correct you?
MARIANO: Je n'en peux plus!
(MARIANO falls onto his back.)
ALMA: Are you sleeping?

MARIANO: No.
(Pause.)
           Who's whispering?
MEN'S CHORUS:
           Like a pale coffin
           on night's tide,
           the drifting moon
           is about to be buried.
           Time is short,
           and what must be done
           is long.
           Let the Mystery be consummated
           now, without delay!
MARIANO: Who are they?
ALMA: Your fathers.
MARIANO: What do they want?
ALMA: They've come to take us away.
MARIANO *(to the CHORUS):*
           Fathers,
           you don't have one
           or two
           to take away.
           I'm not whole.
           See
           how many bloody pieces
           are holding me together.
           There's enough for everyone.
           Welcome,
           all,
           to the feast of the soul.
           Which part would you like?
           Which fragment?
           A river's murmur,
           the attic's sorrow,
           a summer's buzz,
           a girl in France
           I didn't care for
           but who loved me . . . ?
CHORUS: The bloodiest moon,
           the stealthiest steps,
           stifled cries.

MARIANO: You want the worst
of me?

CHORUS: A corpse's pallor,
a drowned boy,
teeth gnashing and sobs.

MARIANO: Alma,
are they murderers?

ALMA: They're what they are,
what they were, and
what they will be.

MARIANO *(terrified):*
Are they demons?

ALMA: They're the earth,
which has suffered so much
and now cries out for vengeance.

MARIANO: Alma,
bearer of sadness,
of crimes
and terror!
When will you forsake me?
When will I be free
of you?
When will I be
a free body,
to graze in the world
in criminal innocence,
glittering,
detached from everything,
shrouded in the common glow
of a conscienceless
creation?

ALMA: That's
how our father was.

MARIANO: Our father
was not like that!
He was guilty!

ALMA: No!
What was he guilty of?
Killing?
That was his nature!
Is the tiger
guilty?

Of what?
Look,
I know him.
I have him inside me,
closed up.
And even me,
the one who loves him,
he destroys me.
That's how he is.
He only wants to be free,
to leap out into the world,
to the pasture
of his butcher's innocence.
Oh, if only I could
open up my body,
his cage,
with a single slash!
If only I could give birth
to him.
Go, Father,
play.

(Pause.)

MARIANO: And inside me is our mother,
the devouress,
biting her way
into the hole in which she nests,
ripping the solid body
from the inside out,
making it porous,
crumbling away
what was once united.
Me, I who was born
to be of a single piece . . .

ALMA: And me, I who was born
to divide and multiply . . .

CHORUS: Children,
time is short,
and our fury is great.
Our knife,
impatient,
love delirious,
glitters and trembles

                    for this warm flesh,
                    for the throat that awaits it.
                    Outside the horses
                    paw the ground,
                    restless, wanting to face
                    the enemy
                    and, outside the city,
                    trample him
                    until his blood
                    rises up to their bridles.
                    Time is short,
                    children,
                    and our fury is great.
MARIANO: Whispers,
                    whispers of death.

(To ALMA.)

                    And you,
                    what do you want from me?
                    The same thing?
ALMA *(drawing forth her knife):*
                    It's time to go,
                    Mariano.
                    To carry on
                    our father's work.
MARIANO: More crimes?
ALMA: Yes,
                    all his henchmen,
                    they must fall
                    to the knife's blade.
                    A knife
                    for the knifed,
                    jail
                    for the jailed.
MARIANO: No,
                    I wasn't born to kill.
                    I wasn't created
                    for that.
                    Besides . . .
                    How am I supposed to kill
                    all those insects?
                    How am I supposed to blacken
                    my hands

on the dried motes
of their blood?
They don't have any juice.
Blow them away
if you don't want to see them.
Or leave them be
in the world
and watch them disappear,
they're fleeting.

ALMA: And yet
I assure you
that nothing will be firm
until they disappear.
Look,
Mariano,
see what those locusts
have done to our land,
how they've eaten it up
until it's left in shreds.
Look
how the earth suffers
and how fat
those moths have gotten.
Come, brother,
help me
frighten them.
Let their fright be such
that they never again dare
to chew through
a naked man's clothes.
Come and rule
the land that belongs to you,
with your steel scepter.

MARIANO: No, sister,
I was born to engender,
to give life.
Now I understand.
And if I should die tonight,
I no longer wish
new shadows
to drag along with me.
I will die my death,

that's enough,
and no others.
(ALMA looks at him, amazed. Pause.)
ALMA *(with an outburst so angry that it almost silences her):*
What a . . .
useless little puppet!
(In a rage.)
What a . . .
an unbearable destiny!
(ALMA runs the side of her blade across her own body, with a slow fury.)
Aaaahhhhhhhh!
This disgusting body!
To be condemned by these breasts!
I'd like to cut them off!
Make myself smooth!
Why am I not a man!
Aaaahhhhhhhh!
If only I could seal up
my humid hole!
Place in my center
that . . .
contemptible solidity,
that . . .
proud impulse!
The wrong body!
An abominable freak!
Aaaahhhhhhhh,
Mother!
(Pause.)

And why can't I
do it,
just as I am?
Go out with a clean knife
and bloody it?
Just like her,
it didn't matter to her,
she did it;
and I,
to whom it matters so much,
I can't?
Do you have to beat me at everything?
Oh, Father,

	you condemned me.
	You gave me the will
	but not the way.
MARIANO:	Enough,
	beast!
	Why do you renounce
	your own self?
ALMA:	Brother,
	I fear
	that you'll never understand . . .
CHORUS:	Look, brothers,
	see how the fire snakes through her.
	Welcome . . .
	How in the gloomy storms
	of her eyes,
	quick sparks slither about.
	Welcome . . .
	How her whole being creaks
	and grinds
	to escape her.
	Welcome, daughter . . .

(Brief pause.)

ALMA:	Brother,
	and what if I told you
	that the old tiger,
	the old dog
	has a new cub,
	a little burning tiger,
	that feeds on my blood?
MARIANO *(changing expression):*	
	What do you mean to say?
	What more do you have for me?
	What do you want to bring to light?
	What do you want to reveal to me?
ALMA:	That during the night
	you dreamt of me
	you lustfully watered
	where you should not have,
	or maybe should have.
	And now there's another bud
	that dreams,
	that feeds off my dreams

	with a hungry, ferocious innocence.
MARIANO:	You lie! You're dreaming like a madwoman! Nothing is real! Not that night, not you, not I, not even that semen of sleep! You're nightmare's womb; only the monstrous can come out of you!
ALMA:	I am the Woman, Mariano, who suffers in labor! And if you see me tormented, it's because I'm giving birth! And you, my husband, you threw the Serpent down to the ground, threw down the seducer who had humiliated me and now lay in the dust, humiliated!
MARIANO:	Blasphemy! I don't want to listen to you!
ALMA:	How the little cursed one trembles and covers his ears! Do you think that my cries of pain can't pass through your hands?
CHORUS:	The horses paw the ground. The hour of Wrath and Judgment has arrived. Because the air has become the forge's smoke, fire and sulfur, and the seas turned into dead man's blood,

into blood the waters of rivers and streams,
and the earth dried up,
dissolving into a dust cloud.
But the hour of Destruction
has arrived,
and the birds will become gorged
upon so much flesh.

MARIANO: Will I never stop
falling?

ALMA: Hurry up,
take the knife;
the day of rage
is about to dawn.

CHORUS: Take the knife
and follow us
to the massacre.

ALMA: Why do you hesitate?
What do you want?
Do you want my body to split open
and my son,
your son,
to come out
of me,
come out complete,
already made,
just as I imagine him,
just as I see him
in my monstrously pregnant head?
So he can do his will,
armed and ferocious?
Take the blade,
Father!
Because now it's not your father
but your son
who condemns you!

(Pause.)

MARIANO: Is that how it is,
my Alma?
I too,
like my father and my son,
I'm submerged in your dream?
Do you have all of us

inside you,
owner of generations?
Living corral
of wolves?
Will we never be free
of you?

(Brief pause.)

Fine,
so be it.
Give me the blade.

Scene Three

Mariano is about to take the knife, but suddenly a slight ray of dawn falls on a figure seated upstage, behind Mariano: it is the young Woman from the prologue. The Chorus shudders.

CHORUS: Dawn is coming . . .

(Mariano faces forward, even though he is addressing the Woman.)

MARIANO: Femme,
             es-tu ici,
             encore?

WOMAN: Yes, Mariano.

MARIANO: Est-ce mon heure?

WOMAN: Yes, it's your hour.

MARIANO: Est-il temps que je meure?

WOMAN: Not your time to die,
             Mariano,
             your time to begin to live.

MARIANO: You mean to say
             that until now
             I was dead?

WOMAN: Just as much as
             the one who has not yet
             been born.

MARIANO: If you have power over this,
             I beg of you,
             lady,
             give me my life.

WOMAN: Come with me,
             give me your hand.

(Mariano turns toward her and gives her his bandaged hand. The Woman takes off the bandage.)

MARIANO: It's still bleeding.

WOMAN: And it will continue to bleed.

(MARIANO rises, hand in hand with the WOMAN. From this moment on, as the morning breaks, the light will gradually grow stronger until it illuminates everything, in a blinding light by the end of the play.)

MEN'S CHORUS *(to the WOMAN)*:

> Why are you taking him away?
> He's ours.

WOMAN: You dare to confront me,
> evil warrior?

MEN: We
> are his fathers.
> We have lovingly
> adopted him.
> For him we went without sleep
> for so long.
> We inspired in him
> a taste for the night,
> the melancholic,
> and the macabre.
> We sought him out,
> crossing the great waters
> where Leviathan lives
> and we are guests.
> We blew sleeplessness into him.
> We stirred him up in the sea,
> we gave him
> seasickness,
> ocean spirit.
> We destroyed his soul
> with our teeth.
> We placed the knife
> in his hands.
> And he killed,
> and the rest.
> He did that
> with a full conscience,
> lady,
> in full possession of himself.
> We possess him;
> he's ours.
> Why are you taking him away?

WOMAN: He was mine
            before.
MEN: But that way there's no tragedy.
WOMAN: No,
            that way no.
MEN: Was not
            what he did
            his own choice?
            He didn't have to do it,
            and he did it,
            out of pride.
            In order to have a destiny.
            So let him pay for it,
            pay for that destiny.
WOMAN: But I crossed the stage.
MEN: Must you always cross?
WOMAN: Yes,
            the cross is in place.
            Now destiny
            belongs to everyone.
            Do you think that you can
            dominate earth
            and heaven?
            Do you think that I made them
            —heaven and earth—
            for your entertainment?
            Do you think that he
            is just your toy?
            I made him
            for myself.
            And he's mine,
            because I want him for myself.
WOMEN'S CHORUS:
            We'd love to have him
            for ourselves.
MEN'S CHORUS:
            Damn you,
            the time for disintegration
            will come soon enough.
            We'll decide how it ends,
            the final "no."
            And in the middle

of your light
and your day,
night will burst forth.
We'll return
to curse
your creation.
We'll laugh,
gritting our teeth.

WOMEN: Out,
who do you think you're scaring?
Denier,
go deny yourself.
Accuser,
accuse yourself.
Out,
light
invades everything.
Light
is the alpha
and the omega.

MEN: No,
darkness.

WOMEN: Light!
To which your eyes
will always be
blind!
Get out of here now!
Don't cloud
the newborn day
with your sad presence!

MEN: Oh, what a dark day . . .
Must we bury ourselves
in nothingness?
Sleep there
and dissolve,
like some inverted fetus?
What are we?
Who are we?
Must we deny ourselves to ourselves?
Like dogs that bite
their own tails?
Our destiny is to negate,

and we negate ourselves.
Lady,
sing us to sleep
in our nothingness.
Alma,
come with us.

ALMA: No,
I'll stay here.
I,
the one dark spot,
I'll resist the light.

WOMAN: I forgive you,
Alma.

ALMA: You too,
Mother?

WOMEN: We forgive you.

ALMA: I don't accept
your forgiveness.

MEN: We take our leave,
no good-byes.

(*The* MEN'S CHORUS *disappears. Pause.*)

WOMAN: Mariano,
Son,
come to me
and awake.

MARIANO: Was I sleeping,
lady?

WOMAN: Yes.

MARIANO: And what I dreamt?

WOMAN: It doesn't exist anymore.
Look, there is
a new heaven
and a new earth,
and the sea you once knew,
Son,
that sea is no more.
The new,
shining,
incorruptible creation
is yours . . .

MARIANO: And the night?

WOMAN: There is no more night;
             it has been destroyed
             forever.
             Night and death
             have died.
             Look at the river of life
             you're swimming in,
             how crystal-clear it shines.
MARIANO: I won't have any more
             hunger or thirst?
WOMAN: Look at the trees of life
             that adorn either side of this river.
             Eat from them
             their fruit.
MARIANO: But, Mother,
             you've just cursed me!
WOMAN: No, Mariano,
             there's no longer
             any curse.
WOMAN/WOMEN'S CHORUS:
             Wake up, Mariano,
             come out of yourself,
             spring forth in the light.
             In me,
             I am waiting for you,
             Son,
             I,
             all light.
             Come,
             dissolve your sorrow
             in light.
             For you, there are
             cathedrals of light
             taller than the highest mountains.
             Universes of light,
             that expand out
             into an endless sea.
ALMA: I,
             the starving,
             dark ray,
             I'll stay here.

WOMAN/WOMEN'S CHORUS:

> Your hunger and thirst
> for light
> will be sated.
> The universe's suns
> are dark
> in this light.
> So much light
> that it will be impossible
> for the shadows to return.
> You won't be able to come back,
> Son,
> even if you wanted to.

ALMA:

> I,
> the dark ray,
> I'll stay here,
> obstinate,
> other.

WOMAN/WOMEN'S CHORUS:

> Come,
> Mariano,
> Lamb,
> our Father's firstfruits,
> without defect.
> Awake
> in the eternally luminous
> bosom
> of the Mother.
> All light
> is for you.
> For you
> it was made;
> and you
> were created
> for it.
> Look
> from above
> the earth,
> from this dawn's
> incandescence.
> See
> how the light

laughingly
transfixes everything.
Come and play in her light.
Come,
dissolve yourself
in light.
Be
yourself,
your laughing self.

ALMA: And I'll sleep
in defeated obscurity.

WOMAN/WOMEN'S CHORUS:
Laugh
in winds of light.
Laugh
in seas of moving light.
Laugh
in transparent mountains
of light.
Newborn light.

ALMA, *crouching on the steps, holds fast to her knife.* MARIANO, *resting motionless on the* WOMAN's *lap, appears to wake up; he slowly gets up, smiling, and submerges himself, dancing in the ever-growing light.*

APPENDIX
English translation of French dialogue

Page 266:

Woman,
are you from here?
Answer me:
Have I arrived?
Are you real?
Do you know me?
Enlighten me

Page 267:

completely.
Look, I'm lost.
Then
from what dream
—to what dream—
have I returned?
Always the mirage?

Page 268:

What uncertain beach,
lady!

And even if I've arrived
I don't find myself.

Could you decipher the enigma

even though I don't know you,
I beg you,

Page 269:

Undeceive my eyes.

Page 275:

My soul,
my sister,
I've found
this brass saber,
rusted, among the debris,
that I played with as a child,
and all the past
fell over me,
demolishing me.

Page 276:

I fell on my knees,
smashed down by the sacred weight
of childhood.

My sister,
my soul,
how empty I was without you,
my soul,
and how incomplete!
What a hole
in the shadow of my body!

I thought myself full,
complete,
and I was only half of myself!

What an agitated marionette,
without history,
I've been!

What a man without truth!
What a furtive inhabitant
of something that's not his!

Page 277:

Even when I die,
my soul
—because you are too true
for such a lie—

even if we come together
I devour you
and you devour me,
and my body
and your soul
explode into pieces,

Page 291:

By God

Page 292:

Yes, my father.

Page 295:

How barbaric!

Page 296:

my uncle?

my son.

Page 297:

I, too,
I'm a poet.

Me, too.

I'm a poet.

Page 298:

"Give light to my word, let God give light to my haze;
your dream refills the hot blood of my pen."

"From the most sacred Gods I will invoke his name:
Mercury the industrious, august Apollo."

Page 300:

Moon, moon
how did you enter
so furtively,
so as to discover
the secrets of my bed?

Page 307:

    I'm a stranger!

Pages 343 & 344:

    Curse it,
    Bless it,
    Sacred Heart,
    sacred devil . . .

Page 344:

    Beddy-bye, Pierrot, my little brother;
    beddy-bye, my little Pierrot . . .
    Mama is upstairs,

Page 345:

    baking cakes,
    Papa is on the water,
    making boats . . ."

    Spoiled child

    Is that you,
    Madeleine?

    A little whore,
    a little whore,

Page 346:

    A little whore,
    a little whore,

    Mama is upstairs
    Papa is on the water . . .

Page 347:

    No.

    Woman,
    who are you?
    Have you come to console me?

    Is that you, Madeleine?
    A little whore,
    a little whore . . .

    What horror!

Page 348:

    Is that you, Madeleine?

    What horror!

I can't take any more!

Page 358:

Woman,
are you here,
again?

Is it my hour?

Is it time for me to die?

Hotel Columbus

(from the "Exemplary Encounters" Series)

No te soltaré hasta que me bendigas premiered on 22 May 2003 in the Cervantes National Theater, Buenos Aires. The production was directed by Mónica Viñao and starred the actors Luis Solanas and Néstor Sánchez.

Characters

CUSTER, a bodyguard
SARAH, a transvestite, dressed in evening wear

ONE ACT

The presidential suite in a five-star hotel. The decor is Empire. Everything is ostentatious, soft, impersonal.

    CUSTER, a bodyguard, sniffs out the place, evaluating its trivial luxury with a certain clumsiness. He sees a whiskey bottle over to one side, on top of a piece of furniture. He goes over to it and sniffs it; he appears to want to serve himself some but hesitates. Finally, he doesn't dare do so. He moves away, yawning, and sits back in one of the armchairs, but something's apparently bothering him: it's his gun holster sticking into his torso. He undoes his jacket, rearranges the holster, takes out his revolver, inspects it. The ringing of his cellular phone surprises him. He leaves the revolver on the coffee table and answers the phone.

CUSTER *(with a self-assurance and authority in direct contrast with what we've just seen):* Custer here. *(He listens. He breaks down into a servile tone.)* Oh, yes, sir, affirmative, sir. Everything's normal . . . And the president, sir, is he feeling better . . . ? *(His face changes color, as if he's just heard some very strong language at the other end of the line.)* Yes, sir, affirm . . . Yes, sir, I understand now that I've no reason to . . . Yes . . . It's just that the president was a little under the weather this morning . . . Sorry,

371

sir, I understand that should have nothing to do with me . . . Affirmative, sir
. . . "There was a delay, and the president will not be returning for the time
being" . . . Understood, sir. Full alert, as always! *(Hurt.)* Sir, please forgive
my earlier behavior . . . What? . . . My name's Custer . . . *(Proud.)* Yes, sir,
I know very well that there was a general by that name . . . *(He listens and
responds, automatically.)* Fought valiantly, killed at Little Big Horn in 1876[1]
. . . Of course, I'm proud . . . *(Growing pale.)* No, sir, no, I do not compare
myself to him . . . Whatever you say, sir . . . Affirmative. *(In a low voice.)*
My name's Crap. What . . . ? *(He shouts, in a military fashion.)* Sir, yes, sir!
My name is Crapper!

*(The other end has already hung up. CUSTER puts the cell phone away. Pause.
In a sudden fury, he kicks an armchair. He's immediately frightened by his
own actions. He squats down in front of the armchair and carefully examines it to see if the toe of his shoe has caused any damage. He rubs the cloth
with his hand as if trying to remove a stain.*

*SARAH enters from another room inside the suite, her back to the body-
guard. She is a mysterious figure, obviously a transvestite. Her makeup is
pathetically piled on, and her sad eyes look desperate, with a certain gleam
that only a delirium can bring. Her entrance is so strange and silent that
CUSTER doesn't notice she's there. SARAH is almost a ghost.*

*CUSTER stands up, his back to SARAH, and looks over to the whiskey
bottle. Seeking to ·make up for his humiliation, he pours himself a drink,
filling the glass to the rim, and then knocks it back in one gulp.)*

SARAH *(very smooth, soft):* Mr. President . . .

*(CUSTER reacts with a huge start. He spits out the whiskey he's just drunk,
lets the glass drop out of his hand, and turns toward SARAH, just as he's
reaching into his holster for the revolver he's left on the table. The revolver
is now closer to SARAH than it is to CUSTER.*

*Then he stares defiantly at SARAH, and his expression begins to change—
from surprise to curiosity and then finally to something else: something
mysterious, the two men enter into a kind of mysterious, secret pact.*

A long silence.)

CUSTER *(finally):* Madam . . . ?

(SARAH smiles, a bit more relaxed, relieved.)

SARAH: For a moment there I thought you didn't recognize me . . . How
absurd, no? I felt like a ghost . . . a strange little moth . . . as if my life
depended on you, on your recognizing me . . . *(SARAH laughs.)* Really, President Custer, power is rather hypnotic, fatal . . . It gives one life, it takes it
away . . . *(Affecting a certain worldliness, SARAH slowly goes toward CUSTER,
her arm outstretched.)* But you finally decided to be generous with me,
mon cher. Yes, it is I, your old friend. Sarah . . . the divine Sarah Bernhardt
. . . *(She has by now moved next to CUSTER, her arm still extended. CUSTER*

does not know how to react. He takes her hand and gives it a hearty shake. SARAH is unable to stifle a pained gesture.) Ow, Mr. President, I didn't expect such a democratic gesture from you. Such a rough handshake . . . ! *(SARAH rubs her hand.)* And with such a strong hand, so used to commanding, to bending in half the strongest will . . . You're just too much for me . . . You almost broke my little bones to pieces . . .

CUSTER: Forgive me, madam . . . You're right . . . Too many military salutes . . . Allow me . . .

(SARAH, smiling, extends her hand once more, and this time CUSTER deposits a kiss on her hand.)

SARAH: Now that's much better, Custer . . . although the slight roughness of your lips is still a bit much for me. But at least you didn't kill me. *(Brief pause.)* One could speak volumes about those lips . . . sometimes they're like daggers . . . at other times, they're so soothing . . . still others, they're like ice . . . and sometimes they burn with a fever . . . But not one of these changes ever had to do with love . . . No, Custer, nothing in you ever has to do with love.

CUSTER: So what then . . . ?

SARAH: Power. And I? Well, we'll talk later about love and me.

CUSTER: But, you, madam . . . ? *(He interrupts himself.)*

SARAH: Yes . . . ? I what . . . ? What's tormenting you, Custer? Ask me, please, ask away . . . I'll answer all your questions, even the cruel ones. After all, isn't it your cruelty that's always been so irresistible to me? I what, Mr. President . . . ?

CUSTER *(laughing, slightly thrown off)*: Well, it's a trivial question . . . practically stupid . . . in reality, a human question . . . More worthy of a bodyguard than a president . . . But anyway, curiosity is insatiable . . . Tell me . . . Sarah . . . how did you get here, how did you get in?

(SARAH lets out a laugh and falls delicately back onto one of the armchairs, facing the coffee table where the revolver is lying. She notices CUSTER's brief glance at the gun. Then she takes the weapon, as if nonchalantly, and during the next speech, she'll continue to play with it, without any consideration for its potential danger, all of which creates great tension in CUSTER.)

SARAH: Custer, President Custer, you never cease to amaze me . . . I must confess that this is yet another source of your fascination . . . Your ability to surprise . . . it's an exquisite art . . . and I, of course, am all too susceptible to all forms of art . . . How did I get in? . . . Your question has two parts . . . First, how did I manage to make my way alive through this neighborhood . . . of scoundrels, prostitutes, ruffians, and transvestites . . . this horrid neighborhood where the Grand Hotel Columbus now stands . . . Strange how such a high-class hotel came to be built in such a neighborhood, don't

you think? Or was it the other way round? The neighborhood just grew up around it . . . Money, luxury, power, they're always dragging around their opposite, in the shadows . . . Darkness and light need one another, they attract each other . . . And I'm not merely speaking metaphorically . . . If all this fauna circles the Grand Hotel Columbus like a ring of filth, well, it's because they'll find their most fervent clients inside . . . De toute façon, that can't be a very big problem, because for the presidential summit surely all the scum was swept away . . . And believe me, they did it with a fine-tooth comb . . . And then you're probably asking yourself, how did I manage to make my way through that army of bodyguards, that iron ring . . . ? Et bien, both questions are very easily answered . . . *(SARAH suddenly points the revolver at CUSTER. Pause.)* I was here the entire time, President Custer, the entire time, the entire time . . . waiting for you . . . *(SARAH continues to point the gun at him, a few seconds of extreme tension.)* What's the matter, Custer, do you think I came here to kill you . . . ? *(SARAH laughs smoothly and lowers the gun. Finally, with great care and deliberation, she puts it back in the same place where she found it, and eases back into the arm-chair. At that very moment, CUSTER throws himself on top of the revolver and takes it. Holding the gun in both hands, he points it at SARAH. SARAH does not look at him. She stretches her neck, her eyes are closed.)* Please, I'm exhausted, would you be a dear and get me something to drink? But not that awful whiskey . . . There's a bottle of champagne over there in that ice bucket, and two flutes . . . *(CUSTER continues to point the gun at SARAH. She opens her eyes and looks at him. With a softly reproachful tone.)* Mr. President, please, that's beneath you . . . *(CUSTER looks at her, at first disconcerted but later trapped by that strange magnetism emanating from her eyes. He slowly begins to put his revolver back in its holster. With elegant naturalness.)* I beg you not to do that . . . *(CUSTER looks at SARAH, questioningly.)* The weapon . . . don't leave it on your person . . . Don't insult your body's delicate anatomy with the rudeness of that thing . . . For so many nights I watched you in the darkness of the moon, I saw your naked, white body shine . . . almost transparent . . . floating in the air, in the immensity of the black plains . . . with the stars as your only crown . . . *(SARAH's lost in her own vision. CUSTER, never taking his eyes off her, puts his gun back onto the table.)* Champagne, please . . .
(Pause.)
CUSTER *(unexpectedly):* Bien sûr, madame . . .
SARAH: Perfect. *(CUSTER removes from a small refrigerator, disguised to look like a piece of furniture, an ice bucket with champagne and two glasses. He places it on the coffee table, takes the bottle of champagne, and uncorks it. He serves them the champagne and then goes to sit on an armchair facing SARAH. SARAH raises her glass.)* To us. Art and power. Politics and theater.

CUSTER: To you, madam, to you . . . for knowing how to breach my solitude and discover the most intimate part of my being . . .

SARAH *(laughing):* But that does not deserve any special merit, Mr. President. After all, I'm a woman.

CUSTER: Yes, of course . . . But it still commands one's attention . . . You appear to know so much about me . . . You, on the other hand, are a complete mystery to me . . .

(SARAH gets up in disgust.)

SARAH: Self-centered . . . ! Typical man. Completely self-involved. The center of the universe! But, my dear sir, there's a power that's much more subtle and mysterious. Many times, Custer, the night's seen you kneel before that center. And how humbly, how religiously, you moistened that center with the tip of your tongue!

CUSTER: Madam, what are you saying!

SARAH: Doesn't it excite you?

CUSTER: No.

SARAH *(ironic):* Then I've failed. I'm a terrible actress.

CUSTER *(with a trace of disappointment):* You were faking it . . . ?

(SARAH laughs.)

SARAH: Don't tell me, Custer, that you're one of those vulgar people who confuse acting with "faking it." *(Brief pause.)* Acting is one of the few states of truth. *(Suddenly frivolous.)* But here I am telling you that, when you're one of the greatest actors of our time . . . ! *(As if without thinking, SARAH takes the gun up again and uses it "innocently" as an accompaniment to her movements.)* Your only flaw, Custer, is that you're an actor with a bad memory. *(She suddenly appears to have discovered something.)* Or are you playacting? Of course, why didn't I realize it? You're acting out forgetfulness. *(She points the gun as if it were her index finger.)* Very well, Mr. President, I'll be your memory.

CUSTER: Yes, madam. You be my memory.

SARAH: But first quit calling me "madam."

CUSTER: And what should I call you?

SARAH: I'll leave that up to your own judgment. You can use the most sublime words, or the foulest. Out of respect for our nights of love, I'll allow you anything.

CUSTER: There were that many?

SARAH: Don't you remember them? Oh, but it's so stingy of me to refer to them as "nights of love," because we also had "mornings of love," afternoons, dawns, noontimes, dusks, twilights, naps . . . how could you forget?

(CUSTER mops the sweat from his brow.)

CUSTER: Yes, I think I'm beginning to remember . . .

SARAH: I taught you everything, Custer. Everything you know. It's not that

I invented you, oh no. You already existed. But you were unformed. A diamond in the rough. I polished you up. I merely gave form to that magnet, that natural seductive force you already possessed, I gave you subtlety . . .
(Pause. CUSTER goes over to SARAH and delicately takes the revolver from her hand. He points it at her as he gazes intently upon her.)
CUSTER: I loved you, Sarah, from the moment the lights came up on that moth-eaten stage.
(SARAH laughs.)
SARAH: Yes, it certainly was in the middle of nowhere.
CUSTER: My troop was quartered there. The entire regiment filled the theater that evening. Please forgive my crudeness, divine Sarah, but the place reeked of men's balls that night. You were incredibly brave. To come on stage like that, in full light. To confront so much male desire. When you appeared, the air stood still, the entire regiment held its breath. The silence washed over you, like oil, it made you shine even more.
SARAH *(laughing):* And I'm certain I played a boy! Because I've always adored male characters: Hamlet, Lorenzaccio . . . *(SARAH takes the revolver out of CUSTER's hands.)*
CUSTER: Yes, you did . . . but that made it even more exciting. Your fragile, liquid voice coming forth from men's clothing was incredibly sensual . . . your pants covering your thighs, rubbing up against you there, rough . . . We could see perfectly well how your crotch grew wet. Did you know that some of the officials even masturbated up there in the boxes?
SARAH: Yes, drops of semen ended up spattering me . . . I incorporated them into the performance . . . they became dewdrops for me . . . I became even more worked up . . . I licked up those salty dewdrops! *(She suddenly begins to walk around in circles, frantic. She points the gun to her temple.)* Ow, my head's exploding! My head's exploding!
(CUSTER goes over to her, stopping her and taking away the gun.)
CUSTER: But I loved you more than anyone else did. I desired you more than anyone else could.
SARAH: Yes? Was that what happened? You saved me . . . ? I've drawn a blank . . . I don't remember anything . . . Yes, I believe I did once fall into the hands of some Indians . . . When this ferocious Indian raid destroyed a frontier town . . . I was the last white captive girl . . .
CUSTER: There weren't any raids then, Sarah. We'd already wiped out all the Indians.
(Pause. SARAH, desolate, looks at him.)
SARAH *(childlike):* Yes? All of them . . . ? *(CUSTER nods yes.)* So I made it all up? All those years in teepees, in the middle of muck, I made all that up? All that suffering, the smallpox, my little boy's death in my arms, I made that up, too? It was just theater? *(CUSTER lowers his gaze. Pause. He places*

the revolver back on the table and walks away. SARAH brushes the tears from her eyes and rapidly regains her composure.) Well, it's possible. I've often confused my performances with reality . . . Reality, hmmph, what's that, anyway? I've never been more real than when I've been onstage. *(Pause.)* But I'm so very tired. I've acted so much. *(Pause.)* Yes, perhaps all that business with the Indians was just playacting, especially since what I remember best are some lines in verse, and I don't think that those poor people spoke to each other in verse . . .

When lilacs last in the door-yard bloom'd,
And the great star early droop'd in the western sky in the night . . .[2]

Even though it is quite possible, because many times and even in the most vulgar of situations I have often sought imaginary refuge in the stage . . . the stage, the stage, Custer! It ruined my life! It took away my spontaneity! It filled my life with falsehoods! *(Pause. Withdrawn.)* Nevertheless, I think that the part about my son was true . . . I see it so clearly . . . I can still feel his weight in my arms . . . He was burning up with fever . . . it was in the middle of a smallpox epidemic . . . those barbarians!

And all my days are trances,
And all my nightly dreams
Are where thy dark eye glances,
And where thy footstep gleams—
In what ethereal dances,
By what eternal streams.[3]

(SARAH silently sobs. Pause. Suddenly CUSTER leaps on top of the revolver and puts it in his mouth as if he were going to shoot himself. SARAH lets out a cry.) Mr. President! *(CUSTER slowly lowers the revolver and returns it to its place on the coffee table.)* I'm a worn-out heart, Custer, don't scare me like that. Why did you do it?
(CUSTER gives out an adolescent laugh.)
CUSTER: I was just playing around.
SARAH *(smiling):* Like a little boy.
CUSTER *(with a strange motivation):* Yes, I was playing around like a little boy.
SARAH: I can understand that.
CUSTER: I understand you, too, Sarah. I've often felt like an actor, lost in some play. I live on a set where everything's simulated . . . An infinite set that the mocking masses try to put up as quickly as they can when I pass by. All those people in cardboard streets . . . They're just rank amateurs, and

I'm sure they laugh behind my back as I move on . . . This unreality I live in scares me, Sarah. I have terrible fears. I'm afraid that my audience will suddenly leave and I'll be left alone in the middle of an empty space . . .

SARAH: But I'll be there with you, mon petit. I'll be your reality. For me, your performance will always be filled with truth.

(CUSTER *slowly goes over to her. He takes her forcefully by her waist, embracing her.*)

CUSTER: Now that excites me. That really excites me. You're my eternity. The chance of keeping the show going until the end. Do you feel how hard it is?

SARAH: The gun? Careful, it could go off.

CUSTER: The gun's on the table.

(CUSTER *holds* SARAH *even tighter.*)

SARAH: You're suffocating me.

CUSTER: Faggot.

(SARAH *appears to have fainted. She doubles over.* CUSTER *carries her over to the armchair, where he deposits her. He waits with great anxiety for* SARAH *to come around. She does so, breathing deeply.*)

Sorry.

SARAH: Sorry for what? It was just a dizzy spell. You held me so tightly it cut off my breath. I didn't even hear what you said. But it doesn't matter what you said, I've already given you permission. Between the two of us, everything's allowed.

CUSTER: Thank you, Sarah. That's a relief. Vulgarity is such a great temptation.

SARAH: I know.

CUSTER: Sometimes, for example, I spy on my bodyguards. There's one in particular who is fascinatingly repulsive. When he thinks nobody's looking, or even sometimes when he forgets that anyone's there, even around prime ministers, kings, presidents, he picks his nose, he scratches his ass or his crotch, he belches, farts . . . I don't know why I keep him on. I suppose it's because he keeps me in touch with some animal part of myself. Also, just between us, I like to imagine that he's capable of all kinds of perverse acts.

SARAH (*suddenly interested*): What kind of perverse acts?

CUSTER (*suddenly cold*): I don't know. Why are you so interested?

SARAH: Because I'm an artist. Everything human is of interest to me.

CUSTER: This guy's a murderer. It's sad to lose yourself in a murderer's dreams.

SARAH: We're all murderers in our dreams.

CUSTER: Yes, but did you ever slice into another body until you saw the intestines jump out? Did you ever shoot a man in the back of the head as he was kneeling on the ground? A man who was crying, drooling, shitting himself? Did you go ahead and squeeze the trigger and have your hand get spattered with blood and brains?

SARAH: That's enough, Custer! That's not like you! You give your murdering orders from a distance, your hands stay clean! You're not an executioner! You're not even a general in a war! You're an elected president now!

(Pause.)

CUSTER: Oh, yes, that's right . . . a president. Just a fleeting salute from far off. A conjecture.

SARAH: A smile that vanishes into thin air as you pass. A symbol without any content.

CUSTER: That's why my simple subjects, my subordinates, intrigue me. The murderer I was talking about earlier, for example . . . a couple of times I found him suffering. Imagine that! He was suffering . . . !

SARAH: Bon, cela suffit . . . ! I didn't come here to talk about your lackeys, your bulldogs, your henchmen!

CUSTER: No, of course not, Sarah. My apologies once again.

SARAH: After all, we all have our own miseries, our scars! A girl can't always enjoy complete freedom in choosing her characters! Even I, even I, a diva like myself, how many times have I had to make concessions? To my public, my critics, the changing times . . . That horrible theater style . . . what was it called . . . oh, naturalism! I acted the streetwalker, I lived in squalid dumps, I played alcoholics, opium addicts . . . I even committed infanticide! I had to perform in a butcher shop! There among real slabs of beef dripping real blood, fetid blood, right there on that sublime abstraction we call the stage! No, my dear Mr. President. I must say that my life hasn't been so easy, either.

CUSTER: But we've finally found each other.

(Pause. They look at each other, needy, each hanging onto the other's sad gaze.)

SARAH: Yes, in the vastness of this cold universe, we found each other. But time's marched on, hasn't it? And we're not what we once were. I don't think you even desire me anymore, Custer. I'm only a shadow for you, something you can barely make out. Although I should confess that you are yourself only a shadow. *(She gives a quick laugh.)* A crappy little shadow of a man.

CUSTER: Why do you say that?

SARAH: I don't know . . . you look so weak, so indecisive . . . Of course you don't have the same violent impulses you had before. That gleam in your eye, that je m'en fou that knocked down everything in your way . . . Tell me the truth, Custer, you don't feel anything anymore, do you? I'm not asking if you love me, of course not, but . . . did you ever love me? *(Pause. With a trace of desperation.)* That's alright, you don't love me, you never loved me. Perhaps you simply can't answer my question. But don't you at least desire me? *(Pause.)* President Custer! General! I order you to answer me! Don't you want me?

CUSTER: Forgive me, but I cannot . . .

SARAH: Do you need a little help, sir? *(She moves determinedly toward the middle of the suite.)*
Something to get your blood flowing? Some pose in particular?

CUSTER *(shyly):* Maybe . . .

(SARAH, on the suite's soft rug, mechanically performs the actions she describes.)

SARAH: What do you prefer? On my back, my legs open? My legs raised up? On all fours? *(She somersaults into position.)* I find this position more exciting. Ça vous plaît?

CUSTER: Sarah, please . . .

SARAH: Please what?

CUSTER: Just sit down . . .

SARAH: Here or . . . ?

CUSTER: Stay over there.

(SARAH sits down on the floor. She looks at CUSTER expectantly.)
Cross your legs.

(SARAH does so.)
Like a yogi.

(SARAH poses like a Buddha.)

SARAH *(a little surprised):* This excites you?

CUSTER: I'm not sure. *(He nonchalantly goes over to her; he yawns.)* Excuse me, may I?

(SARAH looks at him; she doesn't understand.)

SARAH: You can do whatever you want with me.

(CUSTER lies down on his side on the carpet; he's curled up like a baby, his head on SARAH's lap. Long pause. SARAH, a distant look on her face, absent-mindedly strokes CUSTER's hair.)

SARAH: God . . . poor little lost man . . .

(Pause.)

CUSTER: Did I love you, Sarah? Did I ever love you?

SARAH: It's hard to say, mon petit! I only know that you were brutal. Was that love, maybe? Or simply yet another display of power? But sometimes, once in a while, when you'd feel your force weaken, or when you were asleep, like an innocent child, on top of my captive body, my enslaved body . . . Then yes, I think love would flood over you . . . you shook from love . . . and I would calm you with my caresses. I would caress your body until I was worn-out, your body all stirred up by love, tormented by dreams of love. And I would do it without expecting anything in return. In the fullness of my womanly being. You were a child cornered in my womb. A child not yet born, a child full of impatient love, dreaming about the world, about the open spaces of the world, about sniffing the air of the great plains and making those plains shake with his armies. There, inside of me, Custer, you burned with love for the universe.

CUSTER: And your love? Wasn't it enough to accompany me to those open spaces?

SARAH: I hate open spaces. They terrify me. I'm only at home in closed spaces. The world I love fits onto the stage. The only light that moves me comes from footlights. The only universe that I dare to tread in is the one of my dreams.

I'm art, Custer.

And I've dreamt you into being, my little bloody tiger, and sent you out into the world so you can play in it, transform it into one great stage.

Only then will I be able to leave and accompany you. When your fury is no longer needed and theatrical gestures have replaced it. Only then will I be able to accompany you and be your teacher. When the brutality of actions has been domesticated and only fiction remains. When hateful reality no longer exists.

CUSTER: But I love reality!

SARAH: Don't be silly. You only love the reality you've created. Anything else will always be your enemy.

CUSTER: No, Sarah. I love even that reality. Because one of these days it'll belong to me.

(Pause. SARAH continues to stroke CUSTER's hair.)

SARAH: Perhaps . . . But no matter what, Custer, think of the love, the love we shared! How many worlds have we dreamed! When you were my son and we were one, inseparable. And then we were separated, you returned, returned to me to heal the cruelty of that separation. And afterwards as well, when you quit needing me and you invented me like your son . . .

(CUSTER jumps up and stares at her, startled. His cell phone rings. CUSTER notices but doesn't dare answer. In desperation, he begins to pace from one end of the suite to the other, not knowing what to do. Finally, he takes the gun and goes over to SARAH. She has remained in the same place, seated on the floor, her head dropped forward. With incredible violence and ferocity, CUSTER grabs her by the neck and sticks his revolver into the nape of her neck. The cell phone infuriatingly continues to ring.)

CUSTER *(very slowly)*: One . . . two . . . three . . .

(CUSTER cocks the gun. Suddenly the phone stops ringing. There's a long, deep silence. CUSTER slowly relaxes until he finally stops aiming the gun at

SARAH *and releases his grasp. With a labored moan, his arms hanging by his side, the gun still in his hand,* CUSTER *walks hesitantly over to one of the armchairs and collapses into it.)*
Why do you make me suffer like that?
SARAH: Make you suffer, Custer? What do you know about suffering?
(Pause. CUSTER *slowly recovers and regains control of himself.)*
CUSTER: You're wrong, Sarah. It's true that a president can never allow himself any emotion. He must keep a cool head at all times. Think of all the lives that hang upon any erroneous suffering . . . !
SARAH: Yes, it's awful . . . Well, lucky for me I don't have that problem. If I commit an error in suffering onstage, the only fatality will be the audience dying from laughter. Art is so naïve, isn't it, mon ami? Where did I leave my bag?
CUSTER: Over there.
SARAH: Oh, thanks. *(*SARAH *takes her small evening bag, which complements her evening wear, and pulls out a small mirror and compact. She begins to powder her face.)* Oh, but I interrupted you, and I think you were very interested in telling me something.
CUSTER: Only that I have dedicated my life to studying others' emotions in great detail. And it hasn't been very easy. You'll notice that because of my station, I'm used to being surrounded by people accustomed to hiding their feelings. But I've become an expert in decoding traces, small signs . . . though at times when they manifest themselves in a brutal, pure . . .
*(*CUSTER *abruptly cuts himself short, affected by something.* SARAH *has already taken out a lipstick from her bag and begun to apply it while looking into her mirror.* CUSTER *observes, with painful fascination, how* SARAH *runs the thick lipstick over her lips time and again.* SARAH *apparently notices the silence and looks intently at* CUSTER, *even as she continues to apply her makeup. Pause.)*
CUSTER *(hurt):* Don't do that. Don't be so cruel.
SARAH: Do what?
*(*CUSTER *does not answer.)*
Put on my lipstick?
*(*CUSTER *does not answer.)*
Sorry, I didn't know it bothered you. Not a problem. *(She makes a big deal of putting her makeup back into her bag.)* Please, go on.
(Pause.)
CUSTER *(absentminded, almost without expression):* I was telling you about this bodyguard . . .
*(*SARAH *doesn't try to disguise her boredom.)*
SARAH: Oh, please . . .

CUSTER: Don't be intolerant, Sarah. The riffraff can teach us a thing or two as well.

(SARAH laughs.)

SARAH: You just have to accept it, Custer, that you and I are different . . . exceptions . . . resoundingly solitary . . . Sometimes, very occasionally, it happens that we run across each other, two equals, like you and I . . . and what a brief explosion of happiness that is! And I'm saying that conscientiously, because an encounter like that . . . always ends in an explosion. One of the two has to be annihilated. Or both of them . . .

But I understand that . . . that weakness of yours for the simple folk. After all, your mission, Mr. President, your calling as a leader, demands that you know them well. They're the clay for your sculptor's hands. And they should be a very docile clay in your hands. Your intuition, your sense of smell, must be very finely attuned. An expert in sniffing out the changing smells of the masses. If you smell too much adrenaline, you have to knock them down; if there's not enough, you have to wind them up.

(CUSTER laughs.)

Why are you laughing, Custer?

CUSTER: Because you appear to be describing exactly what you do onstage, divine Sarah.

SARAH: A typical line. Are you imitating me, Mr. President?

CUSTER: My dear, you must know that in order for you to develop your art, you need to also know how they behave, how they feel, those simple, vulgar characters . . .

SARAH *(desperately):* No! No! I will never again play a vulgar character! I'd rather die! I'd rather die, do you understand!

(Pause.)

CUSTER *(compassionate):* You could never be vulgar, Sarah . . .

(SARAH relaxes. She smiles.)

SARAH: No, I never could. You are so wise, Custer! You figured out my trick . . . Yes, whenever I found myself obliged to play a vulgar character, I did it with the greatest subtlety, I took such great care, I was so refined . . . that the clumsiest oaf ended up covered in a cape of invisible gold . . .

CUSTER *(applauding):* Brava!

SARAH: Not so very brava. They were all complete failures at the box office. People had a feeling I was tricking them. The producers began to hate me. I began dropping in the ranks. They sent me to theaters farther and farther away. I ended up in those dreary sheds in the provinces, where maybe you saw me for the first time . . .

CUSTER: Where I "saw" myself in you, Sarah. Where I saw my equal. Rather, my teacher, the necessary complement to my own grandeur.

SARAH: Yes, but those times were hard on us, Custer. Well, at least on me. History betrayed me. I sought glory when glory was already an antique. I wanted to play noble characters, heroic, generous, unselfish characters when selfishness was about to become the highest value. I loved poetry as it lay dying and the sublime as it was being ridiculed. I searched for God at a time when His death didn't produce anguish but only bored yawns.

(SARAH goes over to CUSTER, takes away his revolver, expertly checks it for bullets, and then gives it back to him.)

Custer, you are the only one who understands me. Kill me. I can't take any more humiliation. There is no turning back on the road I'm traveling. I come from a cold climate, and I'll end up in the tropics, in some final, terrible whorehouse, covered in sores, with repugnant diseases, with no one to care about me. Please, kill me.

(CUSTER does not take the weapon but instead looks at her, thoughtfully.)

CUSTER: I too wanted glory, Sarah. But even heroes need a hand from tricky Lady Luck. Look at me. I participated in every battle I could, always on the front lines, my chest bared to the artillery shells, to the grenadier's fire. At my side, my friends, my comrades, people far more worthy than I, they all fell like flies. And as for me . . . not even a scratch. Never, not once. In an age when going to the dentist was a heroic act, I suffered terrible illness. And I cured myself. No one knows how.

And when peace came, I, prepared for the greatest deeds . . . I, gifted with a wisdom that could anticipate the changing times . . . what did I discover? That it was my lot to live in an age when the only thing men wanted was to get rich. What could I do, Sarah? A man like I am can't deny his fate, even if it's the wrong fate. History put me in this place, and I, with my infinite nostalgia, allowed her to do so. I did what came naturally to me. With the same facility that you have in knowing what to do on the stage.

There, you see: another thing we have in common.

The big difference is that I'm a politician, not an artist.

My virtue lies in leading the times, not opposing myself to them.

I'm going in the opposite direction from you, Sarah.

The only thing that can hold me back is for you to squeeze that trigger.

SARAH: Are you asking me to kill you?

CUSTER: Out of courtesy, I would say yes, but death disgusts me. She and I don't get along very well. She never chose me, I've never been her favorite. Besides, if you were to kill me, my fighting reflexes, my instincts, would become activated. Automatically. Without any intervention on my part. And you, Sarah, would make very easy prey.

SARAH: Would you devour me whole, Mr. President?

CUSTER: Don't doubt it.

(SARAH slowly, carefully, observes CUSTER. Pause.)
SARAH: Yes, you would . . . Like a man-eating beast.

My skin is very white, did you know that? Perhaps you didn't notice it under all this makeup. And it's very soft. Too soft. Your claws would rip right through it. You'd tear so deep into my flesh, it would be mortal . . . !

I always knew you'd do it, that you were my fate. I always saw in you, in your black eyes, my own murderous double.

Let's get rid of the gun. *(She does so, putting the gun on the table.)* Use your hands, Custer.
(Pause. CUSTER takes a couple of steps toward her.)
CUSTER: Sister, your death is irresistibly attractive.
(SARAH rips open her dress, exposing her chest.)
SARAH: At last, Mr. President. What I came here for. My own annihilation. You're the only one worthy. Let's forget we're in this suite in some silly hotel.

We're in a jungle. And I'm the white prey you've got cornered. I'm your deer, trembling in the moonlight. My heart races. Between terror and pleasure, it feels its death drawing closer and closer. It waits impatiently to be ripped out of my chest. My flesh's last moment. Its final exaltation. The greatest of all mysteries, its most rigorous pleasure.
(CUSTER's cell phone begins to ring.)
Don't answer it.
(CUSTER is upset and doesn't know what to do.)
Turn it off.
(CUSTER, in despair, takes the gun from the table and, pointing it at SARAH, walks to the other end of the room. He answers the phone. He speaks, his gun still pointed at SARAH. With the revolver, CUSTER signals for her to go all the way to the opposite end of the room. SARAH obeys, modestly covering her chest with the torn dress.)
CUSTER *(in a low voice)*: Sir . . . ? Yes, yes, I heard you . . . I was in the bathroom, sir . . . No, I didn't take it with me . . . That long? It didn't seem that long . . . No, sir, I did not have diarrhea. Quite the contrary . . . No, sir, no vomiting either . . . Absolutely, sir, I am very careful about my hygiene . . . Yes, sir, I wash my hands after every time I go . . . Mineral water . . . I would never eat raw fish, sir . . . No, sir, you don't have to worry about my having any symptoms of cholera . . . I'm fully aware that the president cannot afford to be . . . Sir, I know that the president's health and safety are more important than any other consideration . . . Under my breath, sir? No, no, I'm speaking in a normal voice. No, I'm not hoarse, sir. It's that it's very quiet here, and it doesn't seem right to yell. Don't worry, sir. Everything's in order, absolutely in order . . . Sir . . . ? *(There's no reply. It's obvious that the other person has hung up. With a loud, firm voice.)* And

don't fuck around with me any longer. I'm telling you for the last time! I'm with a very important person, and I don't wish to be interrupted. (*CUSTER puts the phone away. To SARAH.*) My apologies. State business.

SARAH: I understand.

CUSTER: It's always like this. I have no privacy. You think that, for example, we're alone here? No, there are surely some hidden microphones. Maybe a closed-circuit camera. Some bored, fat guard could be watching us right now. But don't be afraid, Sarah, you think we mean anything to him? We really exist? No, we're just black-and-white ghosts on his little monitor's screen. Every once in a while, at most, we'll leave the frame . . . Who was it that said, "If you move, you won't show up in the photo"? (*CUSTER's lost in thought. Pause.*)

SARAH (*softly*): Mr. President . . .

CUSTER: Yes . . . ?

SARAH: It pains me to see you like that, all worn-out. Did they tell you something serious?

CUSTER: No, no . . . Only a minor problem . . . having to do with public health matters. Of course, even the most insignificant thing, when it's added to all the other insignificant problems, can end up overwhelming . . .

SARAH: And on top of all that, I show up, to annoy you with my ghost stories.

CUSTER: No, no, you'd never annoy me.

SARAH: If you want me to, I'll go now.

(*SARAH begins to collect her things. CUSTER goes over to her; he's in anguish and still holding the gun.*)

CUSTER: Don't, Sarah, please. Stay. (*Pause. They look at each other. Indicating with the gun.*) I've torn your dress.

SARAH: It's not important.

CUSTER: Deep down I'm so clumsy . . . I only know how to order and be obeyed. And when I find myself with you . . . With freedom's fragile delicacy . . . What do I do? I rip your dress. I imprison you in your own nakedness.

SARAH: I can fly without wings, Mr. President. I can throw myself out that window . . . with the risk that I'll fall for all eternity.

CUSTER: That's because you're so light, Sarah. In the best sense of the word. On the other hand, if I were to follow you, in two seconds I'd smash into the pavement.

SARAH (*fascinated*): Try it, Mr. President! (*She holds her hand out.*) Give me your hand! I'll lead you. We'll fly together.

(*CUSTER looks at her in disbelief.*)

CUSTER: I'm not just one person, Sarah. I'm a nation.

SARAH: You think that your people won't be able to get by without you?

CUSTER *(with a trace of annoyance):* I don't know, it's likely . . . Anyway, why take the risk? *(He nonchalantly points the gun at her.)* But there is a way you can help me.

SARAH: How so, Mr. President? *(She's holding her torn dress shut.)*

CUSTER *(still pointing the gun at her):* Don't close your dress, I beg you. Let your breasts show. That torn dress is like a cry. A desperate declaration of love. Help me, Sarah, lighten the weight of my own vulgarity. Show me the mystery of love.

SARAH *(somewhat tired):* In words or . . . ?

CUSTER: The flesh is tired, my dear friend . . . That's not the revelation I'm longing for.

(Pause. CUSTER is still pointing the gun at SARAH.)

SARAH: I don't know if I can give you an answer now, Custer. I've been so badly wounded. The whole world's played with me as if they were shooting a pigeon. But before, I would have responded that love is a sublime artifice . . . A fiction that feeds upon itself, a performance in which we end up losing ourselves . . . And I tell you that, as a consummate actress and lover.

CUSTER: I don't see it as being much different from anything else. Anyway, Sarah, you're speaking from the point of view of the artist, the refinement of the spirit . . . But there are primitive beings . . .

SARAH *(rapidly):* They don't concern me.

CUSTER: What are you afraid of, Sarah?

SARAH *(exasperated):* That gun! Stop pointing it at me, you're making me nervous!

CUSTER: Oh, sorry . . . *(He puts the revolver back in his holster.)*

SARAH: Why do you go around armed?

CUSTER: I have so many enemies . . . ! But if you want me to, I'll throw it out the window right now.

SARAH: And kill another innocent bystander?

(A very tense pause. CUSTER looks at her, his face disfigured by some old pain.)

CUSTER: Why did you say "another"?

SARAH: I just said it.

(Pause. He pierces her with his look.)

CUSTER: You knew him.

SARAH: Who?

(The phone rings. CUSTER automatically answers, never taking his eyes off of SARAH.)

CUSTER *(firm):* Custer standing by. *(CUSTER instantly realizes his mistake. He bites his lips and moves away from SARAH, trying to speak in a hushed voice.)* Yes, sir . . . Forgive me, sir, I don't mean to be impertinent . . . I did it without thinking, sir, it's my last name . . . Yes, sir, I understand that someone might take it the wrong way . . . Yes, sir, I understand that I said it with an inappropriate tone of authority, and I beg your forgiveness . . . What, sir . . . ? I'm talking in a low voice again? *(He yells out in a military fashion.)* Sir, yes, sir! Affirmative, sir! I'm Crap, sir! *(CUSTER quickly covers the mouthpiece of the phone and turns toward SARAH.)* It's code. *(Back into the phone, in hushed tones.)* Yes sir. Understood, sir. *(He hears something that terrifies him.)* Already? The president is on his way here . . . ? No, no, sir, everything's under control, completely under control . . . *(Desperate.)* Sir, how soon . . . ? *(The other person has already hung up.)* Sir . . . ? Sir . . . ? *(He puts the phone away and turns toward SARAH.)* An emergency.

SARAH: How much time do we have, Mr. President?

CUSTER: I don't know. *(Pause. CUSTER goes over to the bottle of whiskey, serves himself a drink, and downs it in a single gulp. He remembers SARAH and turns toward her, ashamed.)*

I'm sorry . . . would you like one?

(SARAH shakes her head, smiling.)

That's right, you don't like whiskey.

(SARAH looks at the champagne bottle still on the coffee table.)

Champagne . . . ?

(Without waiting for her to answer, CUSTER goes over to the table. He fills both flutes and hands one to SARAH.)

I'm so tired, Sarah . . . tired to death.

SARAH *(raising her glass):* To your being tired to death.

(SARAH and CUSTER clink their glasses together and drink.)

CUSTER: See? It's at moments like this that I'd like to be someone else. You've never wanted to be someone else?

SARAH: All the time.

CUSTER: Of course, you're an actress. How lucky you are! You can run away from yourself, every night . . . Even if it's only for a few hours . . . I envy your freedom!

SARAH *(mechanically):* Yes, I'm so lucky.

CUSTER: But, you know what? I've also pretended I was somebody else, many times. For example, one of my bodyguards . . . Well, I think I already told you that . . .

SARAH: Too many times.

CUSTER: It's just that I got to know a lot about him. Incredibly intimate details that would surprise you, Sarah . . .

SARAH: Nothing surprises me anymore.

CUSTER *(enthusiastic):* No, no, this is something special. A while ago I asked you to talk to me about love—you, someone I consider to be a high priestess—and imagine, I wasn't thinking so much about myself, but about this almost repugnant man . . . Because that's how you'd see him . . .

SARAH: Let me remind you that I don't know this man.

CUSTER: Use your actor's imagination. A disgusting guy. A mercenary, completely without feelings. But intelligent. Not your ordinary thug. It's just that something appears to have snapped inside him. A very deep wound, a tear in his mercy. That is, hard, cold, implacable. A perfect bodyguard. Well, I discovered that this . . . creature was involved in a sublime passion.

SARAH *(mocking):* Tiens!

(Pause.)

CUSTER *(pensive):* Yes, it was a turbulent love story. In reality it went through several phases. Adolescent innocence. He would wait for her on cold, rainy afternoons in front of the courthouse. His soaked jacket weighed a ton on top of his skinny shoulders. He had short, coarse hair. He leaned against the building's wall and tried to light his cigarette with his wet matches, his fingers frozen. When she finally appeared, the raindrops glistened like diamonds on her black hair. Her enormous eyes were lost in his embrace . . . And he hugged her fragility. He felt so powerful holding her in his arms, holding her against his chest, her fragile bones, her smell of dark, wet skin . . .

When it wasn't raining, they'd meet at a bench in the park downtown. It was always cold, and only the cigarette and the caresses could make him forget about it. He'd try unsuccessfully to find her flat breasts under the angora pullover. The angora hairs stuck to his jacket. And stuck to his fingers was the warmth of that hidden skin, so quickly gone, that smooth only once in a lifetime . . .

SARAH *(sourly):* How do you know so many of the details?

CUSTER: It's a puzzle, I put the pieces together, slowly, with the occasional word, the passing comment, the fleeting glances . . .

SARAH: Your powers of divination are impressive. I suppose that you're waiting for me to ask you what happened then . . .

CUSTER: No.

SARAH: What happened then?

CUSTER: Well, what always happens. One day she didn't show up. He looked all over the city for her. Not a sign . . .

SARAH: But that's not the end, is it?

CUSTER: They got together a couple of times. There were moments of sublime ecstasy, and others of complete squalor. Heaven mixed with hell. They had a child.

SARAH: A child!

CUSTER: And she died.

SARAH: She died!

CUSTER: Yes.
(Pause.)
SARAH *(softly):* Did you kill her, Custer?
CUSTER: No. She just died. What do I know? These things happen. Sometimes people die of natural causes.
(Pause.)
SARAH: I have only one question.
CUSTER: Yes?
SARAH: The thing about her flat breasts. Was it because they were smooth or because she didn't have any?
CUSTER: They had a nonexistent roundness, the shadow of a curve. They were a little boy's breasts. I think that that absence, what she hid, surprised me so much that I made them up. I loved her missing breasts, her tiny little nipples. Those childish imitations of womanhood.
SARAH: It's a sad story.
CUSTER: Yes.
(Pause.)
SARAH: I also had my own great love story.
CUSTER: Oh yes?
SARAH: Yes. He was a Nazi, the enemy. A German soldier. It happened at the end of the war. I think they'd wounded him, I don't really know. They shaved my head for collaborating. My parents locked me in the basement. I would scratch the lime off the walls and put a little marble in my mouth. One night I left for Paris on my bicycle. Years later I also ran into him again. I don't know why, but he'd become Japanese.
CUSTER *(lost in thought):* Yes, I saw the movie. *Hiroshima, Mon Amour.*[4]
SARAH: I thought I'd already forgotten it. Everything is forgotten eventually, haven't you noticed? We forget movies, history, people. How many different wars do I have mixed up in my head? How sad, we forget everything. Actors forgetting their lines. Even we're going to be forgotten. Actually, that's already happening, at this very moment. I'm forgetting you. Look at me, Custer, look at how I'm forgetting you!
(SARAH takes CUSTER by the arms and shakes him. Her eyes are full of tears.)
CUSTER *(patient):* It's alright, Sarah, it's alright.
(CUSTER holds SARAH. She cries, her head on his chest, in great distress.)
SARAH: Am I like her? Like the dead girl? Do I smell like rain, like she did?
(She pulls away from CUSTER and opens up her torn dress.) Look, my breasts are like a little boy's.
(CUSTER closes her dress, compassionate.)
CUSTER: Please, Sarah, I'm not that bodyguard.
(Long pause. SARAH appears to have awakened from a dream. She wipes away her tears.)

SARAH: No, of course not. How absurd. I let myself get carried away by a bit of cheap sentimentalism.

It's your fault, President Custer!

How embarrassing! How could I let myself get swept away . . . ?
(SARAH goes to look for her handbag. She takes out the tiny mirror and examines herself.) What a fright! (She goes over to CUSTER and places the mirror in his hands.) Take it, I'm going to need your help.
(CUSTER holds the mirror up in front of her. SARAH takes her time in removing all her makeup and then redoing it. The entire procedure, requiring CUSTER's full attention, is filled with erotic charge.

SARAH first cleans her face with some cream. She then applies another cream, powders herself, applies mascara to her lashes, goes over her eyebrows.

Finally, with a strange, odd manner, she takes out her lipstick and, looking intensely into CUSTER's eyes, begins to paint her lips.

CUSTER suddenly lets the mirror drop onto the floor and abruptly moves away.

SARAH lets out a cry and squats down to retrieve the mirror.

CUSTER picks up the cell phone and frantically dials a number. He listens.)
CUSTER: Why doesn't anyone answer, damn it?
SARAH: Lucky it didn't break, poor little mirror. That would have been seven years of bad luck.
CUSTER: So you think you're going to live for seven more years? What an optimist!
SARAH: Why suddenly so aggressive, Custer?
CUSTER: You knew him, didn't you? That's why you're here . . .
SARAH (biting her words): Who did I know . . . ?
CUSTER: That boy . . . my bodyguard's son.
SARAH (smoothly): I don't know the bodyguard. I don't know the bodyguard's girlfriend. How am I going to know his son?
CUSTER: He's already on his way.
CUSTER: The murderer. You're finally going to get to meet him. Face to face.
(SARAH looks at him, unperturbed. Pause. CUSTER takes out his revolver.)
He was always a delicate child. That's what my bodyguard told me. Took after his mother in everything. Enormous, sad eyes, infinitely sad. Skin with that smooth sheen, sickly . . . He told me that his heart was always in his throat about his son.

He told me that they had a house in some working-class neighborhood on the outskirts, with a dirt road, and that when he returned at night, from who knows where, when he'd see the light of his house, he felt like someone had his hand on his throat.

More than once he found his son burning up with fever, his eyes sunken, wild, as if he were having a vision of some kind . . .

Apparently an aunt used to take care of him, but then she died. He didn't want to have anything more to do with women. They all died on him. Luckily, by then the boy was older. They got by on their own. Sometimes he'd cook, sometimes the kid would cook. He could cook very well. He had a knack for it.

They were very close. Of course, he didn't tell his son anything about his job. The truth—he lied to him. He told him he was the caretaker at a factory, and that sometimes he had to work overtime, or he had to take the night watch.

And when he'd return home, at dawn, or in the late afternoon, walking down those dirt roads, he'd try to clean his soul of everything he'd seen and done, the screams, the smell of burning flesh, the stink.

In the patio sink, he'd scrub his hands and face. And then he'd go into the house. And there he'd be, innocent, his face just like his mother's. Sad, sickly.

(Pause.)

At first, I couldn't understand what'd happened that afternoon, sir. It was summer, hot. Everything was silent, lots of shadows.

The kid wasn't in the kitchen, or in the dining room, or in his bedroom. So I went to my bedroom. The blinds were closed, and a lamp was on.

And there he was, seated on the edge of the bed, in front of the big mirror on the dresser. He saw me and smiled. He was fourteen years old, he was becoming a man. But there was something strange, something that took me a while to pick up on. *(CUSTER laughs, as if it were a prank.)* You know? He had on one of his mother's dresses, which I'd saved . . . and he had his face all made up, just like a woman, and he smiled at me with his sad smile, his lips bright red . . . *(CUSTER laughs again.)* And you think that I caught him in the act? No, sir, he was waiting for me. With that sad smile. What a clown!

(Pause.)

So I went over to him. I stood next to him. The thing that hurt me the most was that he looked exactly like his mother. So I lifted my arm, like this, way up, and I hit him as hard as I could with my fist, hit that beautiful, fragile face I loved so much . . . And a second before I turned away I saw the blood start pouring out of his nose, his mouth.

(Pause.)

I went and sat down on this little bench we have in the kitchen. I just collapsed. I think I lit a cigarette.

I don't know how much time went by.

Then it was like thunder hit the house. I knew right away what it had
been. I ran to my room.

My son, sir, my son was there, dead, sprawled out, his beautiful head
destroyed. Blood, brains, bones scattered everywhere, spattering everything.

(Pause.)

He'd fired the .32 that I keep in a dresser drawer. He'd fired like this, into
his mouth, right between his lipstick-painted lips.

(CUSTER demonstrates.)

SARAH: May I? *(She takes the gun from him.)*

CUSTER: You knew him, didn't you?

SARAH: What does it matter if I knew him or not? Now I know him. But
please, we don't have much time. The murderer is just about to get here.
Hold me, hug me hard.

(CUSTER looks at SARAH in silence.)

What're you waiting for? Hold on to me as if we were wrestling.

*(After a pause, CUSTER suddenly embraces SARAH. It's a strong, long-antici-
pated embrace and might be confused with a fight or a struggle. In the
middle of this embrace, a shot goes off. Long pause. The embrace continues a while longer. It's not apparent who's been wounded.)*

SARAH: He'd tell you, "I love you, Papa. I've always loved you."

*(SARAH starts to slide slowly down to the floor, her arms still tightly hugging
CUSTER's body as she falls. CUSTER remains as erect as a statue. SARAH's
body has left a thick trail of blood that runs from CUSTER's chest down to his
feet. Only after SARAH has hit the ground does CUSTER react. It's as if he
were crumbling, falling to pieces, with a deep despair. He's on his knees.
He pulls SARAH up onto his lap, in a strange Pietà.)*

CUSTER *(softly):* My son, my son, my son.

*Very, very slowly, CUSTER lowers his head over SARAH's and kisses her on
the lips, a long, endless kiss. Until the lights have gone completely to BLACK.
Then, in complete darkness, the cell phone begins to ring.*

TRANSLATOR'S NOTES

1. In the original text, Monti plays with the surname Roca, literally "rock" but also
the name of General Julio Argentino Roca (1843–1914), the nineteenth-century hero of the
"Conquest of the Desert." As minister of war under President Nicolás Avellaneda, he was
instrumental in the Argentinean government's displacement or disappearance of thousands
of gauchos and indigenous peoples as the country cleared the way for white settlers and

investors. As the original text makes clear, Roca was twice president of Argentina (1880–86 and 1898–1904).

In the English translation, "Roca" has been replaced by "Custer," in possible allusion to General George Armstrong Custer (1839–76). Custer's military exploits, notoriety, and participation in the "pacification" of the U.S. West parallel Roca's, although Custer did not live to consider a political career.

2. In the original text, Sarah recites the opening lines of Esteban Echeverría's 1837 romantic epic poem "La cautiva" [The captive woman]: "Era la tarde y la hora / en que el sol la cresta dora / de los Andes." I have substituted the opening lines of Walt Whitman's "When Lilacs Last in the Door-yard Bloom'd" (1865–69).

3. I have substituted lines attributed to José Hernández ("Lo ahogaron en un charco / por causante de la peste. / Tenía los ojos celestes, / como potrillito zarco") with lines from Edgar Allan Poe's poem, "To One in Paradise" (1845).

4. Custer refers to *Hiroshima, Mon Amour,* Alain Resnais's award-winning 1959 film and one of the most powerful works to come out of the French New Wave. Marguerite Duras wrote the screenplay.

Finland

Finlandia was first presented in 2000 as part of the series of staged readings, Teatrísimo, in the Presidente Alvear Theater, Buenos Aires, under the direction of Mónica Viñao. The actors Andrea Bonelli, Rubén Stella, Vanesa Cardella, Jorge Rod, and Ignacio Gadano participated. The following year *Finlandia* received a full staging at La Trastienda, Buenos Aires, once again under the direction of Mónica Viñao and with the actors Jorge Rod, Andrea Bonelli, Ignacio Gadano, and Cutuli.

Characters

BELTRAMI
ASSISTANT
The MEZZOGIORNO TWINS (conjoined twins, a man and a woman, connected at the groin)

PROLOGUE

The frozen plains of Finland, covered by a thick blanket of snow, at the end of the Middle Ages or the beginning of the Renaissance. A rough and precarious wooden structure barely provides any refuge from the inclement weather. In the middle of the darkness, a religious song from the south of Italy is heard, its rhythm frantic, as the plain's howling wind makes it fade in and out.

After a while, the MEZZOGIORNO TWINS appear, whirling in a state of ecstasy, dancing and singing. The male MEZZOGIORNO carries an oil lamp in his hand.

MEZZOGIORNO (M) *(entering):* Lux in tenebris![1]

(Whirling, in a trance, the MEZZOGIORNO TWINS cross the entire stage, disappearing into the wings opposite from where they entered.)

MEZZOGIORNO (M AND F) *(singing):*

> Madonna de la grazia
> ca mbraccio puorte grazia
> a vuje vengo pe' grazia
> o Maria fance grazia.
>
> Fance grazia o Maria
> comme Te fece lu Pateterno
> ca Te fece mamma de Dio
> fance grazia o Maria.
>
> Fammella o Maria
> fammella pe' carità
> pe' li doni ca riceviste
> dalla Santissima Trinità.[2]

Little by little, as the sound of the song grows more distant, the shadows return to hang over the scene. Darkness and silence, except for the sound of the wind and the murmurs of an army making camp.

ONE ACT

Another wavering light begins to take shape, and a few seconds later BELTRAMI, *wrapped in pelts, and his aged* ASSISTANT *enter. The* ASSISTANT *carries a candle in one hand and attempts to maintain his balance while carrying in his other hand a mountain of papers and writing instruments.* BELTRAMI *stops at center stage and looks around the room. The* ASSISTANT *maintains a respectful distance, a few steps behind.*

ASSISTANT *(to* BELTRAMI*):* Is this all right, sir?

BELTRAMI: Yes.

(The ASSISTANT *puts his things on top of a table or on the floor. He remains at* BELTRAMI's *side, waiting, expressionless.)*

BELTRAMI: How long until dawn?

ASSISTANT: A couple of hours, sir.

BELTRAMI: There will be battle.

ASSISTANT: Unknown, sir. The enemy has done nothing but sneak away from us.

BELTRAMI: So they're still moving?

ASSISTANT: They seem to be leaving.

BELTRAMI: Dodges, feints. But they're avoiding the fight. What's happened to the Madman? Why won't he fight us? He came to devour the world, and now he wants to dance?

ASSISTANT: That's how they are, sir.

BELTRAMI: Maybe they're preparing a trap. *(Pause.)* It's cold.

ASSISTANT: Shall I send for a fire?

BELTRAMI: Is the wound deep?

ASSISTANT: No, sir. Just a scratch.

BELTRAMI: Let me see.

(The ASSISTANT draws near. BELTRAMI, without looking, touches the wound. Afterward, he examines his own bloodstained fingers.)

BELTRAMI *(smiling):* Old man's blood.

ASSISTANT: Yes, sir.

BELTRAMI *(teasing):* Watered-down.

ASSISTANT: Not nearly as vigorous as it once was.

(Pause.)

BELTRAMI *(absentmindedly rubbing the blood between his fingers):* How long has it been since I've slept?

ASSISTANT: Two nights, sir.

BELTRAMI: I have a fever. *(Pause.)* Whose lands are these?

ASSISTANT: Enemies, sir. When they heard us coming, they went over to the Madman's army.

BELTRAMI: When we go, set fire to everything.

ASSISTANT: Sir . . .

BELTRAMI: Tell me about these fools.

ASSISTANT: That girl and her little priest, sir?

BELTRAMI *(surprised):* The male freak's a priest?

ASSISTANT: Oh, you mean the Mezzogiornos . . .

BELTRAMI: Yes, yes, the Italians . . .

ASSISTANT: The army came across them in the field. They claim to be lost.

BELTRAMI: Do you believe them?

ASSISTANT: Yes . . . they're from some circus. A pair of unfortunate creatures. They're connected down there. They were showing it off to the soldiers until I put an end to that with a few lashings of my whip.

BELTRAMI: Down there? But it's a man and a woman . . . If they're connected, what sex are they?

ASSISTANT: I didn't go into any details, sir, because frankly it makes me sick . . . but it would appear that they have both sexes, one inside the other, stuck, in the same skin . . . as if they were only one body . . . That's why they get so carried away all the time . . . in the climactic moment, if you get my drift, sir.

BELTRAMI: But they're brother and sister!

ASSISTANT: Yes, it's absolutely immoral. If I were you, sir, I'd have them hanged like dogs.

BELTRAMI: They're circus freaks . . . there's no morality in the circus . . . What the circus puts on display isn't real . . . Send them in, will you?

ASSISTANT: Sir . . .

BELTRAMI: What is it?

ASSISTANT: It's that girl, sir . . .

BELTRAMI: What girl?

ASSISTANT: The one they found . . . She's here.

(Pause.)

BELTRAMI *(remembering a biblical verse):* She who was once lost and now is found? What's she doing here?

ASSISTANT: Your Excellency's orders. Don't you remember?

BELTRAMI: No.

ASSISTANT: That girl and the little priest who seduced her . . . the ones that have caused such a scandal throughout the country . . . Your Excellency ordered that the prisoners be brought back in barred wagons . . .

(Pause.)

BELTRAMI *(exploding):* But what do I have to do with that mess? A laughing matter . . . Go on, I'll take care of it later.

ASSISTANT: Sir.

BELTRAMI: What?

ASSISTANT: The girl . . . *(He makes a gesture over his abdomen indicating that the woman is pregnant.)*

BELTRAMI: That so?

ASSISTANT: This cries out to heaven. It's a shame.

BELTRAMI: Don't worry, man. It's only to set an example. It'll be over soon. Go on, send in those fools.

(The ASSISTANT exits. Pause.)

BELTRAMI: This country . . . always in darkness. Like a sleeping animal. And these people who come from God knows where, like ghosts crossing the snow, starving dogs, wandering like madmen in the desert, pursuing God knows what, a factory of mirages. And here I am with them at the edge. Right where the nobles of Finland have sent me, to guard the border . . . Bastion and prince. These savages don't deserve anything more than our disdain, but nevertheless, here we are, sniffing around in the night. And at dawn, God willing, we'll split each other's skin right open.

(The MEZZOGIORNO TWINS suddenly burst into the room and throw themselves at BELTRAMI's feet. Panting, on their knees, they try to embrace his legs. The ASSISTANT enters behind them and contemplates the scene as if it were a dream. BELTRAMI remains absolutely motionless, like an ice sculpture.)

MEZZOGIORNO (M): Signore! Signore!

MEZZOGIORNO (F) *(excited and amused)*: Sir! Sir! He means "sir"!

MEZZOGIORNO (M): When will I be libero? Signore!

BELTRAMI *(motionless):* Speak in our language, foreigners.

MEZZOGIORNO (F): Libero! Libero!

MEZZOGIORNO (M): Free! She means "free"!

(BELTRAMI lets out a chilling laugh and suddenly grabs MEZZOGIORNO (M) by the hair. The TWIN moans and pants in ecstasy. Pause.)

BELTRAMI: Why do you want to be free, foreigners? So you can go over to the Madman's army of savages?

MEZZOGIORNO (M): Per carità, signore, no!

BELTRAMI: Are you on the Madman's payroll?

MEZZOGIORNO (M): No, no, signore! Ti giuro!

BELTRAMI: So then why did they find you two snooping around?

MEZZOGIORNO (F): I got perduta!

MEZZOGIORNO (M): She got lost!

MEZZOGIORNO (F): Perduta al buio!

MEZZOGIORNO (M): Lost in the night!

BELTRAMI: Well, you got lost in the wrong place, strangers. I think you're enemy spies.

MEZZOGIORNO (M): Nemico, me? Ma cosa dice, signore? Me straniero.

MEZZOGIORNO (F): He's a foreigner!

MEZZOGIORNO (M): Me non capisco never di tutta questa war! Tutti contro tutti!

MEZZOGIORNO (F): Everybody fighting each other!

MEZZOGIORNO (M): Tutti ammazzandosi!

MEZZOGIORNO (F): Everybody killing each other!

MEZZOGIORNO (M): Me, I'm neutrale!

MEZZOGIORNO (F): He's neutral! Neutral!

BELTRAMI: No one's neutral here. If you're not with me, you're against me. *(He releases MEZZOGIORNO (M), and both TWINS remain kneeling on the floor, trying to maintain their balance, moaning histrionically, letting out the occasional orgasmic groan, and rubbing their heads.)*

MEZZOGIORNO (M): Dio, oh Dio, when will this nightmare end, this dream of the assassini?

MEZZOGIORNO (F): When will I wake up, in my sunny terra? Al sole . . .

MEZZOGIORNO (M): Ahhhhh, l'Italia mia, clean, civilizzata. Napoli, Napoli. *(Long pause. The MEZZOGIORNO TWINS are over to one side, turning and turning as they yield to their perpetual orgasm. BELTRAMI does not move.)*

BELTRAMI: Moth, are you awake?

ASSISTANT: Yes, sir.

(BELTRAMI snaps his fingers. The ASSISTANT grabs one of the papers and begins to read.)

ASSISTANT *(reading):* "... sentenced to die at the hands of the firing squad ..."

(BELTRAMI snaps his fingers. The ASSISTANT blindly grabs another sheet of paper.)

ASSISTANT *(reading):* "I have ordered that you be sent the following, without delay ..."

(Another snap of BELTRAMI's fingers.)

ASSISTANT *(reading):* "Declaration regarding the theft of several harnesses ..."

(BELTRAMI snaps his fingers once more, impatiently. The ASSISTANT is flustered.)

ASSISTANT *(reading in a faltering voice, trembling):* "Beltrami, sir, I appeal to you, with a trembling hand, oppressed by and bewildered at this atrocity, unheard of in the country of Finland, this terrible tragedy that has swept down upon my house and me in my old age ..." *(He sneaks a look at BELTRAMI, and, seeing that he has chosen the right document, his voice becomes stronger, taking on a pathetic and indignant tone.)* "... at the hands of my very own daughter and an immoral, unworthy, wicked priest, a vile renegade, who, taking advantage of his position as cleric, managed to worm his way into the sacred enclosure of my home and seduce this evil child, whom I no longer call daughter, making her accomplice to his villainous lust and throwing her headlong into a world of vice ..."

(The MEZZOGIORNO TWINS, who up until now have been softly panting, let out a strident guffaw, joking, obscene, disgusting. BELTRAMI looks at them with repulsion. Time seems to freeze.)

BELTRAMI *(smoothly):* What are you two laughing at?

MEZZOGIORNO (F): At the madness of love, signore.

(The TWINS laugh.)

MEZZOGIORNO (M): Love is too much for one poor man.

MEZZOGIORNO (F): Troppo, troppo. A curse, a thing of the devil.

MEZZOGIORNO (M) *(mysteriously):* And to protect ourselves from it, there's a formula that never fails. Even the pope knows it. Because if not the pope, then who? Anyway, he's just a man.

MEZZOGIORNO (F) *(formal):* Does the signore wish to learn it?

BELTRAMI: Why do I need to learn to cast spells?

MEZZOGIORNO (M): The signore is a leader of men, powerful.

MEZZOGIORNO (F): Love weakens and always arrives unexpected, just like death. We have to stay on our guard.

MEZZOGIORNO (M): The signore makes the war. The signore knows. When the troops sleep, do not the sentinels always keep the watch?

BELTRAMI: I hardly ever sleep.

MEZZOGIORNO (F): Yes, but Nature, she always works on the side of sleep.

MEZZOGIORNO (M): And the minute the man, he falls asleep, love takes him over.

MEZZOGIORNO (F): A man who sleeps is a man in love.

MEZZOGIORNO (M): Because love, signore, love is a figliol' . . .

MEZZOGIORNO (F): A little child, he means to say.

MEZZOGIORNO (M): . . . of the darkness and of sleep. When the body frees itself from the luce . . .

MEZZOGIORNO (F): The light, he means to say.

(The TWINS point to their now-closed eyes.)

MEZZOGIORNO (M): See? When the skin covers the eyes, and the light of God cannot enter the body per gli occhi, through the eyes, then the body returns to its former darkness and becomes one with love.

MEZZOGIORNO (F): And then, the sogni . . .

MEZZOGIORNO (M): Dreams, she means to say.

MEZZOGIORNO (F): . . . those tricky dreams burst open like bubbles on the surface of stagnant water.

MEZZOGIORNO (M): And where do they come from, all stirred up like that?

MEZZOGIORNO (F): From the rotting of the più deep down, the darkness.

MEZZOGIORNO (M): Because il corpo, signore, the body, the darkness, the dreams, and love are all the same thing.

MEZZOGIORNO (F): The same substance in different states.

(The MEZZOGIORNO TWINS' faces are transformed into horrible, laughing masks. They laugh. BELTRAMI cannot avoid a shiver of repulsion.)

BELTRAMI *(to the ASSISTANT)*: Shut these disgusting things up.

(The ASSISTANT gets up and beats the TWINS, who transform their laughter into a histrionic, orgasmic howl of pain.)

BELTRAMI *(laughing):* It hurts that bad, eh, foreigners?

MEZZOGIORNO (M): No, signore. I'm pretending.

MEZZOGIORNO (F): If I pretend, it doesn't really hurt me at all.

MEZZOGIORNO (M): Vede? Ow, ow, ow.

MEZZOGIORNO (M AND F): Ow, ow, ow.

MEZZOGIORNO (F): Il pain si sfuma. *(She laughs, sarcastically.)*

MEZZOGIORNO (M): Theater is such a comfort.

(The ASSISTANT hits the TWINS.)

BELTRAMI *(laughing):* All right, moth. That's enough.

MEZZOGIORNO (F): Let us perform for you, how about it, signore?

MEZZOGIORNO (M): Let us perform in our sleep, so we too can find relief from love.

BELTRAMI: Why do I keep fools around if not to have them perform?

MEZZOGIORNO (F): And if it's good entertainment, it always carries a lesson with it.

BELTRAMI: Very well, Italians, you may create your theater of dreams. How does it all begin?
MEZZOGIORNO (M): In *Inferno*.
MEZZOGIORNO (F): That's how it should be.
BELTRAMI: A good place to start.
(The MEZZOGIORNO TWINS begin an ecstatic dance, sinking down into orgasm and sleep.)
MEZZOGIORNO (M): From the depths of sleep, what happened to that girl?
MEZZOGIORNO (F): To the maiden?
MEZZOGIORNO (M): Yes.
MEZZOGIORNO (F): The one that tempted Evil?
MEZZOGIORNO (M): Yes.
MEZZOGIORNO (F): The one transfixed by love?
MEZZOGIORNO (M): Yes.
(The TWINS laugh in their sleep.)
MEZZOGIORNO (F): In the holy place we see the trace of a cloven hoof.
MEZZOGIORNO (M) *(singing):*

> What did the maid see that day,
> that first time?

(The TWINS dance in orgiastic ecstasy; they're like sleepwalkers.)
MEZZOGIORNO (M AND F) *(singing):*

> What happened?
> What happened?

MEZZOGIORNO (M):   She saw a priest blessing a font
> and hastened quick to be next it;
> and since she knew it naught,
> the priest for her he did wet it.

MEZZOGIORNO (M AND F):
> The priest for her he did wet it.

BELTRAMI: What disgusting crap!
MEZZOGIORNO (F): It comes out the way it comes out.
BELTRAMI: Let's see if you can do any better.

MEZZOGIORNO (M):   What did the maid do then, that day,
> that first time?
MEZZOGIORNO (F):   She looked at it so sweet and calm,
> and sighing, she moistened her palm,

her little fingers holy water did toss,
e dopo she made the sign of the cross.

MEZZOGIORNO (M AND F):
E dopo she made the sign of the cross.

(BELTRAMI shifts in his seat, uncomfortable. The ASSISTANT attempts to stifle his childish giggles.)
BELTRAMI: Well, I never expected this.
MEZZOGIORNO (F): What's that, signore?
BELTRAMI: Obscene little verses, children's dirty jokes.
MEZZOGIORNO (M): That's what Hell is like. May we continue?
BELTRAMI: Let's see where you fools end up.
MEZZOGIORNO (F): Thank you, signore. *(She sings.)*

What did the maid say that day,
that first time?
MEZZOGIORNO (M): She said smooth brother, dear lad,
No one in this world has ever had
within their hand's reach
a mystery so very deep
nor as Communion host to follow
something so very hard to swallow.
MEZZOGIORNO (M AND F):
So very hard to swallow.

BELTRAMI *(gloomy):* That one alone's worth excommunication.
MEZZOGIORNO (M): It's only a dream, signore.
BELTRAMI: A sinner's dream.
MEZZOGIORNO (F): Just like all dreams.
BELTRAMI: This had better not go beyond these walls.
MEZZOGIORNO (M): Don't worry, signore, these are things that live in secret.
MEZZOGIORNO (F) *(interrupts them by singing):*

And what did the priest say that day,
that first time?
MEZZOGIORNO (M): Belovèd child, look and see,
three are one and one is three.
Count, my child, with great care,
two hang down and one's in the air,

the truth is always a mystery,
the Holy Trinity.

MEZZOGIORNO (F):   The Holy Trinity.

BELTRAMI: Enough! Blasphemous spirits! Devil's legion! Get out of this house! Go to the desert!

MEZZOGIORNO (F) *(singing):*

I fear, my father, it does me harm,
this truth, so large and so very warm.

(At a sign from BELTRAMI, the ASSISTANT jumps on top of the TWINS and beats them, but the TWINS continue to sing.)

MEZZOGIORNO (M):   Oh, my child, what is the chance
that pain is worse than ignorance?

MEZZOGIORNO (F):   Oh my father, it is your will:
with your kindness please do me fill.

MEZZOGIORNO (M):   And thus the two bodies one flesh did become.
That's how the will of God is done.

(Without leaving his chair, BELTRAMI slaps and takes a few kicks at the TWINS. In reality, he appears to do all this in a laughing manner.)

MEZZOGIORNO (M AND F):
That's how the will of God is done.

(The TWINS collapse, in deep sleep and orgasmic ecstasy. There is a heavy silence, during which BELTRAMI and the ASSISTANT look at each other.)

BELTRAMI: At dawn, if there's no counterorder, hang them.

ASSISTANT *(pleased):* Yes, sir.

BELTRAMI *(to the ASSISTANT):* What's going on outside?

ASSISTANT: It's snowing heavily, sir.

BELTRAMI: Not letting up, eh?

ASSISTANT: No, sir.

BELTRAMI: And the battle?

ASSISTANT: It's still not certain, sir. We'll probably have to wait until daylight . . .

BELTRAMI: Yes, when it clears up . . .

(Pause. MEZZOGIORNO (F) has opened her eyes and drags herself over to BELTRAMI, trying not to awaken her twin brother.)

MEZZOGIORNO (F) *(in a low voice):* Eh, signore . . .
(BELTRAMI looks at her with curiosity.)
BELTRAMI: What do you want?
MEZZOGIORNO (F): Is it true that you're going to hang us?
BELTRAMI: Yes.
MEZZOGIORNO (F): Don't tell this poor little miss that . . . she's very impressionable.
BELTRAMI: What do you mean "she"? Aren't you the female?
MEZZOGIORNO (F): The truth is we're not sure . . . The juices flow from one body to the other all the time . . . And so, who's who? . . . Per esempio, right now he's asleep and I'm awake . . . But might I not be in reality nothing more than his dream? Now he's having a very powerful dream . . . all about war and glory . . . I can't stand it . . .
(She collapses into a deep sleep. MEZZOGIORNO (M) wakes up, his eyes as if he were hallucinating.)
MEZZOGIORNO (M): Che bello spectacle the war, eh, signore?
ASSISTANT *(to the TWIN):* Don't bother him!
BELTRAMI: Leave him be, he's not bothering anybody. He's an artist. Anyway, he's just dreaming.
(In a rapture of inspiration, MEZZOGIORNO (M) gets up and begins to recite, dragging along his twin sister, who continues sleeping.)
MEZZOGIORNO (M) *(orgasmic):*

> Che bello è when fin'lly at dawn
> the young warriors are unleashèd
> from women's sleep and the pillow's yawn!
>
> Let the drums roll and the playful cub,
> white, freed from memory, rush out,
> to glory's plain, down the slope, to rub.
>
> How it doth stir the ruffled breast!
> How the virile blood streams forth,
> its purple mirth in the golden air blest!
>
> And the mystical bird of war
> hovers over the anguished fields . . .

ASSISTANT: What anguish!

MEZZOGIORNO (M):   . . . spies upon the weak, seizing once more
> the fleshy off'ring this artifice yields.

And deliv'ring to one sole oblivion all,
like a cold, indiff'rent spouse, spurned,
the night dissolves into senseless pall
what had so sensibly in broad daylight burned.

(MEZZOGIORNO (M) takes two long bows and throws himself back down to the floor. The ASSISTANT looks at him with cold hostility. Pause.)
BELTRAMI: Yes, Italian, but that would be fought at high noon, and here, on the border, we wage war differently. Always under the cover of darkness, even in broad daylight. In snow or rain, in the middle of fog or mud. In the hand-to-hand you don't know who's who. There aren't any flashy uniforms, and the only thing that glows is fever. Mud, snow, blood, and fever, all mixed together. Here, foreigner, God never stopped giving breath. Genesis is still in the making. *(Pause.)* Take a letter. *(The ASSISTANT hurries to get his instruments together to take the dictation.)* "Letter to the nobles of Finland: Unhappy is the time of war and destruction, unhappy the time of frontiers and threats! How I would have liked to have lived in gentler times! I answer each movement of that savage, that assassin, the Madman, with one of my own, just like in a mirror. Because now we see through the glass, darkly . . ." Delete that last phrase. "And when I see my own assassin's face in that looking glass, behind that stony mask, I see only the grimaces of anguish and remorse." Delete that last phrase. "And compassion. But I am my own will. And I am the will of all, the nobles and the people of Finland. A peaceful people that, in my hands, become sharp and hard like the edge of a knife. In order to rip open a place in history. In order to become one people." Delete "peaceful." "But how long, friends, will I be able to sustain the general will? When will the spell be broken? When will I see only myself standing in front of the mirror? I await that moment with fear." Delete. "With impatience." Delete. ". . . that moment with concern. The moment when history will finally let me be and I will recover my own true face . . ." *(Brief pause.)* Delete all that. "How I would have liked to have lived in gentler times! But here is where the times have placed me, and I would never let foreign nations, no matter how virile, plunder my land, as if it were a no-man's land." Delete "no matter how virile." "That's why I'm here, friends, riding high on time, weapon in hand, on the lookout for whatever there may be. In order to open the way. To God, the true center of everything."
(Pause.)
BELTRAMI *(to the ASSISTANT):* You may now leave.
(The ASSISTANT clicks his heels and goes to leave. But he vacillates, and turns toward BELTRAMI.)
ASSISTANT *(imploring):* Sir . . .

BELTRAMI: Yes?

ASSISTANT: Allow me to remind you of the girl . . .

BELTRAMI: Yes, yes . . . And I'm going to take care of it. Now get out of here.

(The ASSISTANT exits. The TWINS shiver. The silence is like a tomb's. BELTRAMI paces around the room, in deep thought, his hands interlaced behind his back. On one of his passes, he gives the TWINS a soft nudge with the point of his boot.)

BELTRAMI: Mezzogiornos.

(The TWINS immediately wake up.)

MEZZOGIORNO (F): Signore?

BELTRAMI: You two know something of these things. Why do you suppose that a young woman from a good family . . . ? *(He laughs briefly.)* I'm not asking about the priest, because I'm no kid easily shocked by church scandal. But she . . . It's a mystery, don't you think?

MEZZOGIORNO (M): We can get to the bottom of it.

BELTRAMI: Do it.

MEZZOGIORNO (M) *(enigmatically):*

> If impurity is found in the pure,
> if softness resides in all that endures,
> if in clarity is found the obscure,
> let it all be cleansed by what I now conjure.

(MEZZOGIORNO (F), letting out an exclamation of ecstasy, appears to be in a trance state, her eyes closed.)

MEZZOGIORNO (F): "Nigra sum, sed formosa, filiae Ierusalem . . ."[3]

MEZZOGIORNO (M): We need roses.

BELTRAMI: There aren't any roses here.

MEZZOGIORNO (M): There are always roses.

(The ASSISTANT suddenly appears.)

ASSISTANT: Sir!

BELTRAMI: Get out!

(The ASSISTANT leaves as quickly as he arrived. Pause. MEZZOGIORNO (M) holds a wreath of roses over the MEZZOGIORNO (F)'s head. The roses are transparent, pale in color, and wave in the air as if they were flames just about to go out.)

BELTRAMI: And where did these roses . . . ?

MEZZOGIORNO (M): Silence, signore . . . They're the roses of dreams.

(MEZZOGIORNO (M) slowly crowns his sister with the wreath. Trickles of blood begin to run down her temples. Pause.)

MEZZOGIORNO (F): I'm the girl.

MEZZOGIORNO (M): I'm the priest.
BELTRAMI: And where does this comedy take place?
MEZZOGIORNO (M): In the *World*.
BELTRAMI: First Hell, now the World, makes sense. There's an order to this.
(The MEZZOGIORNO TWINS, like sleepwalkers, begin a dance performance.)
MEZZOGIORNO (M) *(singing):*

> How insidious is love!
> How it does play and plot,
> the whirling demon dove,
> always naked, e'er hot!
>
> Sworn enemy of the chaste,
> no sanctuary enjoys its respect,
> as it swoops down in haste,
> e'en in tombs it may resurrect.
>
> Spreading to all corners
> its ancient, golden flame;
> in the agèd, slow burner,
> mere sparks in a childish game.
>
> As for the young, ah, my lord,
> they are consumed in a trice;
> brighter than the solar orb,
> love in their veins bleeds its price.
>
> How insidious is love!

MEZZOGIORNO (F): Your voice, dark sir, undoes clarity. It comes in shadow, eroding light. And it contains within, a night of recently forged steel, and inside that night, a rough and jagged diamond.
MEZZOGIORNO (M): Your voice, dark lady, arrives drenched in clear liquids. Your voice is open, astonished. Like a bird at dusk, slowly unfolding its dark wings, burnished by water.
MEZZOGIORNO (F): Whence comes your voice, so dark? The light, the clarity that enveloped me was too fragile a protection from your deep sigh that spread throughout me, that filled me forever with darkness. Because, even though I cannot see you, your voice is too deep, too penetrating to be any other color . . .
MEZZOGIORNO (M): Your voice conquered me, my blood's been raised. But

only my blind voice can reach you. What is my blood doing inside me? How can my impassive skin hold back such abundance?

MEZZOGIORNO (F): I found out your eyes, because there in that corner, there was a blackness so thick that it devoured the surrounding shadows. Because your eyes are so dark, they breed clarity.

MEZZOGIORNO (M): And I discovered your eyes, because there where they were, the darkness palpitated and drew apart and made itself so clear that the night of my own eyes could enter and fill you up.

MEZZOGIORNO (F): Dark one, I have marked your rapid and black trace in the shadows: it is one, only one, of your brows.

MEZZOGIORNO (M): And I could see a vertigo of matte brilliance slipping in the shadows: is it your polished forehead?

MEZZOGIORNO (F): And I could see a smooth and burning slope: is it the line of your lips?

MEZZOGIORNO (M): Why should the world wrap you up and shatter you, keep you secret from me? Those luxurious rags that shelter you? That bejeweled shroud with which the dead of the earth tried to rip your live flesh for me?

MEZZOGIORNO (F): What is this black velvet that roughly scrapes your delicate, hidden flesh? This incomprehensible banner?

MEZZOGIORNO (M): I see you only in fragments.

MEZZOGIORNO (F): And I would desire to envelop you and slip through the smallest folds of your skin, and, in order to give you breath, I would kiss you, entering you through your mouth and your throat finally to the depths of your body, unto the limits of your blood, and nestle there, rocked by your heartbeats, sleeping forever, like a forgotten breath.

MEZZOGIORNO (M): I love only the tenuous colors of your darkness. The rest are abominable, bitter, harsh.

MEZZOGIORNO (F): I am very dark, my brother, but comely. I carry within my shadows secret perfumes. I bear within me precious, transparent liquids.

BELTRAMI *(with a hard look, withdrawn):* Enough.

(The TWINS go automatically motionless, waiting.)

MEZZOGIORNO (M): Did you say something, signore?

BELTRAMI *(as before):* I said that was enough.

(The TWINS, now alert, look at BELTRAMI.)

BELTRAMI *(without changing his manner, in a paused fashion):* Where are you going with this, Italians?

MEZZOGIORNO (F): Nowhere. I'm lost, remember?

BELTRAMI: Who are you working for?

MEZZOGIORNO (M): For nobody, signore. I'm unemployed.

BELTRAMI: What's the purpose of your mission?

MEZZOGIORNO (F): But . . .

BELTRAMI: To weaken our soldiers? To insinuate a woman's malice into their hearts?

MEZZOGIORNO (M): It's not my fault. The signore asked us to.

(BELTRAMI stands up and approaches the TWINS in a menacing fashion.)

BELTRAMI: Do you know the Madman?

MEZZOGIORNO (F): We know lots of madmen.

(BELTRAMI lets out a short laugh and slowly takes out from under his pelts a whip. Brandishing it, he goes over to the TWINS.)

MEZZOGIORNO (M) *(trying to maintain a modicum of dignity):* Signore, we are artists. You yourself said so.

(BELTRAMI begins to whip them.)

BELTRAMI: Get out! Get out!

(The TWINS, jumping and yelping, disappear offstage. Pause. The ASSISTANT appears at one side of the stage.)

BELTRAMI: So you were spying on us?

ASSISTANT: No, sir.

BELTRAMI: Then, what are you doing over there, rooted, like the guardian of some tomb? Is it still snowing?

ASSISTANT: No, sir. The snow and wind have stopped.

BELTRAMI: No one's heard any movement from the Madman?

ASSISTANT: Nothing, sir.

BELTRAMI: He must be waiting for the light, too. *(Pause.)* I can picture the Madman. I can see him now, wide awake, with his Madman's eyes. *(Pause.)* What does he want? Why is he fighting me?

ASSISTANT: He's a savage, sir, a madman.

BELTRAMI: Yes, of course. *(Brief pause.)* But there he is, in the candlelight, with his shining eyes wide open. He's feverish and dreaming. What is he dreaming about?

ASSISTANT: Who knows.

BELTRAMI: Leave me, I want to be alone, like him.

ASSISTANT: Yes, sir. *(He goes to leave, but he then stops, hesitating.)* Sir . . . *(At that same moment, the TWINS appear at the other side of the stage.)*

MEZZOGIORNO (M): Eh, signore . . .

BELTRAMI: What is it?

ASSISTANT: That poor young woman, sir . . . all chained up . . .

MEZZOGIORNO (F) *(whining):* We're cold and hungry . . .

ASSISTANT: Sir, just one word from you . . .

MEZZOGIORNO (M): Signore, forgive us . . . Our spirit is weak.

ASSISTANT: Sir, these sinners aren't worth the attention.

MEZZOGIORNO (F): We're sinners, but we're simple people . . . And all of us have un pó of the sinner in us, right, signore?

ASSISTANT: Sir, let them go . . .

MEZZOGIORNO (M): Signore, let us come in . . .

ASSISTANT: Sir . . .

MEZZOGIORNO (M): Signore . . .

(Pause.)

BELTRAMI: I'll see justice is done.

ASSISTANT: Yes, sir.

MEZZOGIORNO (M): Grazie, signore . . .

(The TWINS enter surreptitiously, as the ASSISTANT exits. There is a long silence. The TWINS slowly go over to BELTRAMI.)

MEZZOGIORNO (M): From Inferno to the World. And from the World, where to now, signore?

BELTRAMI: It's your game, Italians.

MEZZOGIORNO (F): Well then, on to *Purgatory.*

(The TWINS immediately go into a trance.)

MEZZOGIORNO (M): I see you, my sister, stretched out on the ground, your loose hair misted by the dew. Your eyes are two dark wells, full of trembling water, expectant.

MEZZOGIORNO (F): I see you, my brother, standing in front of me. Your assassin's eyes shine, dark and hard. My eyes tremble and fill up. And my blood flees deep inside me.

MEZZOGIORNO (M): This is the mystery of the flesh. The eyes slide over the surface, but it's inside, deep inside . . .

MEZZOGIORNO (F): This is the mystery of the flesh. Only slightly more solid than air, its form slips away and takes flight once again, or it descends in a slow rush into hidden corners. But the form is wispy, changing. It's something else that I seek, my sister, something viscous that lies inside, the darkness within, motionless, that which never changes.

MEZZOGIORNO (M): And nevertheless, stretched out on the ground, I await your dark lion's leap, the wounding rub of your cheeks, your fingers sinking into my flesh like claws, your mouth devouring me in a single bite.

MEZZOGIORNO (F): I hunt you, my wife, like I would an enemy. Impatient to rip open your smooth skin, to pierce your surface, to annihilate the form that covers and cloaks you.

MEZZOGIORNO (M): Dissolved in fear, only blind fate binds together my blood and my hair, my nerves, my skin, and my bones.

MEZZOGIORNO (F): Because I was created to wait. In order to be unmade at your hands.

MEZZOGIORNO (M): And in any case, my sister, how could I ever destroy the thing that so sweetly contains you? I am inside my body, torn from yours, and I contemplate you and caress you, with an endless desire for what is deep down inside. And I know that what I desire is beauty.

MEZZOGIORNO (F): And I protect you from myself because I am self-absorbed and greedy, in love with my own excitement brought on by the scent of your unattainable flesh.

MEZZOGIORNO (M): I was made of dark crevices, of ravenous cavities. I was made to envelop and swallow. Peaceful and slight, like the dark night opening up its lips to the impetuous light and then, almost unnoticed, once again closing them.

MEZZOGIORNO (F): Not even my bones will resist your campaign, my brother. Elastic and fragile, they will dismantle their own unnecessary structure. Inside, deep down inside myself, I wait for you, softer and softer.

MEZZOGIORNO (M): I travel around your body, my sister, with the ointment of my fingers and the secret softness of my tongue.

MEZZOGIORNO (F): I breathe, drunk, in the hollow of your neck and your shoulder, and for me, the night watchman, your armpits open, there where the ever-damp moss grows.

MEZZOGIORNO (M): Righteous warrior, my arms will not raise up to cover myself, nor to stop this war against me; instead they encircle your tense back, your arched waist . . .

MEZZOGIORNO (F): And I rest my head between your breasts, that coo like two doves.

MEZZOGIORNO (M): And my lips linger at your nipples, wrinkled and ripe.

MEZZOGIORNO (F): My fingers sink into your hair, my beloved, caressing the stubborn crook of your neck; my fingers are like a laurel wreath anticipating your victory.

MEZZOGIORNO (M): And in the dwindling light of your womb, I become undone in shadows that slither around until they fill up the small chalice that is your navel.

MEZZOGIORNO (F): Your arms, my beloved, enclose me and suffocate me. Your chest weighs like a mountain on top of me.

MEZZOGIORNO (M): What a wide expanse your back is, my sister!

MEZZOGIORNO (F): What a beauty your taut belly is, my brother!

MEZZOGIORNO (M): And what smooth, shining, and abundant haunches you have, my mysterious mare! They burst forth quivering, in their round fullness, they raise up, voluptuous, and suddenly split open the depths of your body.

MEZZOGIORNO (F): What deep and brutal grooves there are in your flanks as you rear up, my colt! With what energy they descend from your hips to meet in hiding, like violent rivers in a primitive jungle! What lofty columns your haunches are, sculpted in the solid night!

MEZZOGIORNO (M): And from what fantastic animal did your legs come, my sister, from what sacred gazelle, so agile, so firm, set upon such delicate ankles?

MEZZOGIORNO (F): And there, my brother, in the very center of your darkness, upon black crags there rises up a dense shower of resplendent blood.

MEZZOGIORNO (M): So dense is this blood that gleams, vermilion! Upright blood! Your most sacred insignia!

MEZZOGIORNO (F): And in the very center of your darkness, my sister, other lips barely open, under the shade of nocturnal laces, and the true, pink flower shyly peeks out, the Mystic Rose.

MEZZOGIORNO (M): Living flesh, blood's most fragile borderline, hidden even from me, so that it can be broken, so that I can enter bleeding and we become one flesh in the communion of blood.

MEZZOGIORNO (F): Because if we have to tolerate the horror of being two bodies and not one . . .

MEZZOGIORNO (M): Because if even the smallest drop of air is not exhaled directly from your mouth, it is unbearable . . .

MEZZOGIORNO (F): The only possibility, my beloved, is for us to devour each other and drink each other up . . .

MEZZOGIORNO (M): So you can quench your thirst with my essences: my saliva, my sweat, my urine . . .

MEZZOGIORNO (F): So you can nourish yourself with my feces . . .

MEZZOGIORNO (M): With my semen . . .

BELTRAMI: This must stop. (*With some effort, BELTRAMI gets up and, vacillating, goes over to the TWINS, but, as if trapped in a dreamlike, unreal zone, they continue moving with an exasperating slowness and ease, entwined in a sleepwalker's dance.*)

MEZZOGIORNO (F): With your viscous, white semen . . . With your cunt's sealike juices . . .

MEZZOGIORNO (M): So I can sniff your rump, like a bitch . . . So I can squeeze your hard breasts until your transparent milk leaps out . . .

MEZZOGIORNO (F): So I can shove my fingers up into the orifice of your ass . . . So I can dilate each one of your holes and penetrate each one of your pores . . .

MEZZOGIORNO (M): So I can mount you, like some fabulous animal with a thousand pricks, and riddle your body until all the blood's run out . . .

MEZZOGIORNO (F): So I can bite into your balls and suck out all your fresh semen . . .

(*A heavy silence suddenly descends upon everything. There is a whirling in the shadows, out of which BELTRAMI emerges, with a crown of blazing red roses on his head. Trickles of blood run down his forehead and cheeks. A long silence, abruptly interrupted by several loud knocks. The MEZZOGIORNO TWINS take the crown from BELTRAMI's head, and then crumble, fall away, plunged into a deep sleep. Pause.*)

BELTRAMI (*his voice weak*): Enter.

(The Assistant enters.)
Beltrami: Why did you knock so hard?
Assistant: Sir, I've been knocking for quite some time.
(Brief pause.)
Beltrami: What do you want?
Assistant: Sir, did you hurt yourself?
Beltrami: No, my friend. *(Smiling.)* It's only the blood of sleep. What do you want?
Assistant: There's been enemy movement, sir.
Beltrami *(absently):* Yes? *(Pause.)* Tell me about these youngsters, will you?
Assistant: The accused?
Beltrami: Yes, the accused. You've met them before, haven't you?
Assistant: Once or twice, yes, sir, our paths crossed . . .
Beltrami: And what impression did they make on you?
Assistant: Nothing out of the ordinary.
Beltrami: Tell me what they're like.
Assistant: Well, he is young, rather short. He appears to be strong but has delicate manners. Black, curly hair. His skin is dark, and he has very lively eyes. Overall, very nice.
Beltrami: And what about her?
Assistant: Well, she . . . *(His look takes on an intense inner concentration.)* She has dark eyes, with long lashes . . . and her hair is black and full . . . *(Brief pause.)* She walked with so much ease and grace. Well, she's in irons at the moment.
Beltrami: You've seen them . . . recently?
Assistant: Yes, of course. Both of them.
(Pause.)
Beltrami: And how did they meet?
Assistant: Well, at confession.
Beltrami: At confession?
Assistant: At confession.
(The two men look at each other, tentatively, and then suddenly burst out laughing heartily.)
Beltrami: What a cheeky pair! A couple of rascals!
Assistant *(still laughing):* It appears that he began to visit her every day. At her own home.
Beltrami *(splitting his sides):* Right under her father's nose!
Assistant *(also dissolved in laughter):* Right under the entire world's nose! And she would go to meet him at church.
Beltrami *(pointing his thumb up):* Right under the Lord's nose!
(Both split their sides laughing. They calm down. Pause.)

ASSISTANT: Well, and then finally they eloped.

BELTRAMI *(admiringly):* They eloped!

ASSISTANT: They eloped.

BELTRAMI: Just like that?

ASSISTANT: Just like that.

BELTRAMI *(severely):* Did they steal anything?

ASSISTANT *(quickly):* No, sir. They left everything behind.

(Pause.)

BELTRAMI: Nobody told me about it.

ASSISTANT: Everyone was terrified. They kept thinking they'd return.

BELTRAMI: They thought they'd return?

ASSISTANT: Yes, sir. Until her father finally sent a letter to Your Excellency.

BELTRAMI: Which I read. What a weakling.

ASSISTANT: And then the vicar-general wrote you.

BELTRAMI: Yes. He called it a "horrid occurrence."

ASSISTANT: And then His Grace, the bishop of the diocese.

BELTRAMI: Another asshole. And the youngsters?

ASSISTANT: It appears that they were making for the South.

BELTRAMI: The South?

ASSISTANT: Yes, they wanted to get to the South . . . *(Pause.)* Who knows why? They were caught on the banks of a river. *(Pause.)* The rest of it, Your Lordship surely recalls.

BELTRAMI: No.

ASSISTANT: They brought them in chains.

(Pause.)

BELTRAMI: And now, how are they?

ASSISTANT: Calm.

BELTRAMI: They're brave.

(Pause.)

BELTRAMI *(softly):* Old man . . .

ASSISTANT *(surprised):* Yes, sir?

BELTRAMI: Don't you ever rest, old man? What's your secret, old age? Does this blood ever become thinner?

ASSISTANT: Sir, it gradually becomes thinner, yes, it becomes light itself, but with a light that never stops giving off heat.

BELTRAMI: Do our passions ever grow old?

ASSISTANT: I don't know, sir, if our passions grow old, or if it's just the memory of old passions that keeps us alive, or if old age itself has its own weak passion.

BELTRAMI: And just what kind of passion might you still have, old man?

ASSISTANT: To become light itself.

BELTRAMI: Oh, yes? And how might you go about doing that?

ASSISTANT: By cleansing myself of even the smallest stain of desire. But that in itself is a desire. And so we go on, always in the dark, we travel through this earth, hungry for light. Yes, sir, I ache, I long to be pure light. And that is what still makes me burn. And it is my longing to extinguish myself that fans the fire. But don't think that it's a docile, kind fire. When I wake up in the morning and the light jumps up and smiles in my direction, I smile back and I tell the light I'm going to make it; I'm going to make it. *(Pause.)*

BELTRAMI *(astounded):* I didn't know that you were so crazy, too. So you really do that? Talk to the light?

ASSISTANT *(smiling, his eyes lit up by a sweet dementia):* Yes, sir. Sometimes this madness is very strong. And I become furious with impatience, because of this little patch of darkness and fear that separates me from . . . all that light that just hovers there . . . huge, unyielding . . . over the earth. Then my thoughts take me into the future. And I see the moment in which my veins, my lips, rapidly burst into repugnant bubbles. But that will not be more than just a . . . an instant of indignity, of disgust . . . My bones will stay behind to reestablish my respectability . . . Clean, dry, free from all that filthy liquid . . . They will grow old and gray, respectably, growing whiter and clearer all the while . . . All the while more porous to the light . . . Until they're nothing more than illuminated specks of dust. And then not even that. Nothing but light.

BELTRAMI: What a crazy old man! And God?

ASSISTANT: Well, that's God, isn't it? That's heaven.

(Pause.)

BELTRAMI: But right now everything is so dark.

ASSISTANT: Yes, sir.

BELTRAMI: It's so difficult to get one's bearings in this darkness, to find one's way, and, on top of that, lead this pack of fools.

ASSISTANT: Yes, sir.

BELTRAMI: And to be just!

ASSISTANT: Yes, sir.

BELTRAMI: For that, one would need to live thousands of years, because it's only out of world-weariness that justice is born. *(Pause.)* How much longer till dawn?

ASSISTANT: Not long, sir.

(Pause.)

BELTRAMI: Did you hear that?

ASSISTANT: I heard nothing, sir.

BELTRAMI: The Madman, he's beginning to stir. He's getting ready to fight.

ASSISTANT: I don't hear anything, sir.

(Pause. The TWINS begin to get up, restless.)
BELTRAMI: And you don't smell anything either?
ASSISTANT: No, sir.
BELTRAMI: I do. I smell battle. Soon everything will begin, the blood, fever
. . . Look out, everything's about to happen. We don't want the Madman
taking us by surprise. *(He goes over, frantic, to the table and grabs a hand-
ful of papers.)* Take these, convey my orders.
ASSISTANT: Sir, what orders?
BELTRAMI: You already know. Everyone on the alert! Get out! Get out! Out!
*(He pushes the ASSISTANT toward offstage. BELTRAMI is agitated. In the pro-
found silence, the lighting begins to change. It becomes golden, strange,
resplendent. The TWINS go to the center of the stage and solemnly announce:)*
MEZZOGIORNO (M AND F): *Paradise*, signore!
*(BELTRAMI bows and moves away from the center of the stage. The TWINS go
into an orgasmic trance.)*

MEZZOGIORNO (F):	One afternoon we were in our full flight
	by an old and lum'nous river delayed.
MEZZOGIORNO (M):	"Look, Sister dear," said I, "The tree of life
	across the river grows beauteous and straight.
	Go you alone, or does your path join mine?"
MEZZOGIORNO (F):	"Brother," I replied, "I go with my mate,
	our roads will run together ever right."
	Thus our feet as one broke the river's light.
MEZZOGIORNO (M):	And sinking down into the clarity great
	of the waters, we were two impostor fish,
	already cleansed of mortal rust's plate,
	as our clothes the river had stripped,
	and with them went all our shifts
	and days and the world. We did wake
	all polished and naked; afloat, adrift
	on the opposite shore, our eyes on each other lit.
MEZZOGIORNO (F):	How strangely our soft, milky skin did shine
	in the silent, silver air of a grand,
	lush, eternal dawn! It rained and rained light.
MEZZOGIORNO (M):	And the nearby sun was all golden sand,
	we never knew if it chose to decline
	or rise up. Nor knew we what divine hand
	placed it there forever, e'er unrestrained
	from time, keeping our tender sun enchained.
MEZZOGIORNO (F):	Our eyes burning, aflame from our innocence
	and pure astonishment, we wandered lonely
	into a virgin jungle. No insistence,

our voices forgotten, now listening only
to the limpid sounds. A strange, unknown science
guided us in our footsteps. When forlornly
the air moved, its sigh carried us along;
once calm in the light, it calmed us, too, strong.

MEZZOGIORNO (M): Peace-drunk animals still meandering
brushed up against our skin, in love, lovesick.

MEZZOGIORNO (F): We saw tigers satisfy their hungering
in the soft, snowy combs of honey stick.

MEZZOGIORNO (M): We saw both lambs and jackals in a clearing,
dwelling together, blessed, heaven's pick.

MEZZOGIORNO (F): And we dreamt a dream of a venom'd serpent,
cradling a child, the viper's skin transparent.

MEZZOGIORNO (M): Each shining, each resplendent stone unveiled
the clear path to the center, still, mysterious.

MEZZOGIORNO (F): And the translucent, glitt'ring earth displayed
her veins of metal . . .

MEZZOGIORNO (M):   In a wide, rigorous
labyrinth of light we slowly made way
to the last tree. I saw its fronds, luxurious,
glory's outburst, the corn's great tasseling picket,
grace's crown residing there in the thicket.

MEZZOGIORNO (F): As I lie down at his feet, on a bower
of eternity, under sacred wood,
he falls over me, falls like a shower,
this severe owner o'erpower me should,
o'er my being he has absolute power,
he falls like mist, a cloak, a dream, a hood.
And I am he, we are one and the same,
there's no other, no borders, nothing unnamed.

MEZZOGIORNO (M): And I am she. My annihilated skin
sets loose the juicy dizziness, uproarious.
Finally freed from my delicate, thin
jail, I die and I am reborn victorious,
in our own transparent blood, illumin'd.
I am, and in her, my own body glorious.
Dissolved in the brilliance of lover's fire,
I am time unfettered, timeless desire.

MEZZOGIORNO (F): Words have run away from us, each one flees,
their selfish pride no longer freely blows.

MEZZOGIORNO (M): Nothing mars aged wisdom, swollen on dreams.
Of the exploit of flight, like the bird knows,

	of the thunder of pounding, churning steeds,
	of the spider's ritual as its fan grows.
Mezzogiorno (F):	Immortal home of every dawn and animal,
	of all games shared, and of all games perpetual.
Mezzogiorno (M):	In slow spirals, we go down, disembark
	the tree's sleep . . .
Mezzogiorno (F):	And in the tenacious center
	of its mystery, we become the night's dark.
	Where the heartbeat is born, we deeply enter,
	submerged in sap, we become the tree's bark.
Mezzogiorno (M):	Fruit and flower nuptials, amorous presenter,
	encounter of petals and lips; the wood
	made flesh, the mane in full-flowering brood.
Mezzogiorno (F):	And in the primal mud, in dust, in clay,
	our bodies are unborn . . .
Mezzogiorno (M):	To him the sigh
	returns, He who first gave it, He, the days'
	Seed. And at peace, each element alive
	renews its dream of earth . . .
Mezzogiorno (F):	The dry shine plays
	on metal, lightness floats in the wind's eye.
Mezzogiorno (M):	All wetness returns to live water's weft[4]
	and woof, all hot things to the flame are left.
Mezzogiorno (F):	And in shadows, at the end of the feast,
	the awful face of God, seeing and seen,
	surrounded by both the Lamb and the Beast.
	And the knots come untied, of all that's been
	wrought from the last day back to the first, least.
Mezzogiorno (M):	We're the remains, Genesis undone, green.
Mezzogiorno (F):	Fragments of water and light.
Mezzogiorno (M):	Shadow, frothing.
Mezzogiorno (F):	Even less than its remains.
Mezzogiorno (M):	Nothing, nothing.

(*Pause. The light gradually returns to normal. The* Twins *have thrown themselves on the ground, and* Beltrami *looks at them with a tranquil expression on his face. The* Assistant *appears. Pause.*)

Beltrami: Come in, man. Don't just stand there in the doorway.

(*The* Assistant *slowly enters.*)

Beltrami: Is everything quiet?

Assistant: Yes.

Beltrami: But I know that the Madman is out there, crouching.

Assistant: Yes, sir. There will surely be battle. I feel it, too, now.

(BELTRAMI expels all the air out of his mouth, slowly, and sags into his chair. Pause.)

BELTRAMI: What peace! What enormous and simple peace! Now everything has its order. *(He stretches.)* Let me rest, will you? It's been a long night.

(Pause. The ASSISTANT vacillates.)

ASSISTANT: Sir . . . now that battle is certain . . . and it's only a little while until dawn, and Your Lordship said . . . Forgive me for reminding you that you have to make a decision about that irritating matter. But it's just that having those youngsters here is a nuisance. And furthermore, if it gets rough, they'll be in danger.

(Brief pause.)

BELTRAMI: It's an irritating matter.

ASSISTANT: Yes, sir.

BELTRAMI: And what do you recommend?

ASSISTANT *(smiling):* And how should I know, sir?

BELTRAMI: Then why do I have you on my staff, man? Venture some advice.

ASSISTANT *(coming to attention):* Yes, sir. I believe, sir, that they should be punished.

BELTRAMI: Aha.

ASSISTANT: They have much offended and scandalized society with their crime.

BELTRAMI: Aha.

ASSISTANT: So I would advise Your Excellency to be strong.

BELTRAMI: And what would you do?

ASSISTANT: I would stick the renegade priest in jail for a while, until the dust settles, and then I would hand him over to the Holy Church and let them decide what he has coming to him.

BELTRAMI: And as for her?

ASSISTANT *(vacillating):* Well, sir, given her delicate condition and her dishonor, I think she's already been punished enough . . . Anyway, her parents will know what to do with her . . .

(Pause. BELTRAMI gets up, laughing.)

BELTRAMI: The Madman has finally decided! I was getting tired of looking at myself in the mirror, darkly . . . Now we'll see each other face-to-face. What's the morning like?

ASSISTANT: It's snowing again.

BELTRAMI *(laughing):* Always the same old snow and mud. Won't it ever dry up? What does God want from us?

ASSISTANT: We'll know soon enough.

BELTRAMI: Right, soon enough.

(Pause.)

ASSISTANT: And, sir? Have you made a decision?

BELTRAMI: Execute them.

(The ASSISTANT looks at him in astonishment. The TWINS wake up with a start; they sit up and remain paralyzed, with their anguished eyes wide open.)

ASSISTANT *(reacting):* No, sir, I meant those crazy-headed youngsters.

BELTRAMI: Yes, execute them.

(The ASSISTANT, pale and terrified, looks at him.)

BELTRAMI *(exploding):* What's wrong with you? Don't you understand?

(He suddenly goes over to the ASSISTANT and slaps his face, knocking him to the ground.)

BELTRAMI: Moron! Look at them all, how they ran away to their homes, afraid, trembling, when that stain appeared. It's a scandal, yes. Because any enormous passion like that scandalizes the world. Because it turns it upside down and disintegrates it. Because the world is nothing more than an infinite web of petty cowardices. And here the web broke. *(Brief pause.)* What irony, moth, that I in all my bravery would be the representative of all that cowardice!

ASSISTANT: But, sir . . . what about compassion?

BELTRAMI: They were . . . too close to Nature. And if we're here, trying to create a world at its frontiers, it's because someone, sometime, split Nature in two . . . Because we were expelled forever from Paradise . . . And because on the road we're on, there's no turning back. This way the Madman will know that I too am a civilizer . . .   •

ASSISTANT: And compassion, sir?

BELTRAMI: Now go.

ASSISTANT: Sir.

BELTRAMI: Do as I said.

ASSISTANT: Sir.

BELTRAMI: That's an order.

ASSISTANT *(with a howl of heartbreaking anguish):* Sir!

(There is no answer. A pause. The ASSISTANT leaves. The TWINS leap up.)

MEZZOGIORNO (M): Sir, we'll trade our lives for theirs.

MEZZOGIORNO (F): We're not worth anything.

MEZZOGIORNO (M): We don't even know if we're happy or sad. We're in perpetual ecstasy, beyond time . . .

BELTRAMI: You two aren't real . . . you're barely a curiosity.

MEZZOGIORNO (M): And you think this is real?

BELTRAMI: This is the world.

MEZZOGIORNO (F): A hollow shell with some paint!

MEZZOGIORNO (M): Reality, resplendent, eternal, lies behind this painted world!

(BELTRAMI *leaps onto* MEZZOGIORNO (M), *takes him by the neck with his arm, and drags both* TWINS *toward one of the walls.*)

BELTRAMI: And here, what's painted here?

MEZZOGIORNO (F): It's some painting on a wall.

MEZZOGIORNO (M): The painted wall of a tomb.

(BELTRAMI *brutally slams the* TWINS' *heads against the wall. He lets them go, and they fall down on their knees, stunned and bleeding.*)

BELTRAMI: And now?

MEZZOGIORNO (F): Forgive me, sir . . . but it's still paint. (*She runs her fingers through the blood on her face.*)

MEZZOGIORNO (M): And this is painted blood.

(*The discharge of rifles is heard outside. A violent death rattle shakes the* TWINS.)

MEZZOGIORNO (M): Sir . . .

(*Pause.*)

BELTRAMI: I'll be known forever for my cruelty. Let God show no mercy on me.

MEZZOGIORNO (M): O Dio, un altro pazzo ancor'.

MEZZOGIORNO (F) (*translating, neutral, possibly facing the audience*): He means, "My God, another fool."

(*The cry of a child is heard, coming closer. The* ASSISTANT *enters, carrying in his outstretched arms, like an offering, a newborn child, swaddled in a bloodstained white rag.*)

ASSISTANT: It's the woman's son. I don't know how to carry him. I think he's cold.

(*On his knees, without turning around,* BELTRAMI *hands him his pelts. He is possibly left naked.*)

BELTRAMI: Cover him up.

(*While the* ASSISTANT *dresses the child, cannon fire is heard.*)

BELTRAMI: What's that thundering?

ASSISTANT: Battle.

TRANSLATOR'S NOTES

1. See *A South American Passion Play*, n. 1.

2. "Oh Madonna of Grace / You who hold Grace in your hands / I come to you for grace / Oh Mary, grant us grace. / Grant us grace, oh Mary / As the Eternal Father did to you / He who made you mother of God / Grant us grace, oh Mary. / Grant it to me, oh Mary / Grant it to me, I beseech you / For the gifts that you received / from the most Holy Trinity."

I am indebted to Erasmo Gerato and Reinier Leushuis for the translation from the Neapolitan. The prologue's song comes from *Madonna della Grazia*, part of the repertory of the Neapolitan Nuova Compagnia di Canto Popolare. According to the playwright, the verses sung during the "Inferno" scene were written to the tune of *La zita*, recorded in 1971 by the same Neapolitan musical group.

    3. See *A South American Passion Play*, n. 2.
    4. See *A South American Passion Play*, n. 10.